D0210485

Ichigo Takano presents

Dreamin'
Sun

9

volume
nine

Dreamin'
Sun

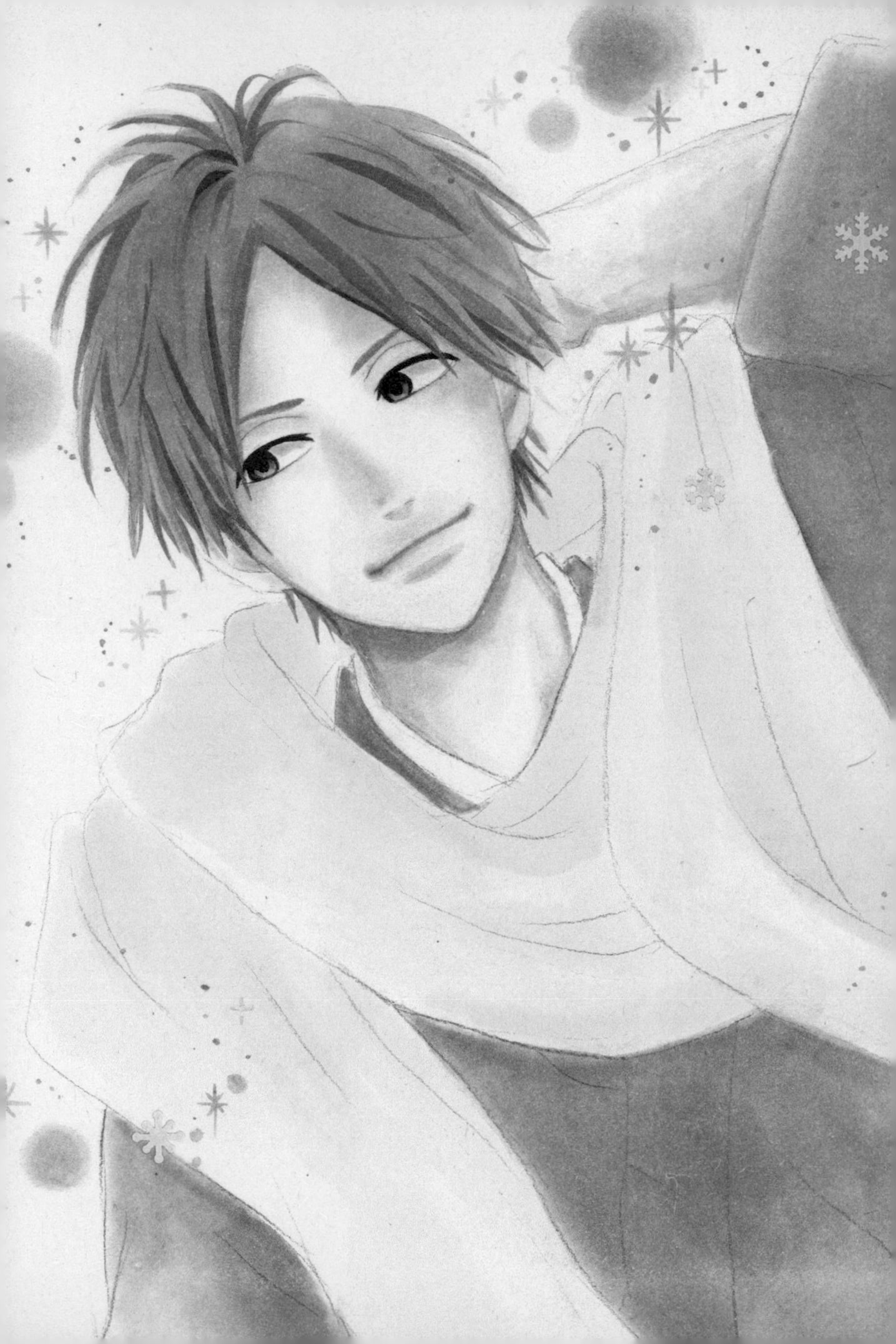

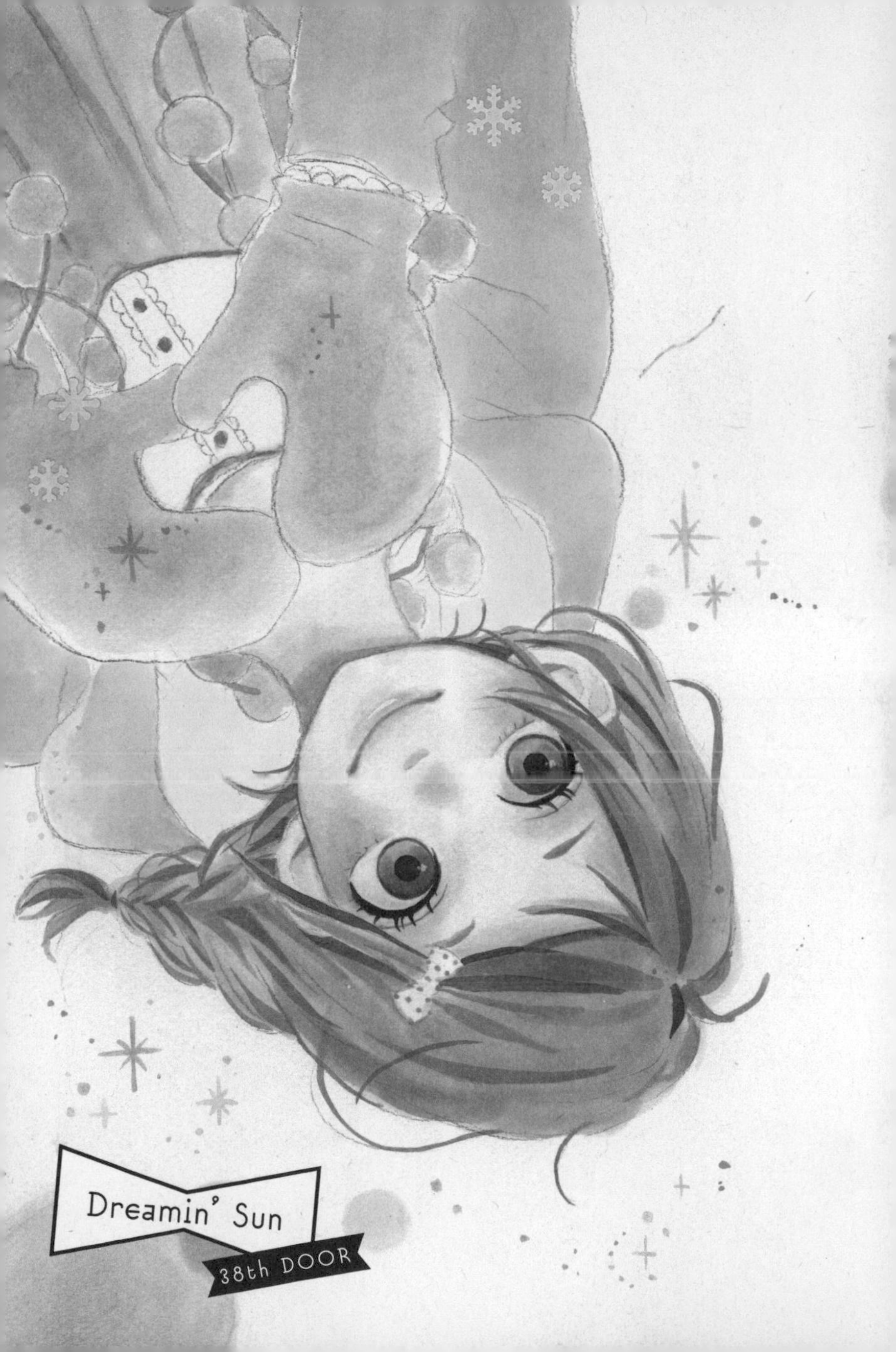
Dreamin' Sun
38th DOOR

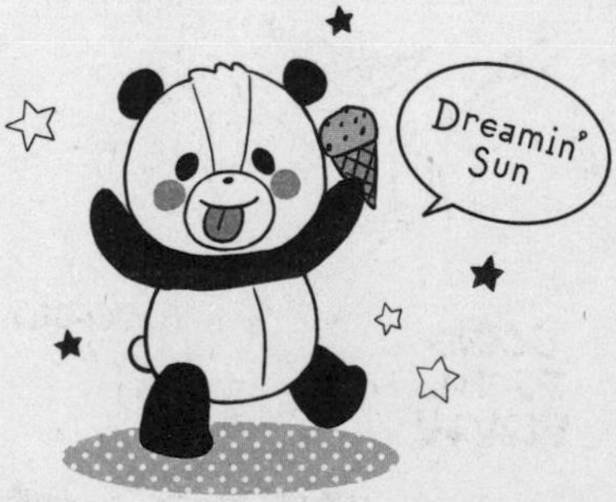
Dreamin' Sun

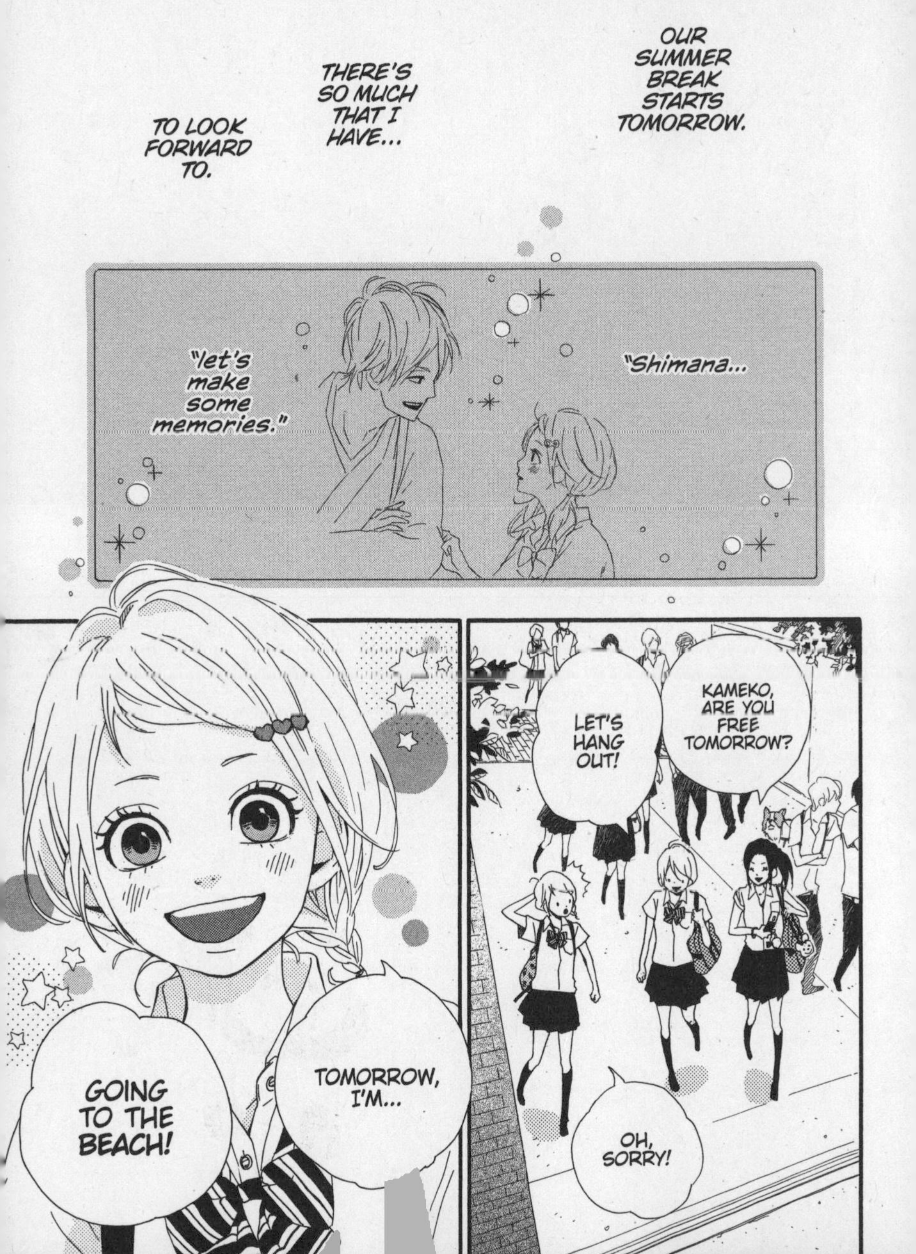
OUR SUMMER BREAK STARTS TOMORROW.
THERE'S SO MUCH THAT I HAVE...
TO LOOK FORWARD TO.
"Shimana...
"let's make some memories."
KAMEKO, ARE YOU FREE TOMORROW?
LET'S HANG OUT!
OH, SORRY!
TOMORROW, I'M...
GOING TO THE BEACH!

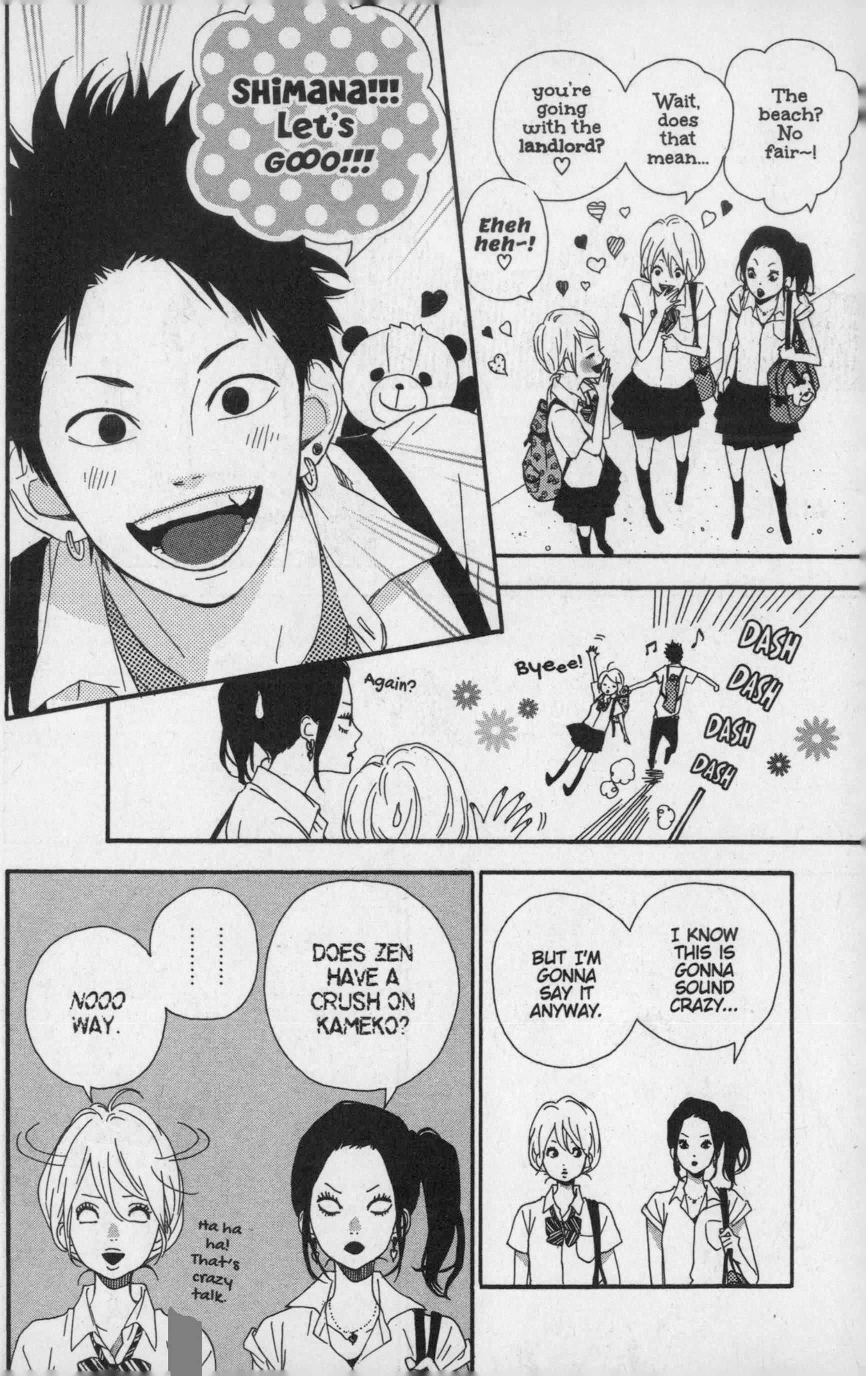

The beach? No fair~!
Wait, does that mean...
you're going with the landlord? ♡
Eheh heh~! ♡
SHIMANA!!! Let's GOOO!!!
DASH
DASH
DASH
DASH
Byeee!
Again?
I KNOW THIS IS GONNA SOUND CRAZY...
BUT I'M GONNA SAY IT ANYWAY.
DOES ZEN HAVE A CRUSH ON KAMEKO?
......
NOOO WAY.
Ha ha ha! That's crazy talk.

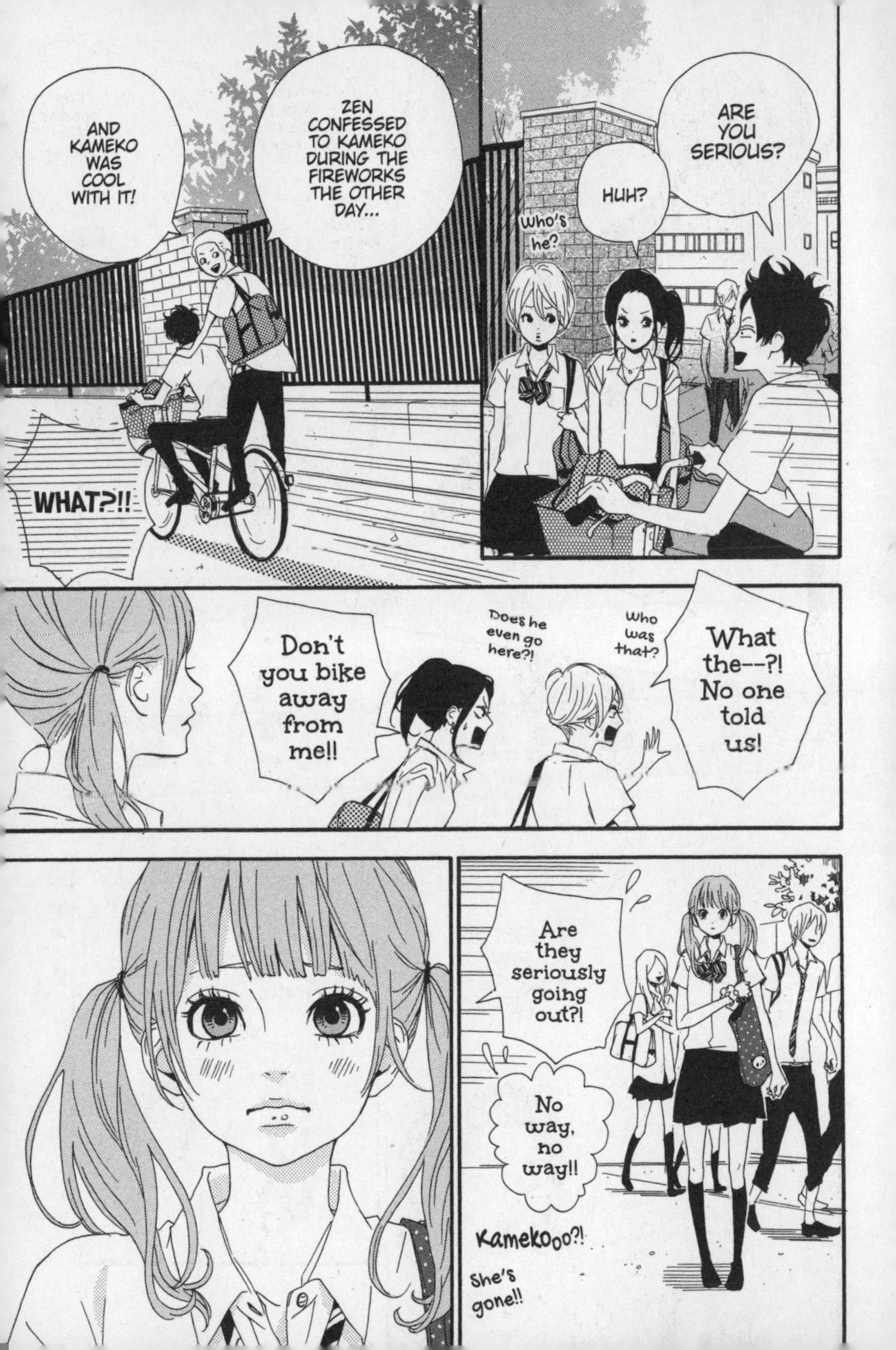
ARE YOU SERIOUS?
HUH?
Who's he?
ZEN CONFESSED TO KAMEKO DURING THE FIREWORKS THE OTHER DAY...
AND KAMEKO WAS COOL WITH IT!
WHAT?!!
What the--?! No one told us!
Who was that?
Does he even go here?!
Don't you bike away from me!!
Are they seriously going out?!
No way, no way!!
Kamekooo?!
She's gone!!

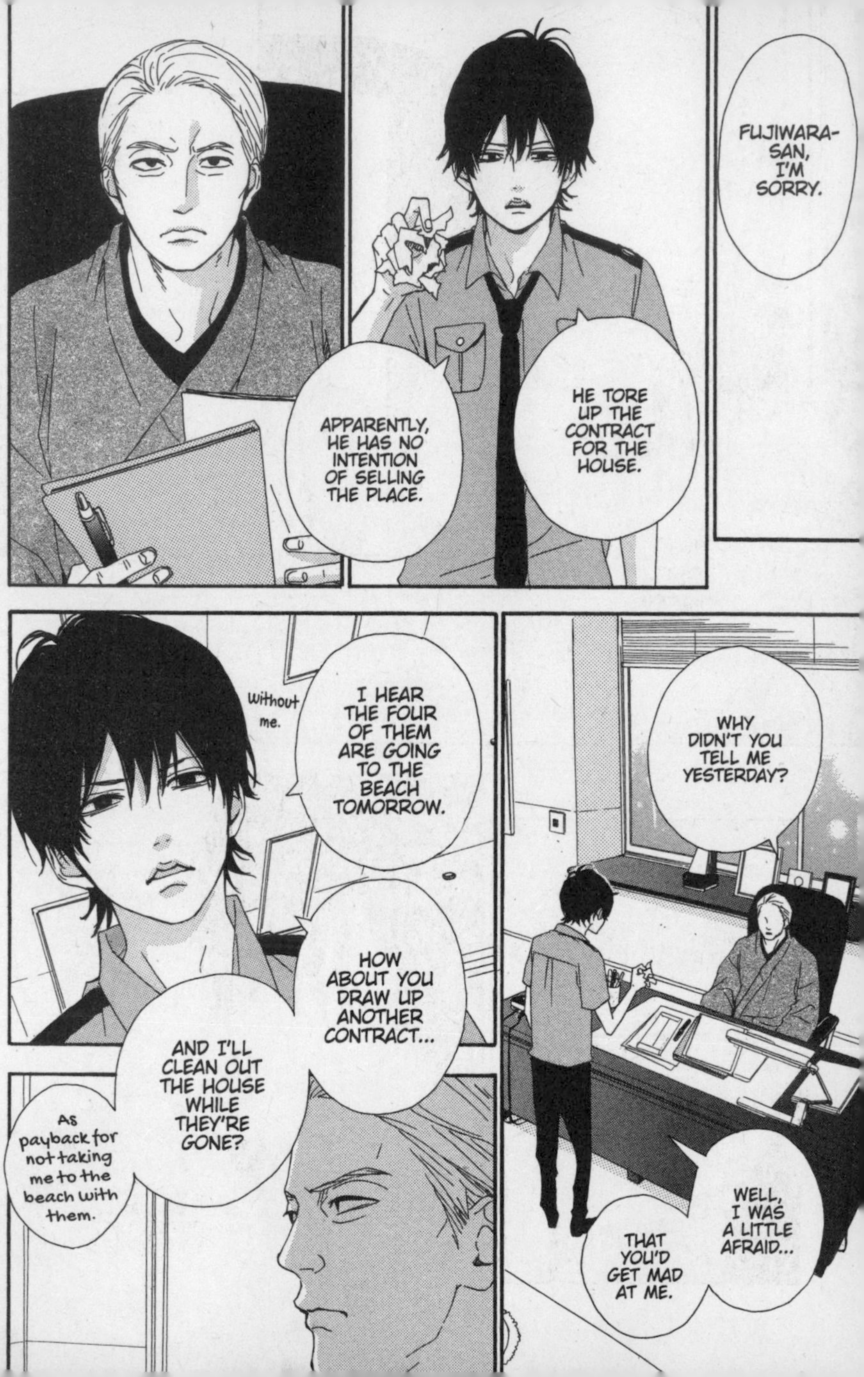
FUJIWARA-SAN, I'M SORRY.
HE TORE UP THE CONTRACT FOR THE HOUSE.
APPARENTLY, HE HAS NO INTENTION OF SELLING THE PLACE.
WHY DIDN'T YOU TELL ME YESTERDAY?
WELL, I WAS A LITTLE AFRAID...
THAT YOU'D GET MAD AT ME.
I HEAR THE FOUR OF THEM ARE GOING TO THE BEACH TOMORROW.
without me.
HOW ABOUT YOU DRAW UP ANOTHER CONTRACT...
AND I'LL CLEAN OUT THE HOUSE WHILE THEY'RE GONE?
As payback for not taking me to the beach with them.

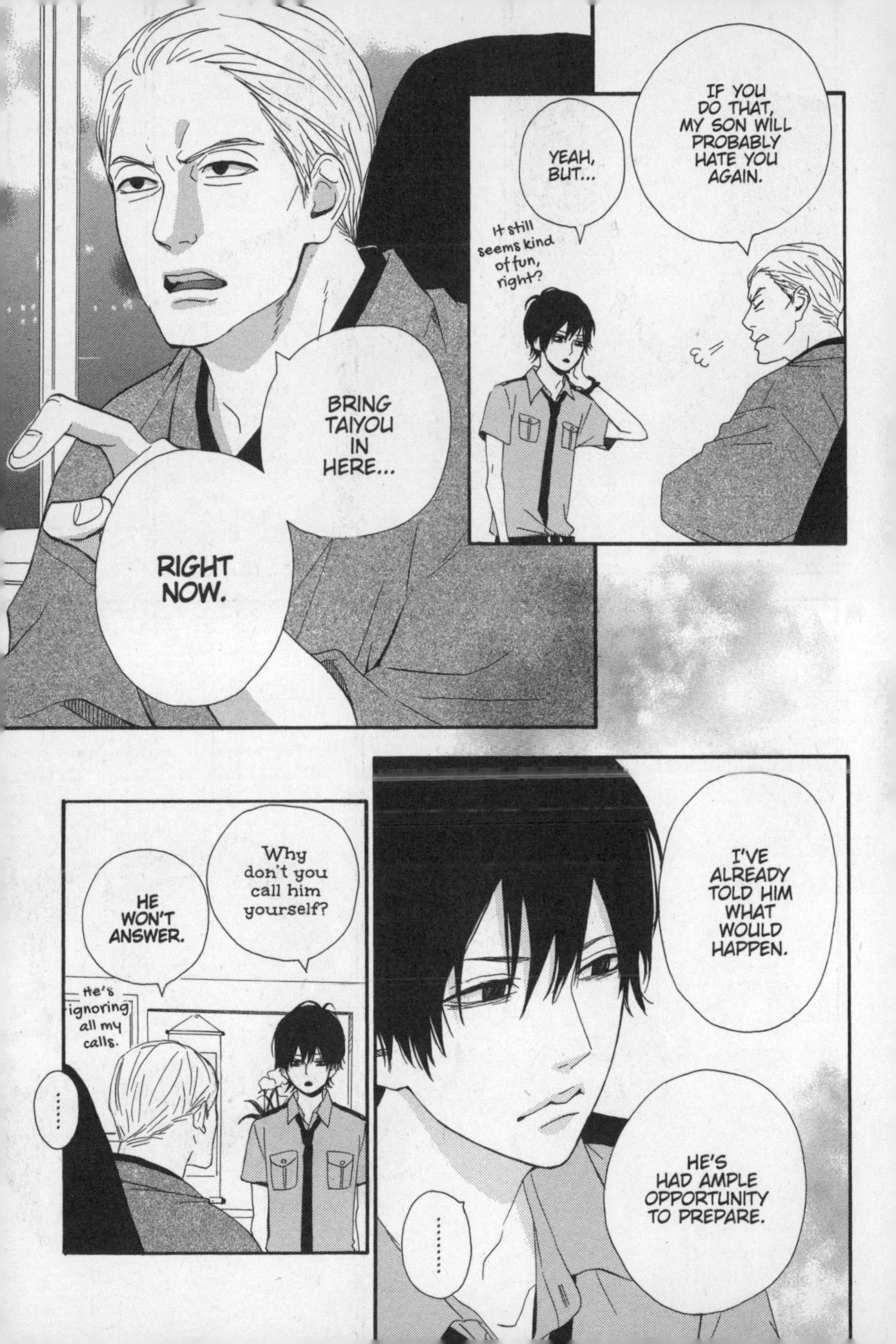
BRING TAIYOU IN HERE...
RIGHT NOW.
IF YOU DO THAT, MY SON WILL PROBABLY HATE YOU AGAIN.
YEAH, BUT...
It still seems kind of fun, right?
I'VE ALREADY TOLD HIM WHAT WOULD HAPPEN.
HE'S HAD AMPLE OPPORTUNITY TO PREPARE.
......
Why don't you call him yourself?
HE WON'T ANSWER.
He's ignoring all my calls.
......

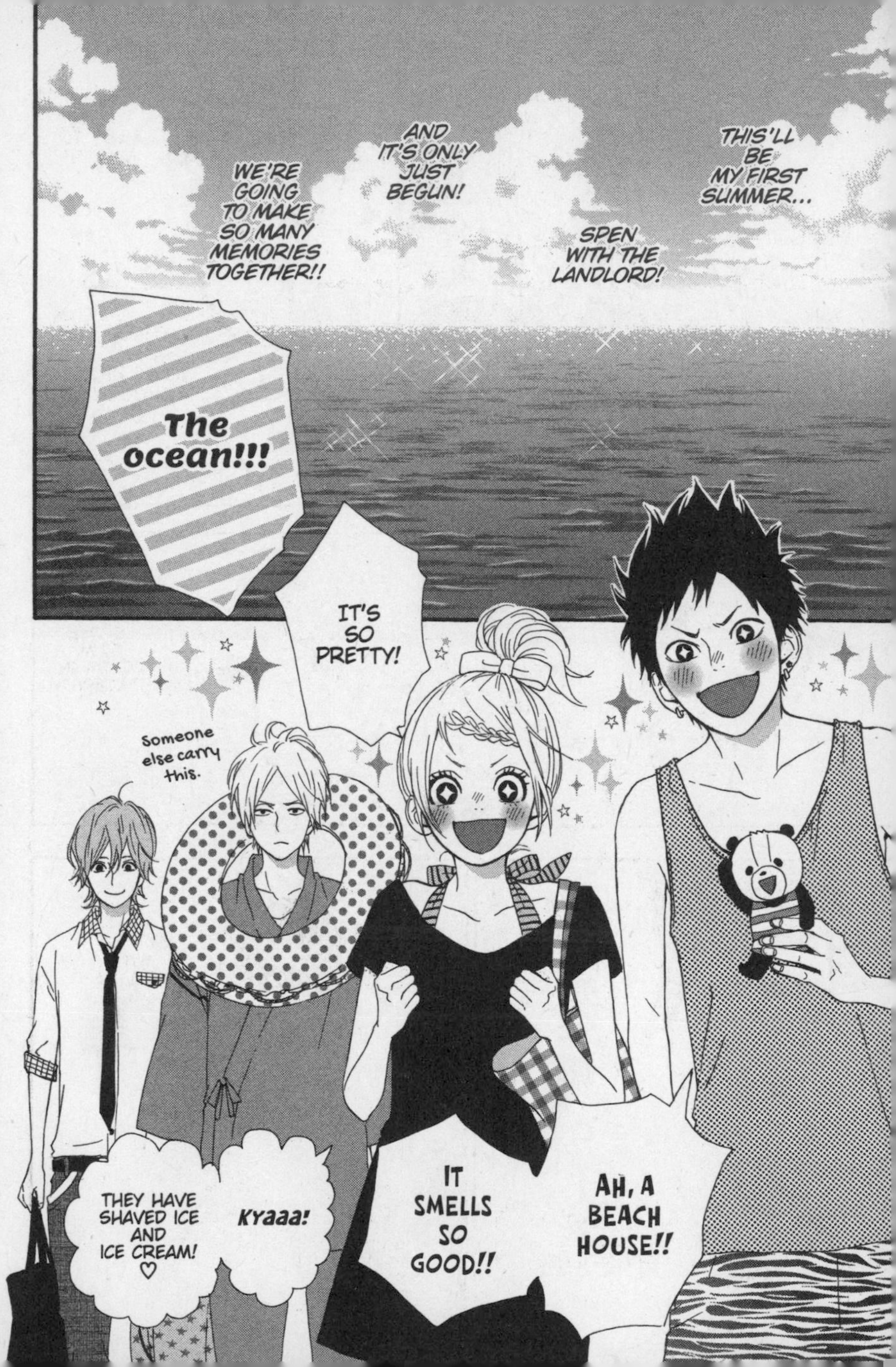
THIS'LL BE MY FIRST SUMMER...
SPEN WITH THE LANDLORD!
AND IT'S ONLY JUST BEGUN!
WE'RE GOING TO MAKE SO MANY MEMORIES TOGETHER!!
The ocean!!!
AH, A BEACH HOUSE!!
IT'S SO PRETTY!
IT SMELLS SO GOOD!!
Kyaaa!
THEY HAVE SHAVED ICE AND ICE CREAM! ♡
Someone else carry this.

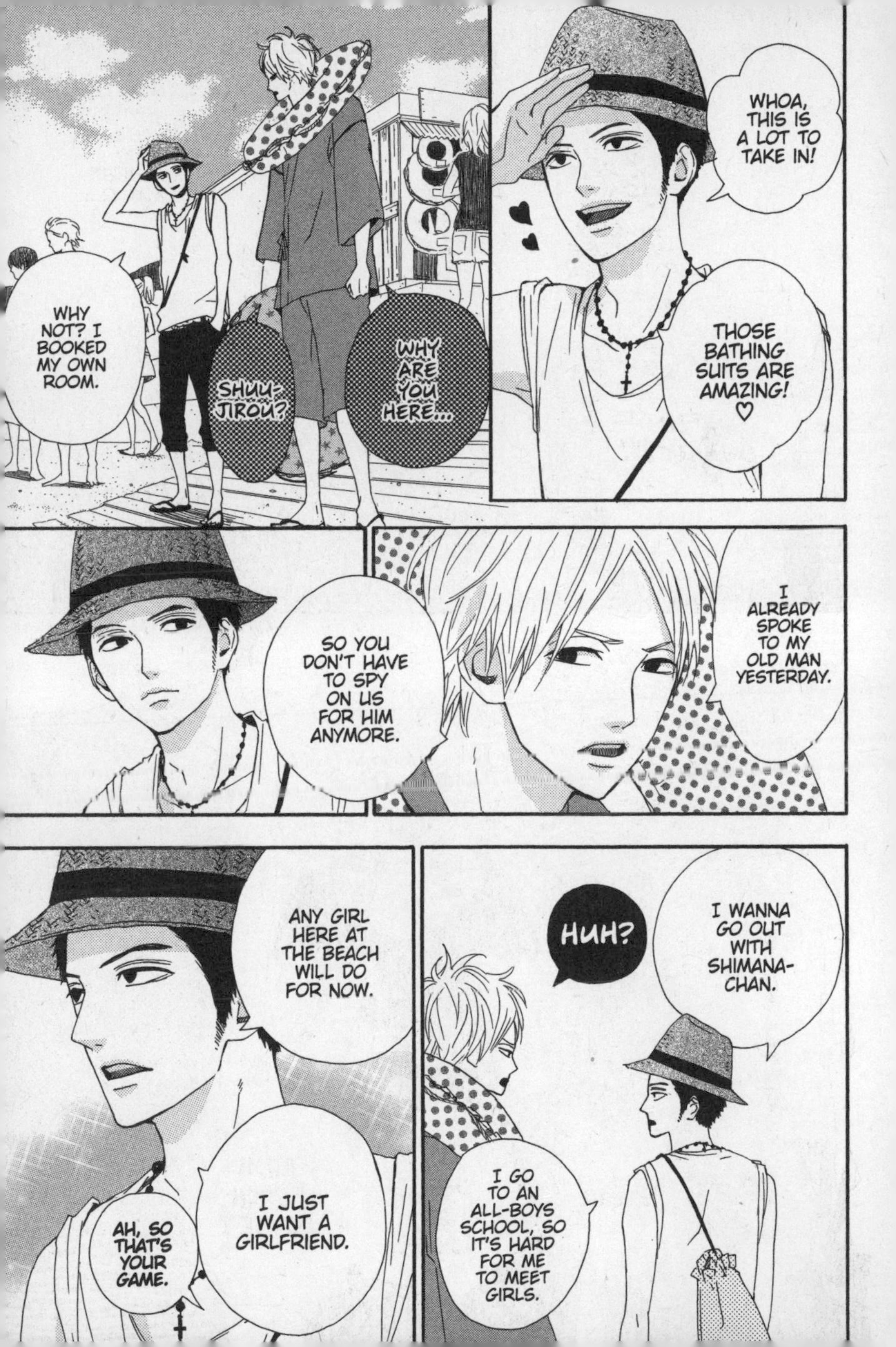
WHOA, THIS IS A LOT TO TAKE IN!
THOSE BATHING SUITS ARE AMAZING! ♡
WHY ARE YOU HERE...
SHUU-JIROU?
WHY NOT? I BOOKED MY OWN ROOM.
I ALREADY SPOKE TO MY OLD MAN YESTERDAY.
SO YOU DON'T HAVE TO SPY ON US FOR HIM ANYMORE.
I WANNA GO OUT WITH SHIMANA-CHAN.
HUH?
I GO TO AN ALL-BOYS SCHOOL, SO IT'S HARD FOR ME TO MEET GIRLS.
ANY GIRL HERE AT THE BEACH WILL DO FOR NOW.
I JUST WANT A GIRLFRIEND.
AH, SO THAT'S YOUR GAME.

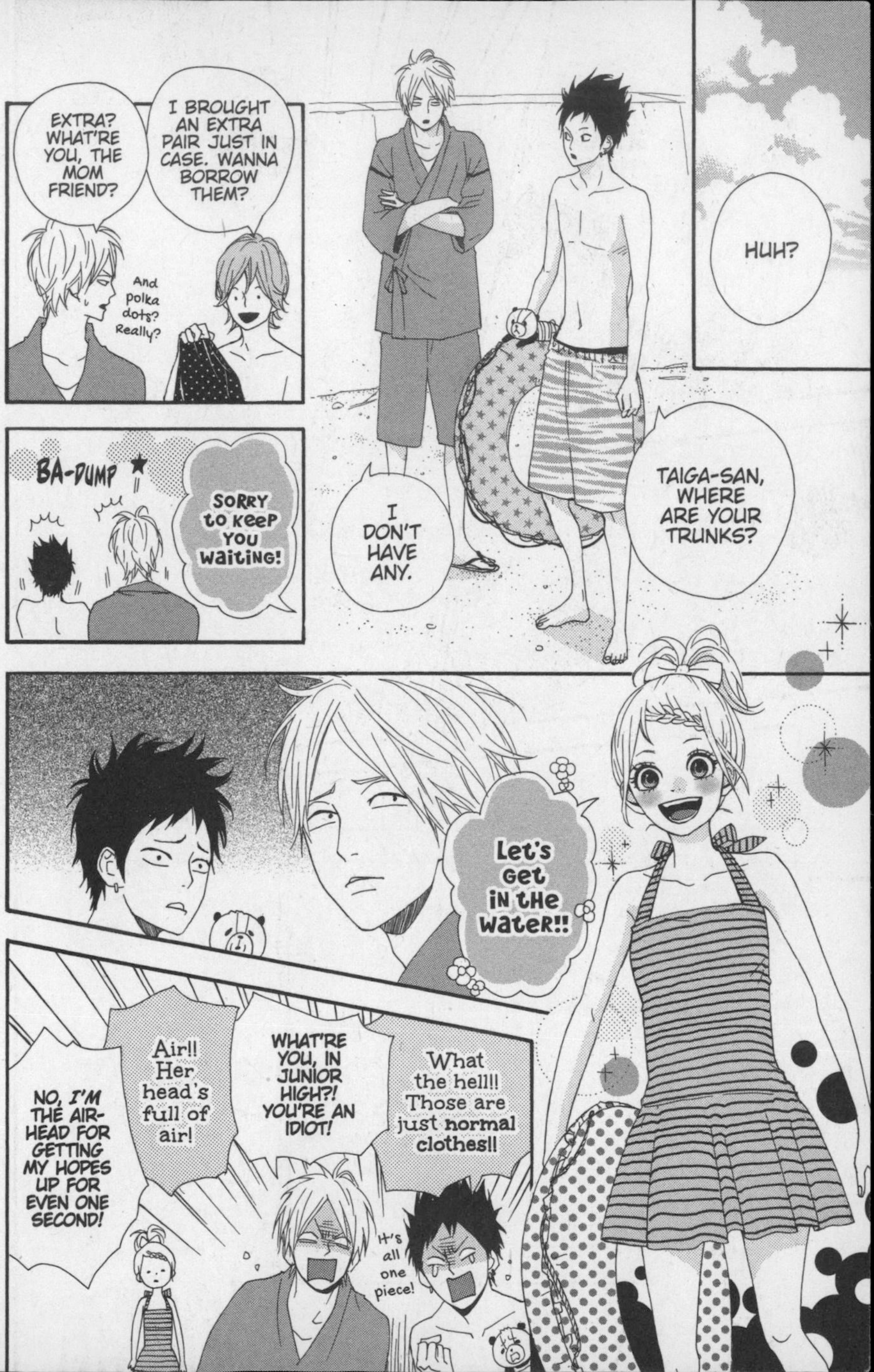
HUH?
TAIGA-SAN, WHERE ARE YOUR TRUNKS?
I DON'T HAVE ANY.
I BROUGHT AN EXTRA PAIR JUST IN CASE. WANNA BORROW THEM?
EXTRA? WHAT'RE YOU, THE MOM FRIEND?
And polka dots? Really?
SORRY to KEEP YOU Waiting!
BA-DUMP ★
Let's Get in tHe water!!
What the hell!! Those are just normal clothes!!
WHAT'RE YOU, IN JUNIOR HIGH?! YOU'RE AN IDIOT!
Air!! Her head's full of air!
NO, I'M THE AIR-HEAD FOR GETTING MY HOPES UP FOR EVEN ONE SECOND!
It's all one piece!

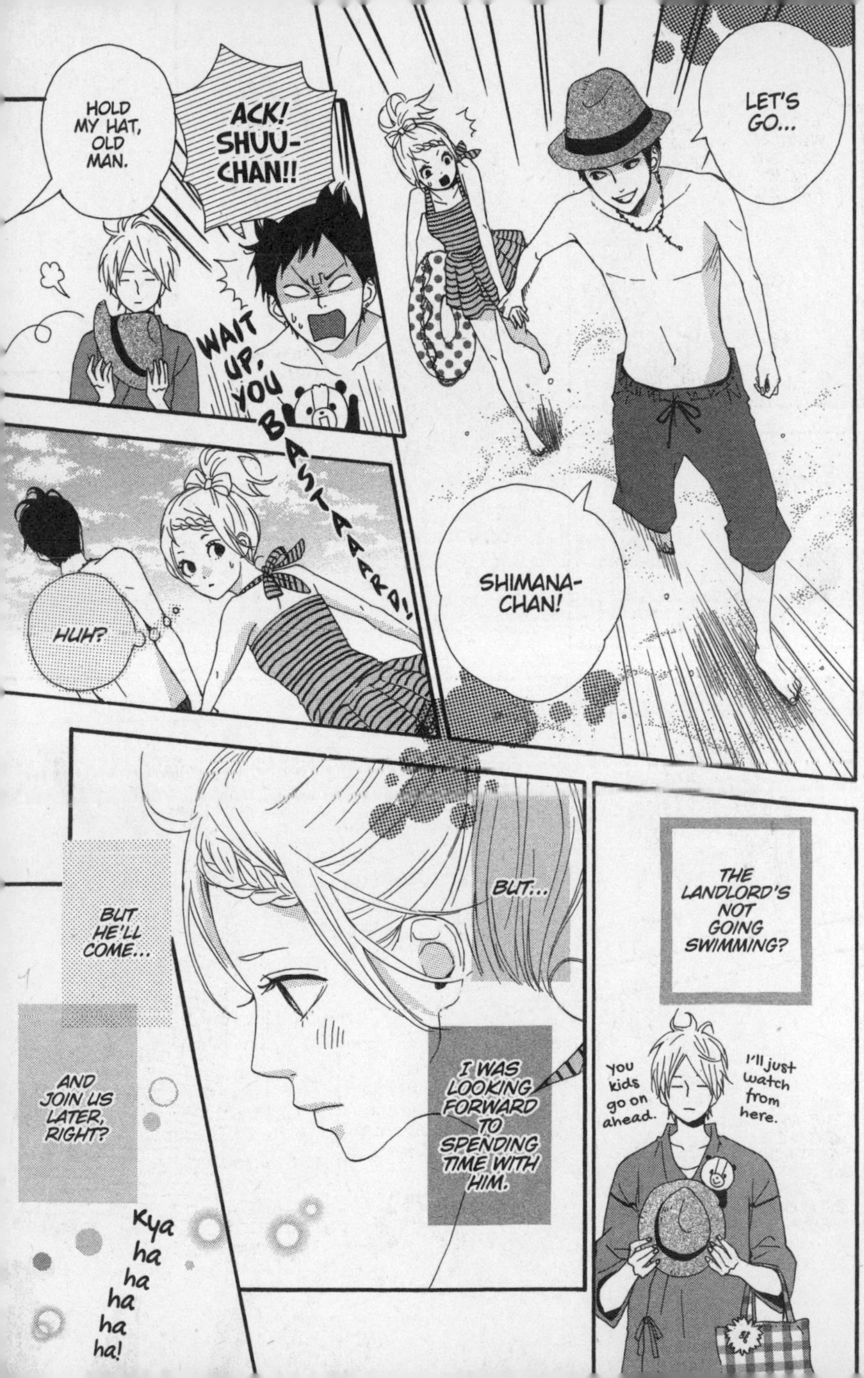

LET'S GO...
SHIMANA-CHAN!
ACK! SHUU-CHAN!!
HOLD MY HAT, OLD MAN.
WAIT UP, YOU BASTAAARD!!
HUH?
THE LANDLORD'S NOT GOING SWIMMING?
I'll just watch from here.
You kids go on ahead.
BUT...
I WAS LOOKING FORWARD TO SPENDING TIME WITH HIM.
BUT HE'LL COME...
AND JOIN US LATER, RIGHT?
Kya ha ha ha ha ha!

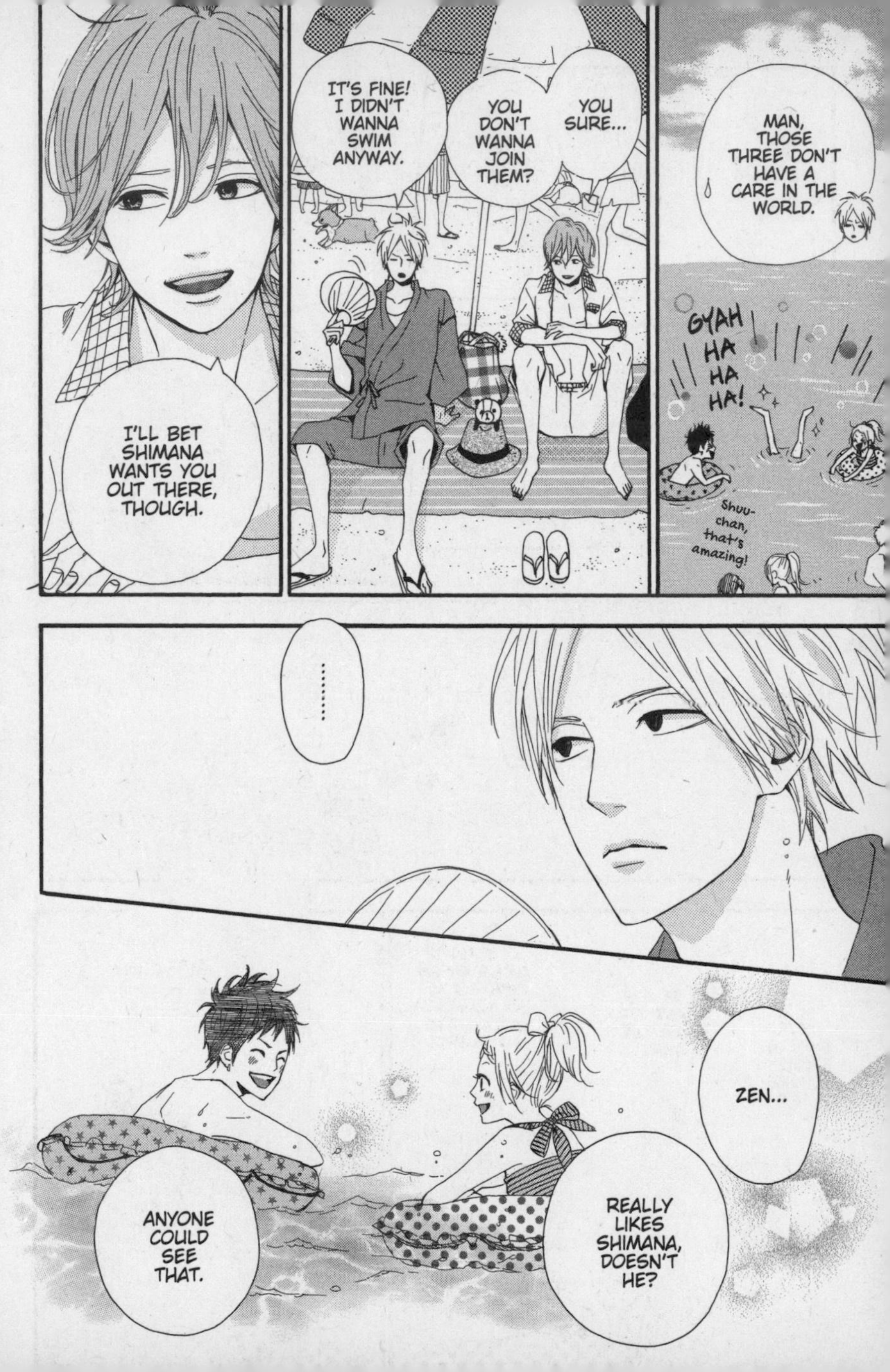
MAN, THOSE THREE DON'T HAVE A CARE IN THE WORLD.
GYAH HA HA HA!
Shuu-chan, that's amazing!
YOU SURE...
YOU DON'T WANNA JOIN THEM?
IT'S FINE! I DIDN'T WANNA SWIM ANYWAY.
I'LL BET SHIMANA WANTS YOU OUT THERE, THOUGH.
......
ZEN...
REALLY LIKES SHIMANA, DOESN'T HE?
ANYONE COULD SEE THAT.

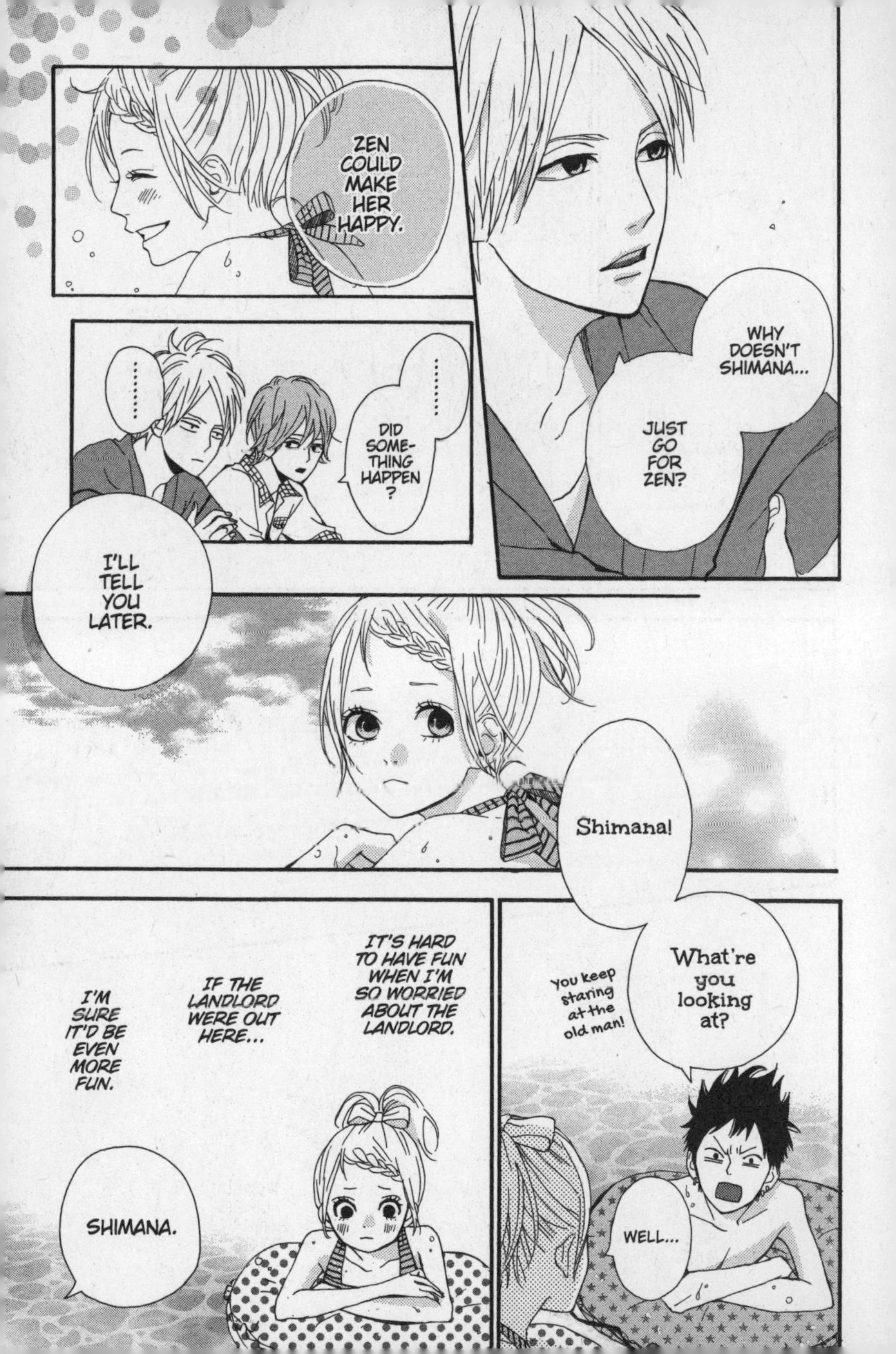

WHY DOESN'T SHIMANA...
JUST GO FOR ZEN?
ZEN COULD MAKE HER HAPPY.
......
DID SOMETHING HAPPEN?
......
I'LL TELL YOU LATER.
Shimana!
What're you looking at?
You keep staring at the old man!
WELL...
IT'S HARD TO HAVE FUN WHEN I'M SO WORRIED ABOUT THE LANDLORD.
IF THE LANDLORD WERE OUT HERE...
I'M SURE IT'D BE EVEN MORE FUN.
SHIMANA.

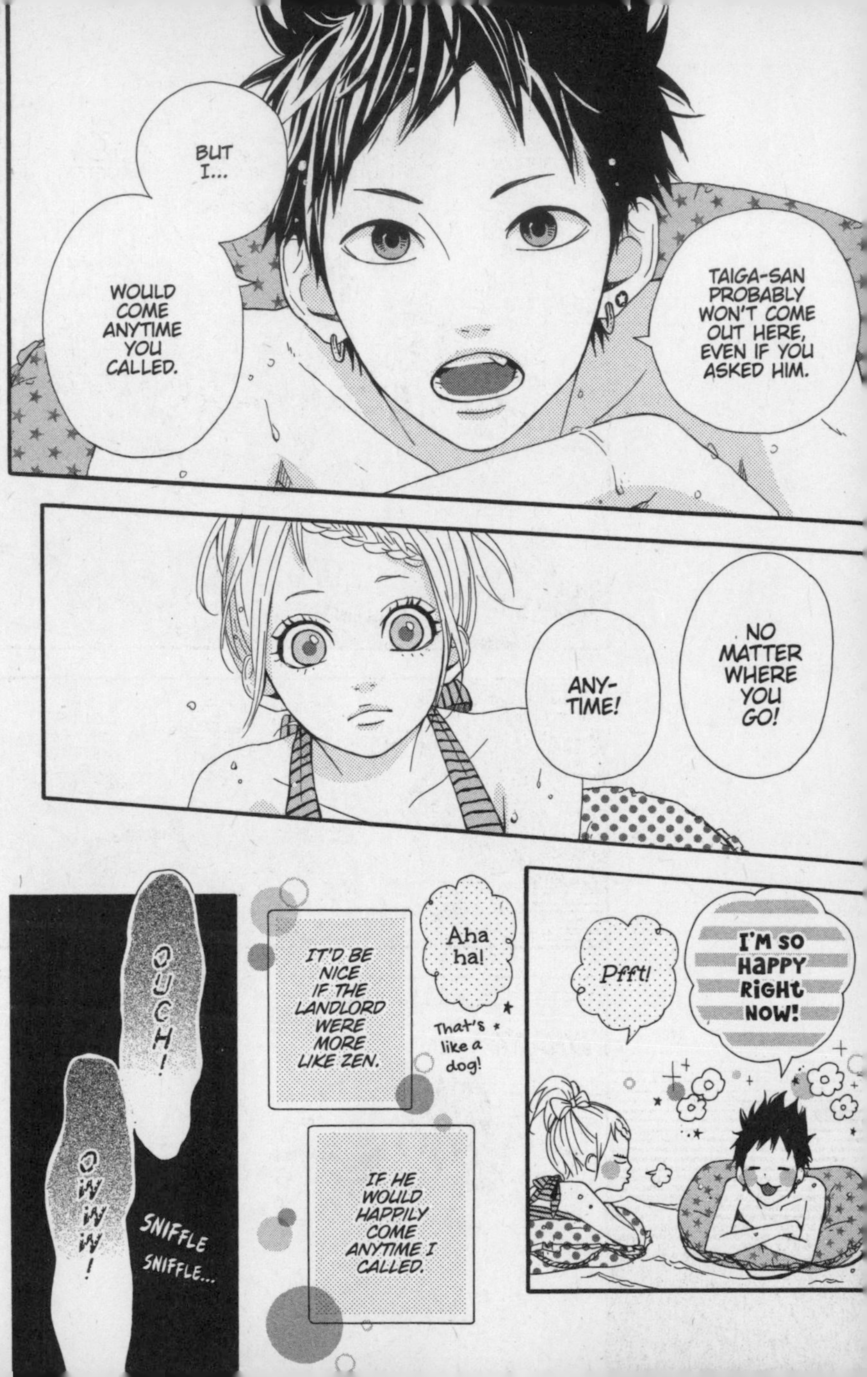
TAIGA-SAN PROBABLY WON'T COME OUT HERE, EVEN IF YOU ASKED HIM.
BUT I...
WOULD COME ANYTIME YOU CALLED.
NO MATTER WHERE YOU GO!
ANY-TIME!
I'M SO HAPPY RIGHT NOW!
Pfft!
Aha ha!
That's like a dog!
IT'D BE NICE IF THE LANDLORD WERE MORE LIKE ZEN.
IF HE WOULD HAPPILY COME ANYTIME I CALLED.
OUCH!
OWWW!
SNIFFLE SNIFFLE...

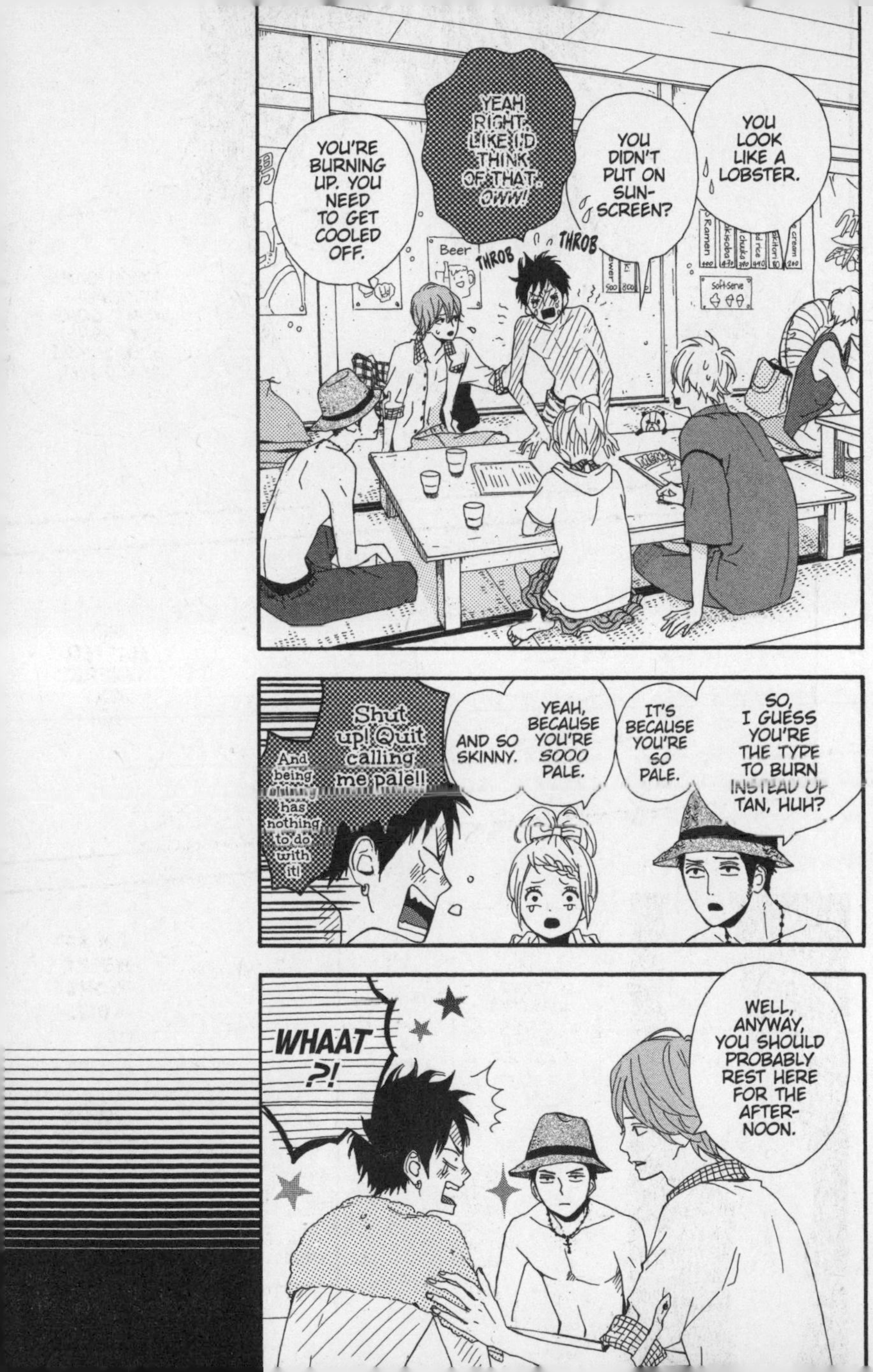
YOU LOOK LIKE A LOBSTER.
YOU DIDN'T PUT ON SUN-SCREEN?
THROB
YEAH RIGHT. LIKE I'D THINK OF THAT. OWW!
THROB
YOU'RE BURNING UP. YOU NEED TO GET COOLED OFF.
Beer
Soft-Serve
SO, I GUESS YOU'RE THE TYPE TO BURN INSTEAD OF TAN, HUH?
IT'S BECAUSE YOU'RE SO PALE.
YEAH, BECAUSE YOU'RE SOOO PALE.
AND SO SKINNY.
Shut up! Quit calling me pale!!
And being skinny has nothing to do with it!
WELL, ANYWAY, YOU SHOULD PROBABLY REST HERE FOR THE AFTER-NOON.
WHAAT?!

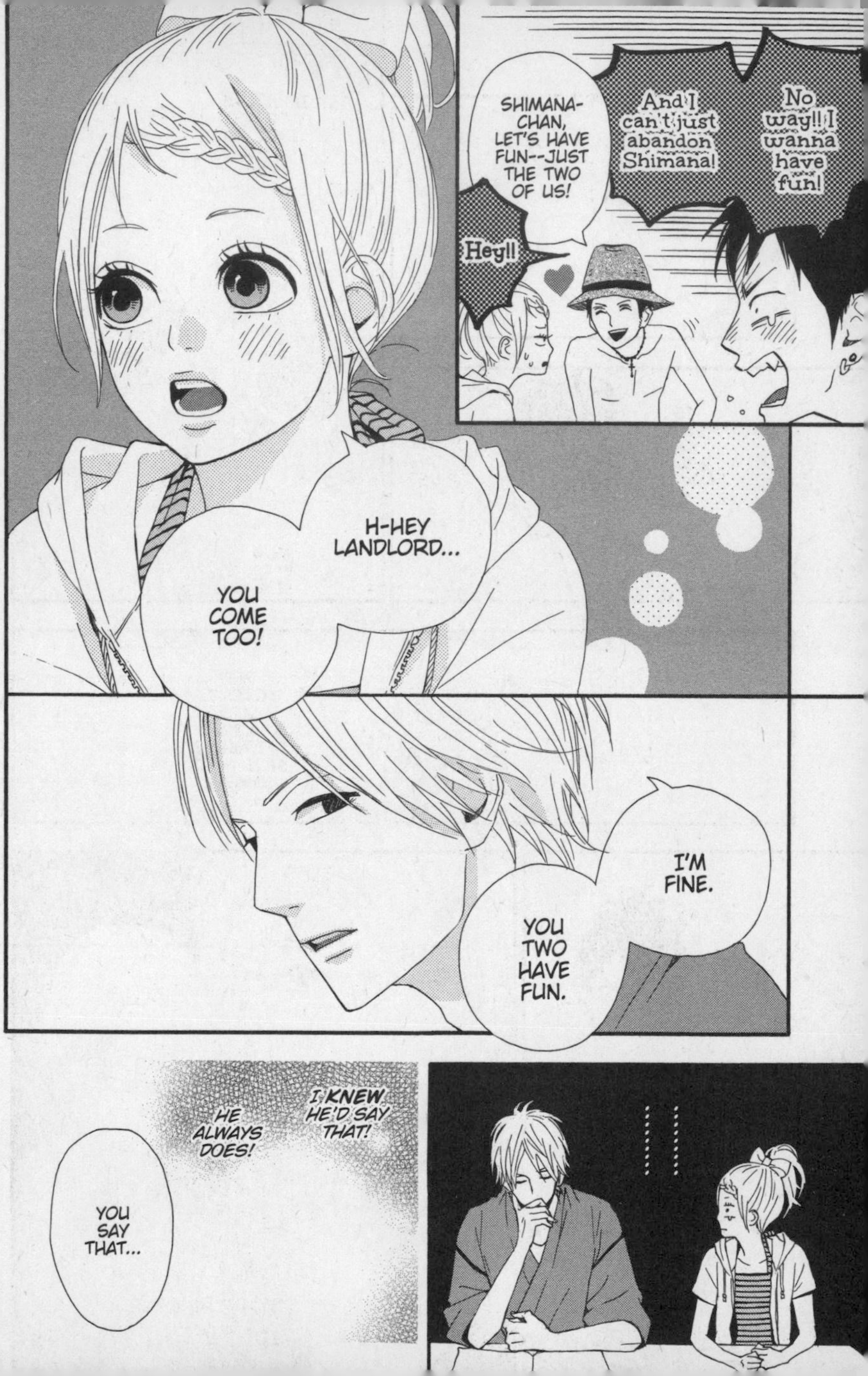
No way!! I wanna have fun!
And I can't just abandon Shimana!
SHIMANA-CHAN, LET'S HAVE FUN--JUST THE TWO OF US!
Hey!!
H-HEY LANDLORD...
YOU COME TOO!
I'M FINE.
YOU TWO HAVE FUN.
......
I KNEW HE'D SAY THAT!
HE ALWAYS DOES!
YOU SAY THAT...

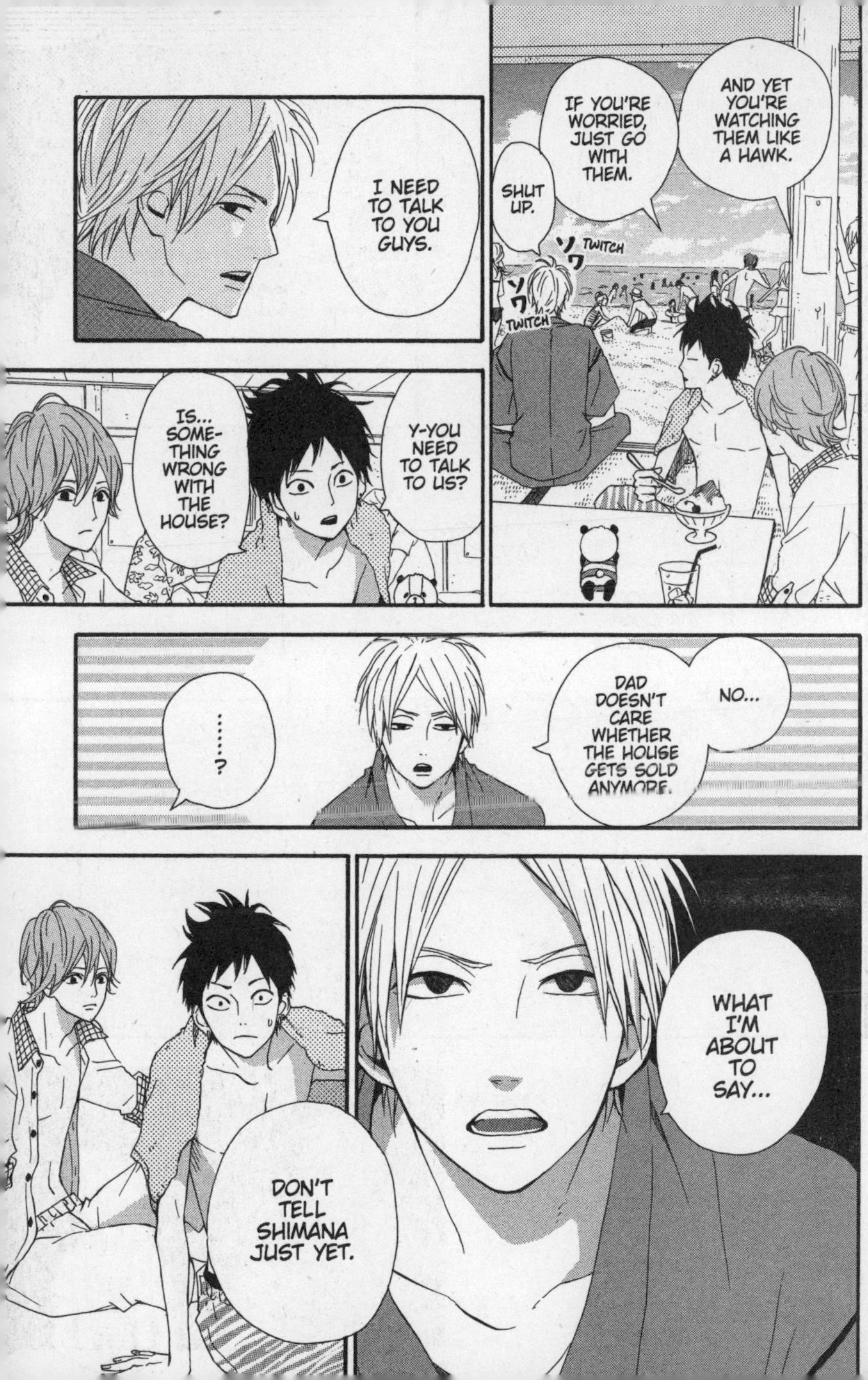
AND YET YOU'RE WATCHING THEM LIKE A HAWK.
IF YOU'RE WORRIED, JUST GO WITH THEM.
SHUT UP.
ソワ TWITCH
ソワ TWITCH
I NEED TO TALK TO YOU GUYS.
Y-YOU NEED TO TALK TO US?
IS... SOME-THING WRONG WITH THE HOUSE?
NO...
DAD DOESN'T CARE WHETHER THE HOUSE GETS SOLD ANYMORE.
......?
WHAT I'M ABOUT TO SAY...
DON'T TELL SHIMANA JUST YET.

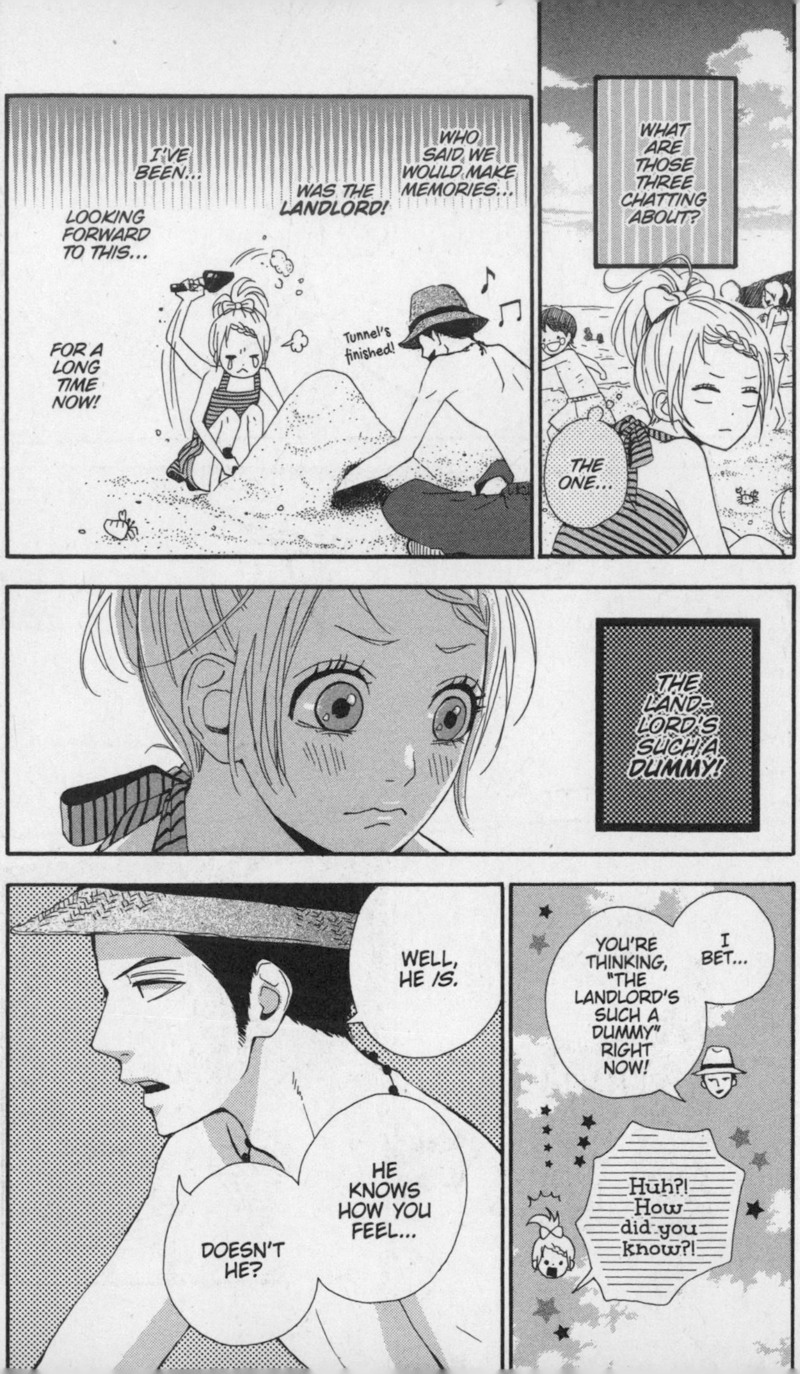

WHAT ARE THOSE THREE CHATTING ABOUT?
THE ONE...
WHO SAID WE WOULD MAKE MEMORIES...
WAS THE LANDLORD!
I'VE BEEN...
LOOKING FORWARD TO THIS...
FOR A LONG TIME NOW!
Tunnel's finished!
THE LANDLORD'S SUCH A DUMMY!
I BET...
YOU'RE THINKING, "THE LANDLORD'S SUCH A DUMMY" RIGHT NOW!
Huh?! How did you know?!
WELL, HE IS.
HE KNOWS HOW YOU FEEL...
DOESN'T HE?

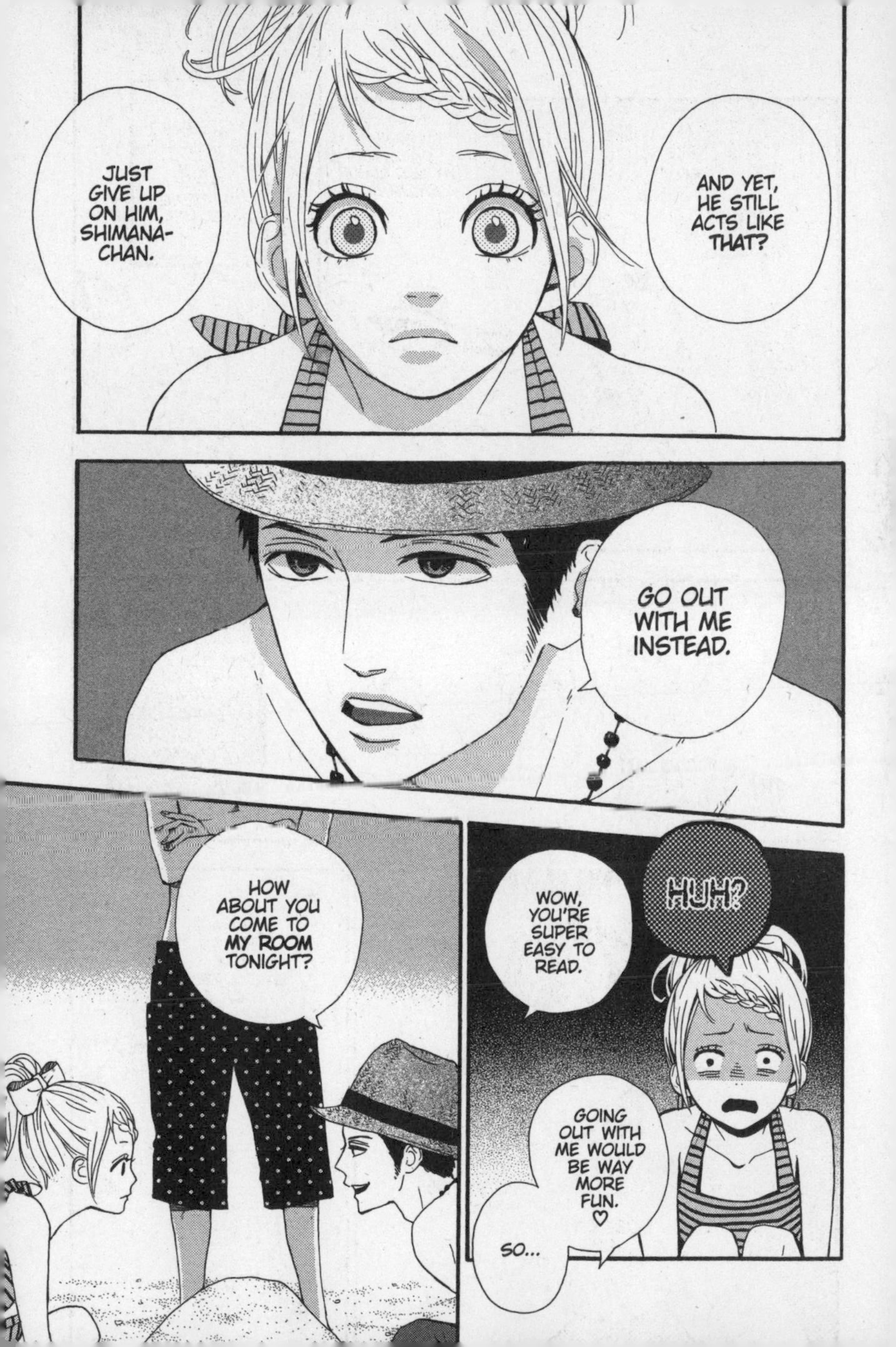
AND YET, HE STILL ACTS LIKE THAT?
JUST GIVE UP ON HIM, SHIMANA-CHAN.
GO OUT WITH ME INSTEAD.
HUH?
WOW, YOU'RE SUPER EASY TO READ.
GOING OUT WITH ME WOULD BE WAY MORE FUN. ♡
SO...
HOW ABOUT YOU COME TO MY ROOM TONIGHT?

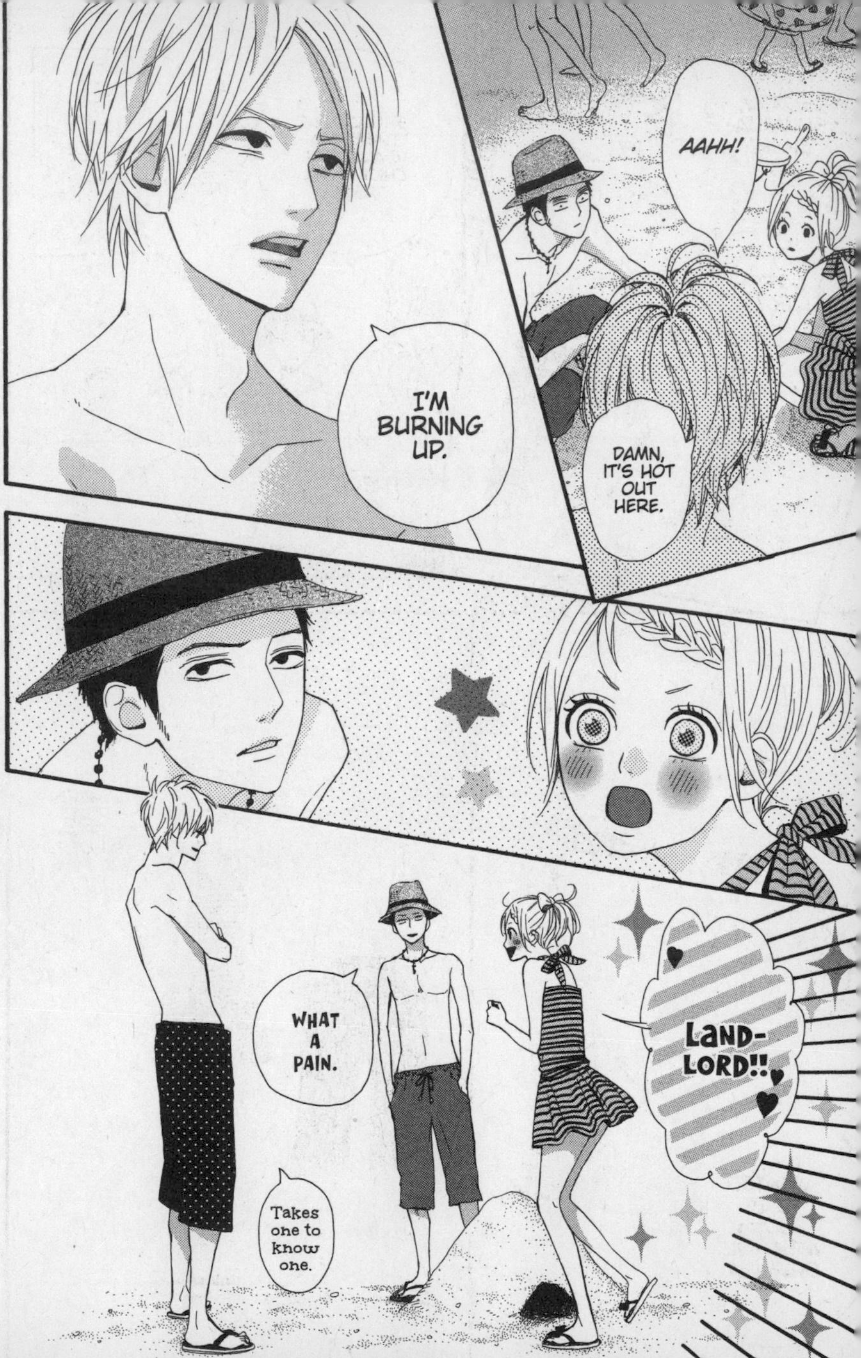
AAHH!
DAMN, IT'S HOT OUT HERE.
I'M BURNING UP.
LAND-LORD!!
WHAT A PAIN.
Takes one to know one.

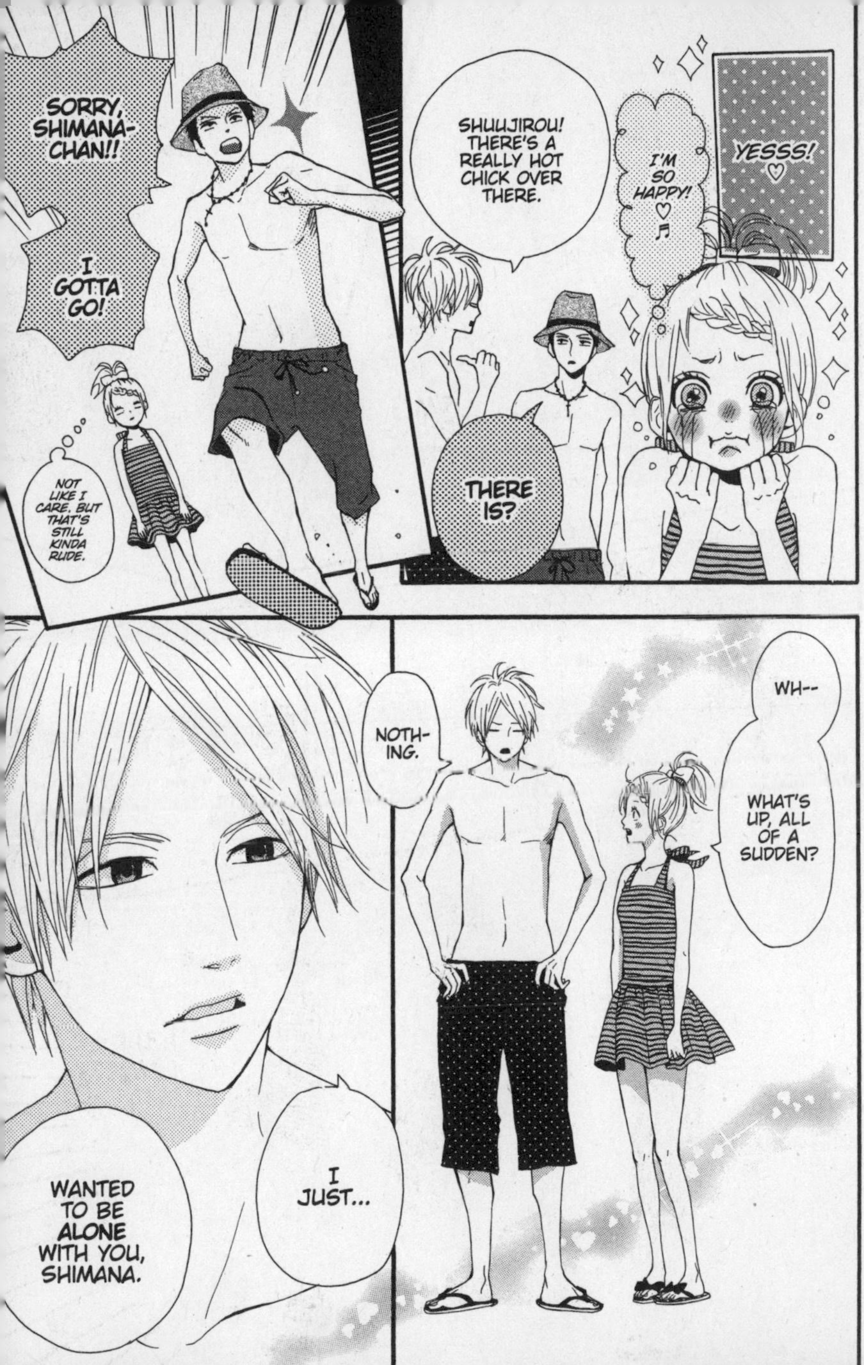
YESSS! ♡
I'M SO HAPPY! ♡ ♫
SHUUJIROU! THERE'S A REALLY HOT CHICK OVER THERE.
THERE IS?
SORRY, SHIMANA-CHAN!!
I GOTTA GO!
NOT LIKE I CARE. BUT THAT'S STILL KINDA RUDE.
WH--
WHAT'S UP, ALL OF A SUDDEN?
NOTH-ING.
I JUST...
WANTED TO BE ALONE WITH YOU, SHIMANA.

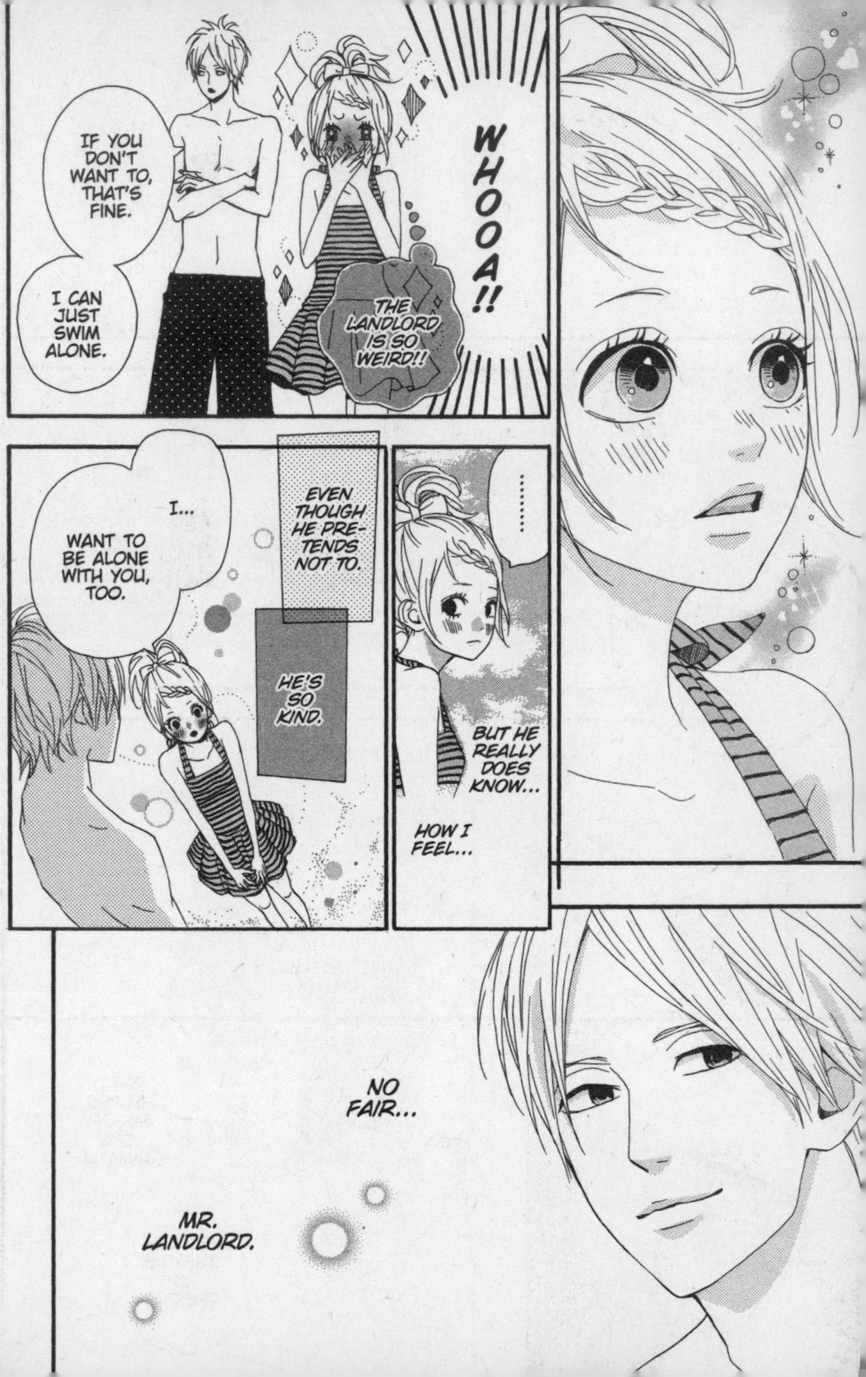
IF YOU DON'T WANT TO, THAT'S FINE.
I CAN JUST SWIM ALONE.
WHOOOA!!
THE LANDLORD IS SO WEIRD!!
....
BUT HE REALLY DOES KNOW...
HOW I FEEL...
EVEN THOUGH HE PRETENDS NOT TO.
HE'S SO KIND.
I...
WANT TO BE ALONE WITH YOU, TOO.
NO FAIR...
MR. LANDLORD.

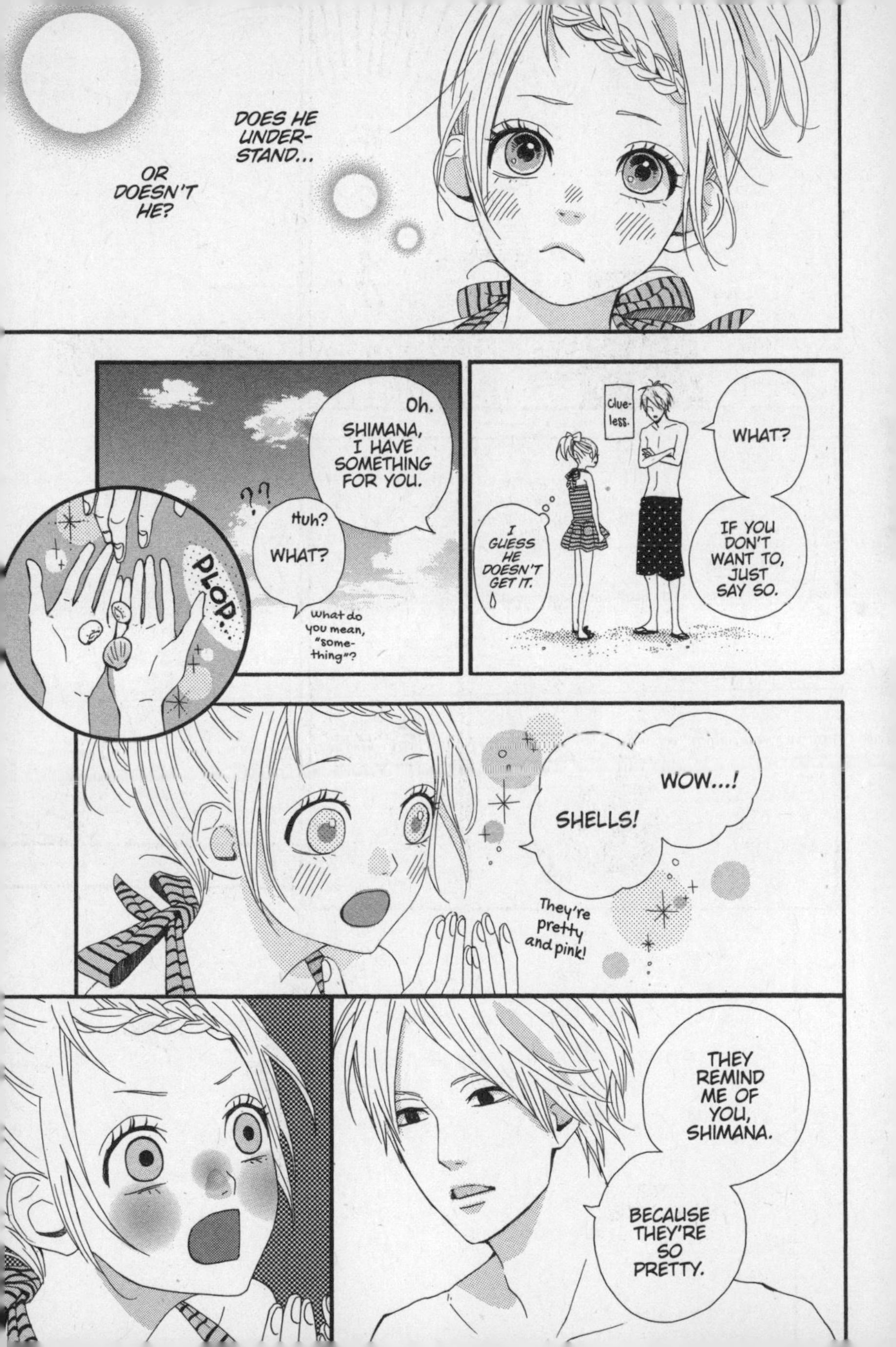

DOES HE UNDER-STAND...
OR DOESN'T HE?
Clue-less.
WHAT?
IF YOU DON'T WANT TO, JUST SAY SO.
I GUESS HE DOESN'T GET IT.
Oh.
SHIMANA, I HAVE SOMETHING FOR YOU.
Huh?
WHAT?
What do you mean, "some-thing"?
PLOP...
WOW...!
SHELLS!
They're pretty and pink!
THEY REMIND ME OF YOU, SHIMANA.
BECAUSE THEY'RE SO PRETTY.

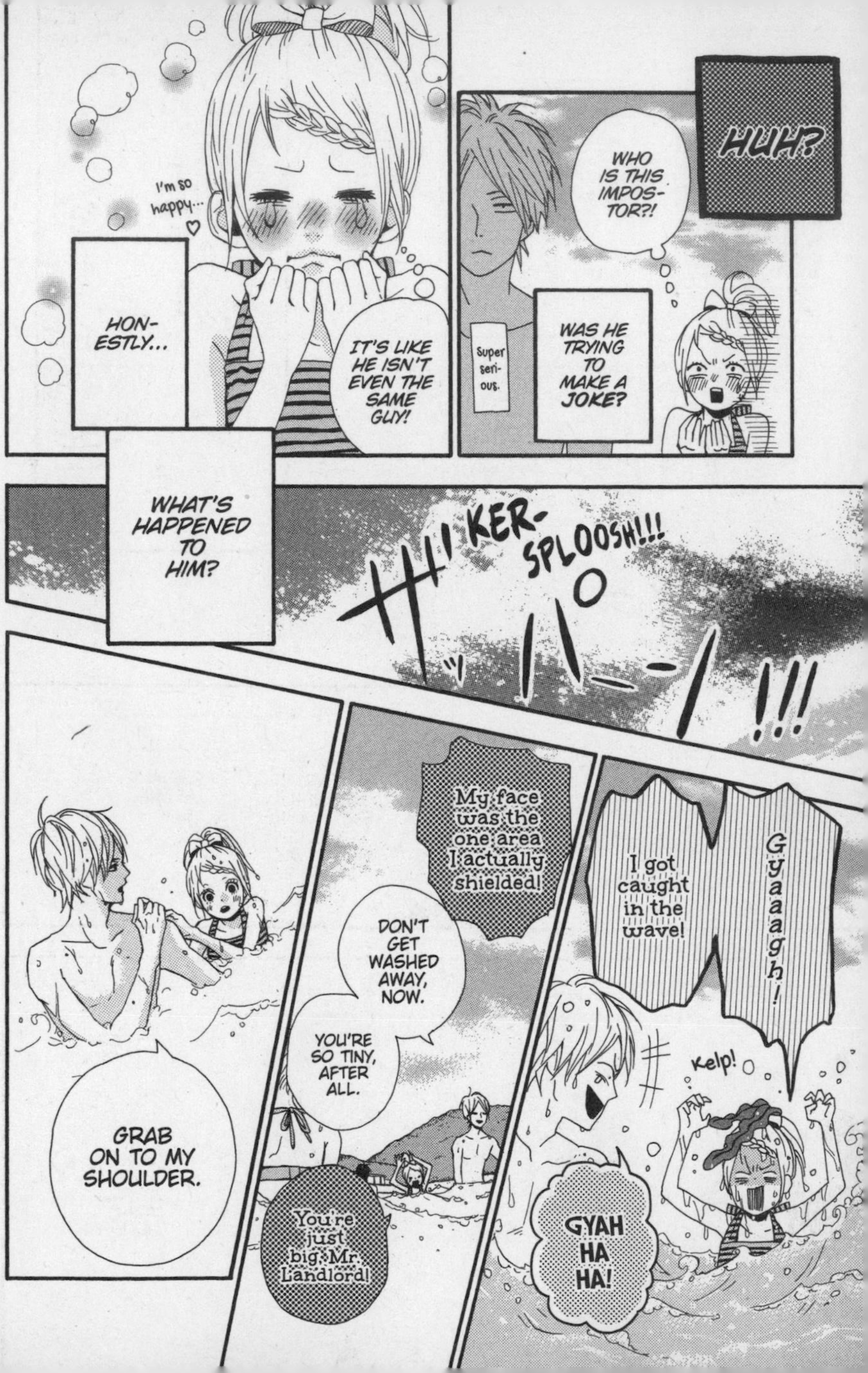
HUH?
WHO IS THIS IMPOSTOR?!
Super serious.
WAS HE TRYING TO MAKE A JOKE?
IT'S LIKE HE ISN'T EVEN THE SAME GUY!
I'm so happy... ♡
HONESTLY...
WHAT'S HAPPENED TO HIM?
KER-SPLOOSH!!!
Gyaaagh!
I got caught in the wave!
Kelp!
GYAH HA HA!
My face was the one area I actually shielded!
DON'T GET WASHED AWAY, NOW.
YOU'RE SO TINY, AFTER ALL.
You're just big, Mr. Landlord!
GRAB ON TO MY SHOULDER.

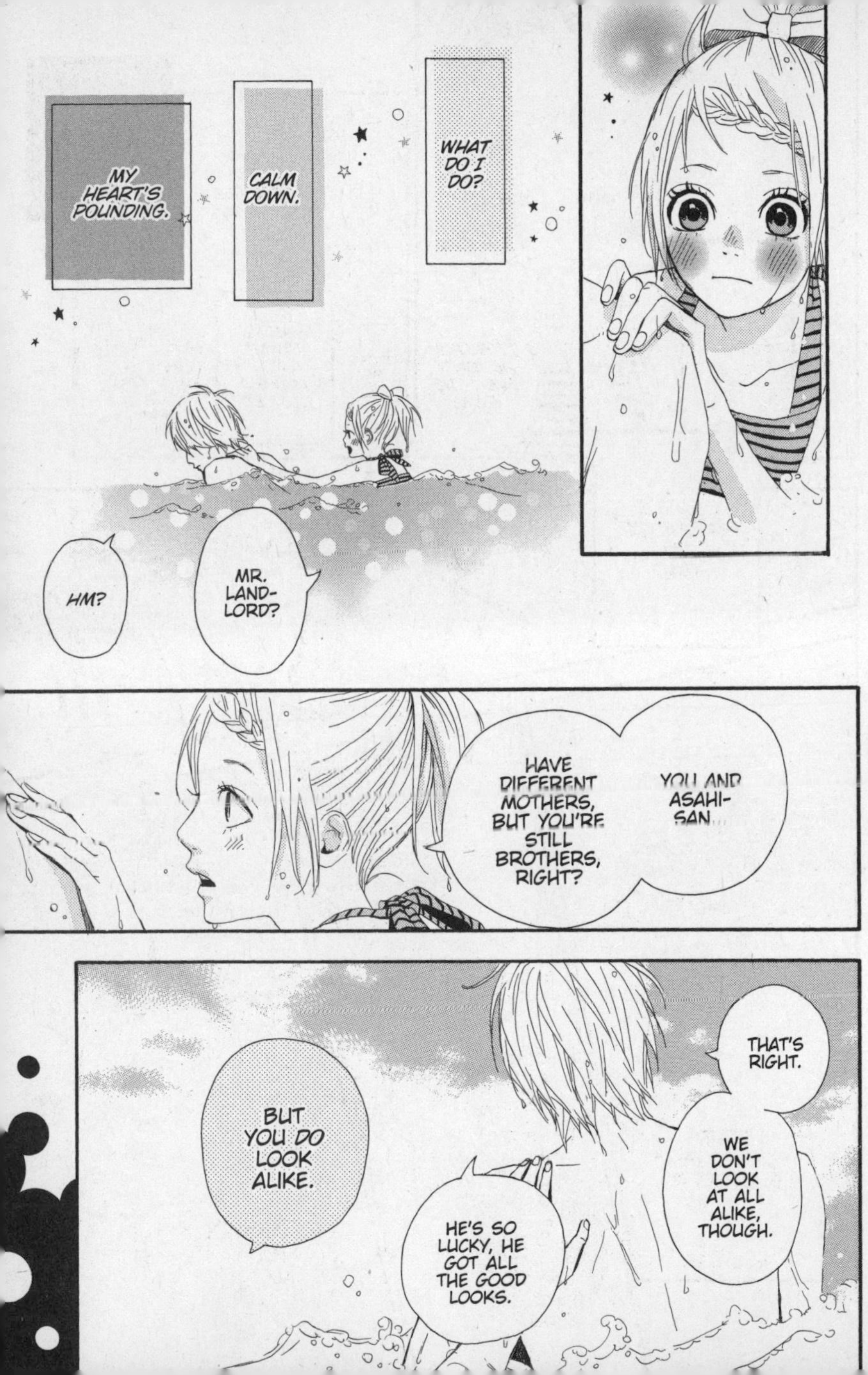
WHAT DO I DO?
CALM DOWN.
MY HEART'S POUNDING.
MR. LANDLORD?
HM?
YOU AND ASAHI-SAN...
HAVE DIFFERENT MOTHERS, BUT YOU'RE STILL BROTHERS, RIGHT?
THAT'S RIGHT.
WE DON'T LOOK AT ALL ALIKE, THOUGH.
BUT YOU DO LOOK ALIKE.
HE'S SO LUCKY, HE GOT ALL THE GOOD LOOKS.

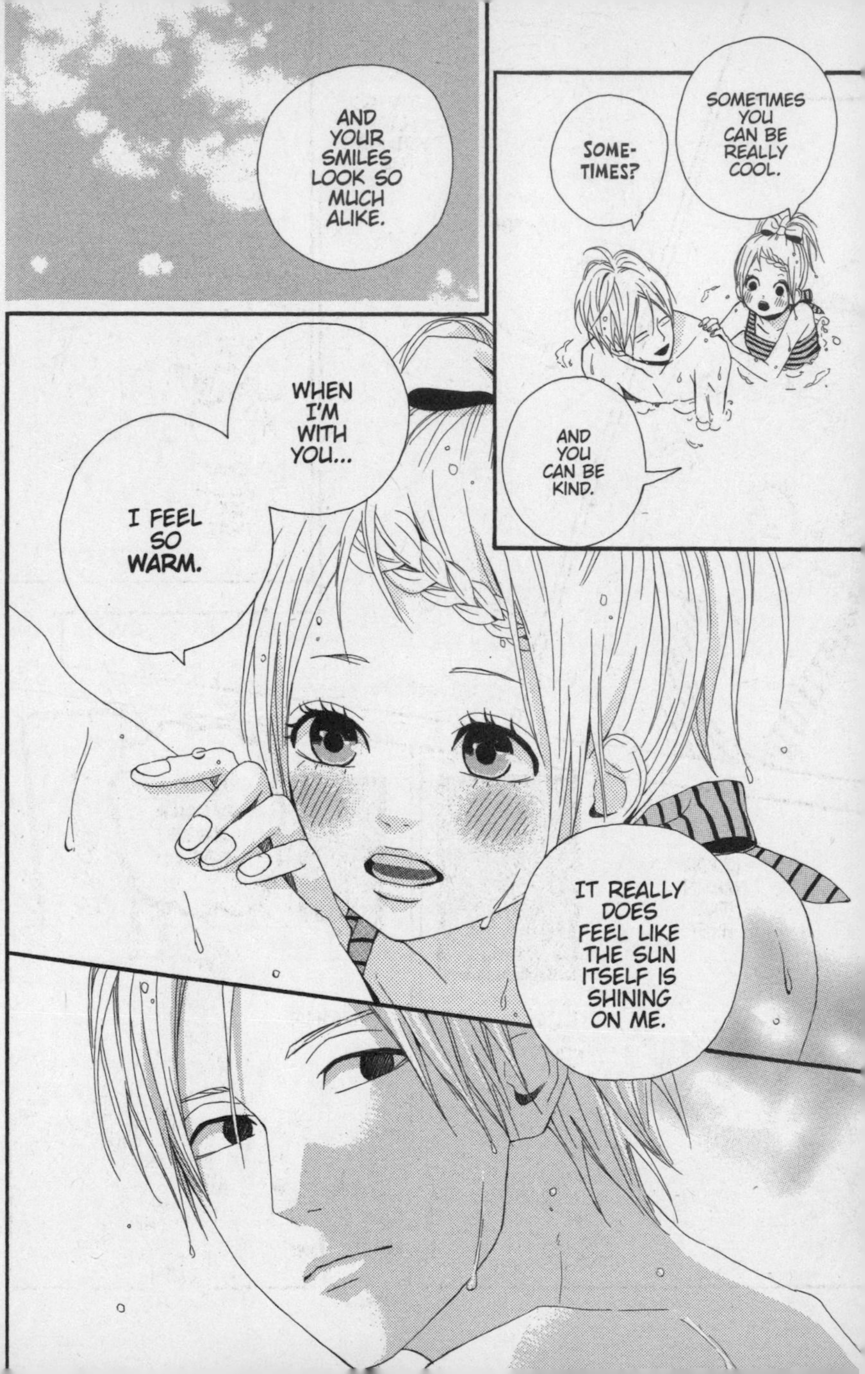
SOMETIMES YOU CAN BE REALLY COOL.
SOME-TIMES?
AND YOU CAN BE KIND.
AND YOUR SMILES LOOK SO MUCH ALIKE.
WHEN I'M WITH YOU...
I FEEL SO WARM.
IT REALLY DOES FEEL LIKE THE SUN ITSELF IS SHINING ON ME.

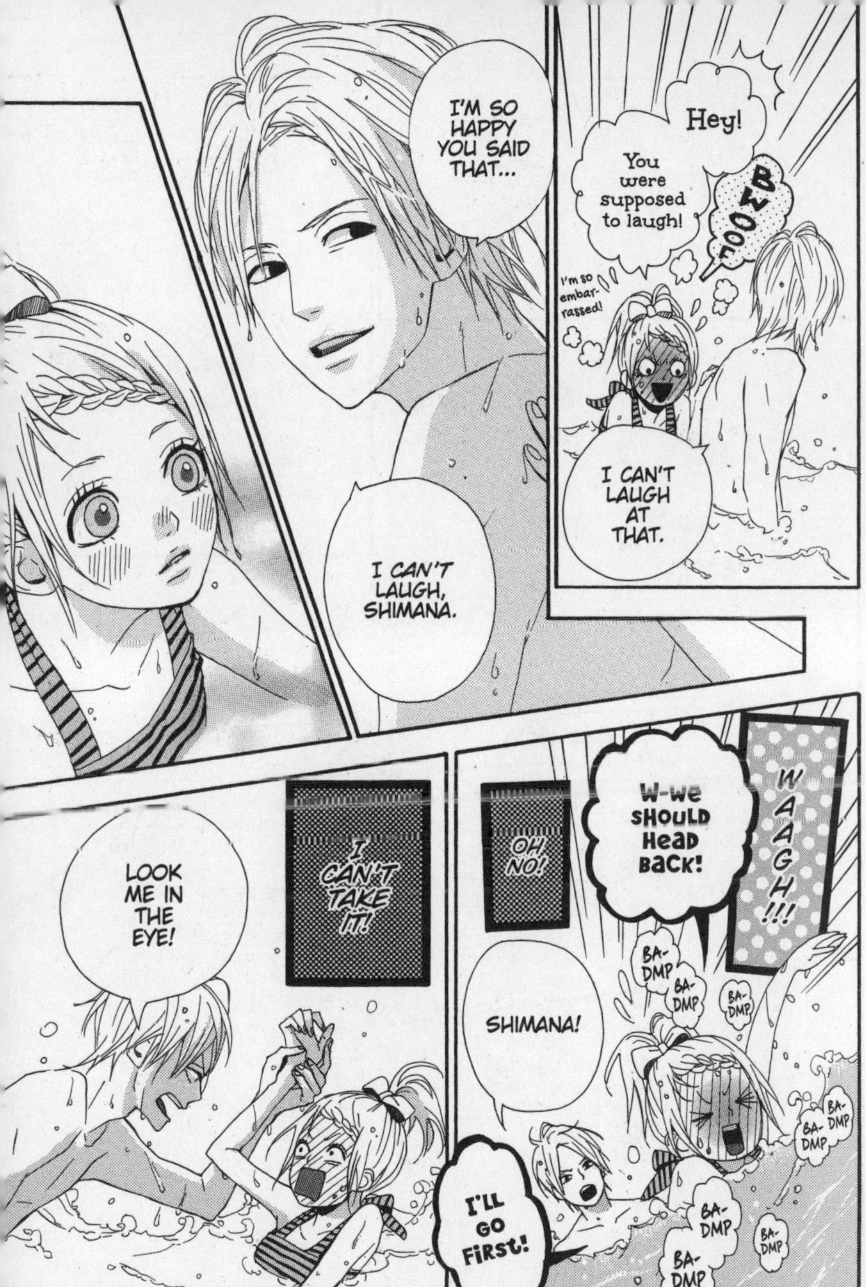
Hey!
You were supposed to laugh!
BWOOF
I'm so embarrassed!
I CAN'T LAUGH AT THAT.
I'M SO HAPPY YOU SAID THAT...
I CAN'T LAUGH, SHIMANA.
WAAGH!!!
W-WE SHOULD HEAD BACK!
OH NO!
BA-DMP
BA-DMP
BA-DMP
SHIMANA!
BA-DMP
BA-DMP
BA-DMP
BA-DMP
BA-DMP
I'LL GO FIRST!
I CAN'T TAKE IT!
LOOK ME IN THE EYE!

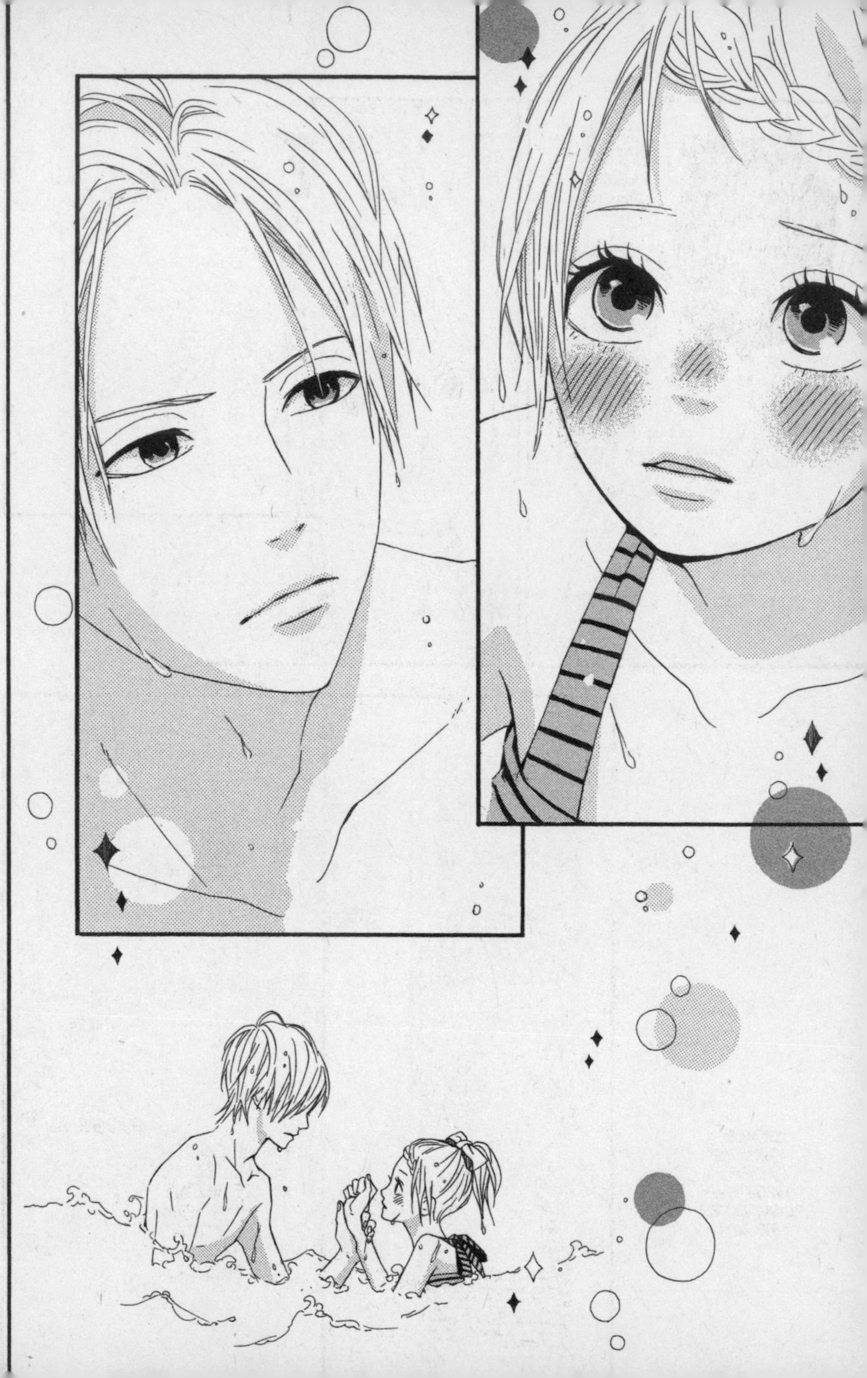

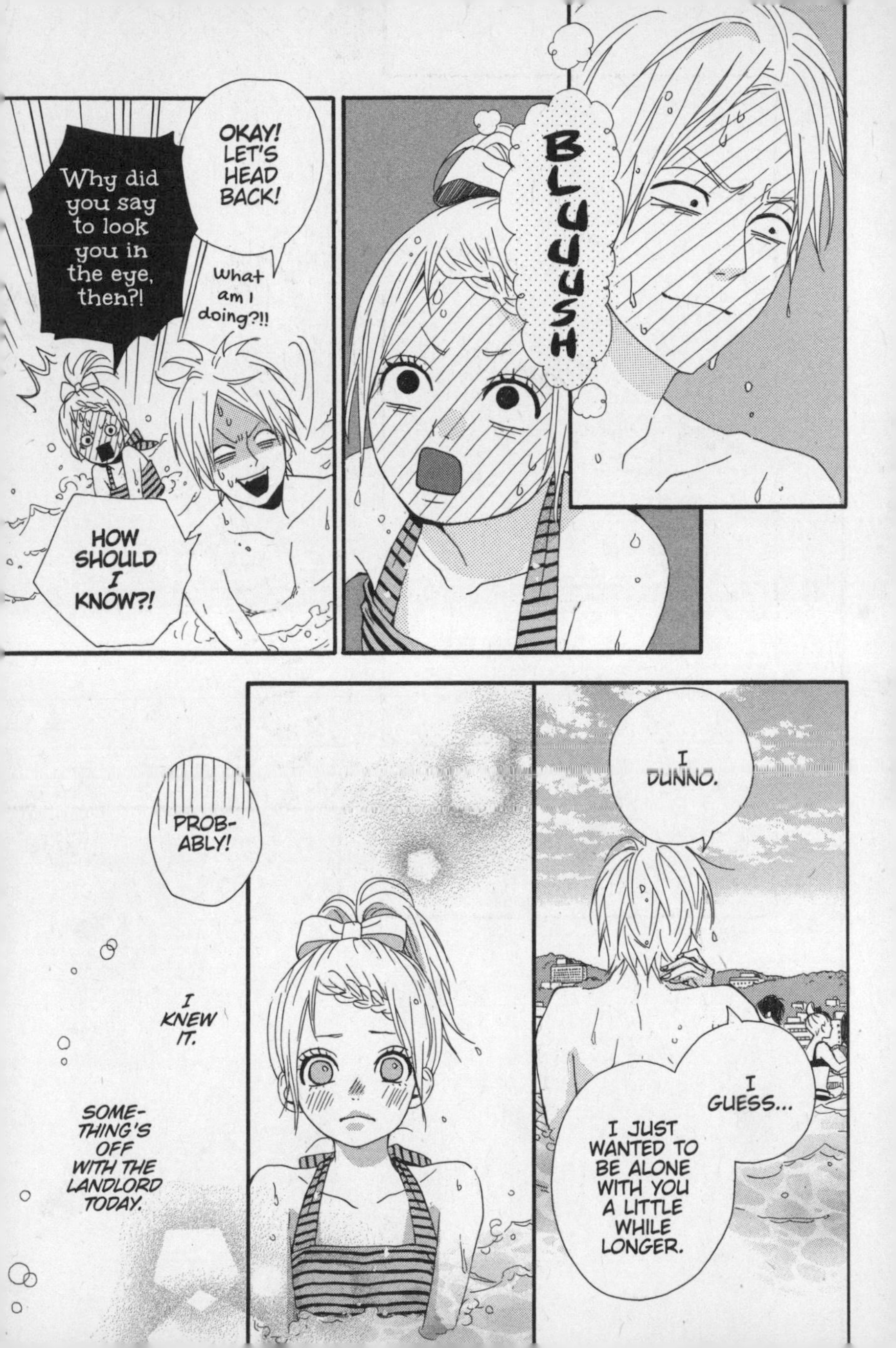
BLUUUSH
OKAY! LET'S HEAD BACK!
What am I doing?!!
Why did you say to look you in the eye, then?!
HOW SHOULD I KNOW?!
I DUNNO.
I GUESS...
I JUST WANTED TO BE ALONE WITH YOU A LITTLE WHILE LONGER.
PROB-ABLY!
I KNEW IT.
SOME-THING'S OFF WITH THE LANDLORD TODAY.

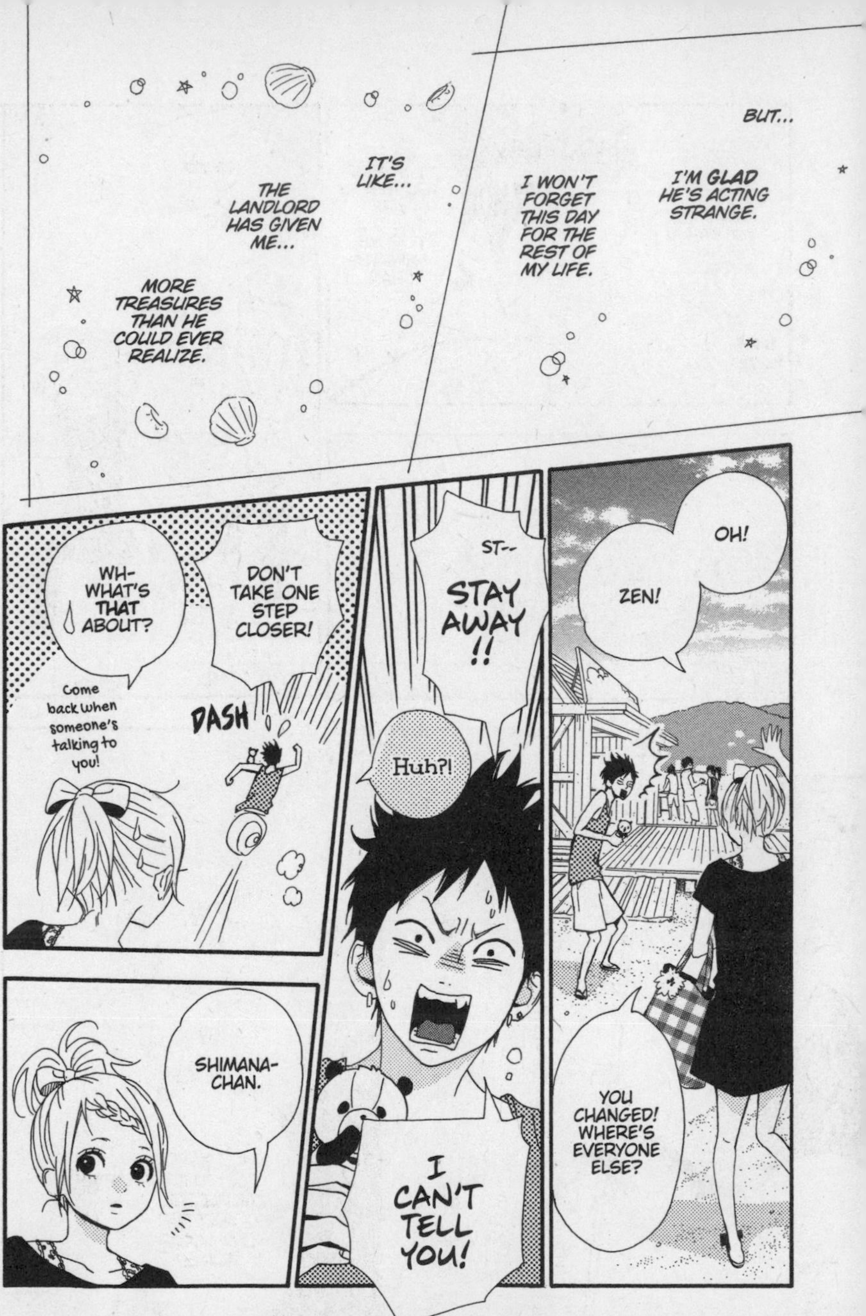
BUT...
I'M GLAD HE'S ACTING STRANGE.
I WON'T FORGET THIS DAY FOR THE REST OF MY LIFE.
IT'S LIKE...
THE LANDLORD HAS GIVEN ME...
MORE TREASURES THAN HE COULD EVER REALIZE.
OH!
ZEN!
YOU CHANGED! WHERE'S EVERYONE ELSE?
ST--
STAY AWAY!!
Huh?!
I CAN'T TELL YOU!
DON'T TAKE ONE STEP CLOSER!
WH-WHAT'S THAT ABOUT?
DASH
Come back when someone's talking to you!
SHIMANA-CHAN.

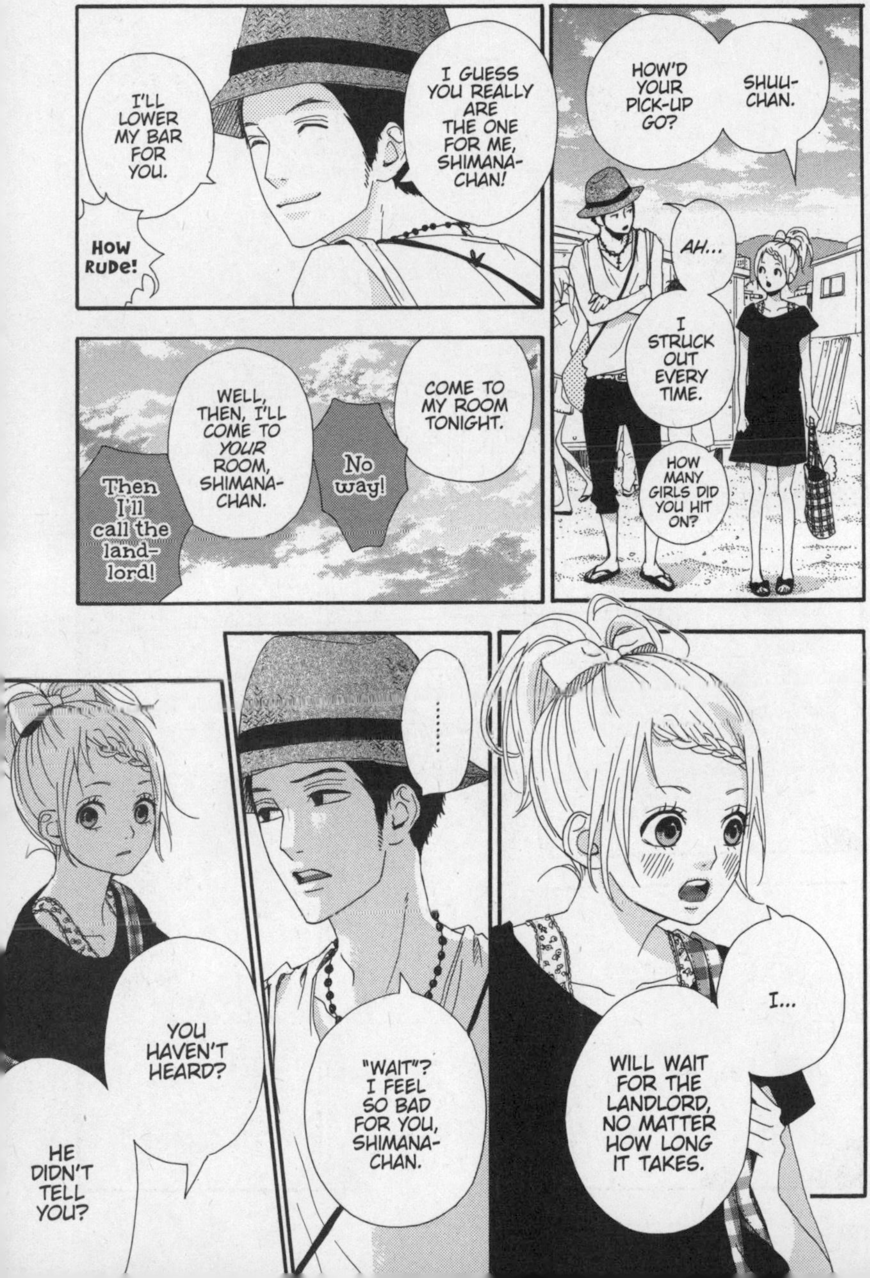
SHUU-CHAN.
HOW'D YOUR PICK-UP GO?
AH...
I STRUCK OUT EVERY TIME.
HOW MANY GIRLS DID YOU HIT ON?
I GUESS YOU REALLY ARE THE ONE FOR ME, SHIMANA-CHAN!
I'LL LOWER MY BAR FOR YOU.
HOW RUDE!
COME TO MY ROOM TONIGHT.
No way!
WELL, THEN, I'LL COME TO *YOUR* ROOM, SHIMANA-CHAN.
Then I'll call the land-lord!
I...
WILL WAIT FOR THE LANDLORD, NO MATTER HOW LONG IT TAKES.
......
"WAIT"? I FEEL SO BAD FOR YOU, SHIMANA-CHAN.
YOU HAVEN'T HEARD?
HE DIDN'T TELL YOU?

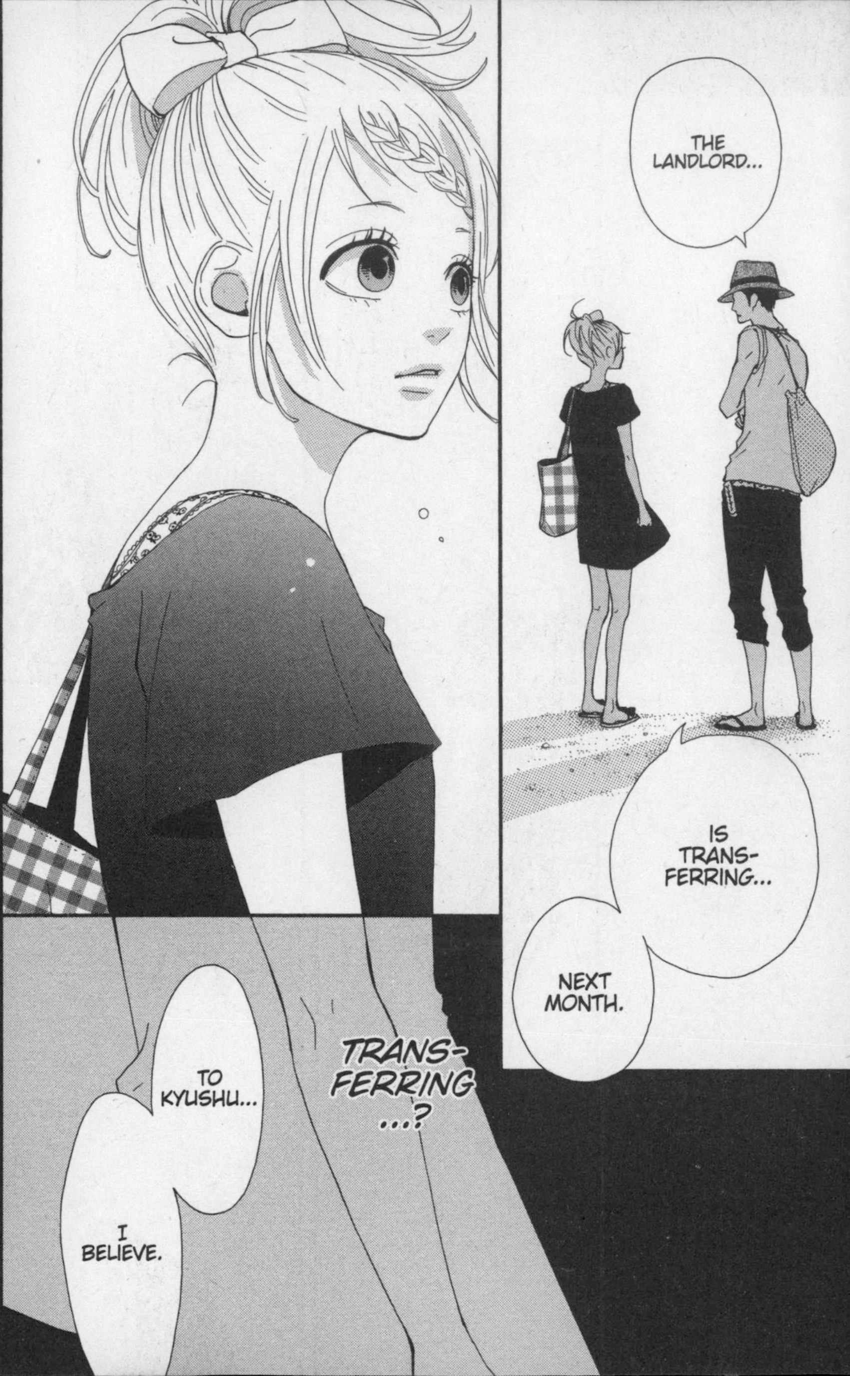
THE LANDLORD...
IS TRANS-FERRING...
NEXT MONTH.
TRANS-FERRING ...?
TO KYUSHU...
I BELIEVE.

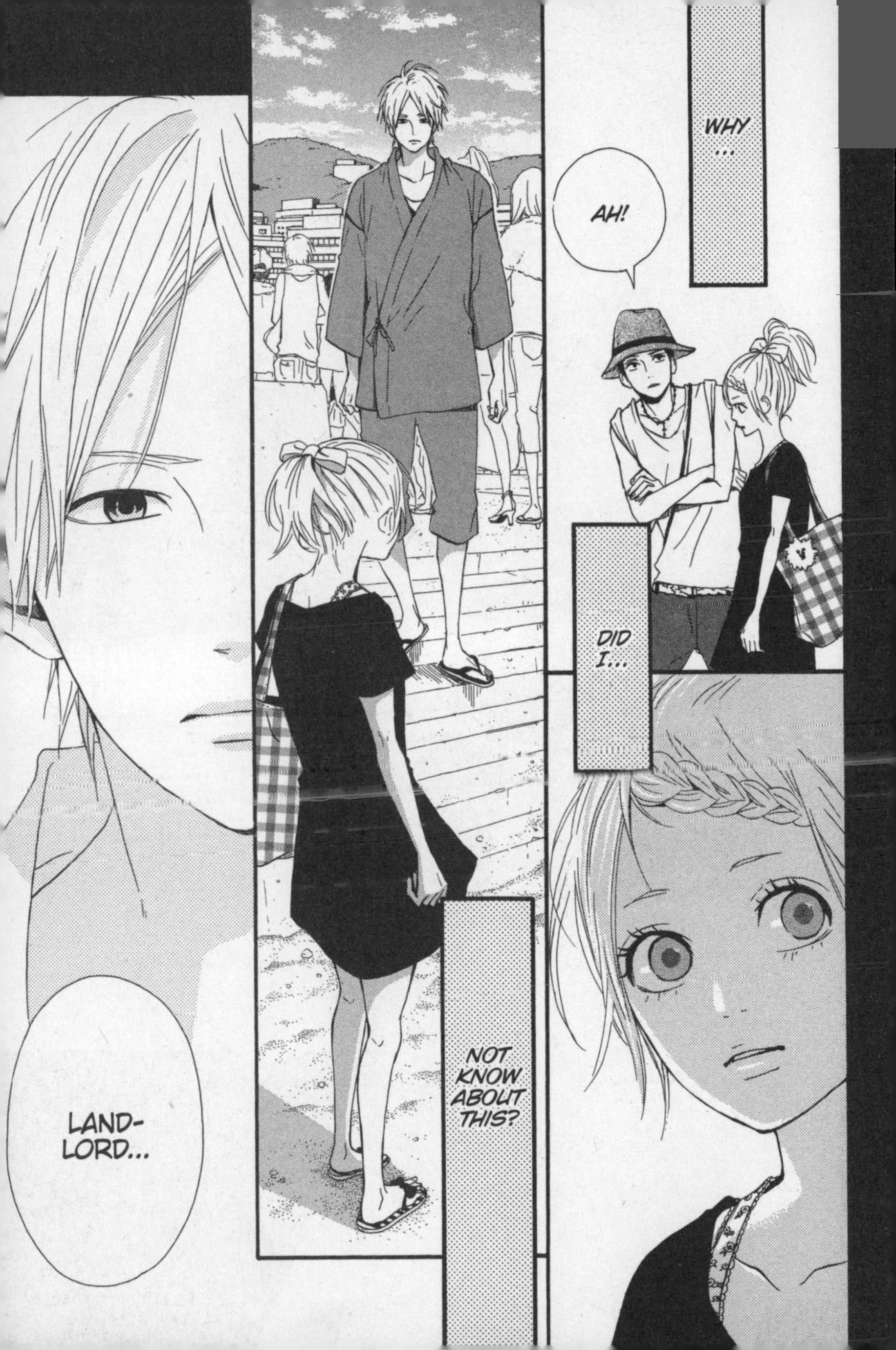
WHY ...
AH!
DID I...
NOT KNOW ABOUT THIS?
LAND-LORD...

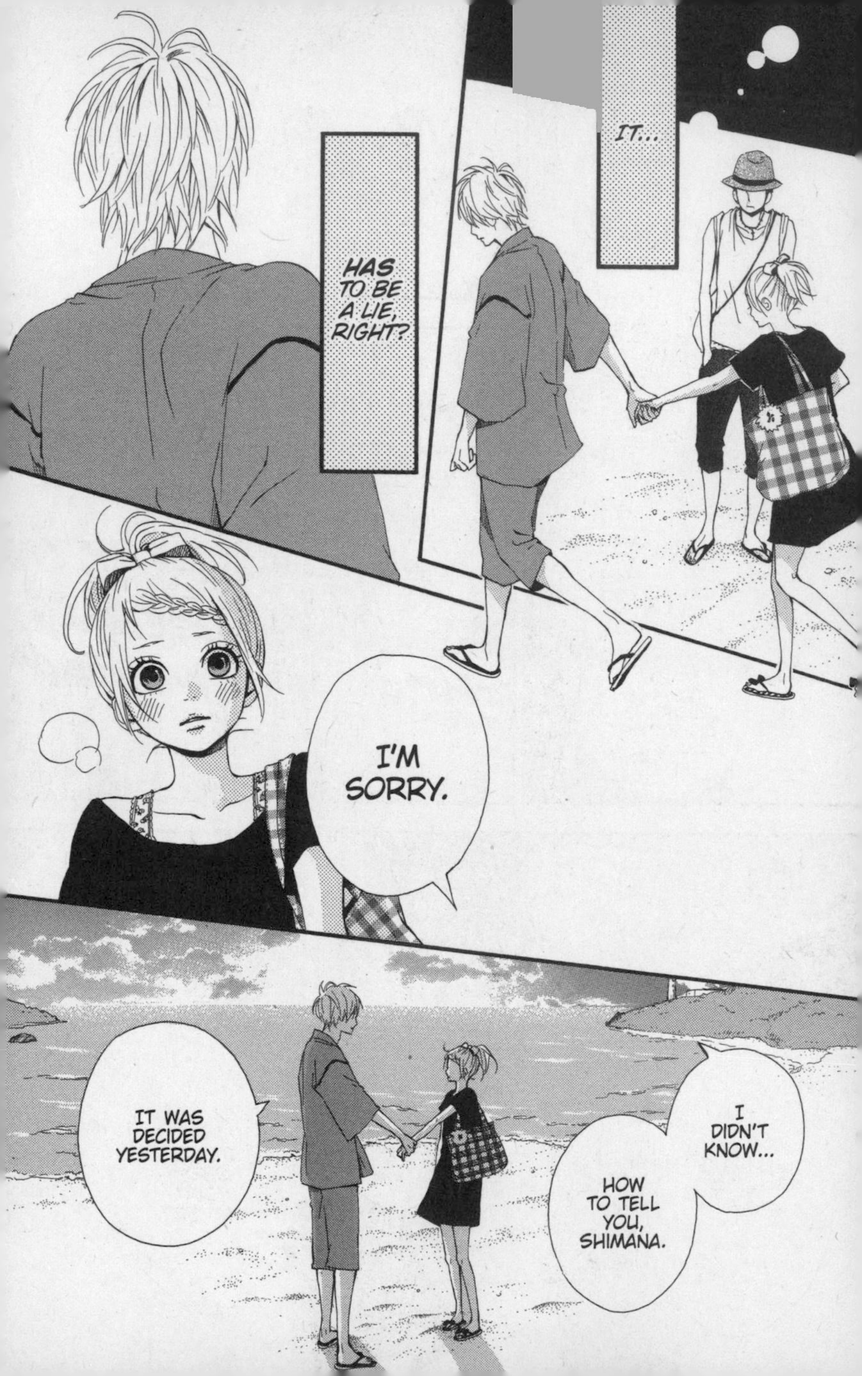
IT...
HAS TO BE A LIE, RIGHT?
I'M SORRY.
I DIDN'T KNOW...
HOW TO TELL YOU, SHIMANA.
IT WAS DECIDED YESTERDAY.

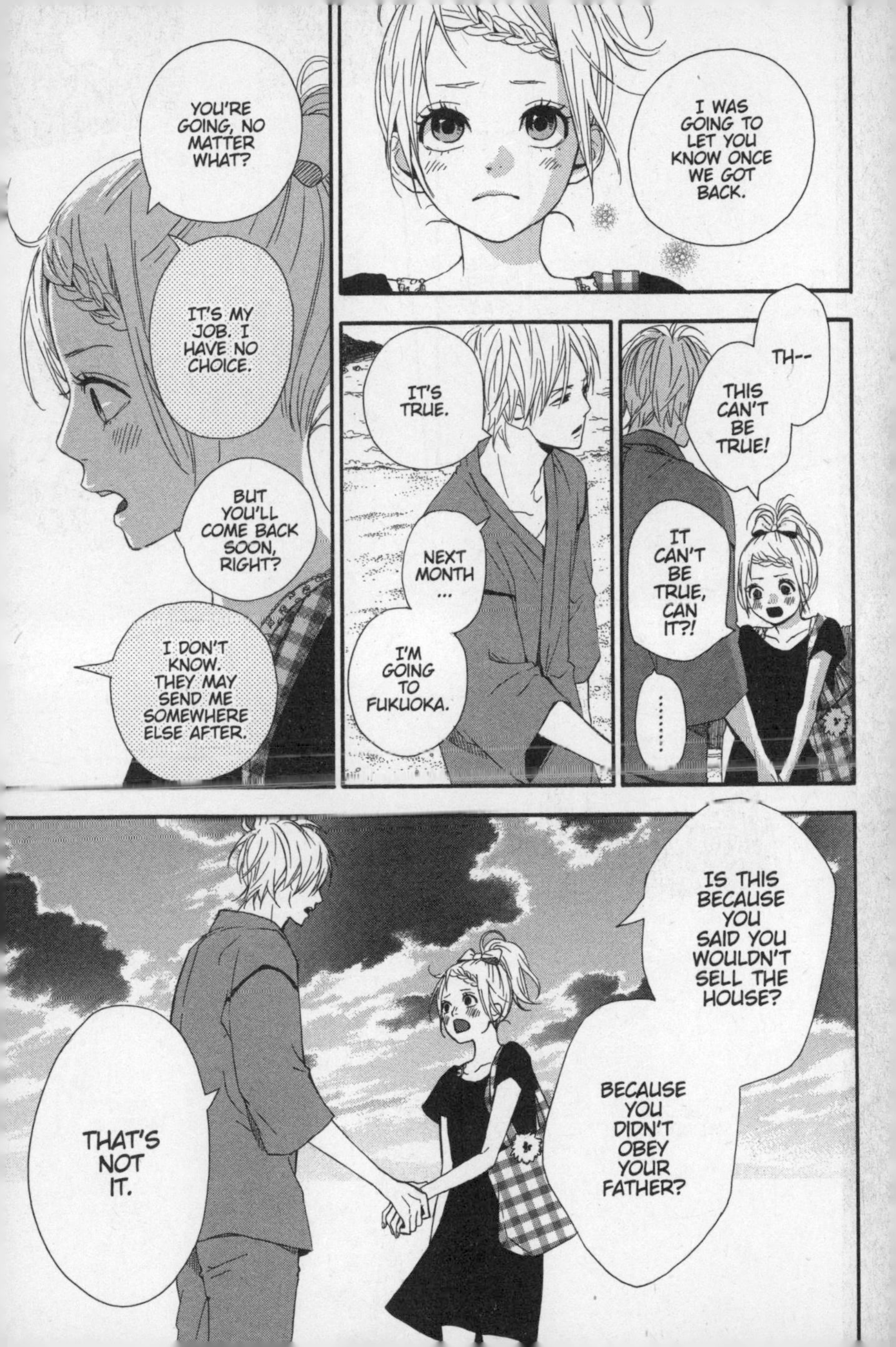
I WAS GOING TO LET YOU KNOW ONCE WE GOT BACK.
TH--
THIS CAN'T BE TRUE!
IT CAN'T BE TRUE, CAN IT?!
......
IT'S TRUE.
NEXT MONTH ...
I'M GOING TO FUKUOKA.
YOU'RE GOING, NO MATTER WHAT?
IT'S MY JOB. I HAVE NO CHOICE.
BUT YOU'LL COME BACK SOON, RIGHT?
I DON'T KNOW. THEY MAY SEND ME SOMEWHERE ELSE AFTER.
IS THIS BECAUSE YOU SAID YOU WOULDN'T SELL THE HOUSE?
BECAUSE YOU DIDN'T OBEY YOUR FATHER?
THAT'S NOT IT.

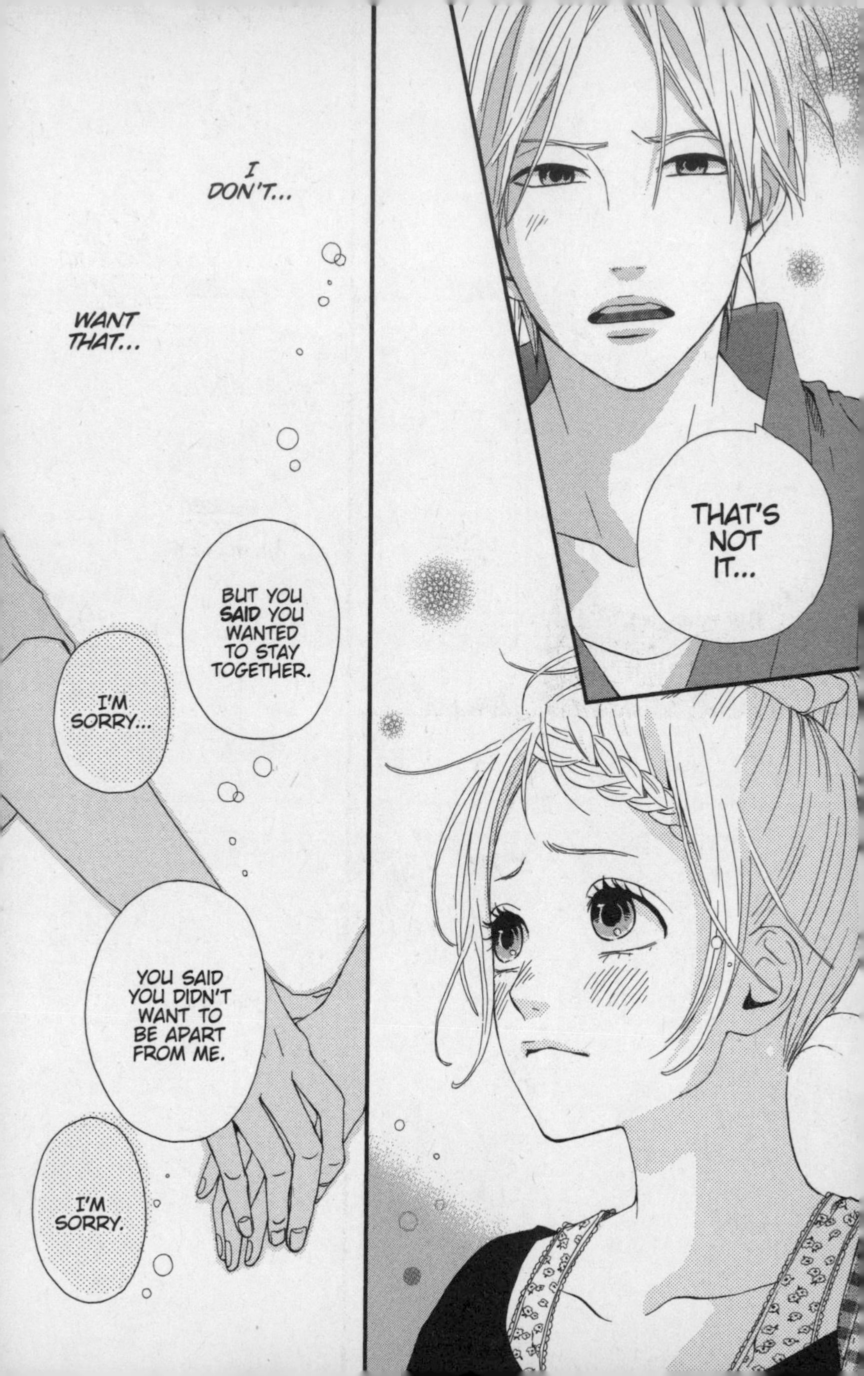

THAT'S NOT IT...
I DON'T...
WANT THAT...
BUT YOU SAID YOU WANTED TO STAY TOGETHER.
I'M SORRY...
YOU SAID YOU DIDN'T WANT TO BE APART FROM ME.
I'M SORRY.

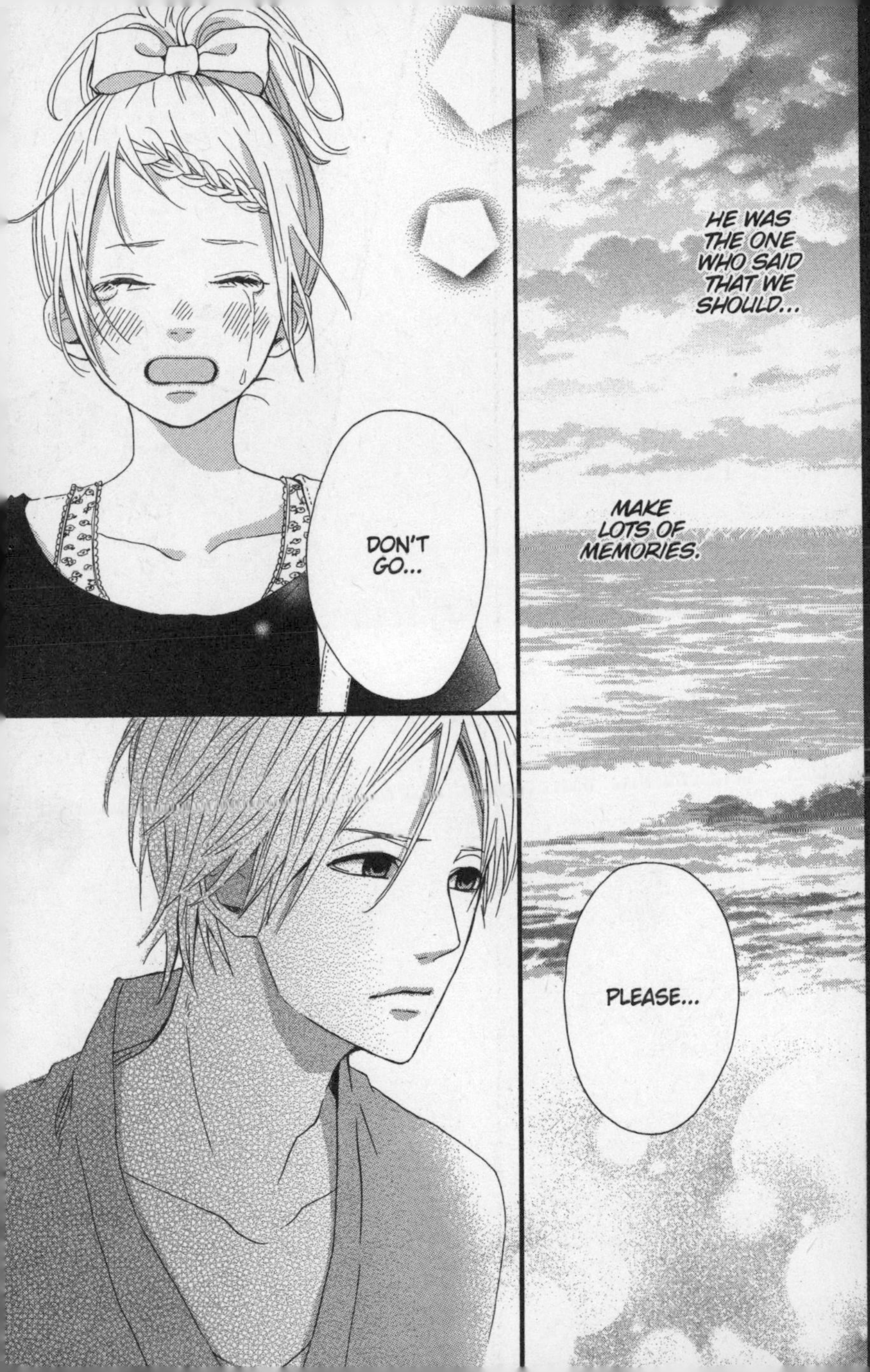
HE WAS THE ONE WHO SAID THAT WE SHOULD...
MAKE LOTS OF MEMORIES.
PLEASE...
DON'T GO...

I'M SO SORRY, SHIMANA.

MEMORIES...

CAN BE FUN IN THE MOMENT...

BUT THEY MAKE THE PAIN OF PARTING EVEN HARDER.

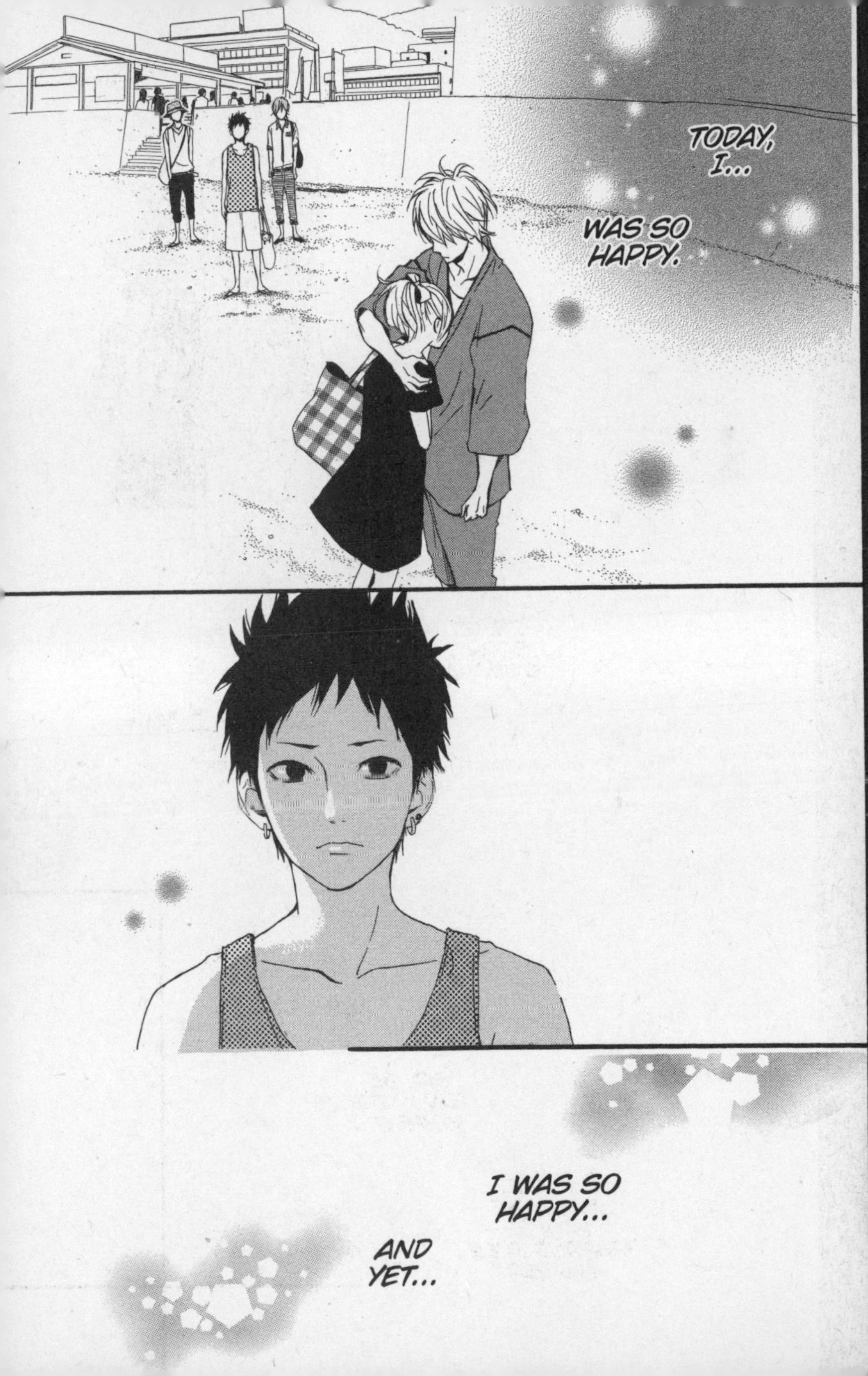
TODAY, I...
WAS SO HAPPY.
I WAS SO HAPPY...
AND YET...

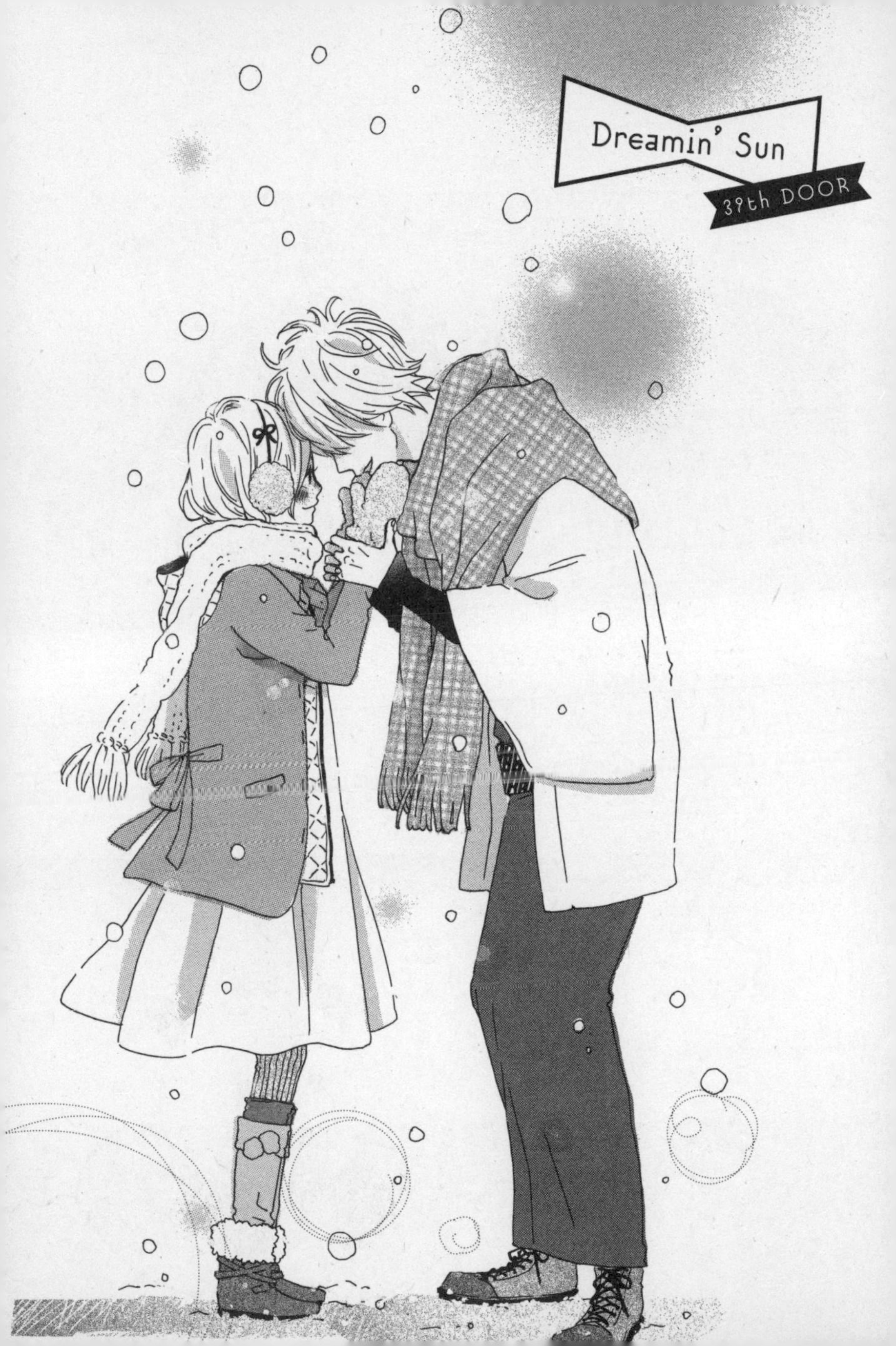
Dreamin' Sun
39th DOOR

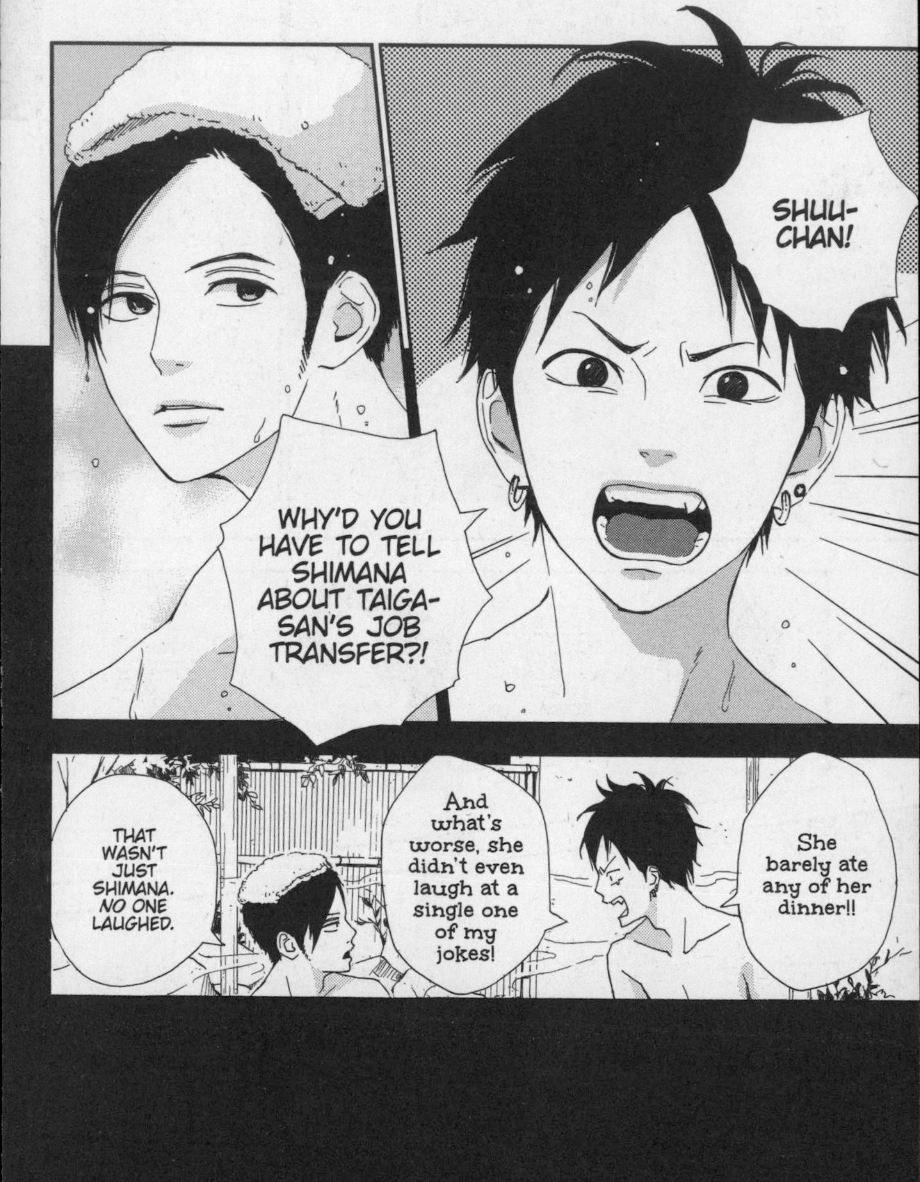
SHUU-CHAN!
WHY'D YOU HAVE TO TELL SHIMANA ABOUT TAIGA-SAN'S JOB TRANSFER?!
She barely ate any of her dinner!!
And what's worse, she didn't even laugh at a single one of my jokes!
THAT WASN'T JUST SHIMANA. NO ONE LAUGHED.

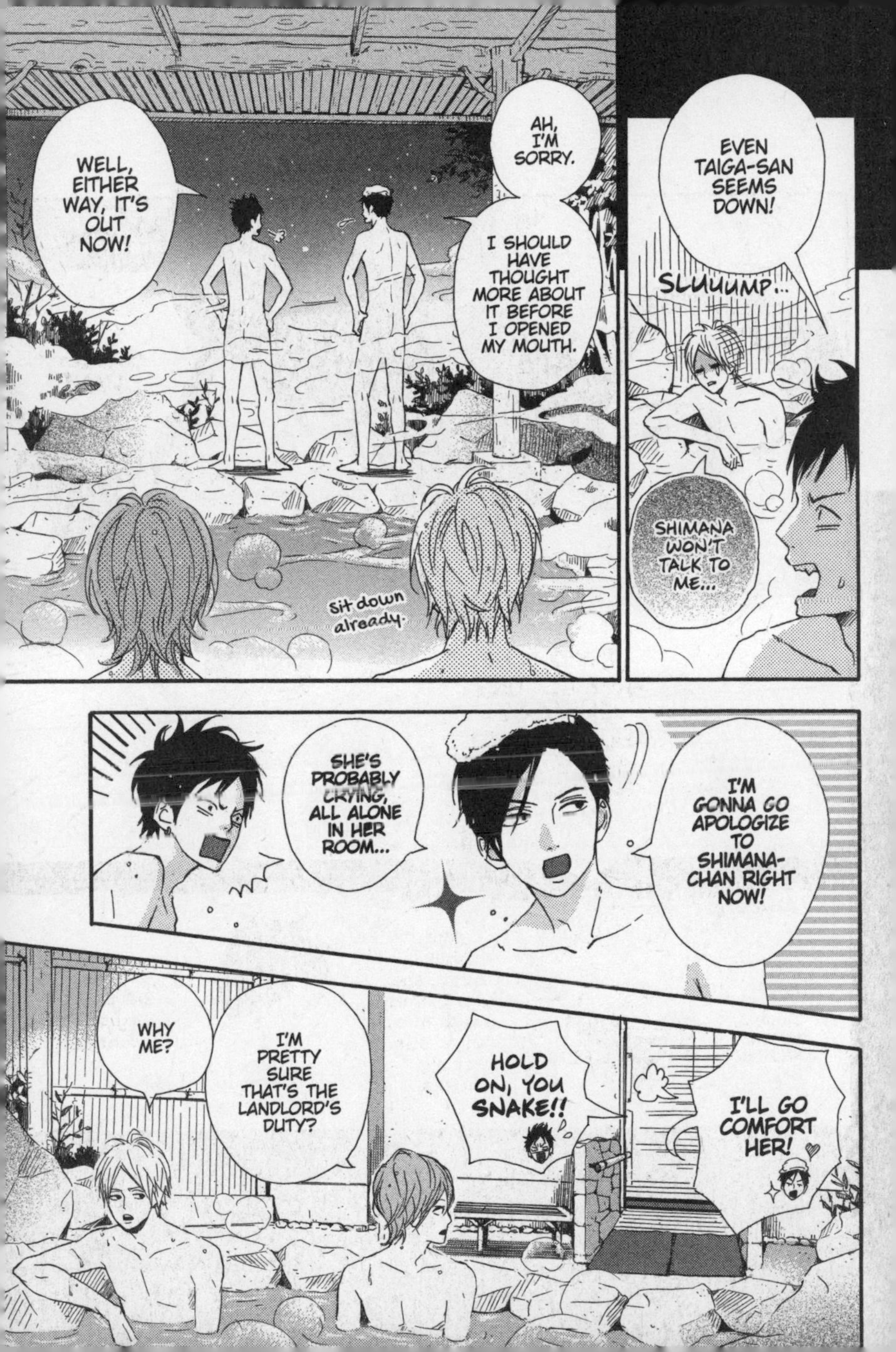
EVEN TAIGA-SAN SEEMS DOWN!
SLUUUMP...
SHIMANA WON'T TALK TO ME...
AH, I'M SORRY.
I SHOULD HAVE THOUGHT MORE ABOUT IT BEFORE I OPENED MY MOUTH.
WELL, EITHER WAY, IT'S OUT NOW!
sit down already.
I'M GONNA GO APOLOGIZE TO SHIMANA-CHAN RIGHT NOW!
SHE'S PROBABLY CRYING, ALL ALONE IN HER ROOM...
I'LL GO COMFORT HER!
HOLD ON, YOU SNAKE!!
I'M PRETTY SURE THAT'S THE LANDLORD'S DUTY?
WHY ME?

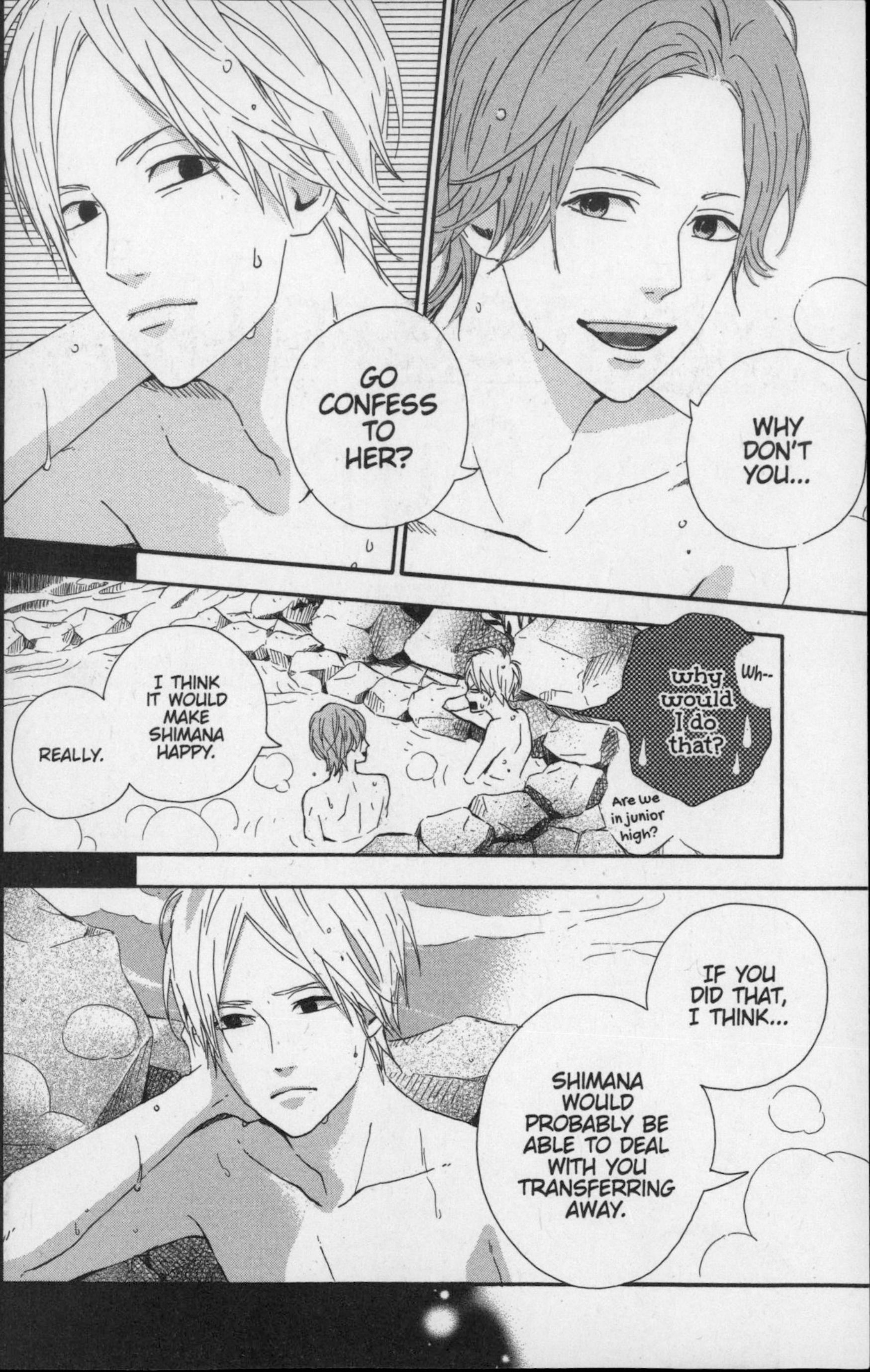
WHY DON'T YOU...
GO CONFESS TO HER?
Wh--
why would I do that?
Are we in junior high?
I THINK IT WOULD MAKE SHIMANA HAPPY.
REALLY.
IF YOU DID THAT, I THINK...
SHIMANA WOULD PROBABLY BE ABLE TO DEAL WITH YOU TRANSFERRING AWAY.

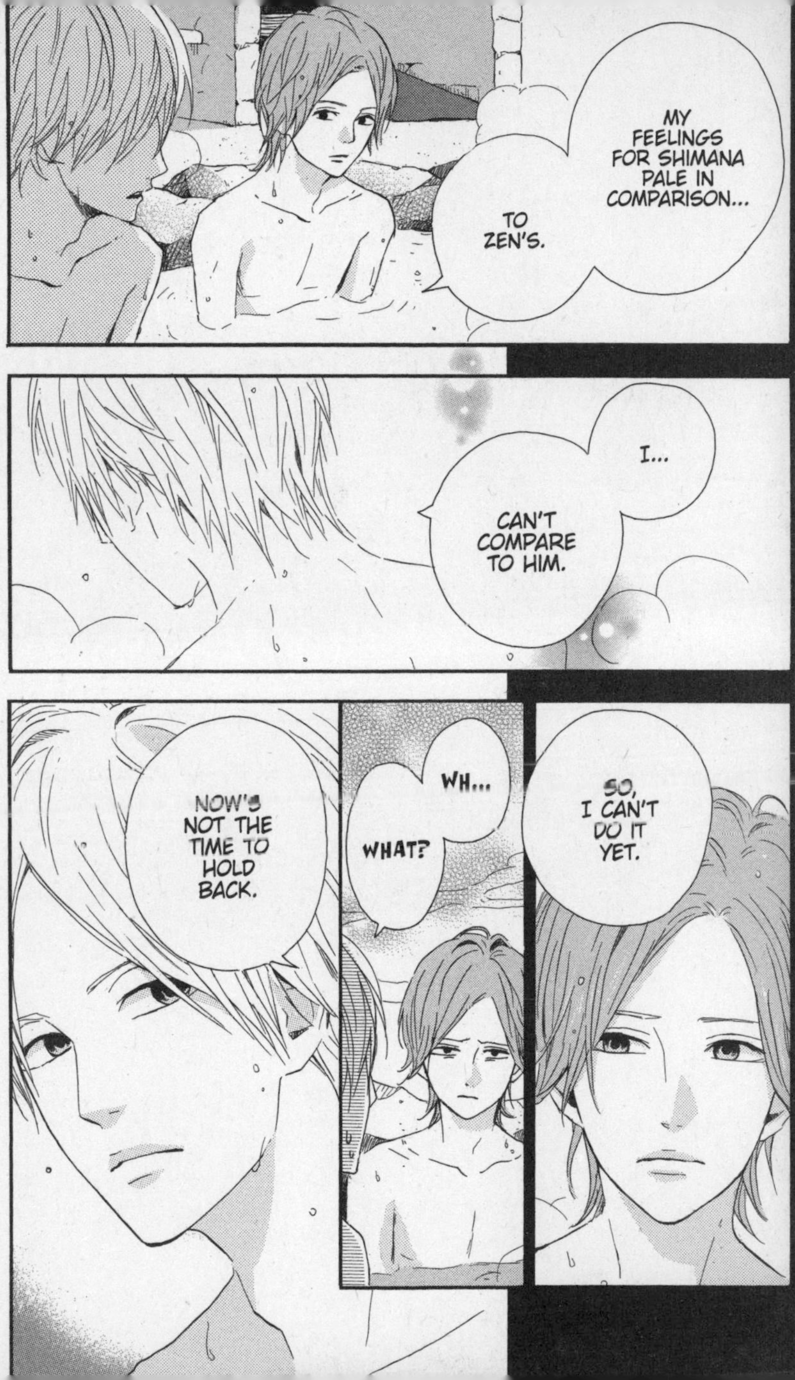
MY FEELINGS FOR SHIMANA PALE IN COMPARISON...
TO ZEN'S.
I...
CAN'T COMPARE TO HIM.
SO, I CAN'T DO IT YET.
WH...
WHAT?
NOW'S NOT THE TIME TO HOLD BACK.

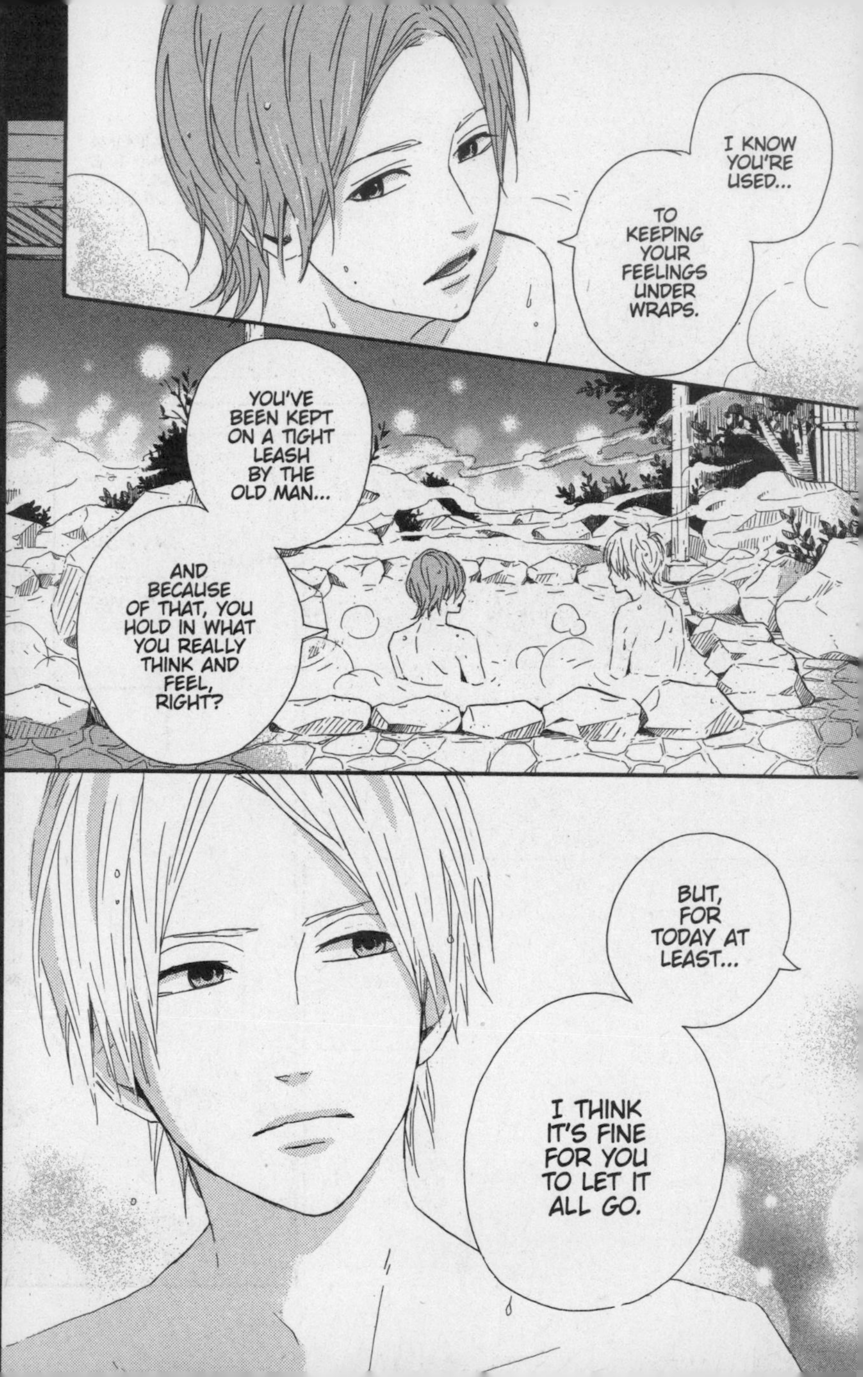

I KNOW YOU'RE USED...
TO KEEPING YOUR FEELINGS UNDER WRAPS.
YOU'VE BEEN KEPT ON A TIGHT LEASH BY THE OLD MAN...
AND BECAUSE OF THAT, YOU HOLD IN WHAT YOU REALLY THINK AND FEEL, RIGHT?
BUT, FOR TODAY AT LEAST...
I THINK IT'S FINE FOR YOU TO LET IT ALL GO.

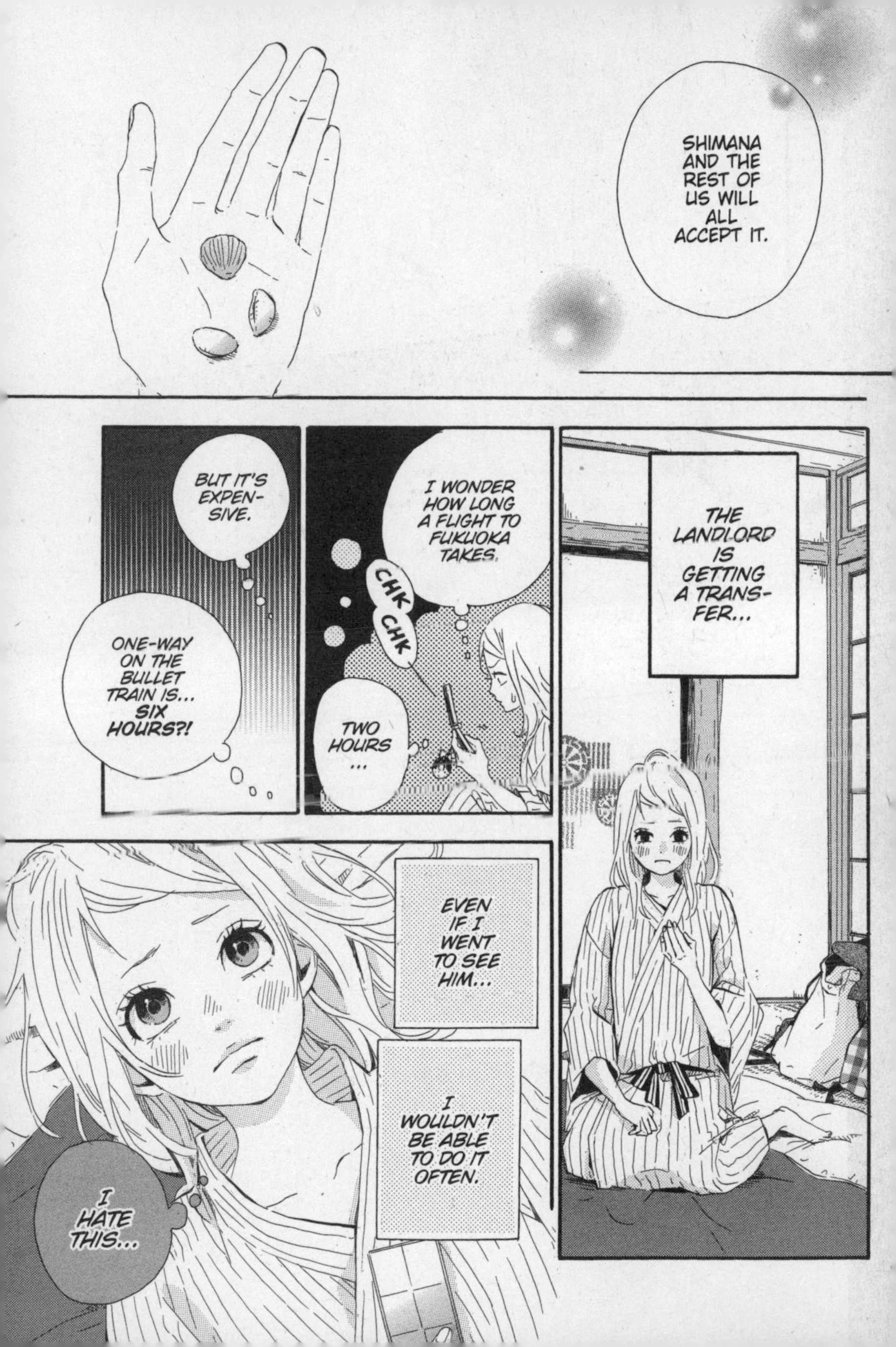
SHIMANA AND THE REST OF US WILL ALL ACCEPT IT.
THE LANDLORD IS GETTING A TRANS-FER...
I WONDER HOW LONG A FLIGHT TO FUKUOKA TAKES.
CHK CHK
TWO HOURS ...
BUT IT'S EXPEN-SIVE.
ONE-WAY ON THE BULLET TRAIN IS... SIX HOURS?!
EVEN IF I WENT TO SEE HIM...
I WOULDN'T BE ABLE TO DO IT OFTEN.
I HATE THIS...

I DON'T WANT TO BE APART FROM HIM.

SHIMANA-CHAN, ARE YOU THERE?

I SHOULDN'T HAVE BEEN THE ONE TO TELL YOU.

I'M SORRY ABOUT THE TRANSFER.

I'M SORRY.

ZOK ZOK

HE TOLD ZEN AND ASAHI-SAN.

IT'S NOT YOUR FAULT, SHUU-CHAN.

I WAS THE ONLY ONE HE WOULDN'T TELL...

IT'S THE LANDLORD'S FAULT FOR NOT TELLING ME.

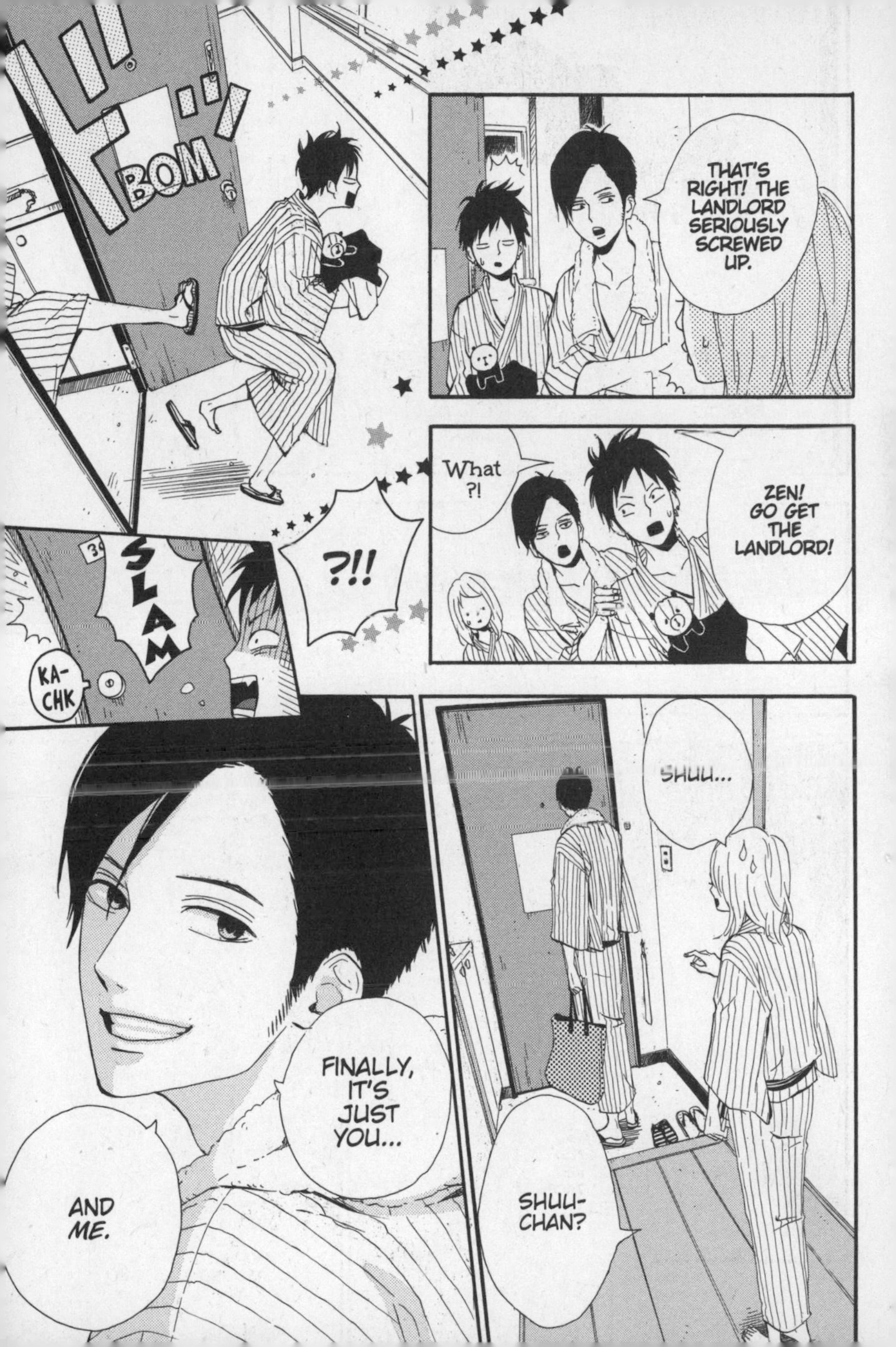
THAT'S RIGHT! THE LANDLORD SERIOUSLY SCREWED UP.
ZEN! GO GET THE LANDLORD!
What ?!
BOM
?!!
SLAM
KA-CHK
SHUU...
SHUU-CHAN?
FINALLY, IT'S JUST YOU...
AND ME.

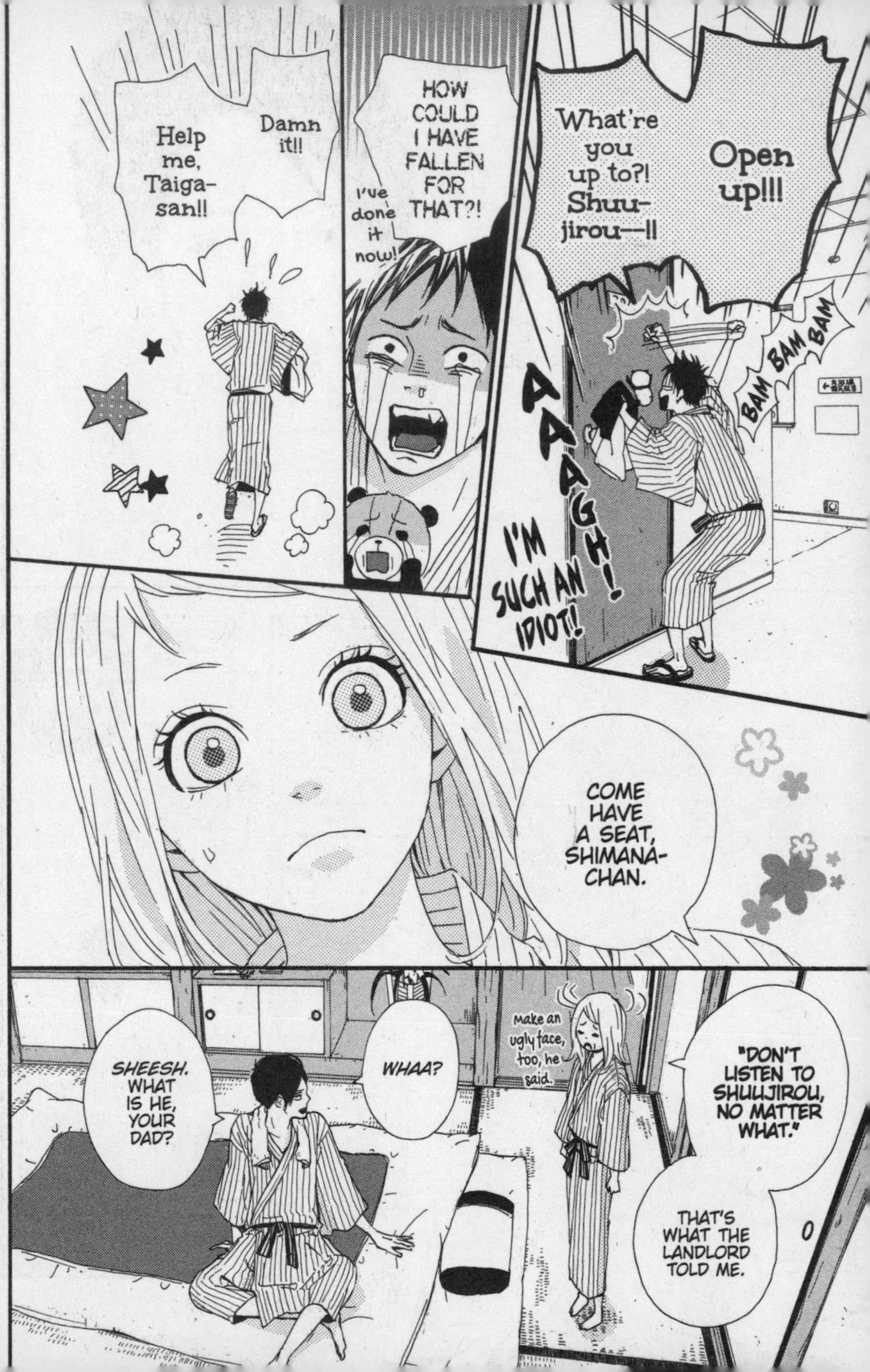

What're you up to?! Shuu-jirou--!! Open up!!!
BAM BAM BAM
AAAGH!
I'M SUCH AN IDIOT!!
HOW COULD I HAVE FALLEN FOR THAT?!
I've done it now!
Damn it!!
Help me, Taiga-san!!
COME HAVE A SEAT, SHIMANA-CHAN.
"DON'T LISTEN TO SHUUJIROU, NO MATTER WHAT."
THAT'S WHAT THE LANDLORD TOLD ME.
Make an ugly face, too, he said.
WHAA?
SHEESH. WHAT IS HE, YOUR DAD?

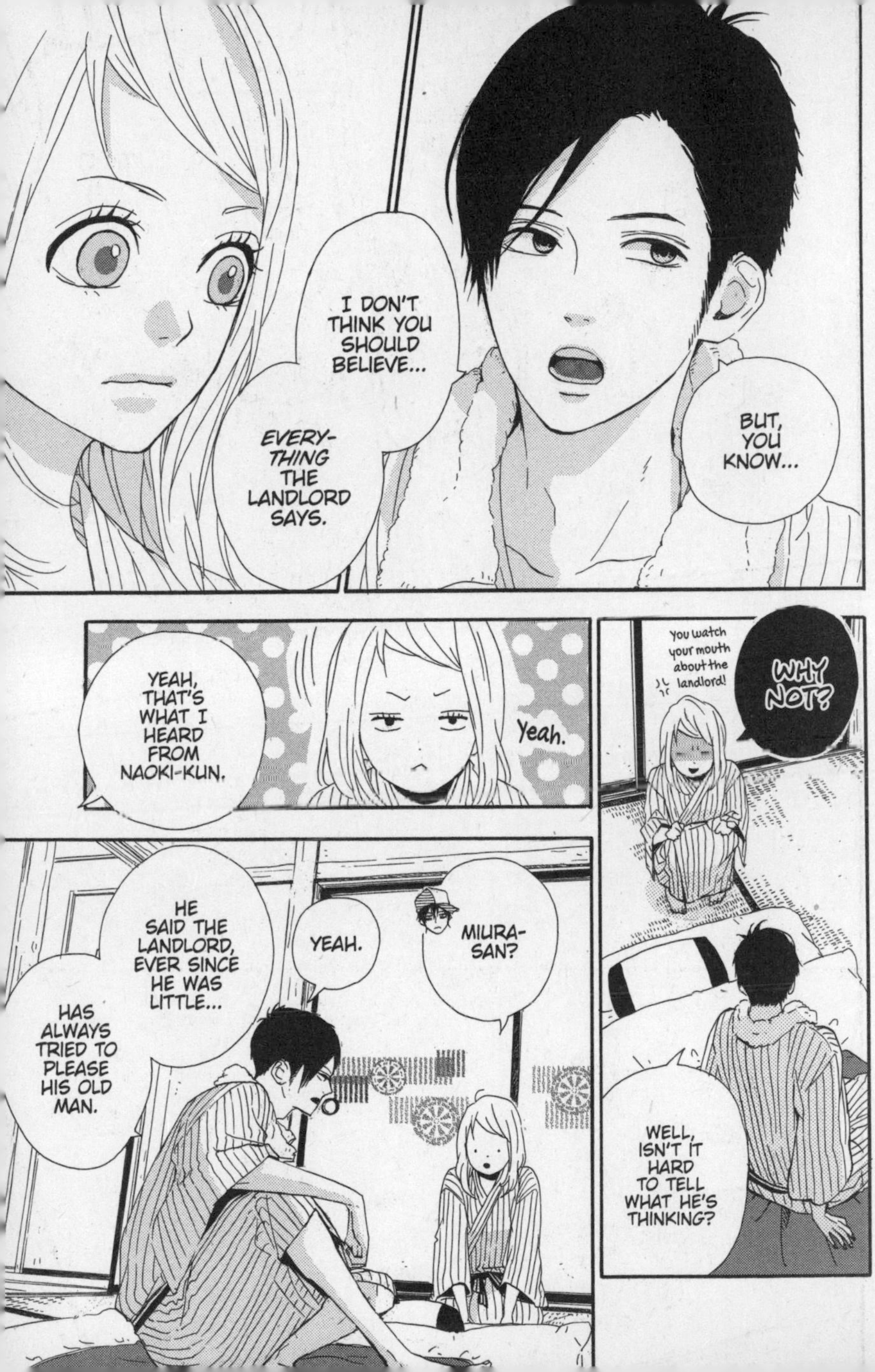
BUT, YOU KNOW...
I DON'T THINK YOU SHOULD BELIEVE...
EVERYTHING THE LANDLORD SAYS.
WHY NOT?
You watch your mouth about the landlord!
WELL, ISN'T IT HARD TO TELL WHAT HE'S THINKING?
Yeah.
YEAH, THAT'S WHAT I HEARD FROM NAOKI-KUN.
MIURA-SAN?
YEAH.
HE SAID THE LANDLORD, EVER SINCE HE WAS LITTLE...
HAS ALWAYS TRIED TO PLEASE HIS OLD MAN.

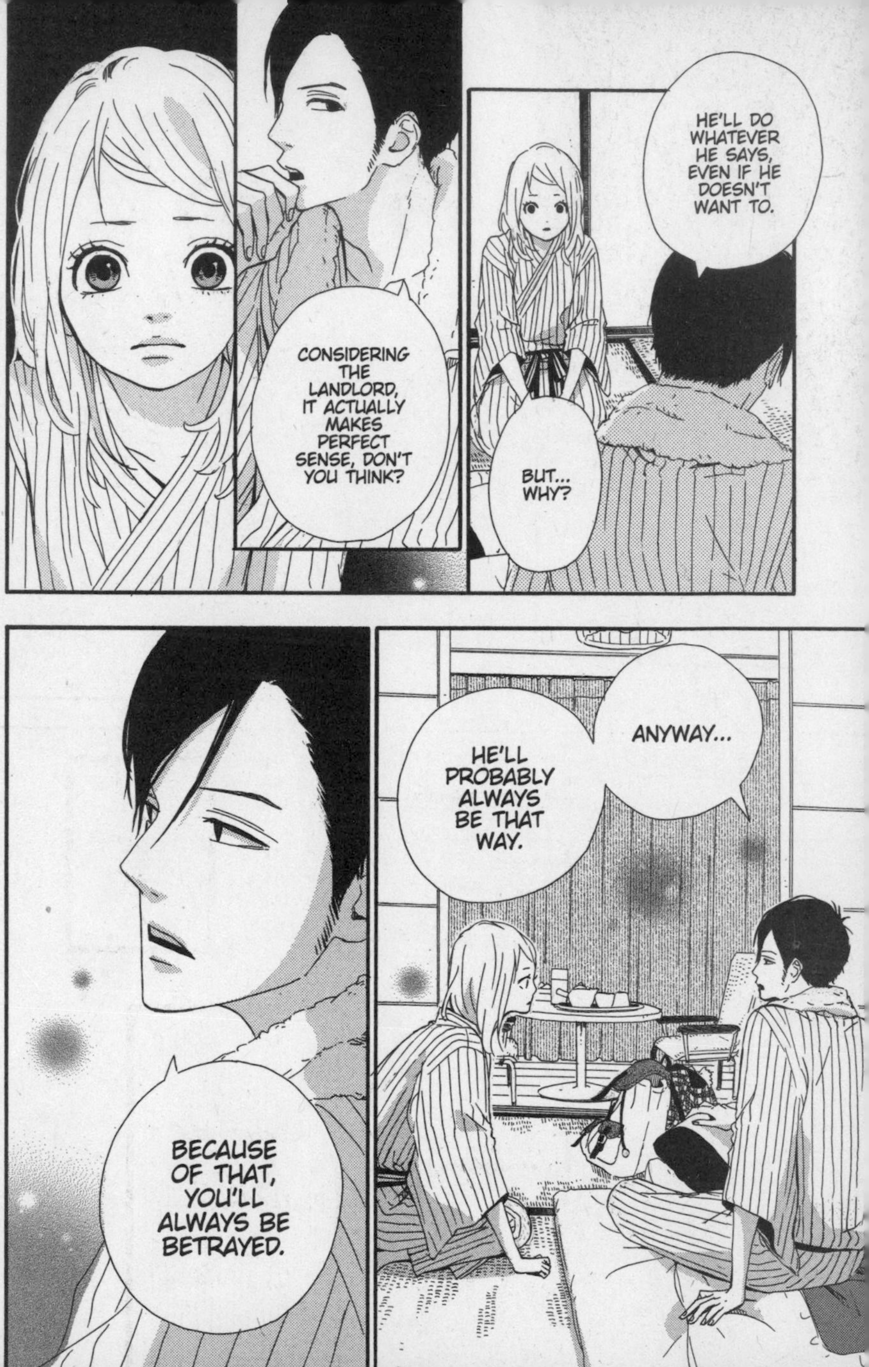
HE'LL DO WHATEVER HE SAYS, EVEN IF HE DOESN'T WANT TO.
BUT... WHY?
CONSIDERING THE LANDLORD, IT ACTUALLY MAKES PERFECT SENSE, DON'T YOU THINK?
ANYWAY...
HE'LL PROBABLY ALWAYS BE THAT WAY.
BECAUSE OF THAT, YOU'LL ALWAYS BE BETRAYED.

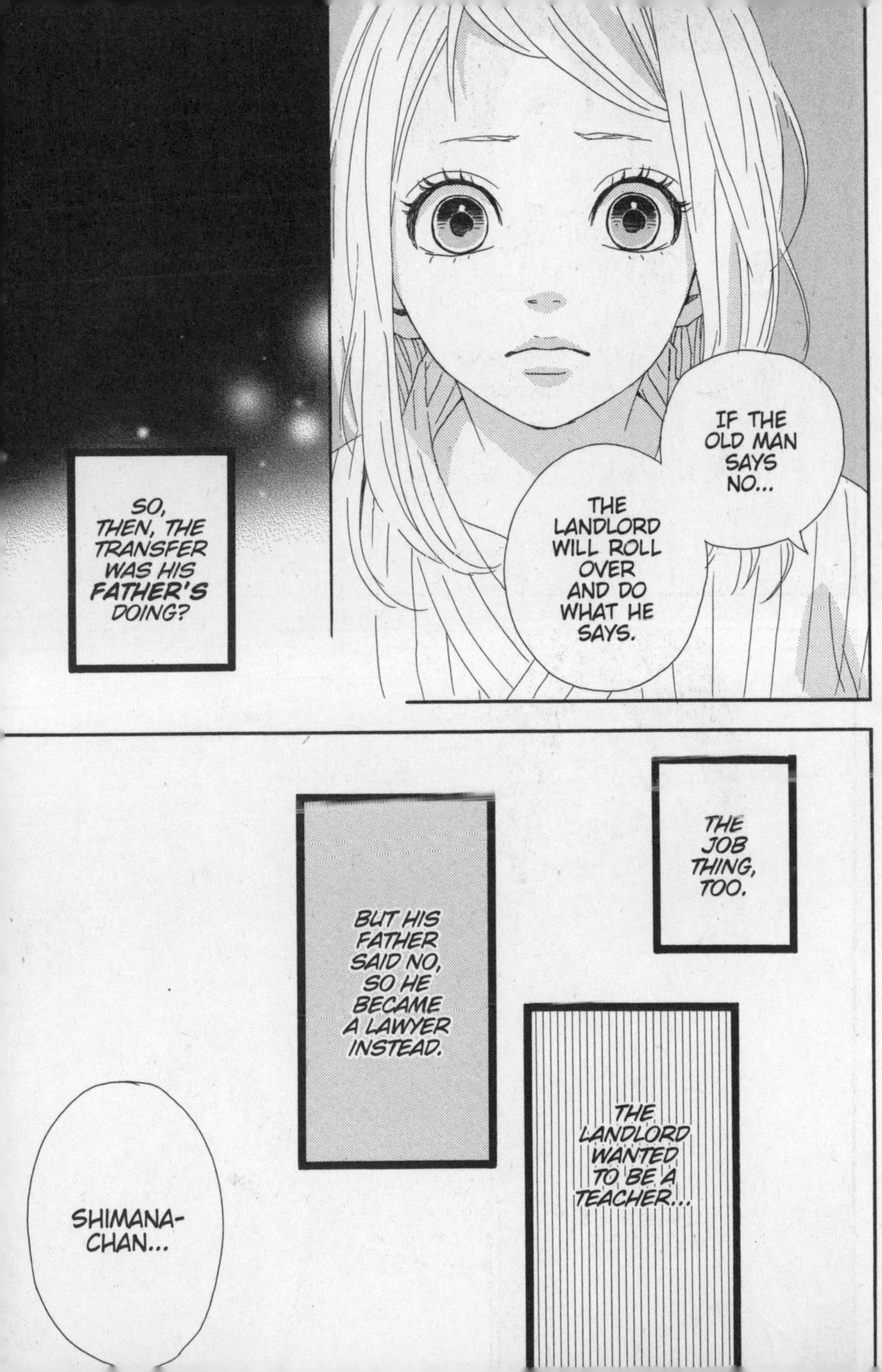
IF THE OLD MAN SAYS NO...
THE LANDLORD WILL ROLL OVER AND DO WHAT HE SAYS.
SO, THEN, THE TRANSFER WAS HIS FATHER'S DOING?
THE JOB THING, TOO.
THE LANDLORD WANTED TO BE A TEACHER...
BUT HIS FATHER SAID NO, SO HE BECAME A LAWYER INSTEAD.
SHIMANA-CHAN...

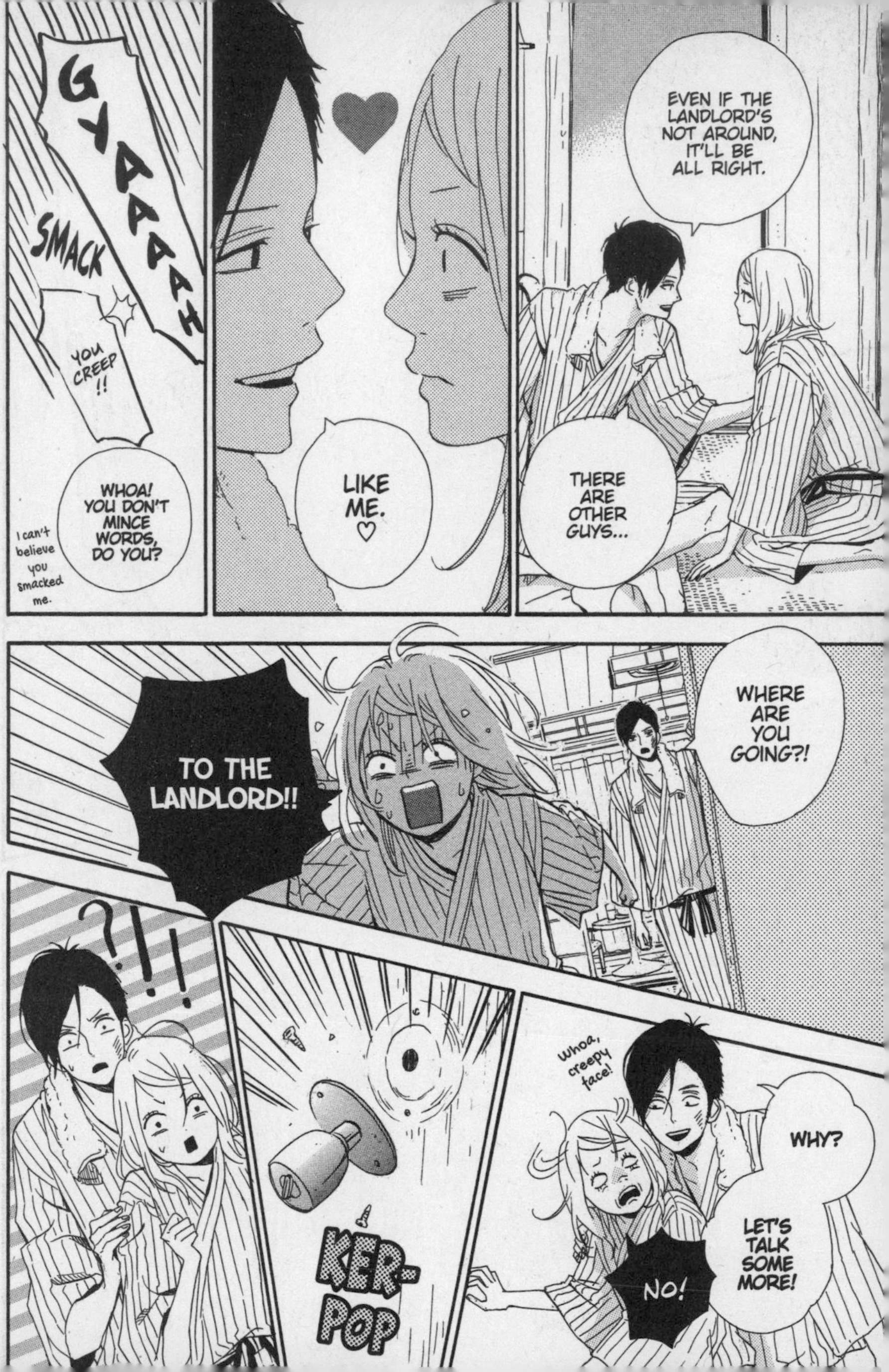
EVEN IF THE LANDLORD'S NOT AROUND, IT'LL BE ALL RIGHT.
THERE ARE OTHER GUYS...
LIKE ME. ♡
GYAAAAH
SMACK
YOU CREEP!!
WHOA! YOU DON'T MINCE WORDS, DO YOU?
I can't believe you smacked me.
WHERE ARE YOU GOING?!
TO THE LANDLORD!!
WHY?
LET'S TALK SOME MORE!
NO!
Whoa, creepy face!
KER-POP
?!!

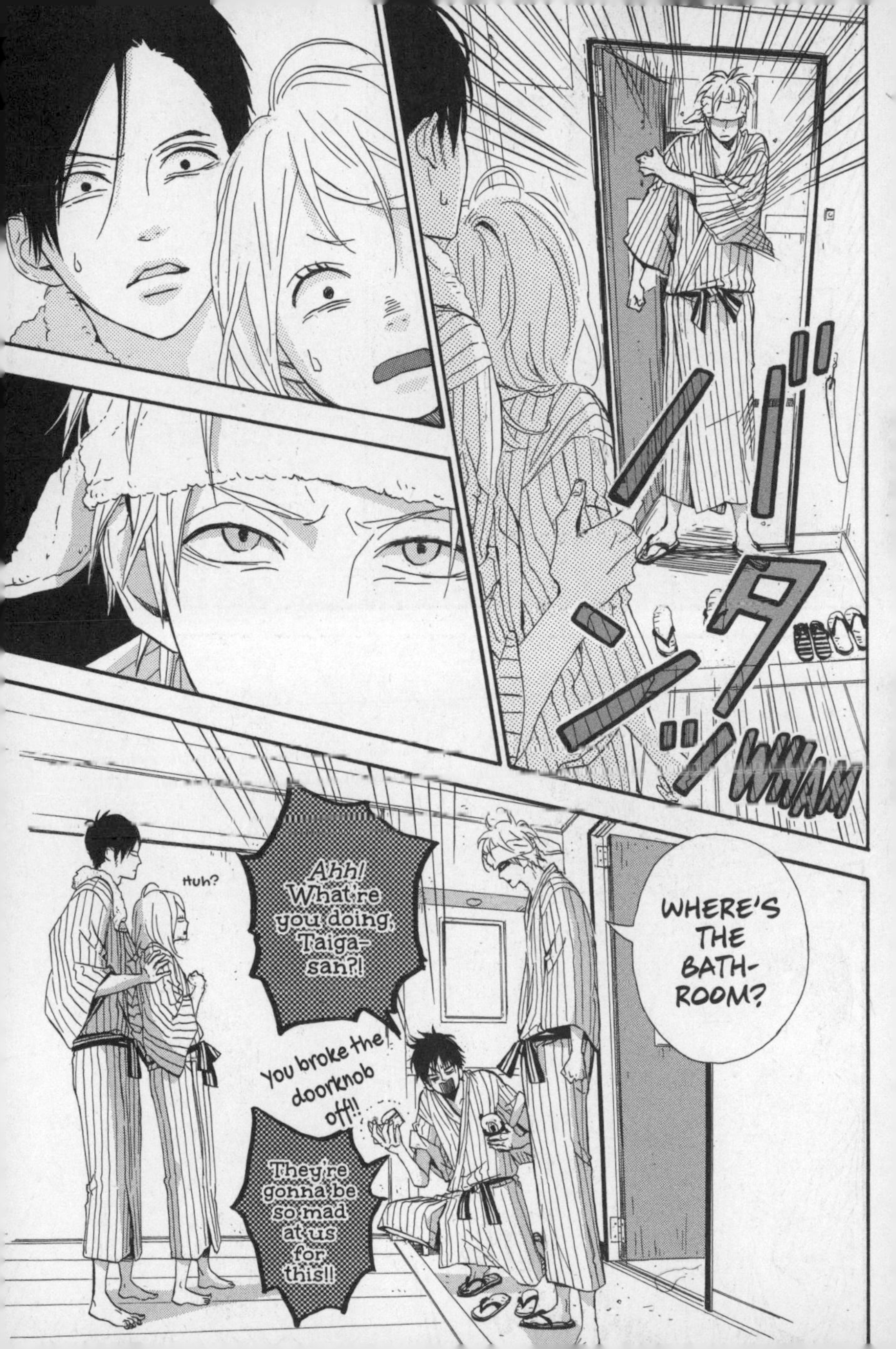
WHAM
WHERE'S THE BATHROOM?
Ahh! What're you doing, Taiga-san?!
You broke the doorknob off!!
They're gonna be so mad at us for this!!
Huh?

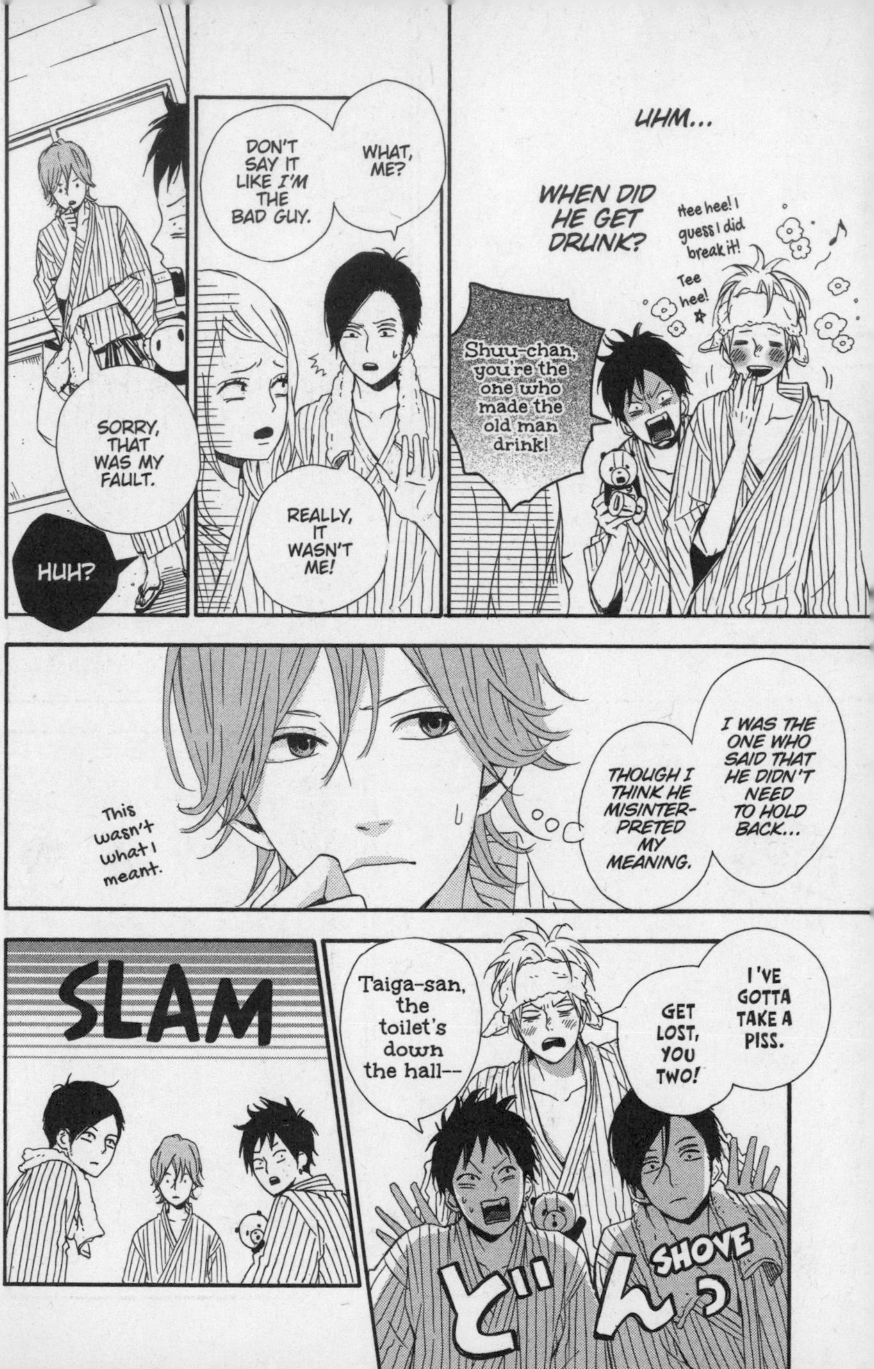
UHM...
WHEN DID HE GET DRUNK?
thee hee! I guess I did break it!
Tee hee! ☆
Shuu-chan, you're the one who made the old man drink!
WHAT, ME?
DON'T SAY IT LIKE I'M THE BAD GUY.
REALLY, IT WASN'T ME!
SORRY, THAT WAS MY FAULT.
HUH?
I WAS THE ONE WHO SAID THAT HE DIDN'T NEED TO HOLD BACK...
THOUGH I THINK HE MISINTER-PRETED MY MEANING.
This wasn't what I meant.
I'VE GOTTA TAKE A PISS.
GET LOST, YOU TWO!
Taiga-san, the toilet's down the hall--
SHOVE
どんっ
SLAM

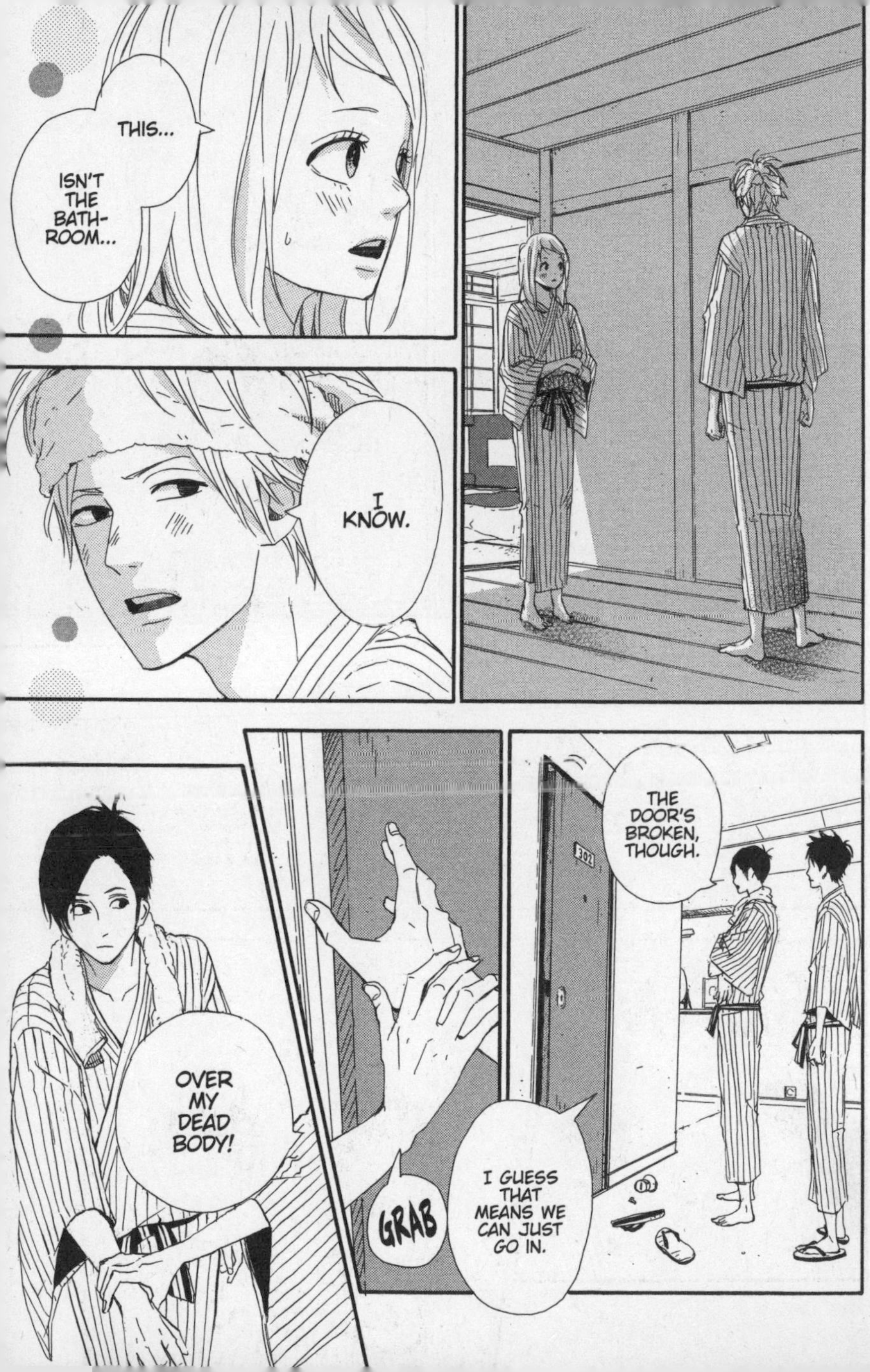
THIS...
ISN'T THE BATH-ROOM...
I KNOW.
THE DOOR'S BROKEN, THOUGH.
302
I GUESS THAT MEANS WE CAN JUST GO IN.
GRAB
OVER MY DEAD BODY!

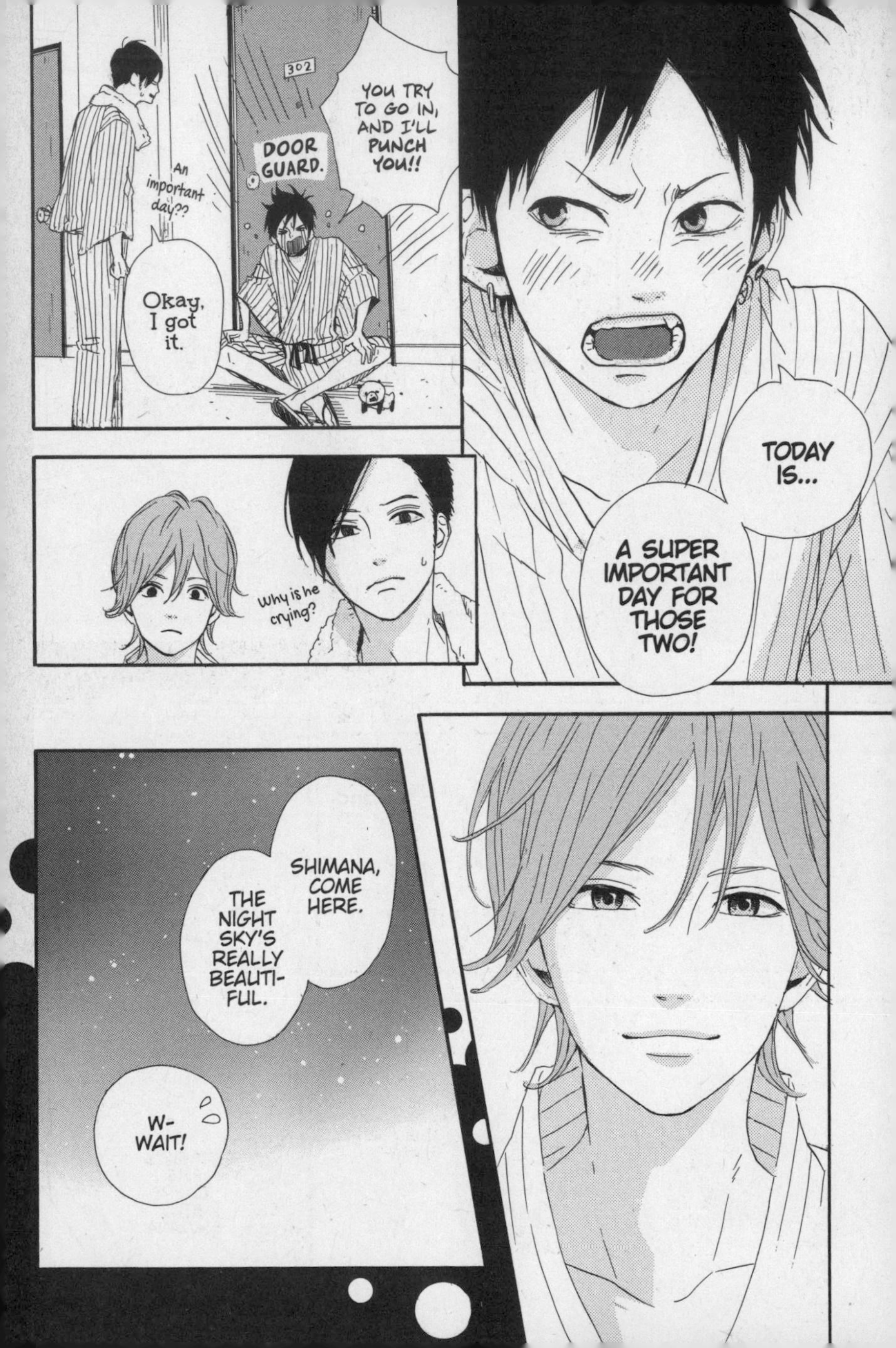
TODAY IS...
A SUPER IMPORTANT DAY FOR THOSE TWO!
YOU TRY TO GO IN, AND I'LL PUNCH YOU!!
DOOR GUARD.
An important day??
Okay, I got it.
Why is he crying?
SHIMANA, COME HERE.
THE NIGHT SKY'S REALLY BEAUTI-FUL.
W-WAIT!

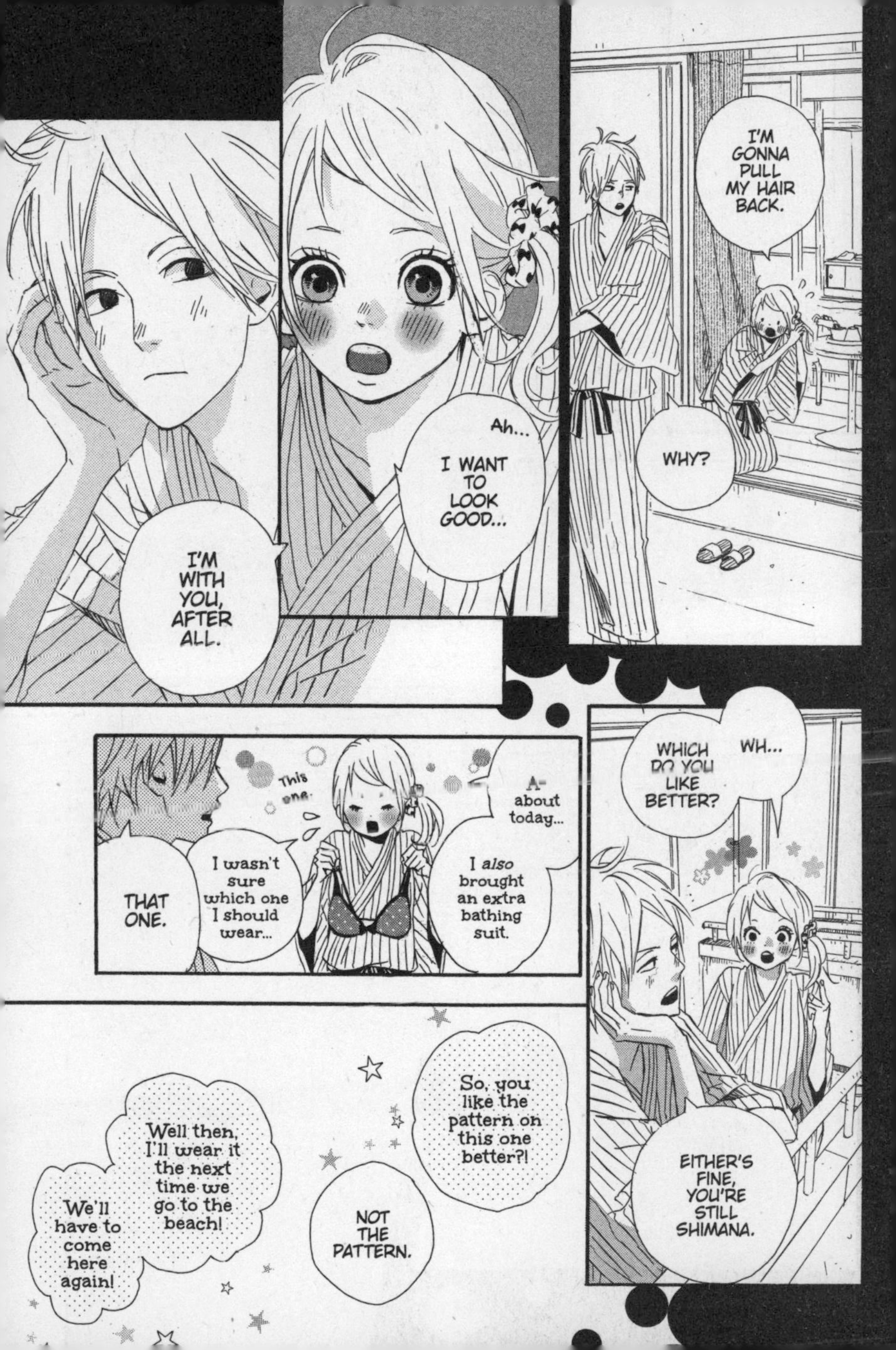
I'M GONNA PULL MY HAIR BACK.
WHY?
Ah...
I WANT TO LOOK GOOD...
I'M WITH YOU, AFTER ALL.
WH...
WHICH DO YOU LIKE BETTER?
EITHER'S FINE, YOU'RE STILL SHIMANA.
A- about today...
I also brought an extra bathing suit.
This one.
I wasn't sure which one I should wear...
THAT ONE.
So, you like the pattern on this one better?!
NOT THE PATTERN.
Well then, I'll wear it the next time we go to the beach!
We'll have to come here again!

WE DEFINITELY...

SHOULD.

BUT...

I DON'T THINK THAT'S GONNA HAPPEN.

....

NO. TRANSFERS ARE COMMON FOR PROSECUTORS.

IT'S MY JOB, SO I CAN'T REFUSE.

THE TRANSFER...

ARE YOU DOING IT BECAUSE YOUR FATHER TOLD YOU TO?

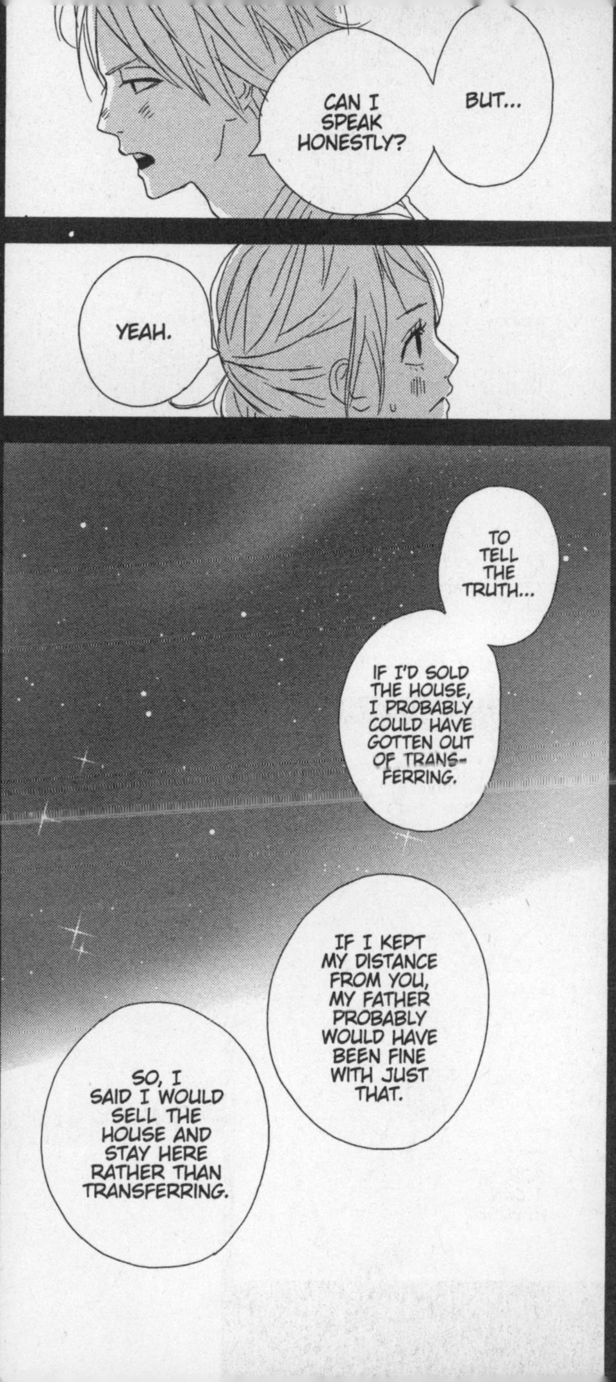
BUT...
CAN I SPEAK HONESTLY?
YEAH.
TO TELL THE TRUTH...
IF I'D SOLD THE HOUSE, I PROBABLY COULD HAVE GOTTEN OUT OF TRANS-FERRING.
IF I KEPT MY DISTANCE FROM YOU, MY FATHER PROBABLY WOULD HAVE BEEN FINE WITH JUST THAT.
SO, I SAID I WOULD SELL THE HOUSE AND STAY HERE RATHER THAN TRANSFERRING.

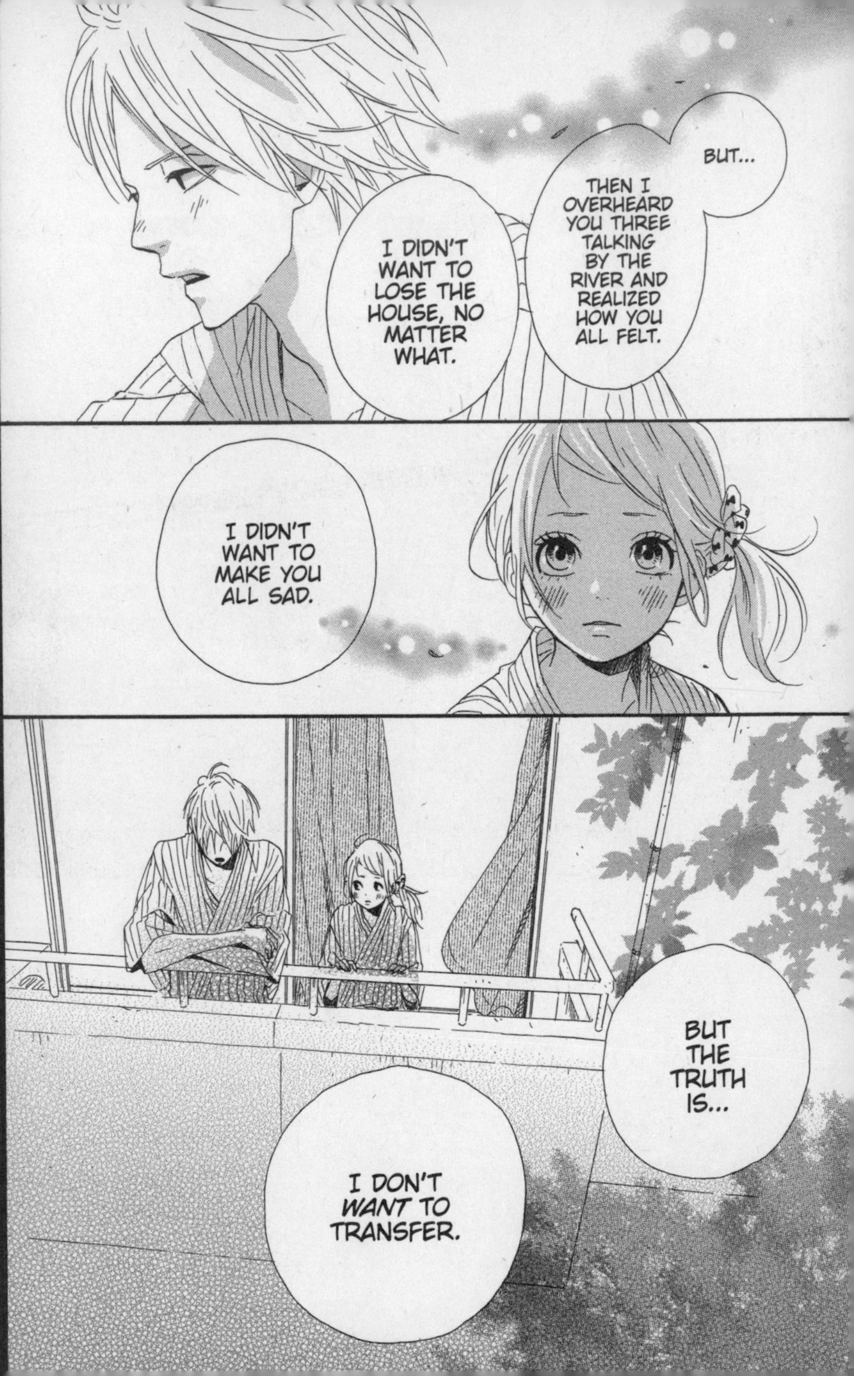
BUT...
THEN I OVERHEARD YOU THREE TALKING BY THE RIVER AND REALIZED HOW YOU ALL FELT.
I DIDN'T WANT TO LOSE THE HOUSE, NO MATTER WHAT.
I DIDN'T WANT TO MAKE YOU ALL SAD.
BUT THE TRUTH IS...
I DON'T *WANT* TO TRANSFER.

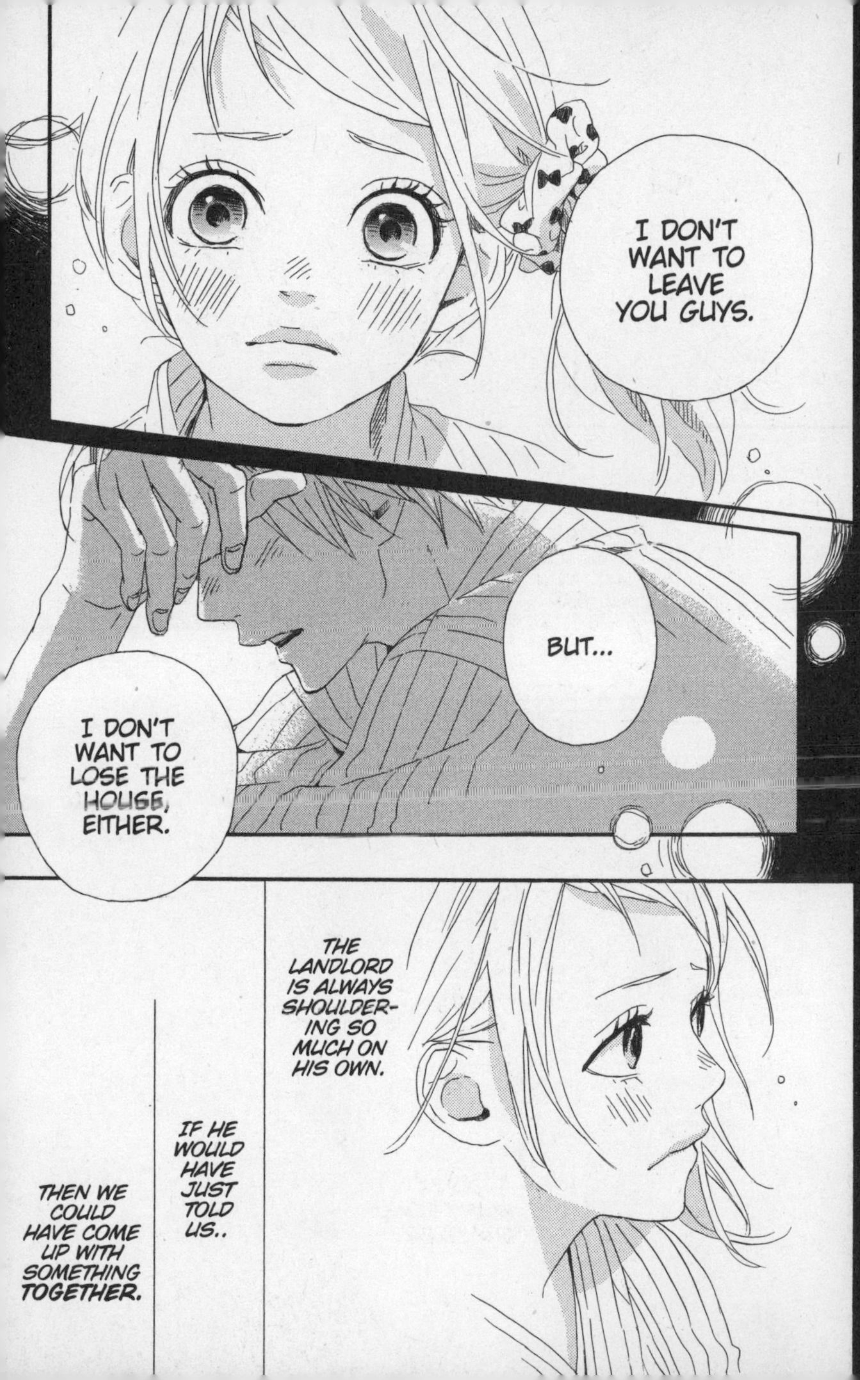
I DON'T WANT TO LEAVE YOU GUYS.
BUT...
I DON'T WANT TO LOSE THE HOUSE, EITHER.
THE LANDLORD IS ALWAYS SHOULDER-ING SO MUCH ON HIS OWN.
IF HE WOULD HAVE JUST TOLD US..
THEN WE COULD HAVE COME UP WITH SOMETHING TOGETHER.

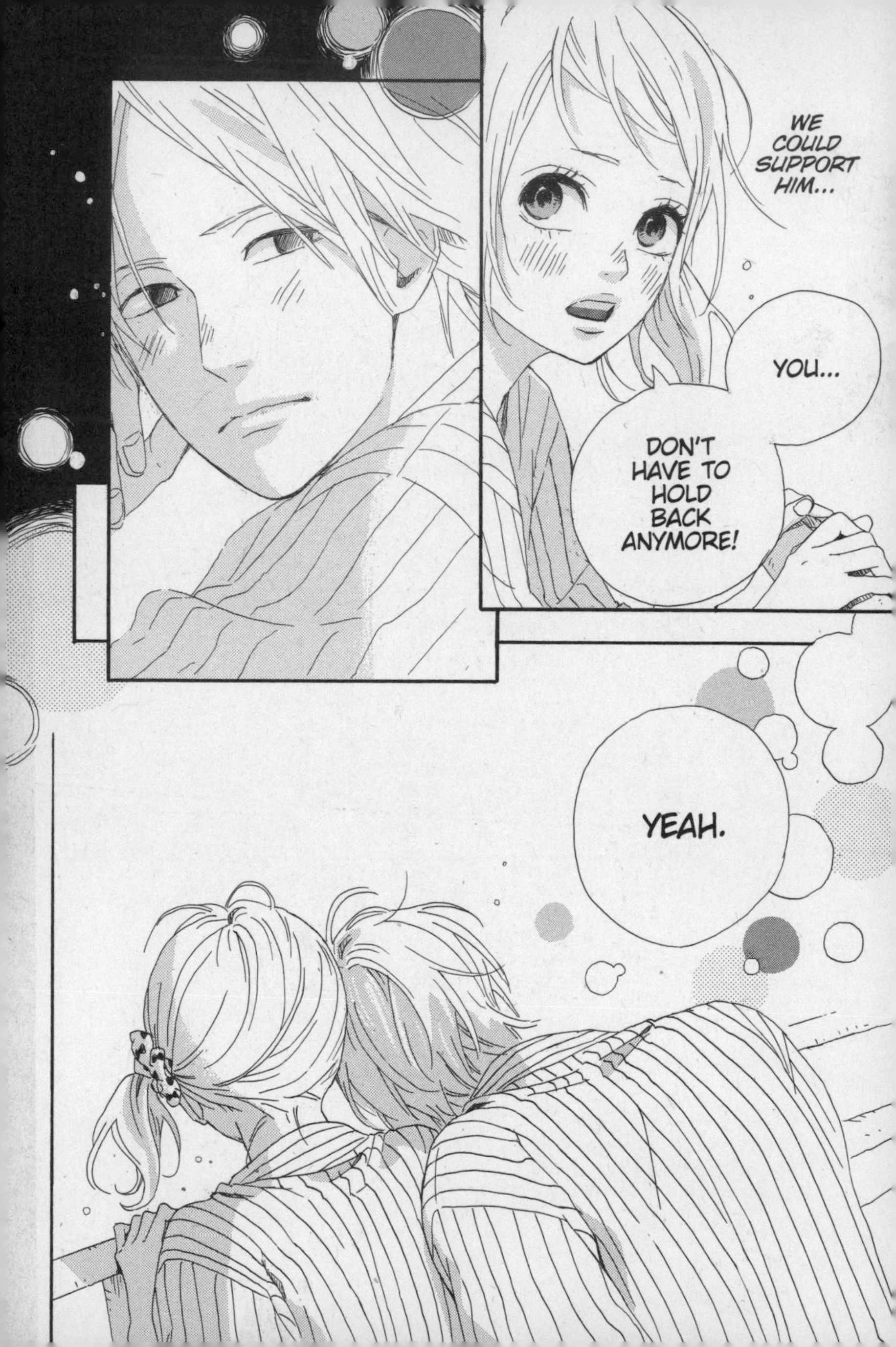
WE COULD SUPPORT HIM...
YOU...
DON'T HAVE TO HOLD BACK ANYMORE!
YEAH.

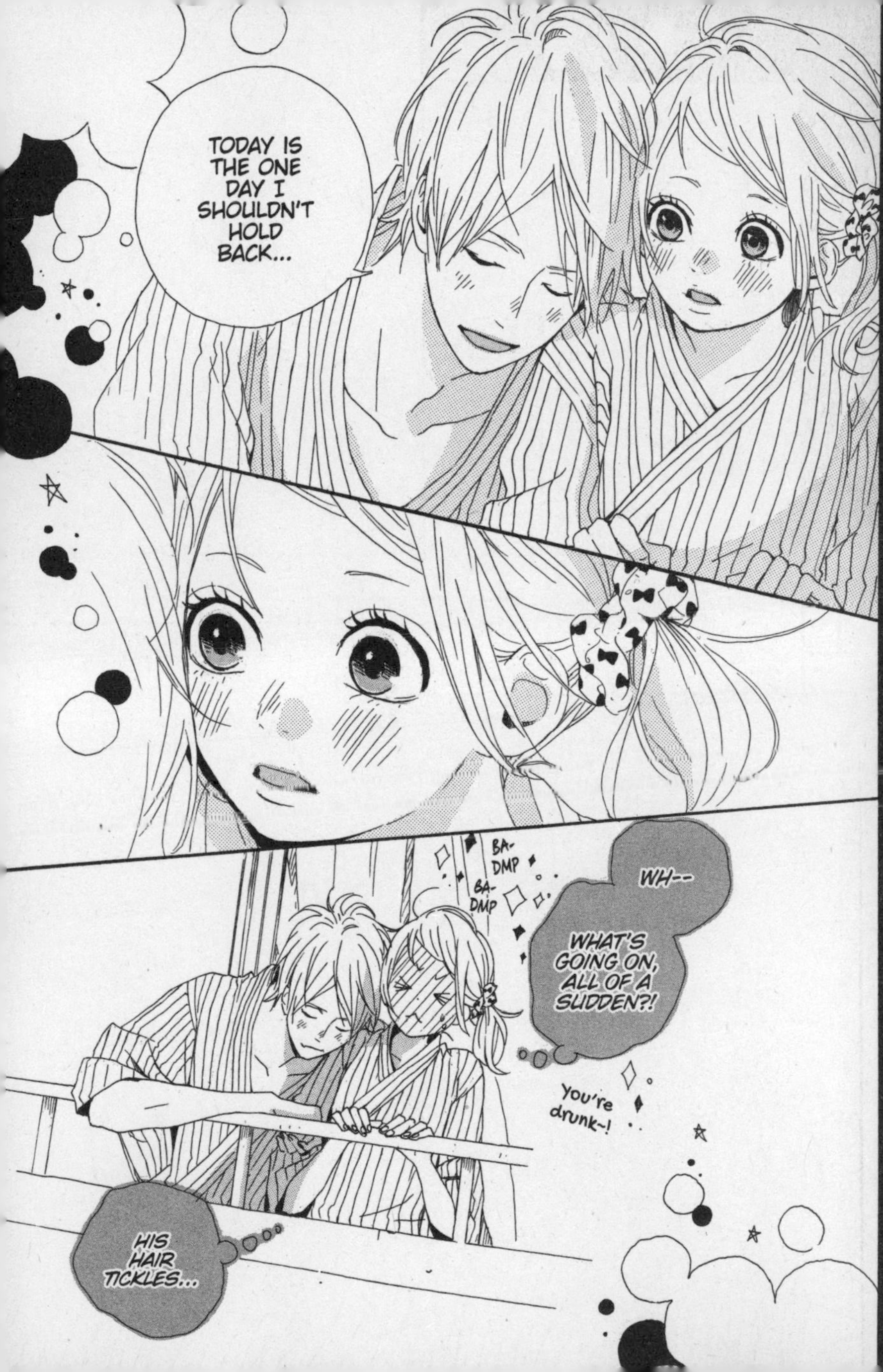
TODAY IS THE ONE DAY I SHOULDN'T HOLD BACK...
BA-DMP BA-DMP
WH-- WHAT'S GOING ON, ALL OF A SUDDEN?!
You're drunk~!
HIS HAIR TICKLES...

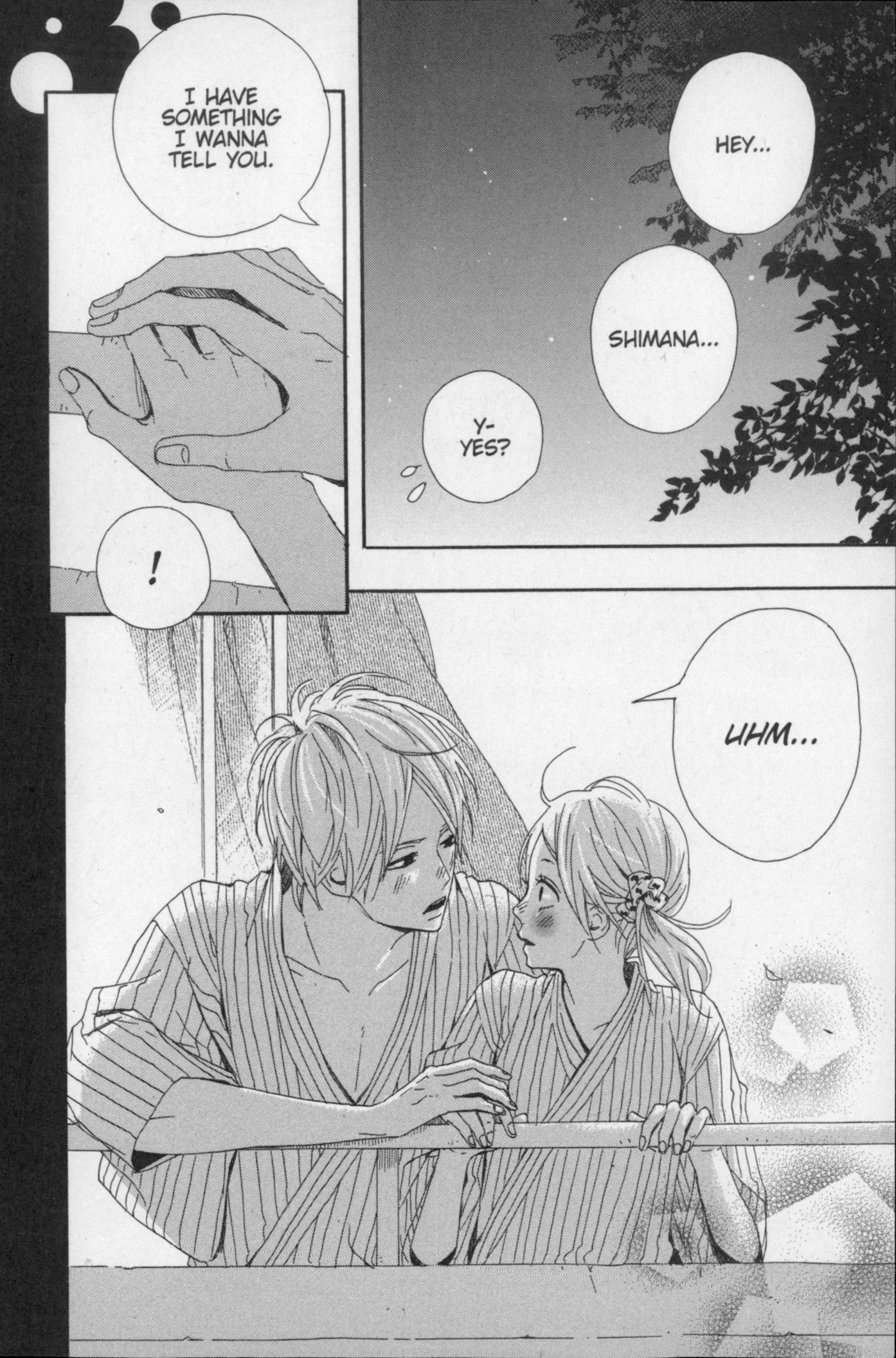
HEY...
SHIMANA...
Y-YES?
I HAVE SOMETHING I WANNA TELL YOU.
!
UHM...

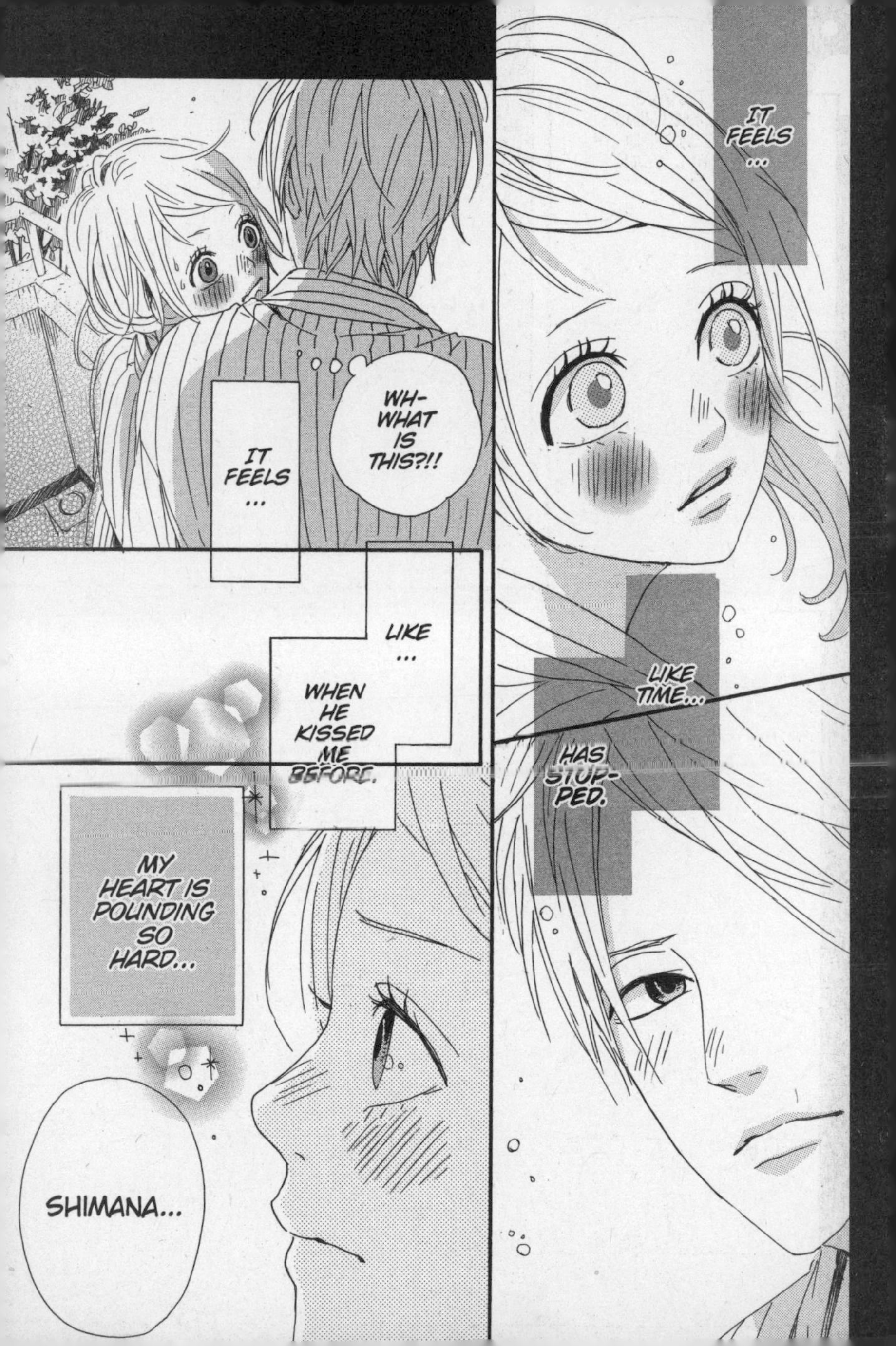
IT FEELS...
LIKE TIME...
HAS STOPPED.
WH-WHAT IS THIS?!!
IT FEELS...
LIKE...
WHEN HE KISSED ME BEFORE.
MY HEART IS POUNDING SO HARD...
SHIMANA...

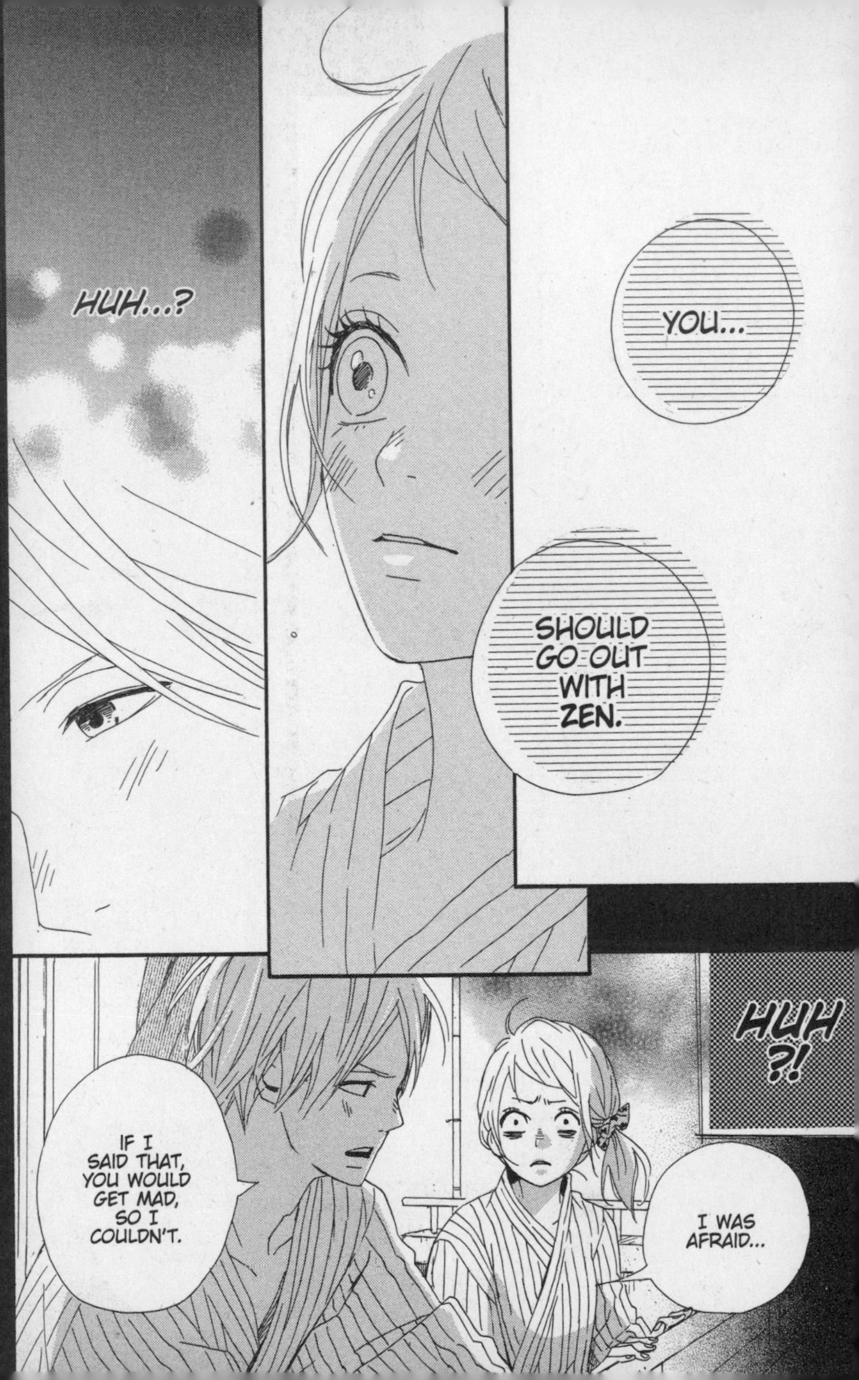
YOU...
SHOULD GO OUT WITH ZEN.
HUH...?
HUH ?!
I WAS AFRAID...
IF I SAID THAT, YOU WOULD GET MAD, SO I COULDN'T.

IF YOU'RE WITH ZEN, I BET EVERY DAY WILL BE FUN.

......

BUT I CAN'T KEEP ASKING YOU TO WAIT FOR ME.

I MIGHT NOT BE ABLE TO COME BACK... WE MIGHT NOT BE ABLE TO SEE EACH OTHER...

I CAN'T DO THAT...

I'LL **ALWAYS** LOVE THE LANDLORD.

MOREOVER, YOU KNOW HOW ZEN FEELS ABOUT YOU...

RIGHT?

IF YOU TRIED GOING OUT WITH HIM, YOU MIGHT COME TO LIKE HIM BACK.

THERE'S NO WAY...
YOU SAID YOU WOULD DO WHATEVER I SAID, RIGHT, SHIMANA?
ON THIS...
One Ticket 3 for Me to Do Anything You Want!
"Will you really do anything I ask?"
"Yeah! Sure! Anything!"
FALL IN LOVE WITH ZEN FOR ME.

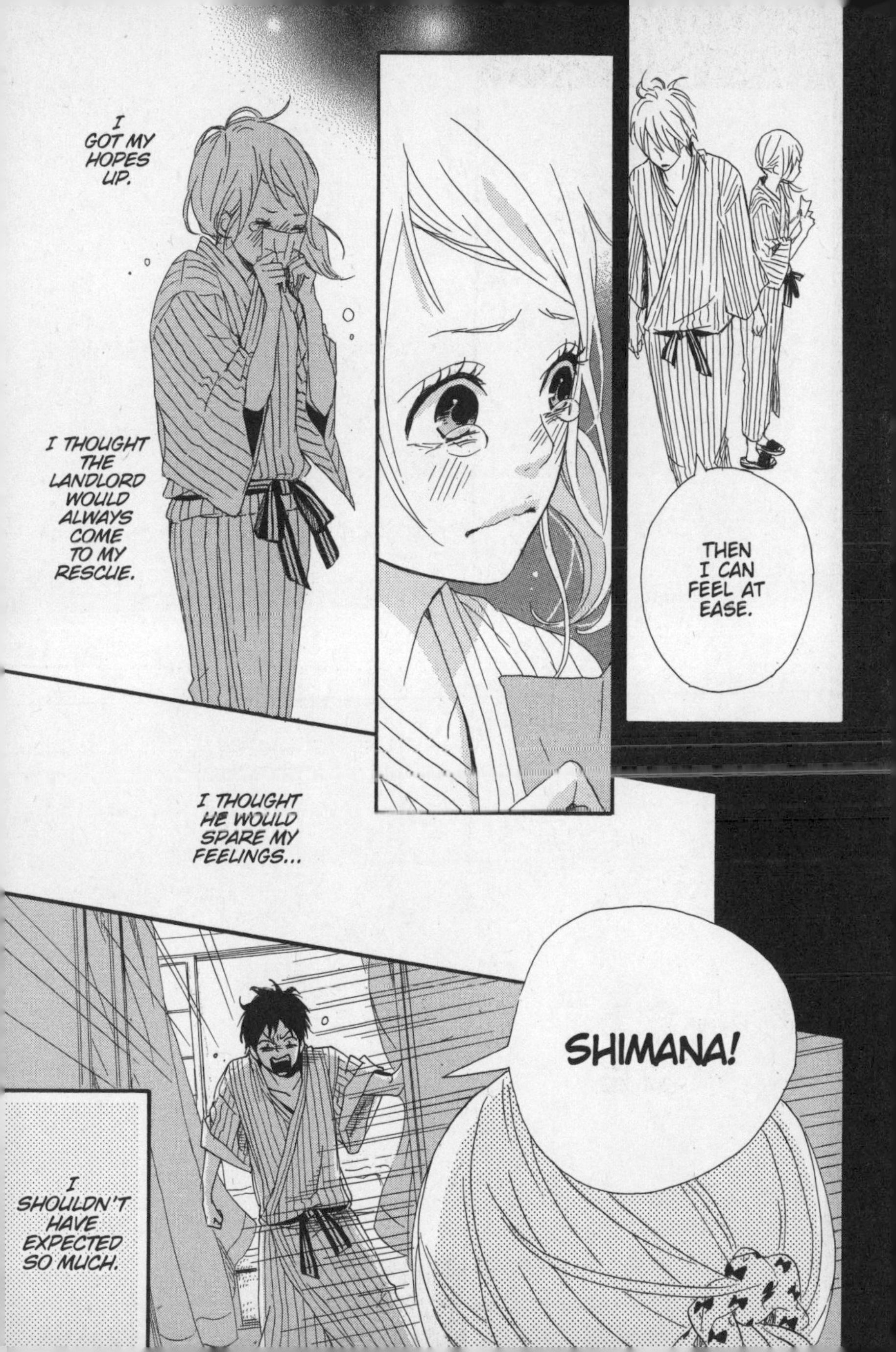
THEN I CAN FEEL AT EASE.
I GOT MY HOPES UP.
I THOUGHT THE LANDLORD WOULD ALWAYS COME TO MY RESCUE.
I THOUGHT HE WOULD SPARE MY FEELINGS...
SHIMANA!
I SHOULDN'T HAVE EXPECTED SO MUCH.

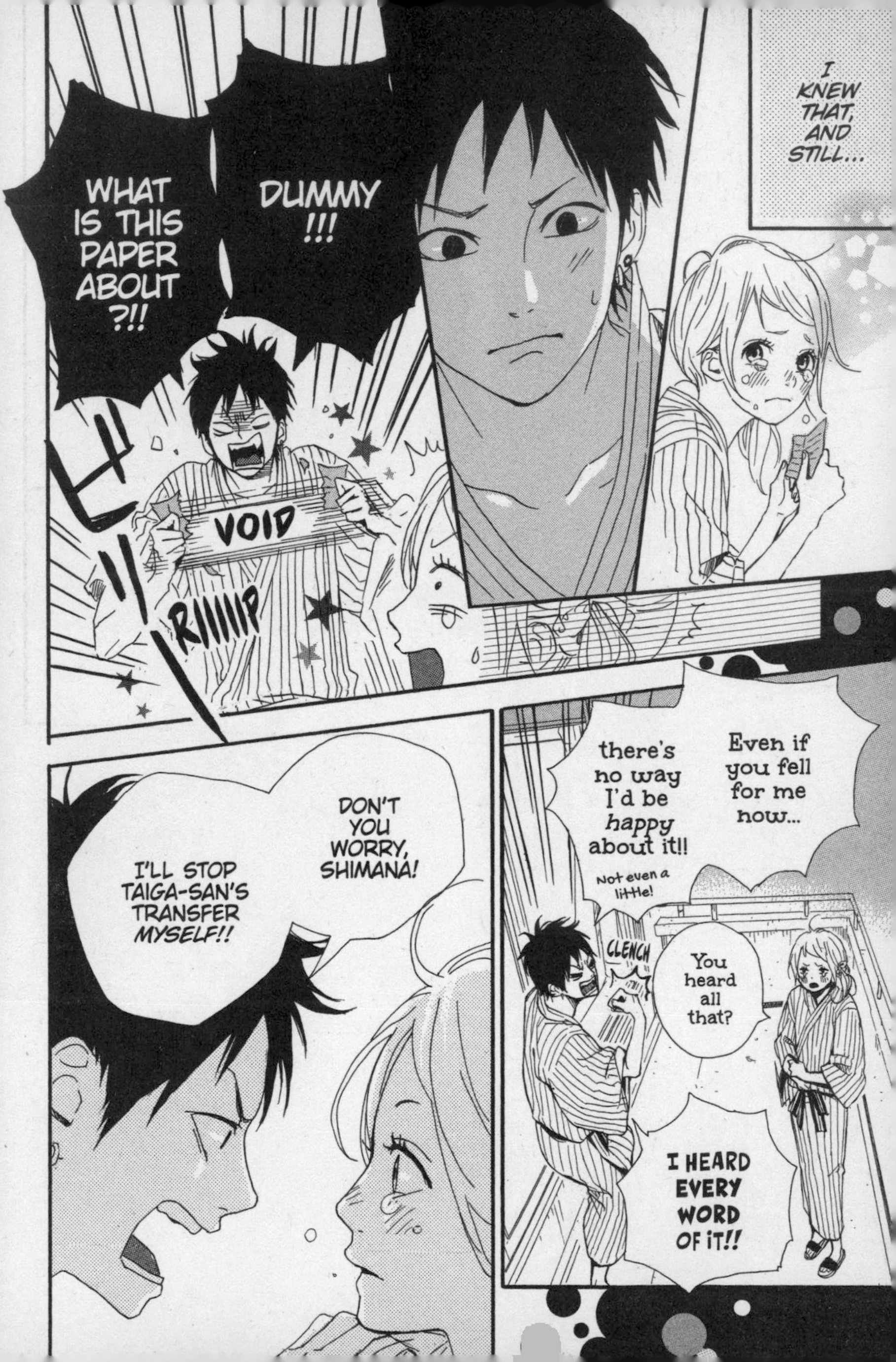
I KNEW THAT, AND STILL...
DUMMY!!!
WHAT IS THIS PAPER ABOUT?!!
VOID
RIIIIIP
Even if you fell for me now...
there's no way I'd be *happy* about it!!
Not even a little!
CLENCH
You heard all that?
I HEARD EVERY WORD OF IT!!
DON'T YOU WORRY, SHIMANA!
I'LL STOP TAIGA-SAN'S TRANSFER *MYSELF*!!

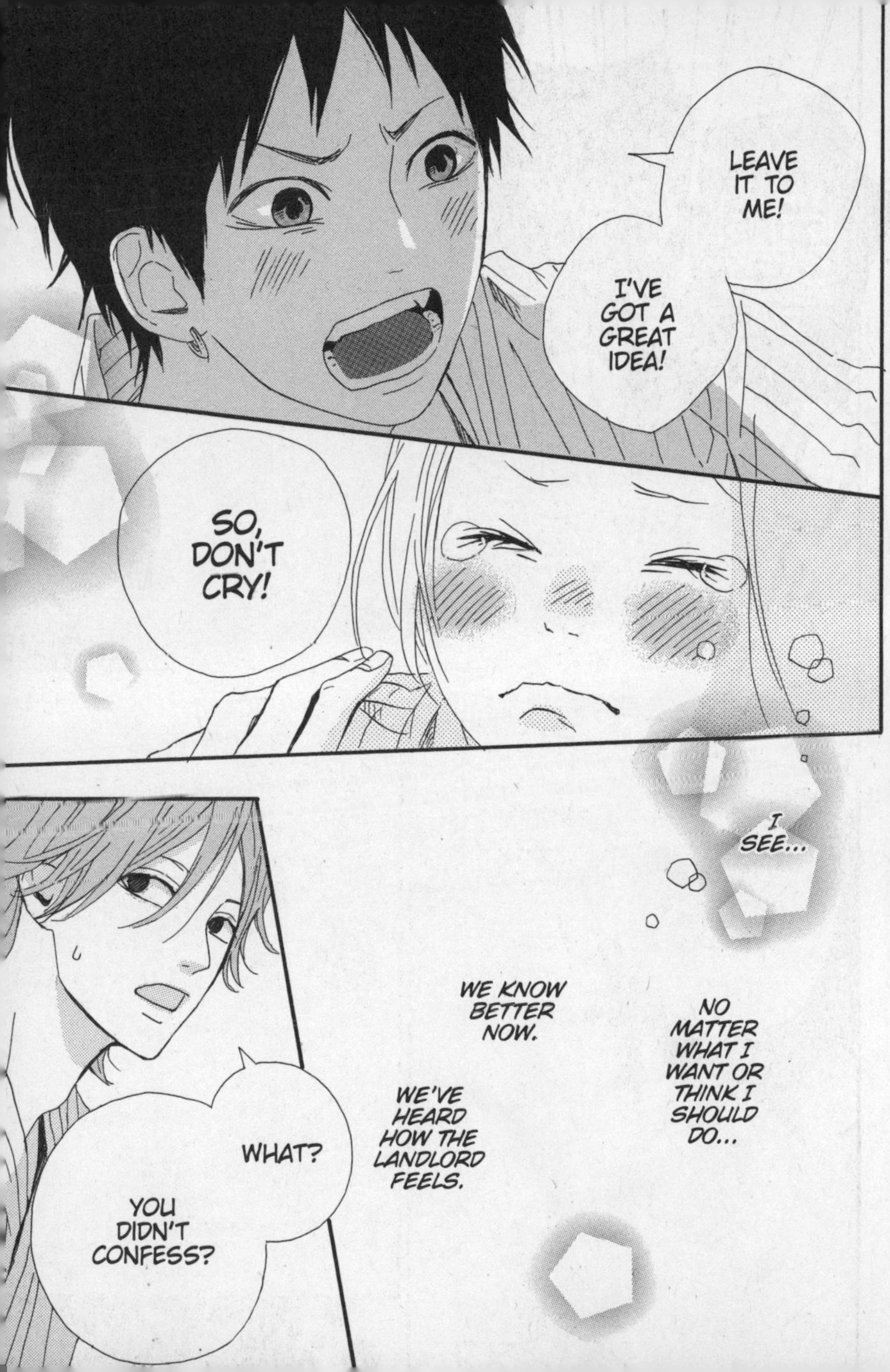
LEAVE IT TO ME!
I'VE GOT A GREAT IDEA!
SO, DON'T CRY!
I SEE...
NO MATTER WHAT I WANT OR THINK I SHOULD DO...
WE KNOW BETTER NOW.
WE'VE HEARD HOW THE LANDLORD FEELS.
WHAT?
YOU DIDN'T CONFESS?

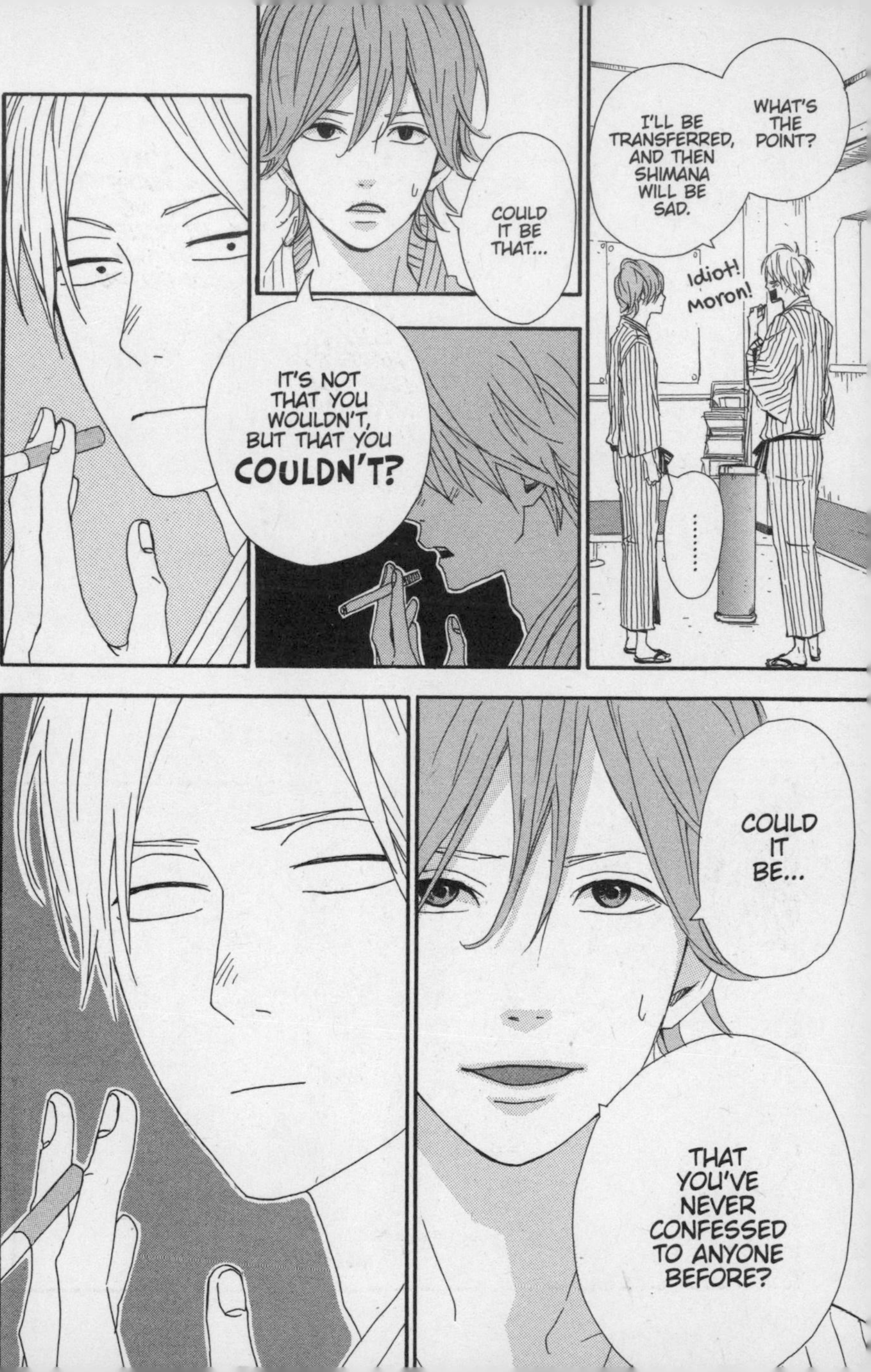
WHAT'S THE POINT?
I'LL BE TRANSFERRED, AND THEN SHIMANA WILL BE SAD.
Idiot! Moron!
......
COULD IT BE THAT...
IT'S NOT THAT YOU WOULDN'T, BUT THAT YOU COULDN'T?
COULD IT BE...
THAT YOU'VE NEVER CONFESSED TO ANYONE BEFORE?

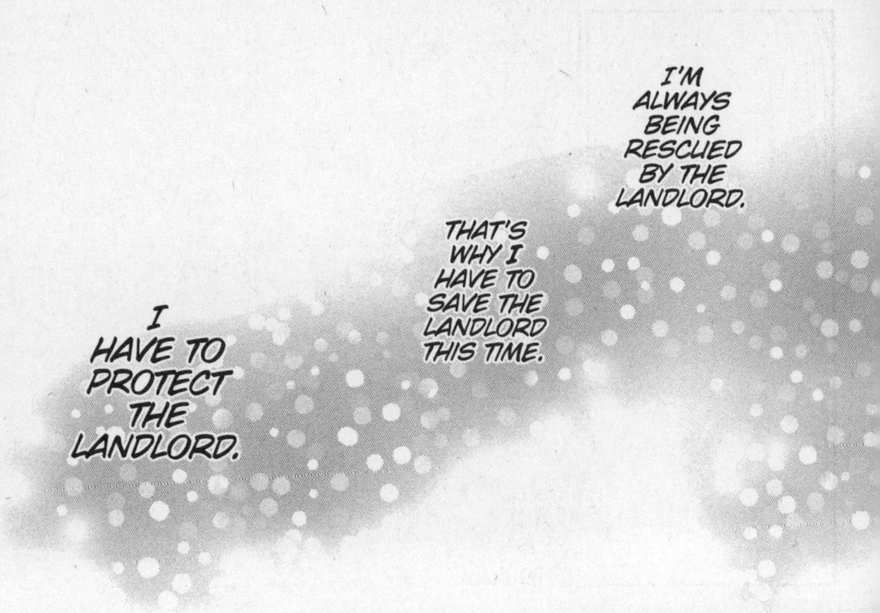
I'M ALWAYS BEING RESCUED BY THE LANDLORD.
THAT'S WHY I HAVE TO SAVE THE LANDLORD THIS TIME.
I HAVE TO PROTECT THE LANDLORD.

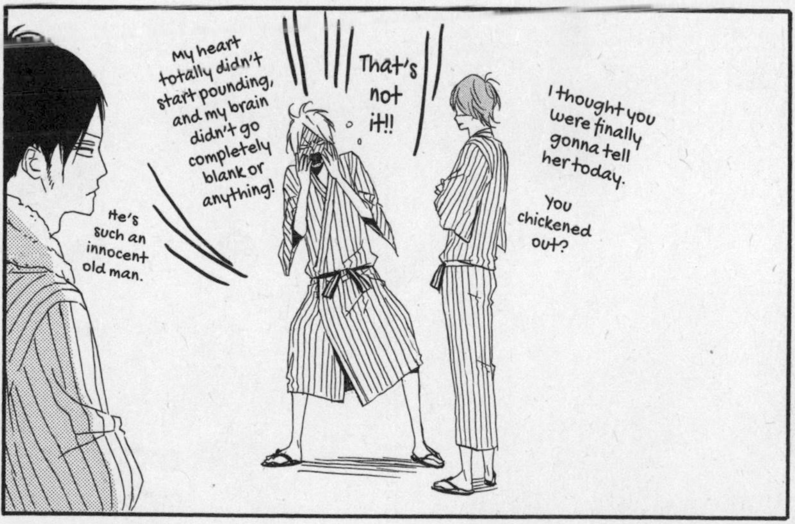
I thought you were finally gonna tell her today.
You chickened out?
That's not it!!
My heart totally didn't start pounding, and my brain didn't go completely blank or anything!
He's such an innocent old man.

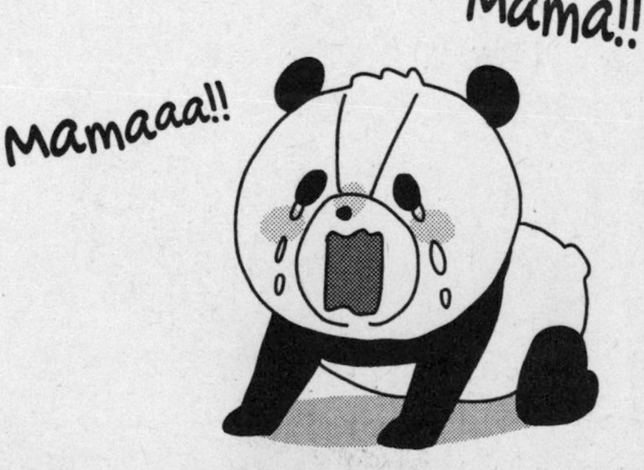
Mama!!
Mamaaa!!

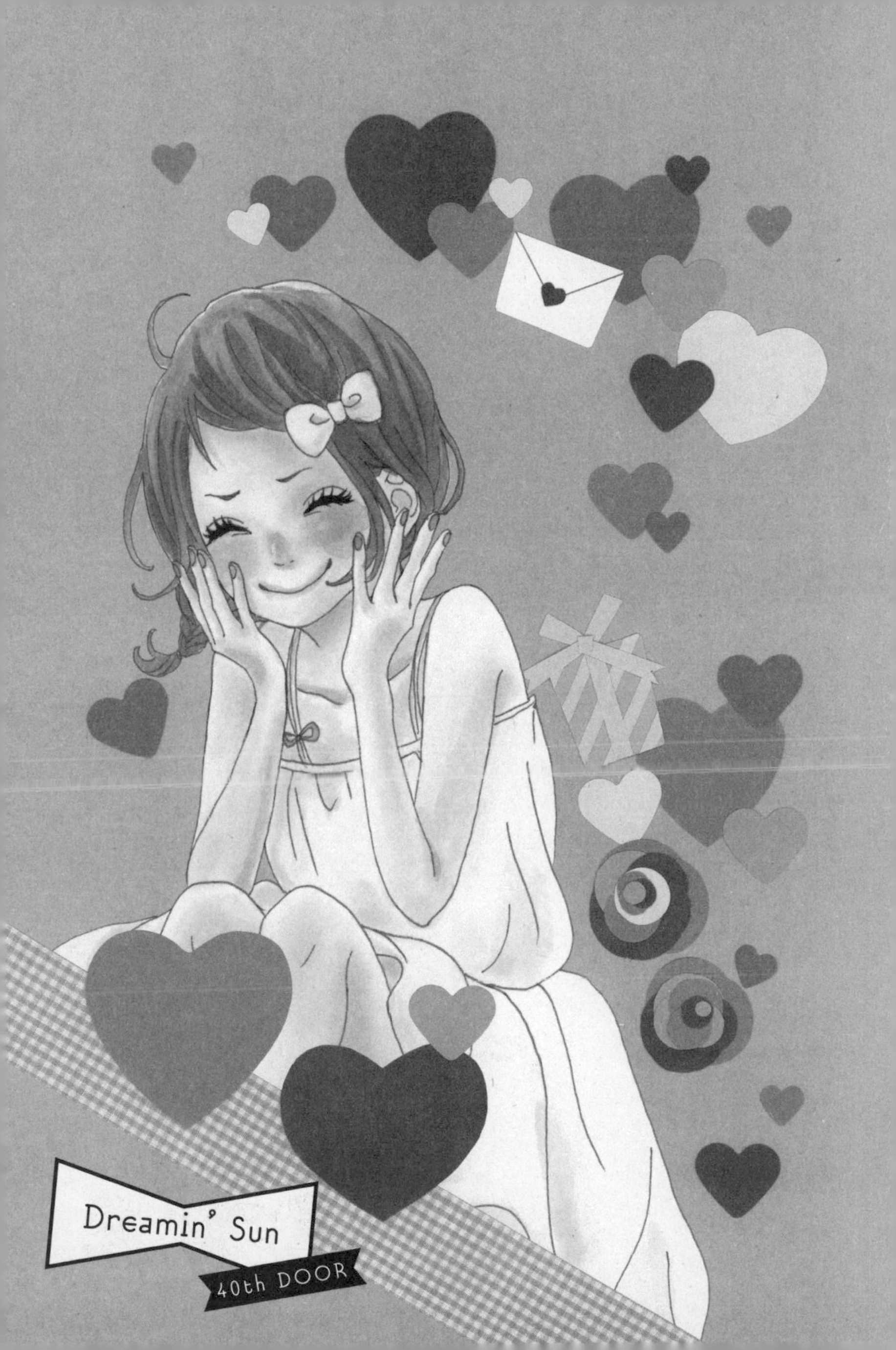
Dreamin' Sun
40th DOOR

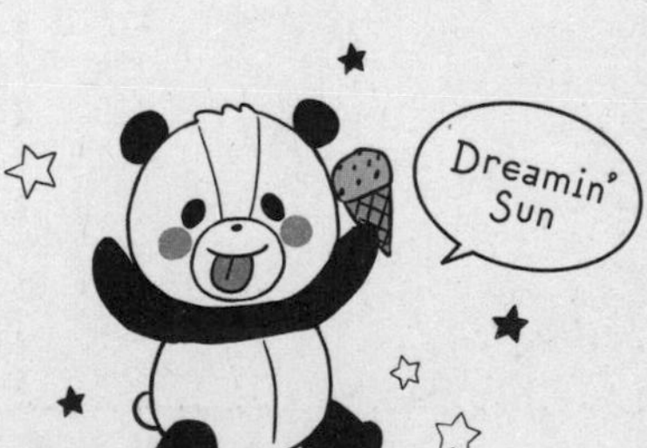
Dreamin' Sun

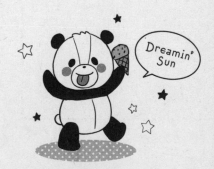

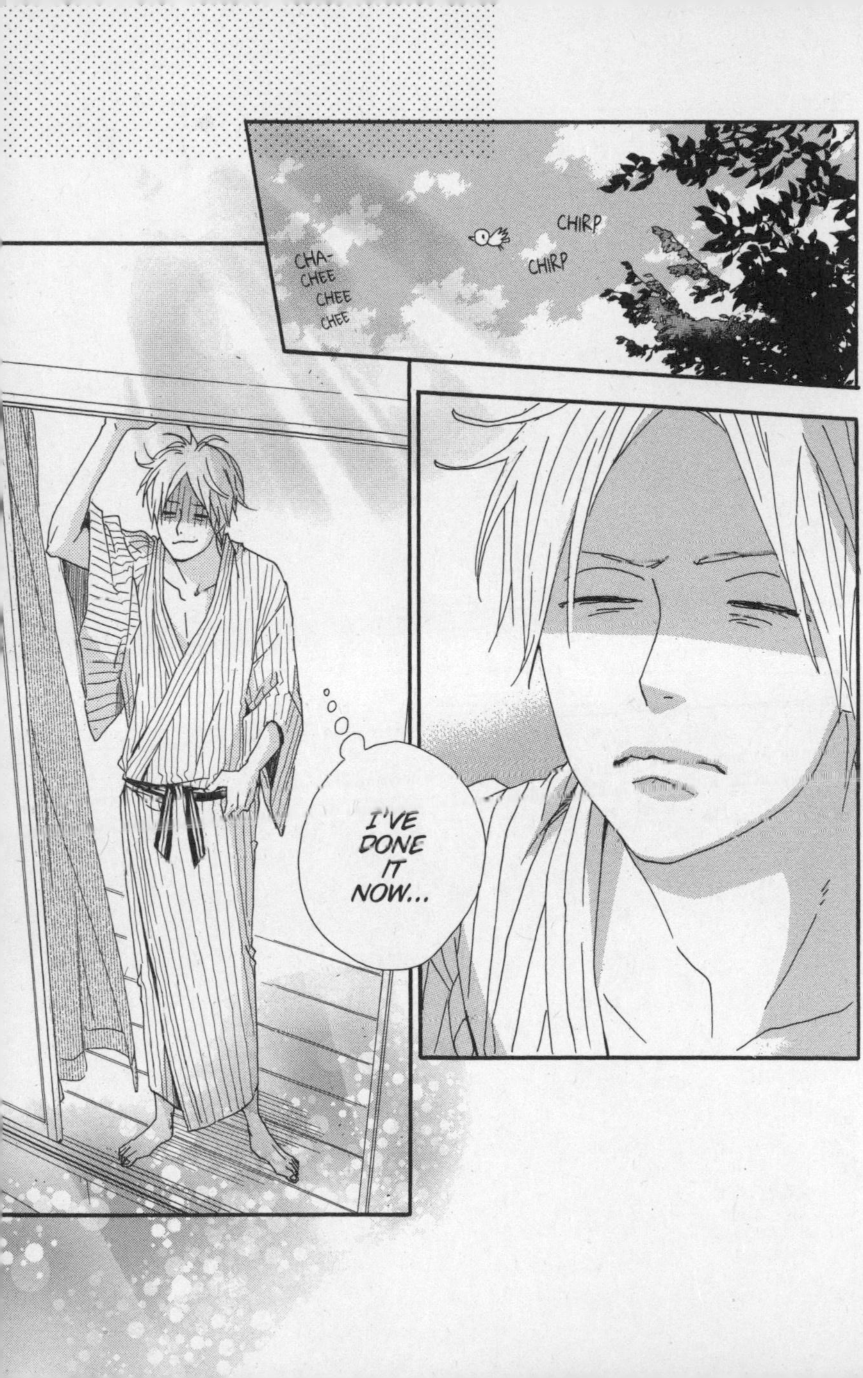
CHIRP
CHIRP
CHA- CHEE CHEE CHEE
I'VE DONE IT NOW...

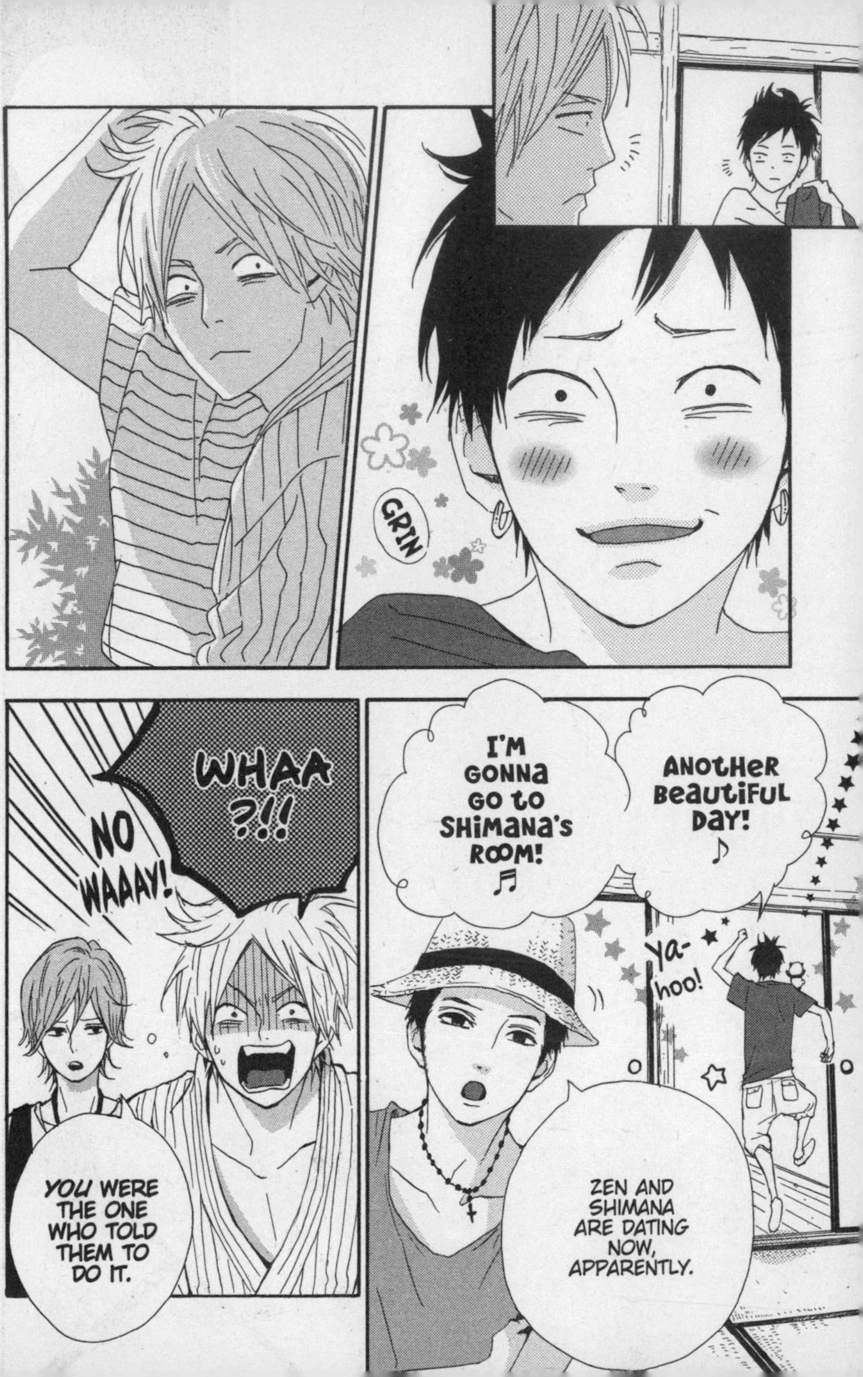
GRIN
ANOTHER BEAUTIFUL DAY! ♪
I'M GONNA GO TO SHIMANA'S ROOM! ♬
Ya-hoo!
ZEN AND SHIMANA ARE DATING NOW, APPARENTLY.
WHAA ?!!
NO WAAAY!
YOU WERE THE ONE WHO TOLD THEM TO DO IT.

I KNOW YOU CAN'T BE HAPPY LEAVING THINGS LIKE THIS.

THEN TAKE IT BACK.

·········

YOU DIDN'T EVEN CONFESS TO HER.

YEAH, I DID...

BUT, ASAHI...

·········

Like I care.

I was drunk!

I CAN'T...

SO LONG AS I'M BEING TRANS-FERRED.

NO. IT'S FINE.

EVERY-THING'S FINE.

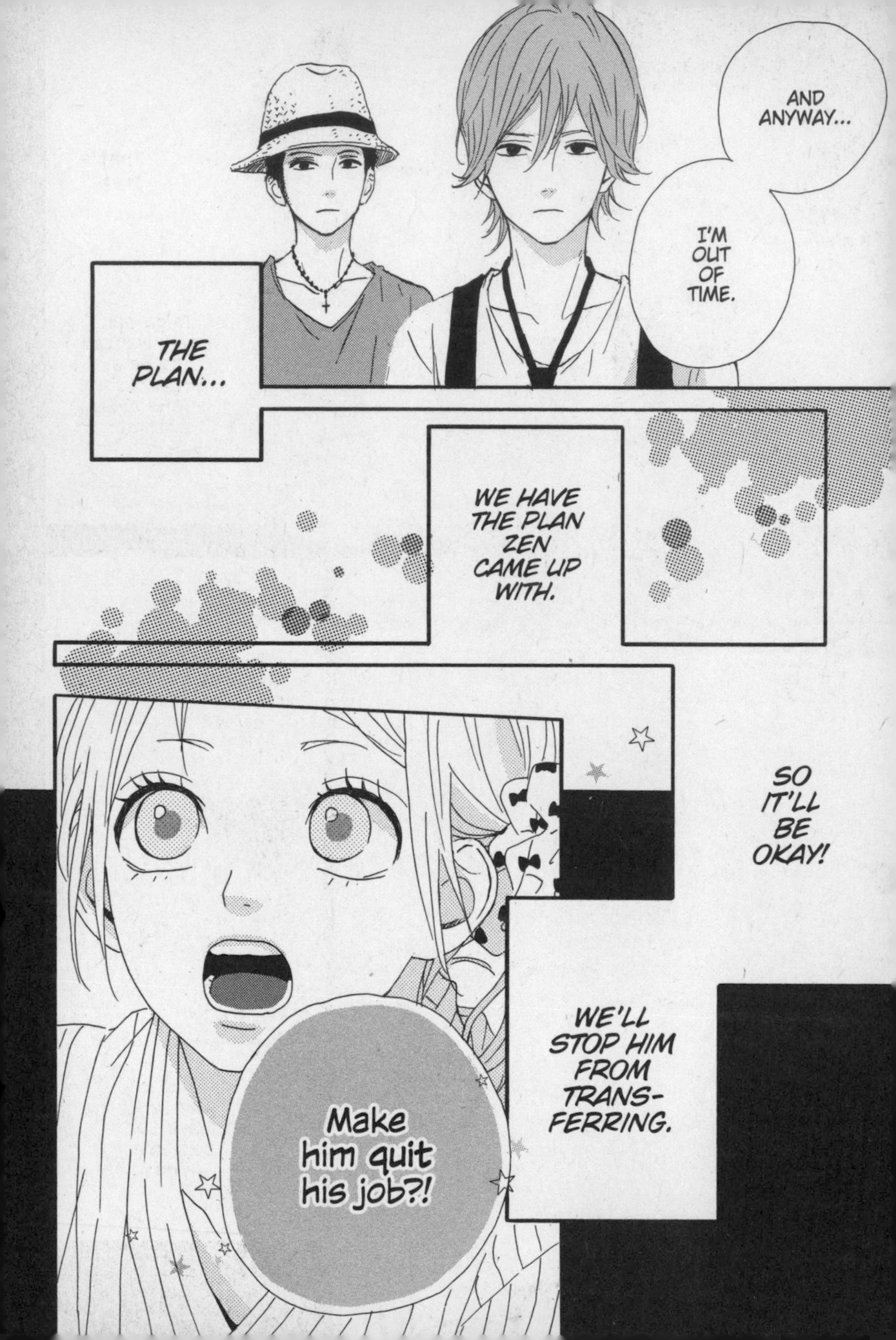
AND ANYWAY...
I'M OUT OF TIME.
THE PLAN...
WE HAVE THE PLAN ZEN CAME UP WITH.
SO IT'LL BE OKAY!
WE'LL STOP HIM FROM TRANS-FERRING.
Make him quit his job?!

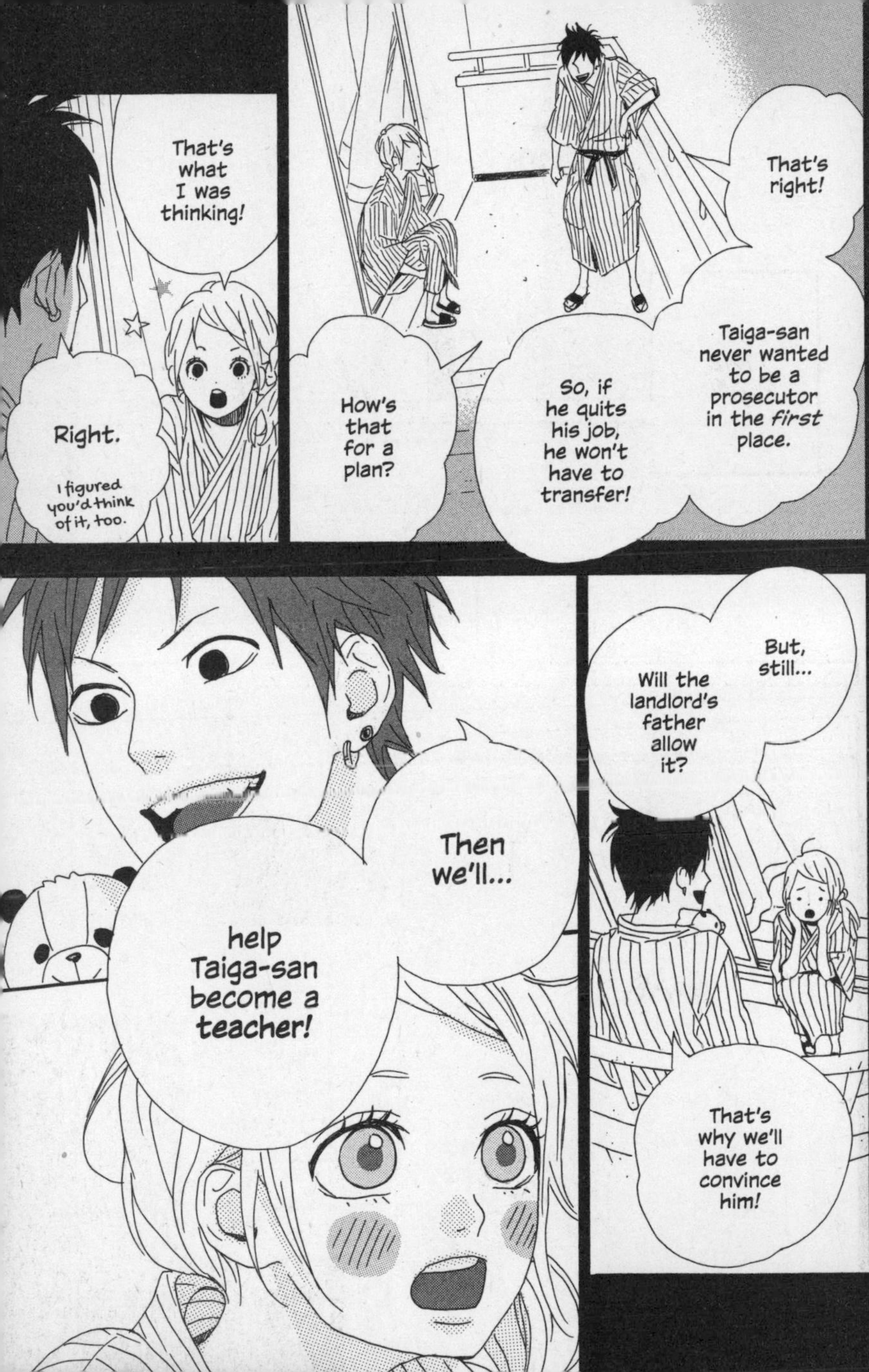
That's right!
Taiga-san never wanted to be a prosecutor in the *first* place.
So, if he quits his job, he won't have to transfer!
How's that for a plan?
That's what I was thinking!
Right.
I figured you'd think of it, too.
But, still...
Will the landlord's father allow it?
That's why we'll have to convince him!
Then we'll...
help Taiga-san become a teacher!

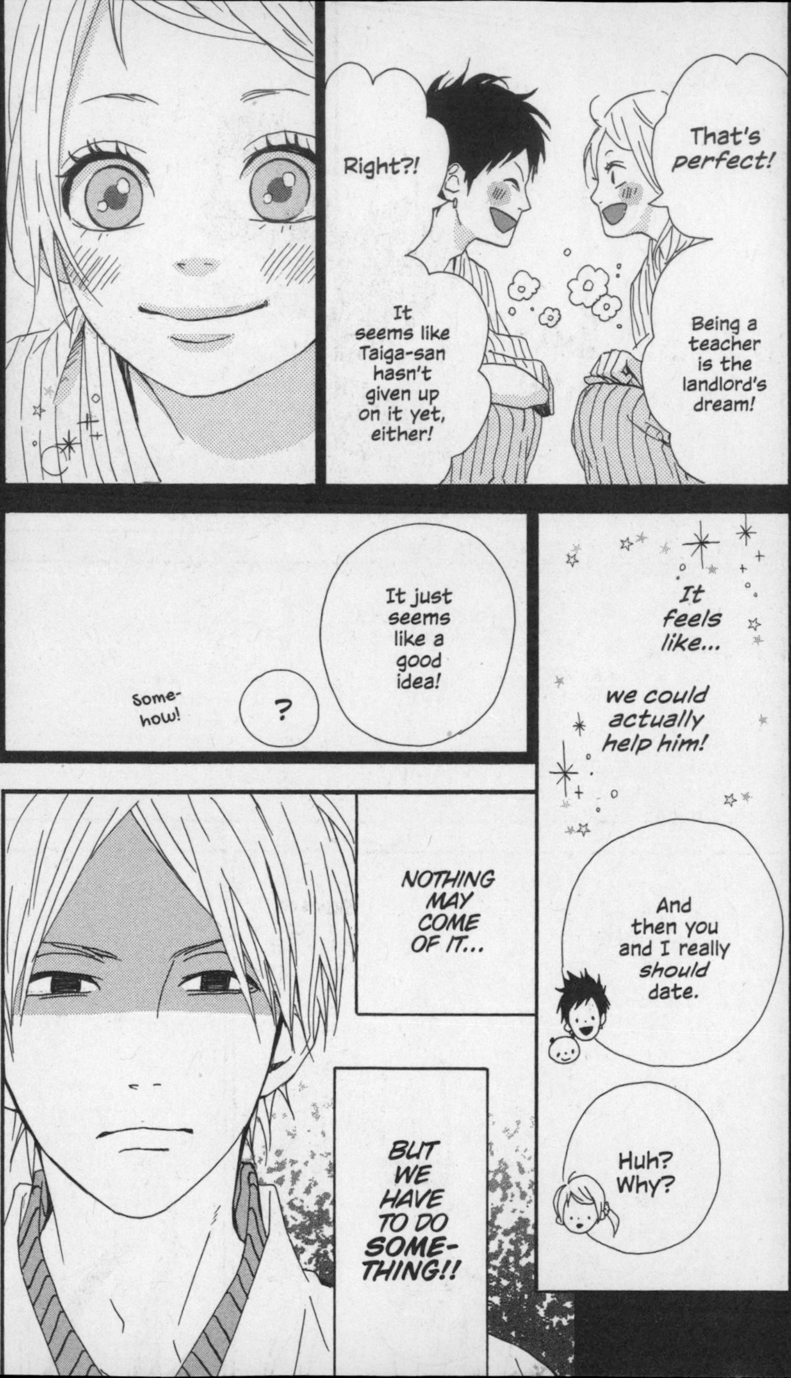
That's perfect!
Right?!
Being a teacher is the landlord's dream!
It seems like Taiga-san hasn't given up on it yet, either!
It feels like...
we could actually help him!
And then you and I really should date.
Huh? Why?
It just seems like a good idea!
?
Some-how!
NOTHING MAY COME OF IT...
BUT WE HAVE TO DO SOMETHING!!

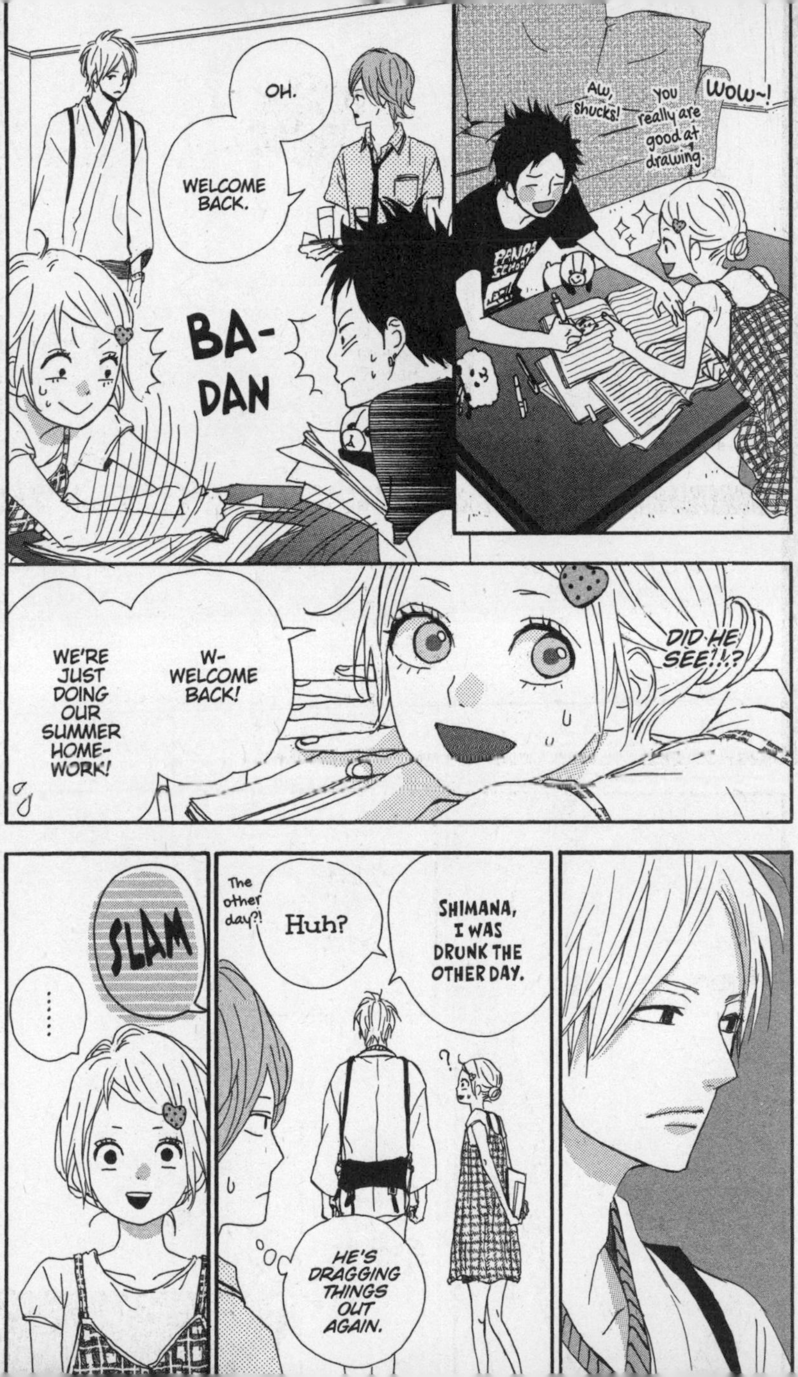
WOW~!
You really are good at drawing.
Aw, shucks!
OH.
WELCOME BACK.
BA-DAN
DID HE SEE!!?
W-WELCOME BACK!
WE'RE JUST DOING OUR SUMMER HOMEWORK!
SHIMANA, I WAS DRUNK THE OTHER DAY.
Huh?
The other day?!
HE'S DRAGGING THINGS OUT AGAIN.
SLAM
......

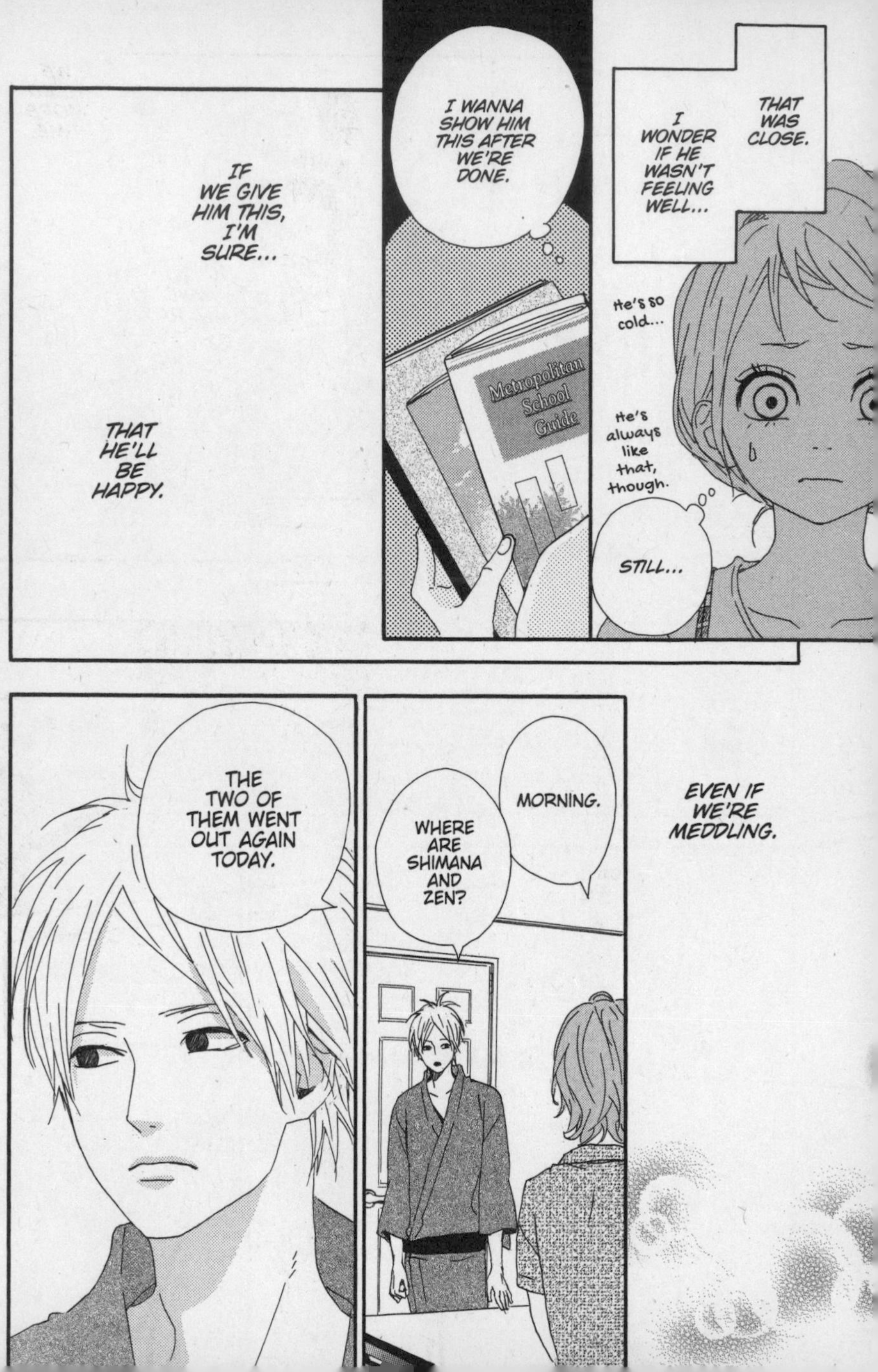
THAT WAS CLOSE.
I WONDER IF HE WASN'T FEELING WELL...
He's so cold...
He's always like that, though.
STILL...
I WANNA SHOW HIM THIS AFTER WE'RE DONE.
Metropolitan School Guide
IF WE GIVE HIM THIS, I'M SURE...
THAT HE'LL BE HAPPY.
EVEN IF WE'RE MEDDLING.
MORNING.
WHERE ARE SHIMANA AND ZEN?
THE TWO OF THEM WENT OUT AGAIN TODAY.

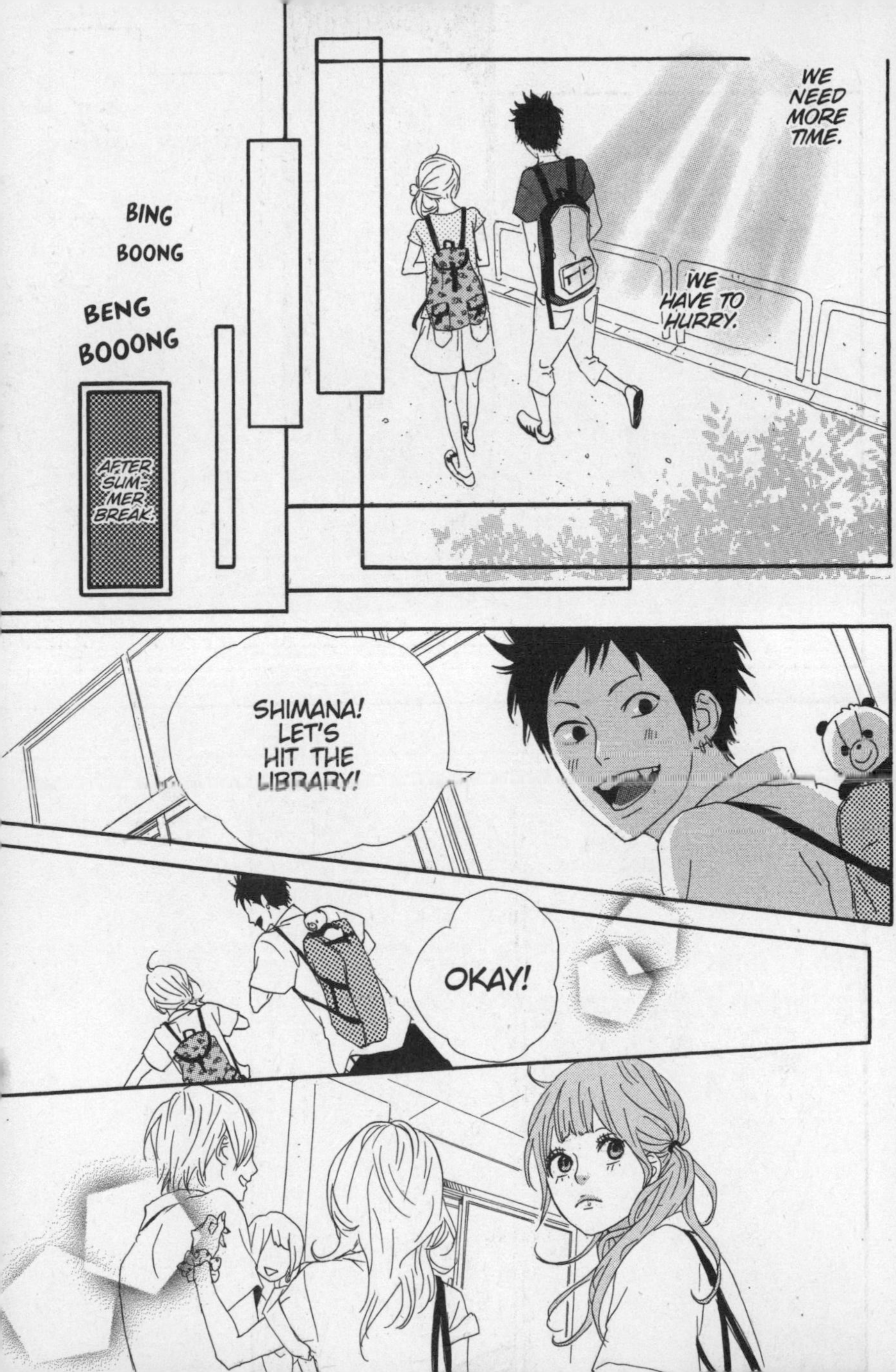
WE NEED MORE TIME.
WE HAVE TO HURRY.
BING BOONG
BENG BOOONG
AFTER SUM-MER BREAK.
SHIMANA! LET'S HIT THE LIBRARY!
OKAY!

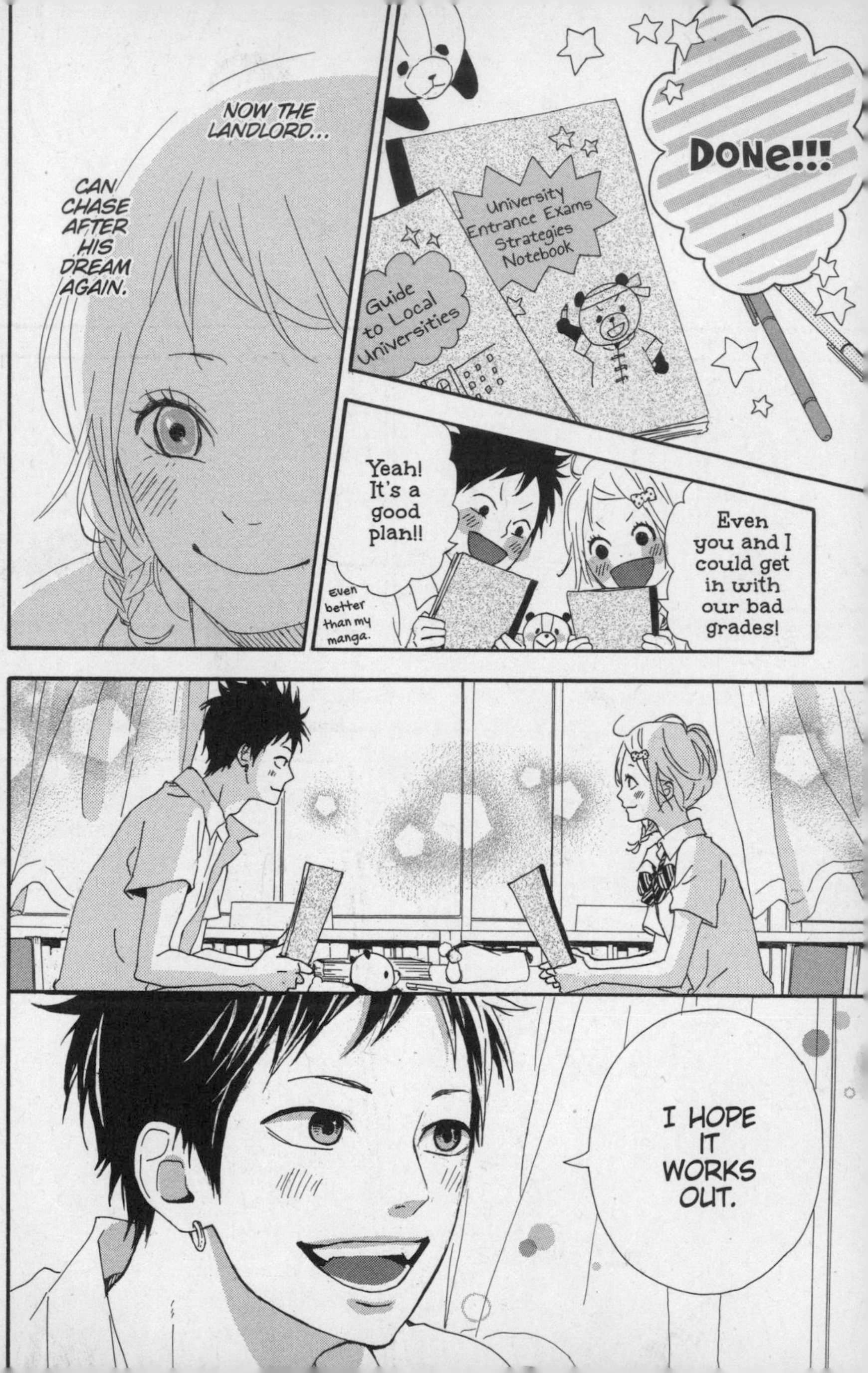
DONE!!!
University Entrance Exams Strategies Notebook
Guide to Local Universities
Even you and I could get in with our bad grades!
Yeah! It's a good plan!!
Even better than my manga.
NOW THE LANDLORD...
CAN CHASE AFTER HIS DREAM AGAIN.
I HOPE IT WORKS OUT.

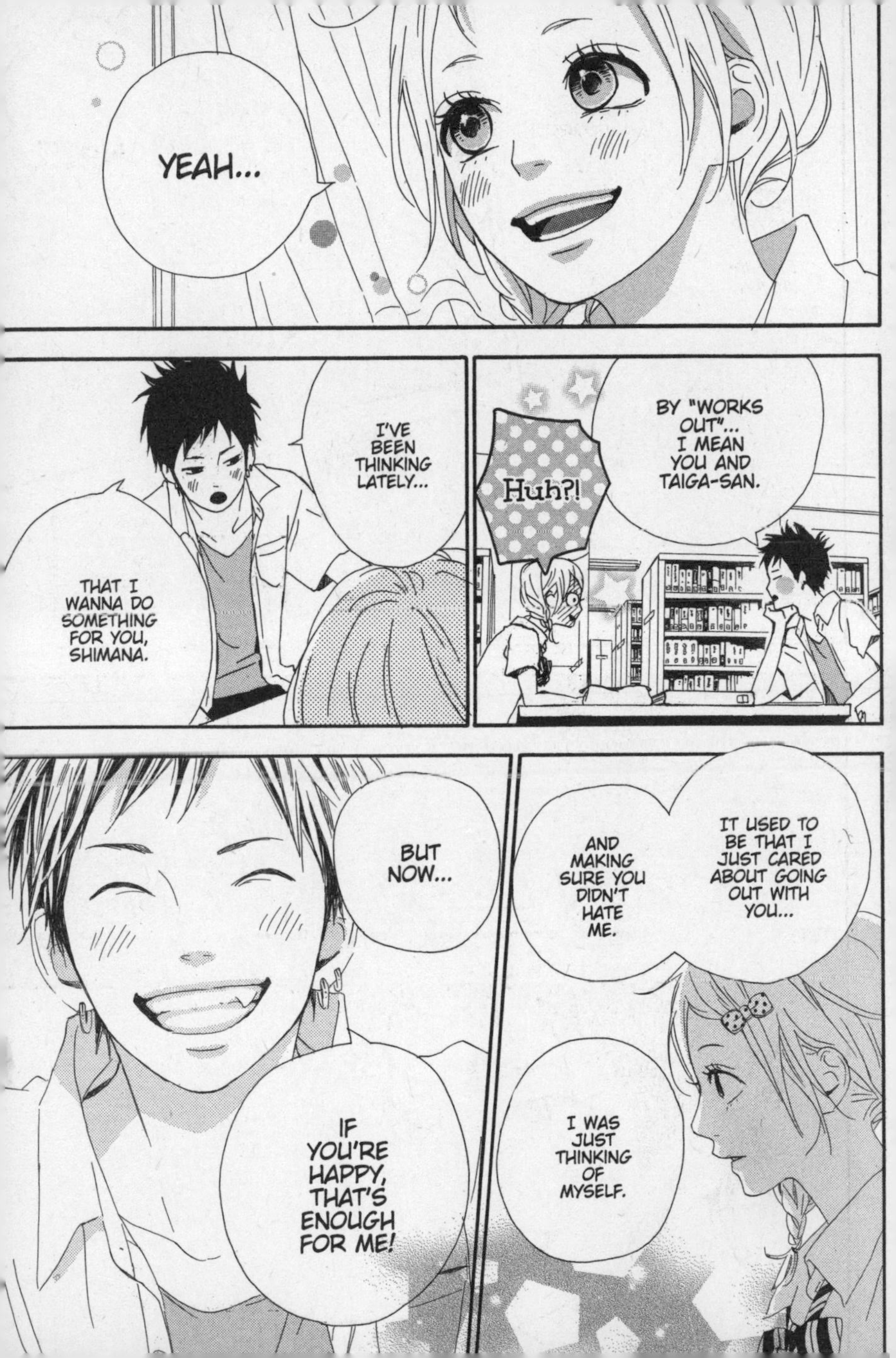
YEAH...
BY "WORKS OUT"... I MEAN YOU AND TAIGA-SAN.
Huh?!
I'VE BEEN THINKING LATELY...
THAT I WANNA DO SOMETHING FOR YOU, SHIMANA.
IT USED TO BE THAT I JUST CARED ABOUT GOING OUT WITH YOU...
AND MAKING SURE YOU DIDN'T HATE ME.
I WAS JUST THINKING OF MYSELF.
BUT NOW...
IF YOU'RE HAPPY, THAT'S ENOUGH FOR ME!

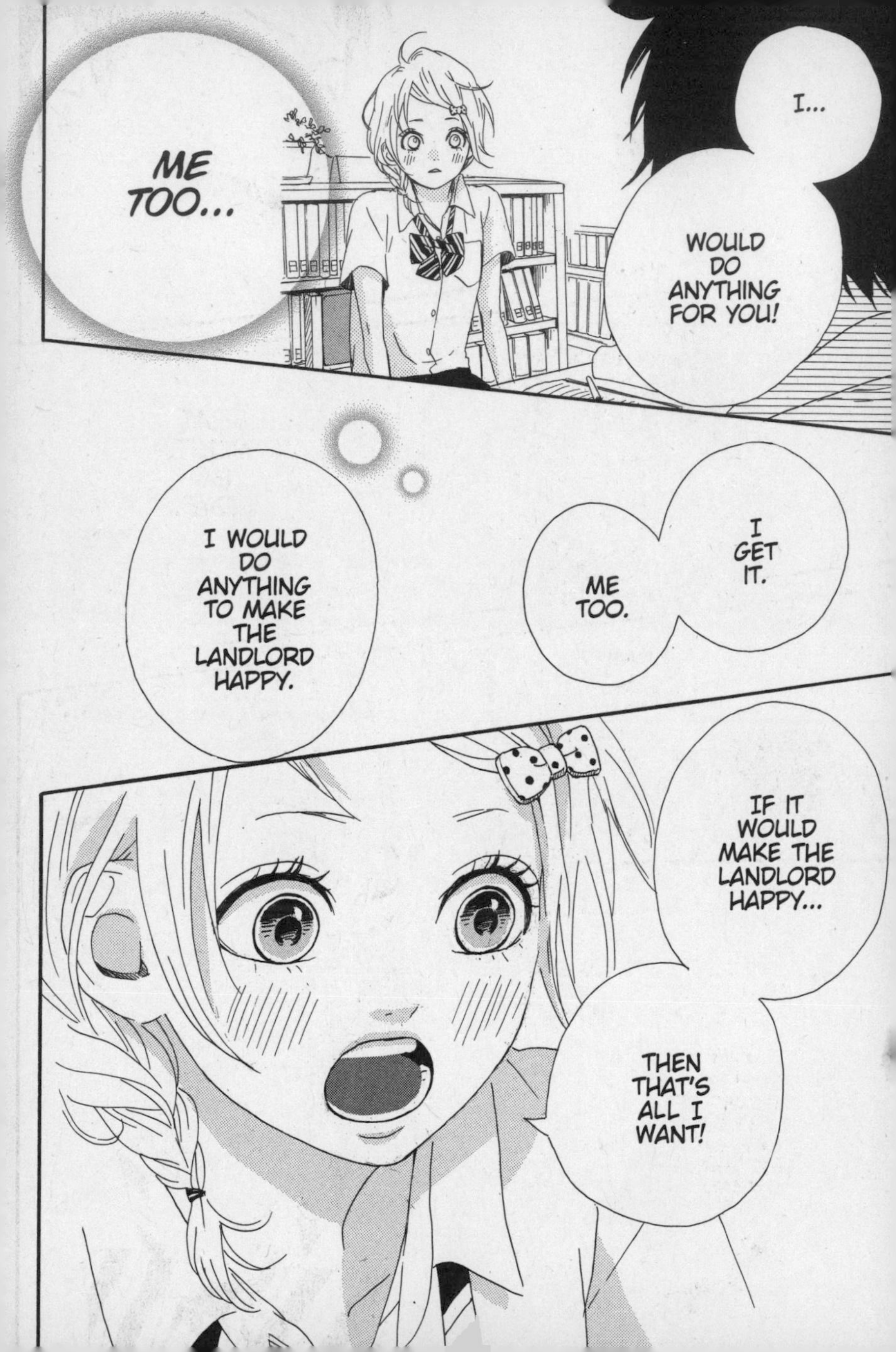
I...
WOULD DO ANYTHING FOR YOU!
ME TOO...
I GET IT.
ME TOO.
I WOULD DO ANYTHING TO MAKE THE LANDLORD HAPPY.
IF IT WOULD MAKE THE LANDLORD HAPPY...
THEN THAT'S ALL I WANT!

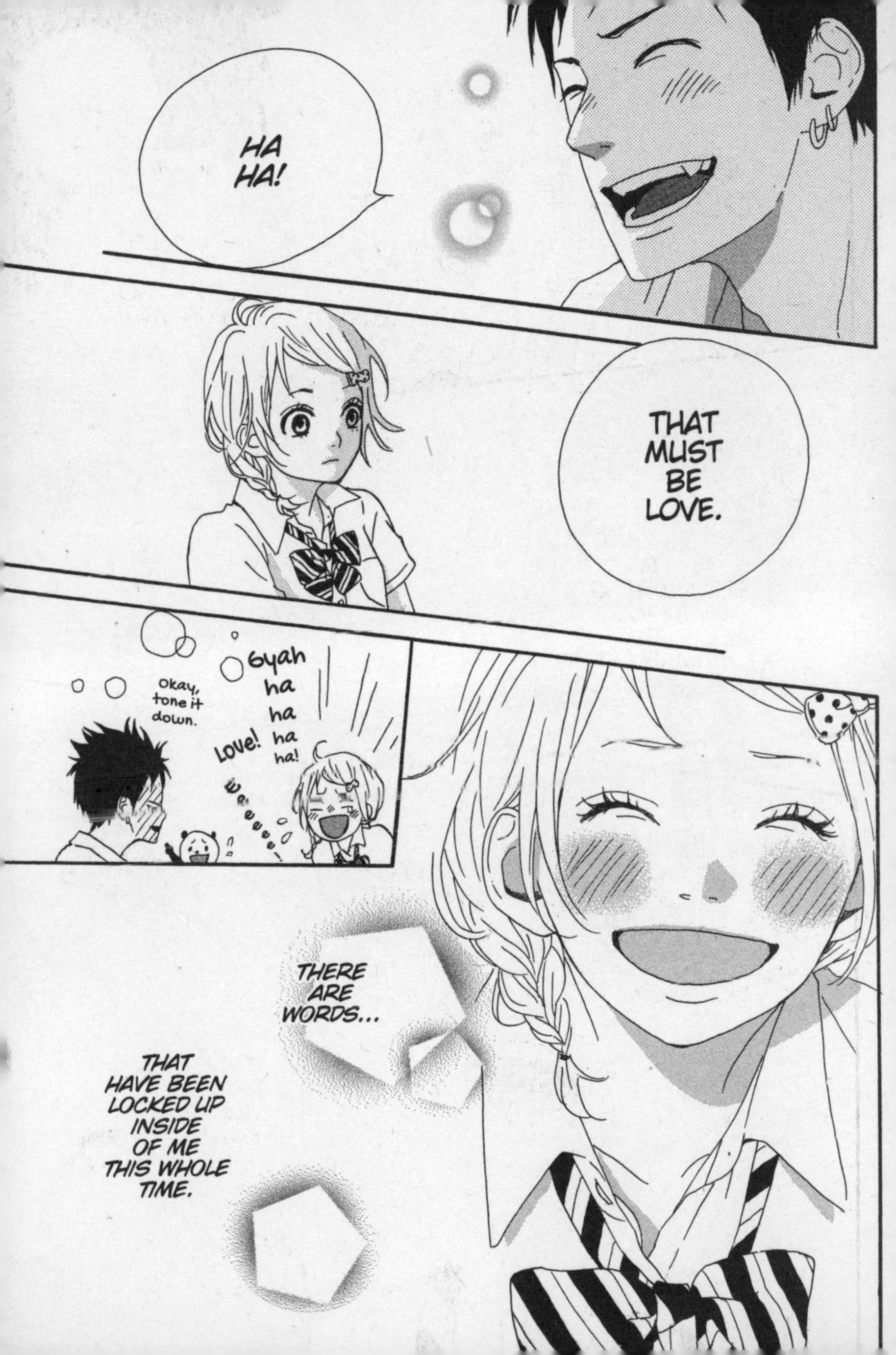
HA HA!
THAT MUST BE LOVE.
Gyah ha ha ha ha!
Love!
Weeeee!
Okay, tone it down.
THERE ARE WORDS...
THAT HAVE BEEN LOCKED UP INSIDE OF ME THIS WHOLE TIME.

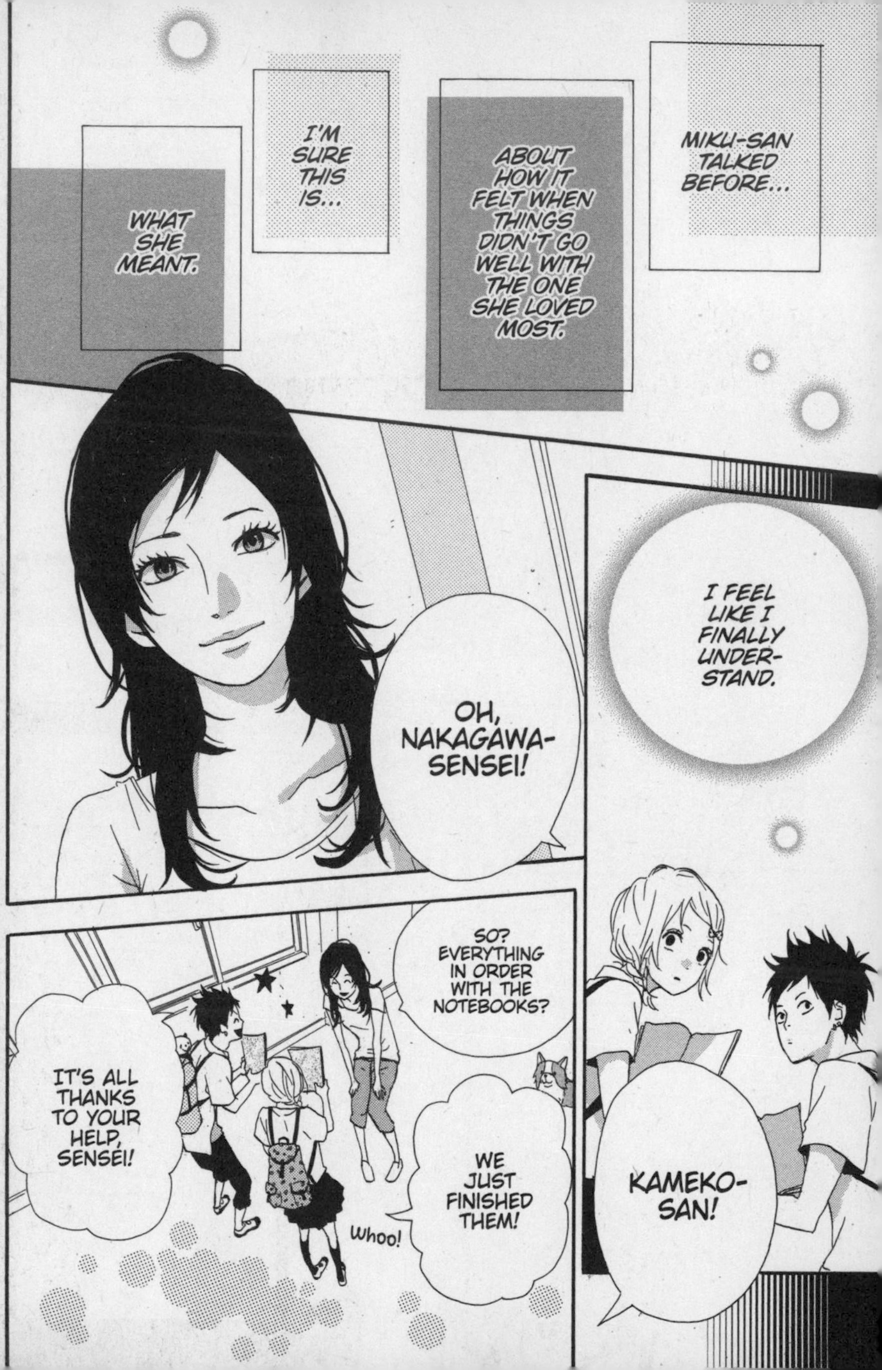
MIKU-SAN TALKED BEFORE...
ABOUT HOW IT FELT WHEN THINGS DIDN'T GO WELL WITH THE ONE SHE LOVED MOST.
I'M SURE THIS IS...
WHAT SHE MEANT.
I FEEL LIKE I FINALLY UNDER-STAND.
KAMEKO-SAN!
OH, NAKAGAWA-SENSEI!
SO? EVERYTHING IN ORDER WITH THE NOTEBOOKS?
WE JUST FINISHED THEM!
Whoo!
IT'S ALL THANKS TO YOUR HELP, SENSEI!

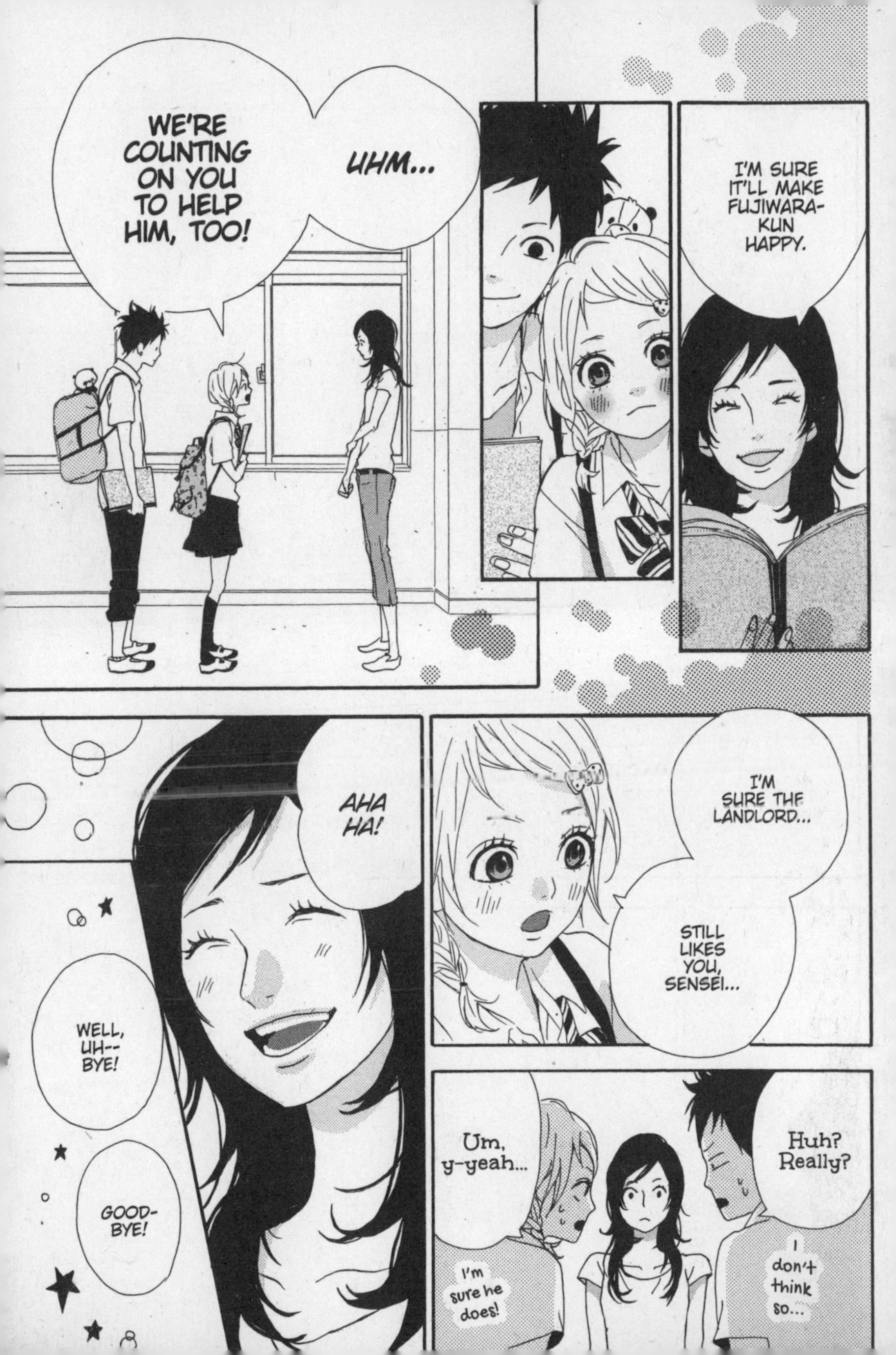
WE'RE COUNTING ON YOU TO HELP HIM, TOO!
UHM...
I'M SURE IT'LL MAKE FUJIWARA-KUN HAPPY.
I'M SURE THE LANDLORD...
STILL LIKES YOU, SENSEI...
Huh? Really?
I don't think so...
Um, y-yeah...
I'm sure he does!
AHA HA!
WELL, UH-- BYE!
GOOD-BYE!

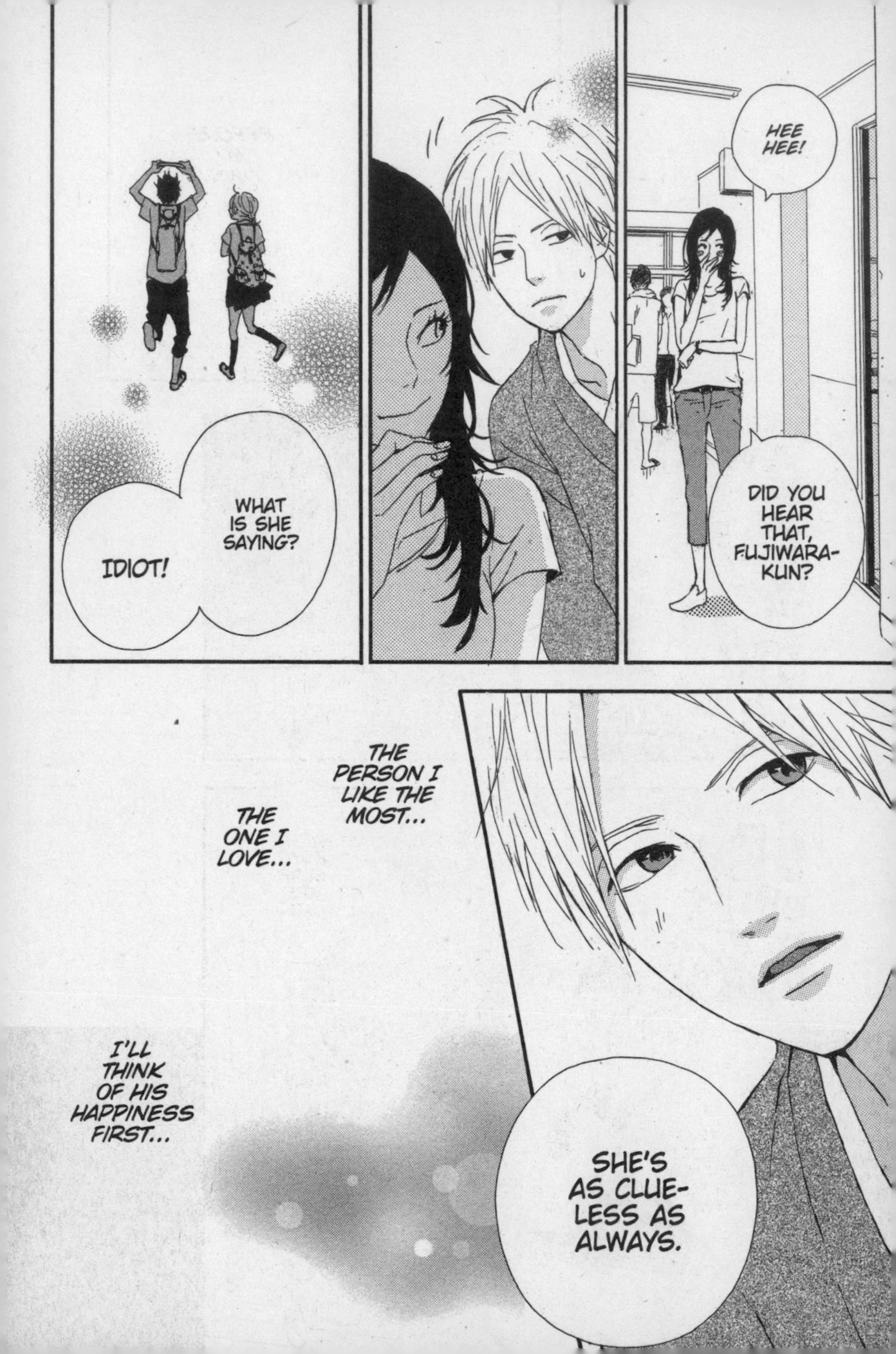
HEE HEE!
DID YOU HEAR THAT, FUJIWARA-KUN?
WHAT IS SHE SAYING?
IDIOT!
THE PERSON I LIKE THE MOST...
THE ONE I LOVE...
SHE'S AS CLUELESS AS ALWAYS.
I'LL THINK OF HIS HAPPINESS FIRST...

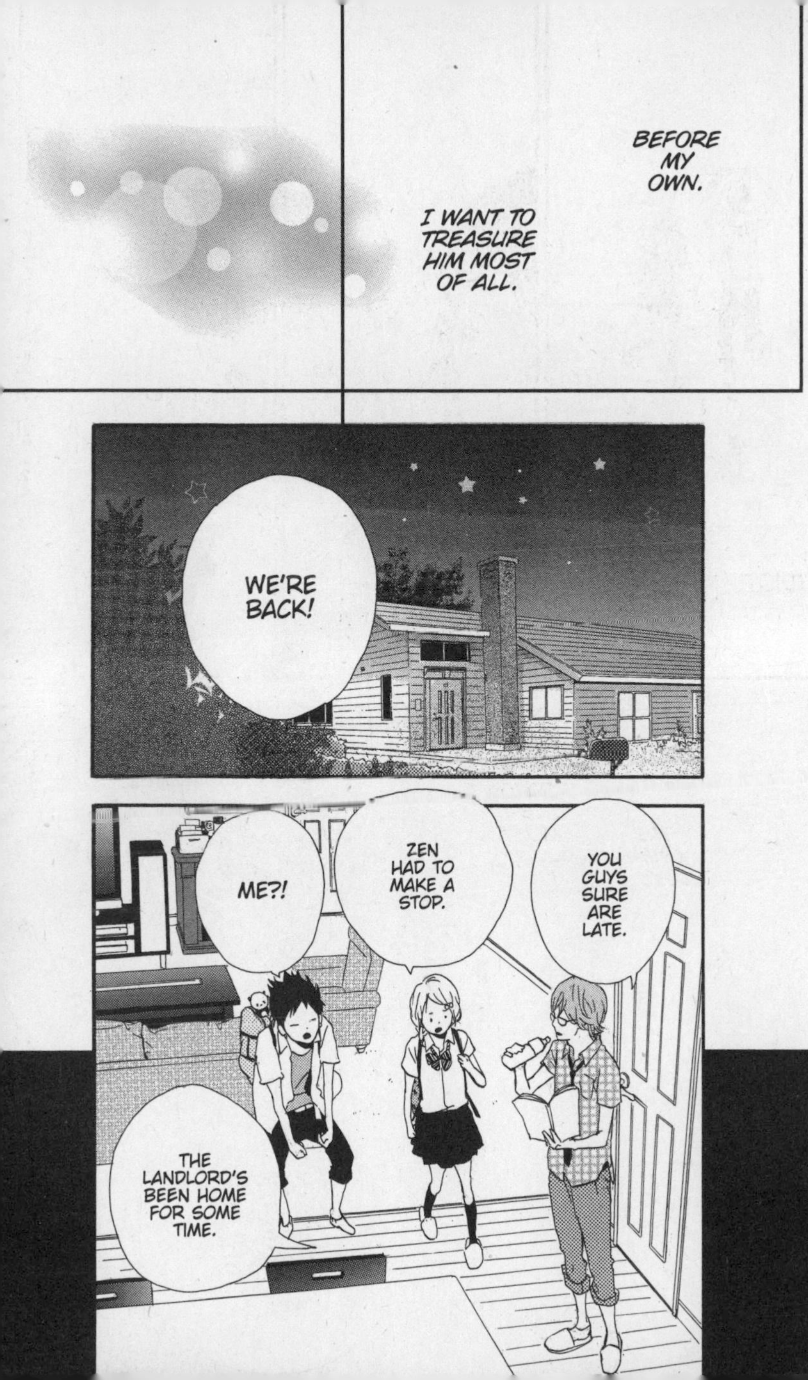
BEFORE MY OWN.
I WANT TO TREASURE HIM MOST OF ALL.
WE'RE BACK!
YOU GUYS SURE ARE LATE.
ZEN HAD TO MAKE A STOP.
ME?!
THE LANDLORD'S BEEN HOME FOR SOME TIME.

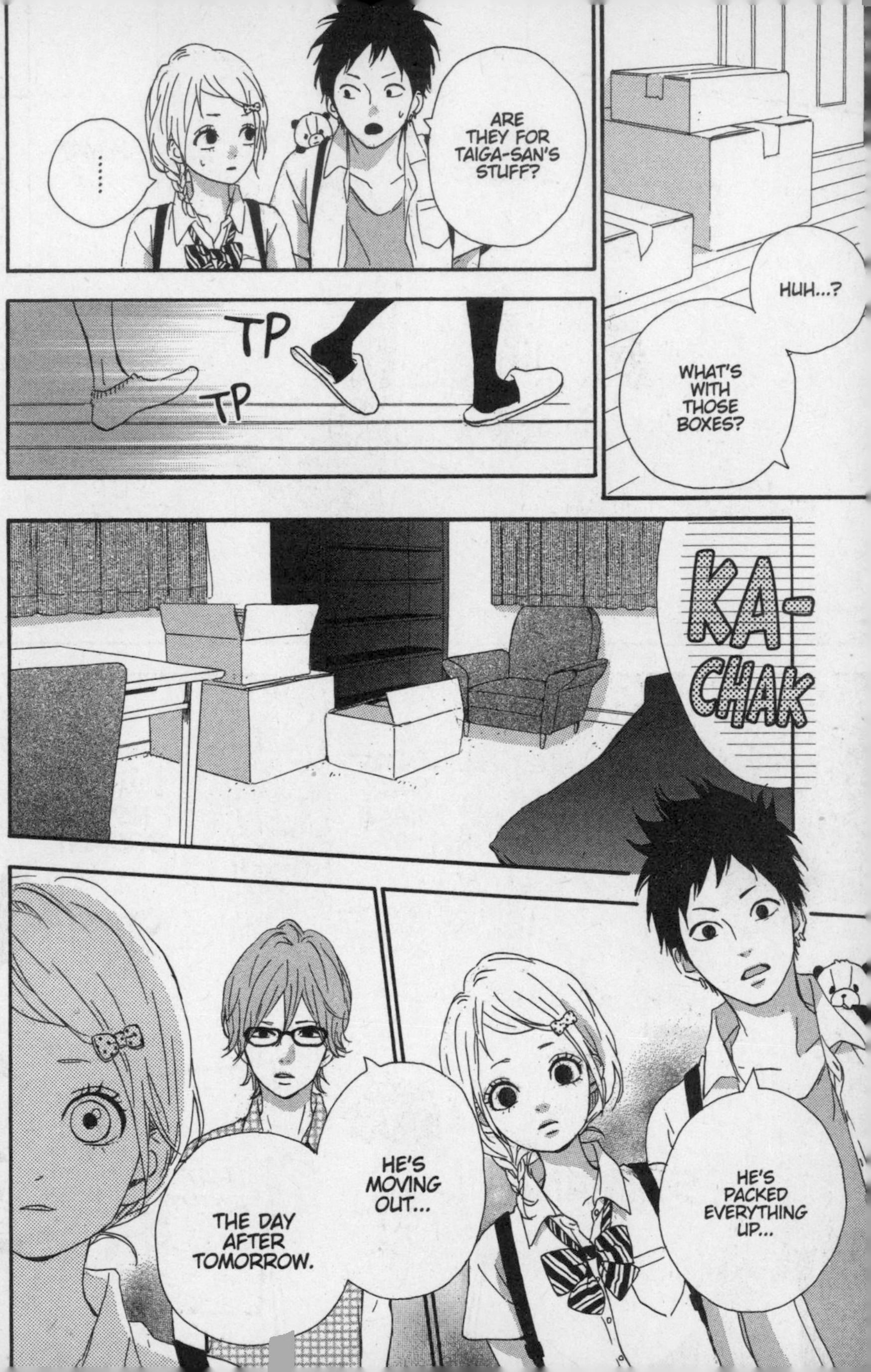
HUH...?
WHAT'S WITH THOSE BOXES?
ARE THEY FOR TAIGA-SAN'S STUFF?
......
TP
TP
KA-CHAK
HE'S PACKED EVERYTHING UP...
HE'S MOVING OUT...
THE DAY AFTER TOMORROW.

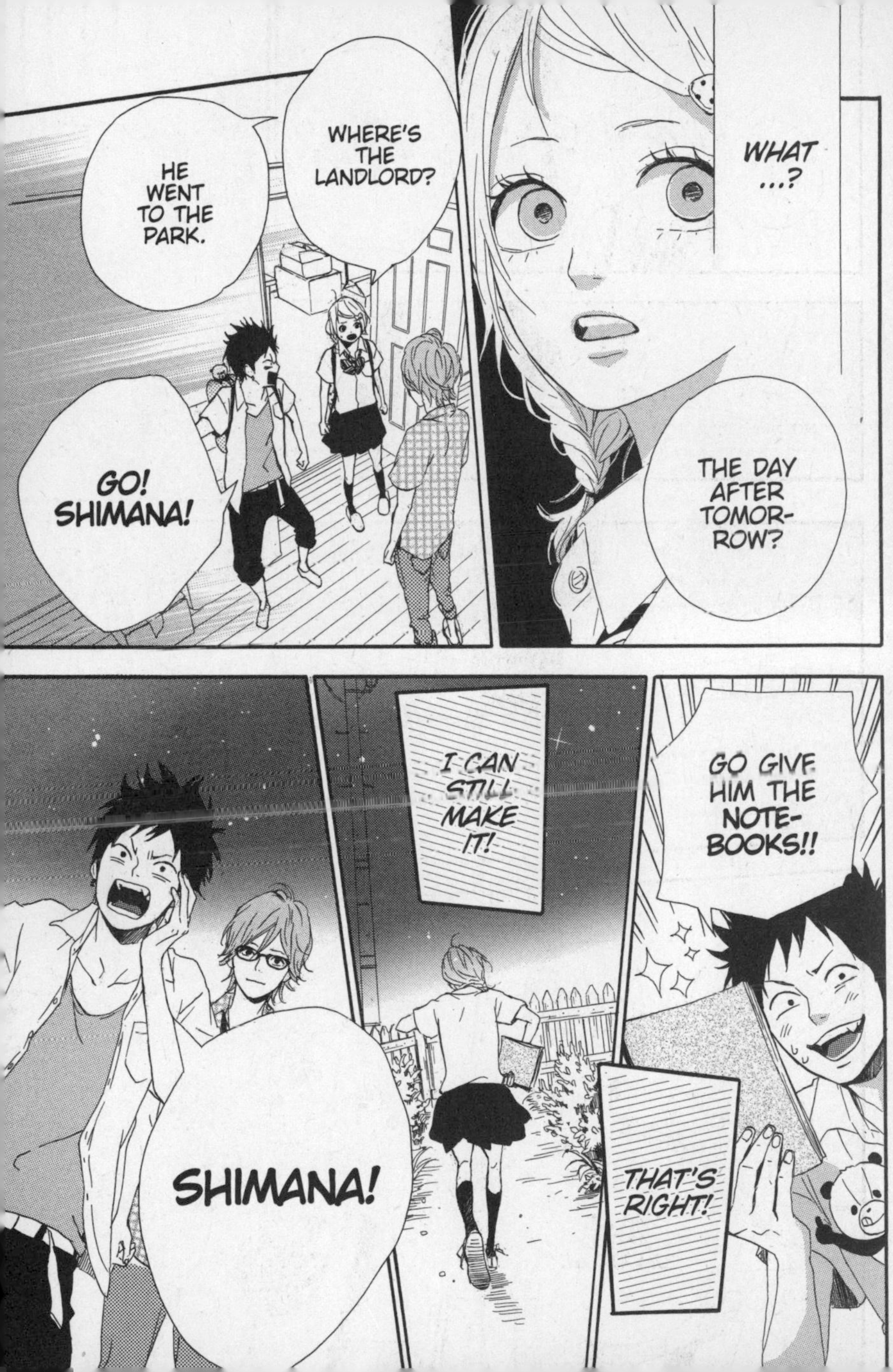
WHAT ...?
THE DAY AFTER TOMOR-ROW?
WHERE'S THE LANDLORD?
HE WENT TO THE PARK.
GO! SHIMANA!
GO GIVE HIM THE NOTE-BOOKS!!
THAT'S RIGHT!
I CAN STILL MAKE IT!
SHIMANA!

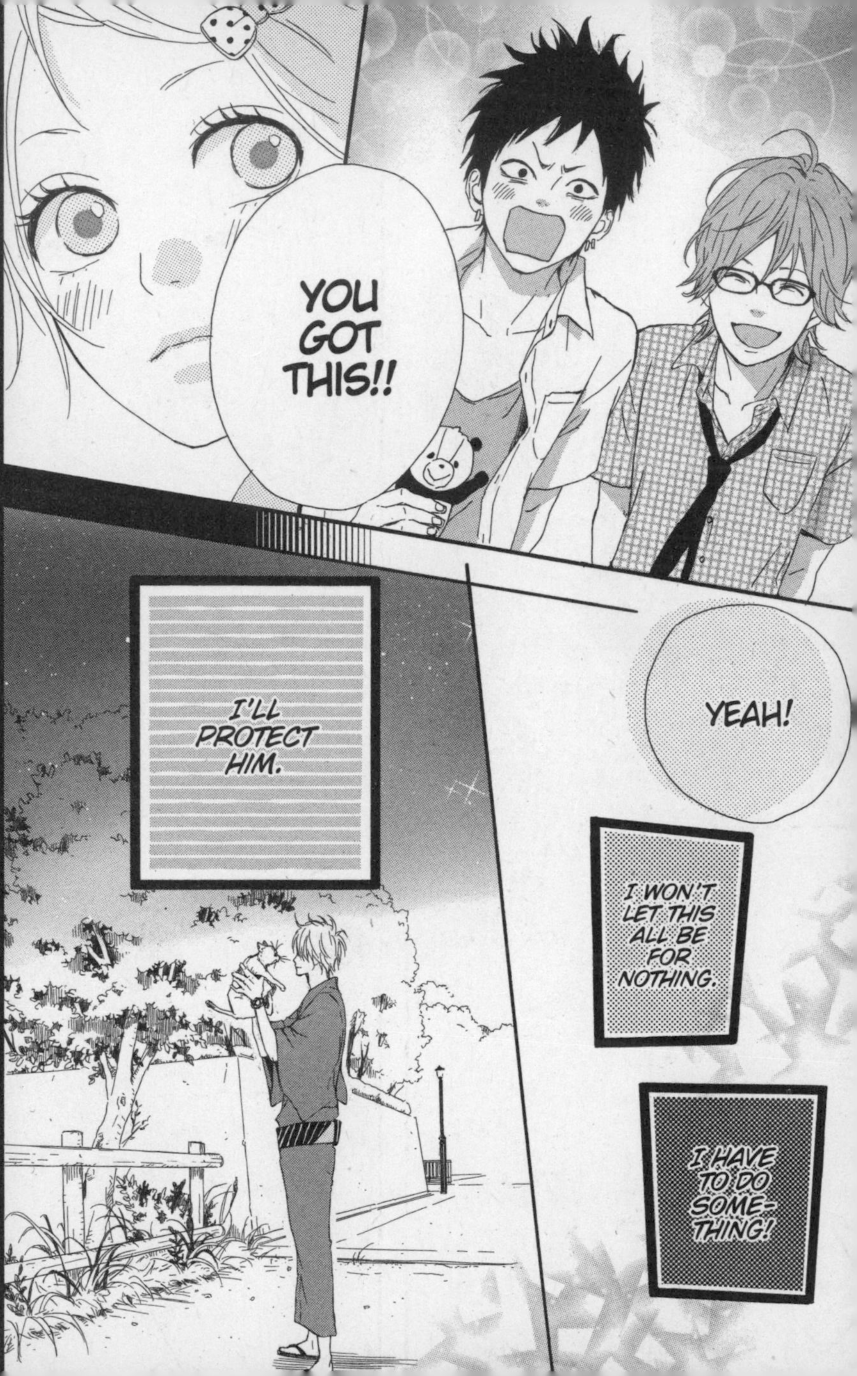
YOU GOT THIS!!
YEAH!
I WON'T LET THIS ALL BE FOR NOTHING.
I HAVE TO DO SOME-THING!
I'LL PROTECT HIM.

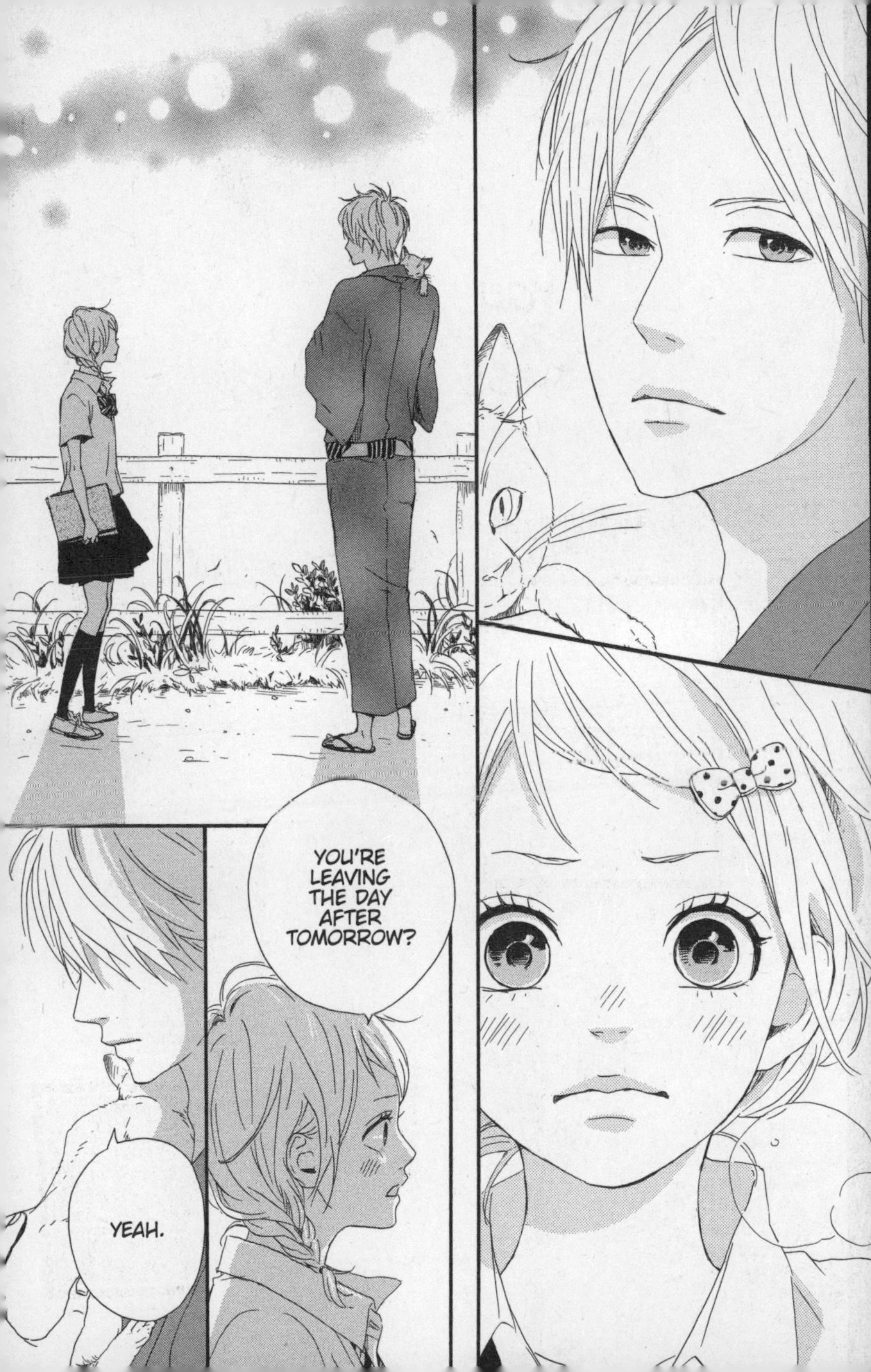
YOU'RE LEAVING THE DAY AFTER TOMORROW?
YEAH.

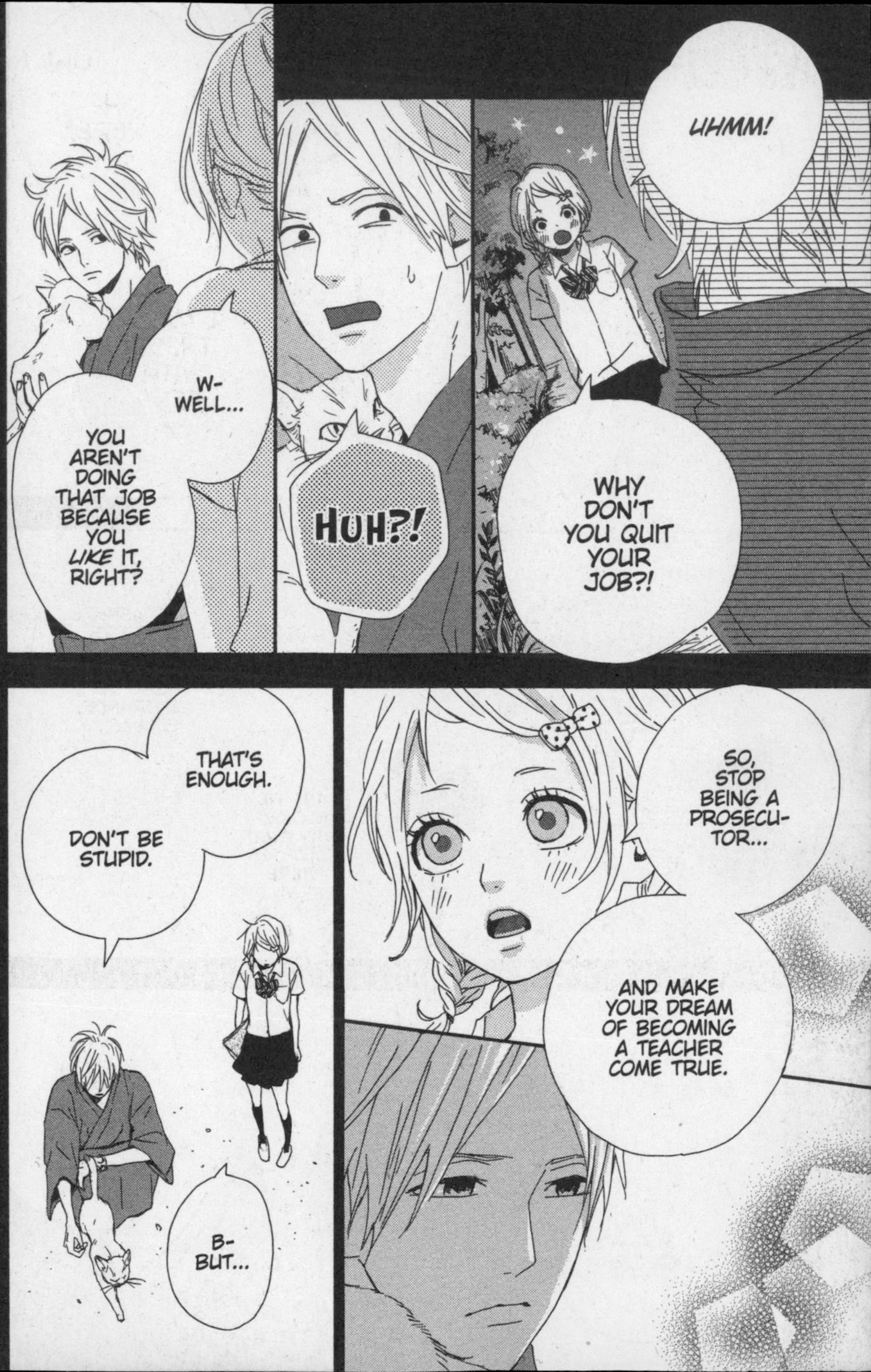
UHMM!
WHY DON'T YOU QUIT YOUR JOB?!
HUH?!
W-WELL...
YOU AREN'T DOING THAT JOB BECAUSE YOU *LIKE* IT, RIGHT?
SO, STOP BEING A PROSECU-TOR...
AND MAKE YOUR DREAM OF BECOMING A TEACHER COME TRUE.
THAT'S ENOUGH.
DON'T BE STUPID.
B-BUT...

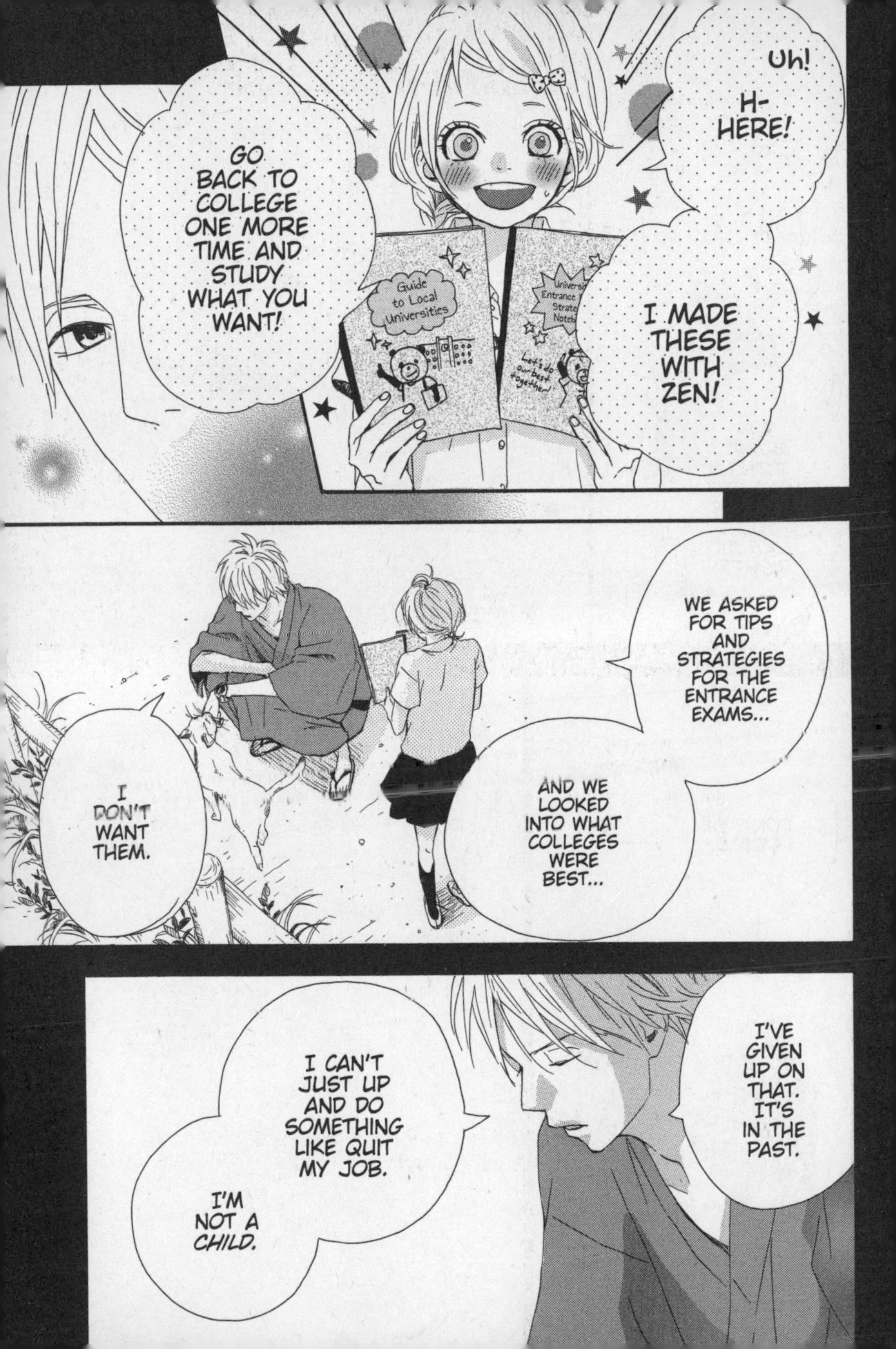
Uh! H-HERE!
I MADE THESE WITH ZEN!
Guide to Local Universities
Let's do our best together!
GO BACK TO COLLEGE ONE MORE TIME AND STUDY WHAT YOU WANT!
WE ASKED FOR TIPS AND STRATEGIES FOR THE ENTRANCE EXAMS...
AND WE LOOKED INTO WHAT COLLEGES WERE BEST...
I DON'T WANT THEM.
I'VE GIVEN UP ON THAT. IT'S IN THE PAST.
I CAN'T JUST UP AND DO SOMETHING LIKE QUIT MY JOB.
I'M NOT A CHILD.

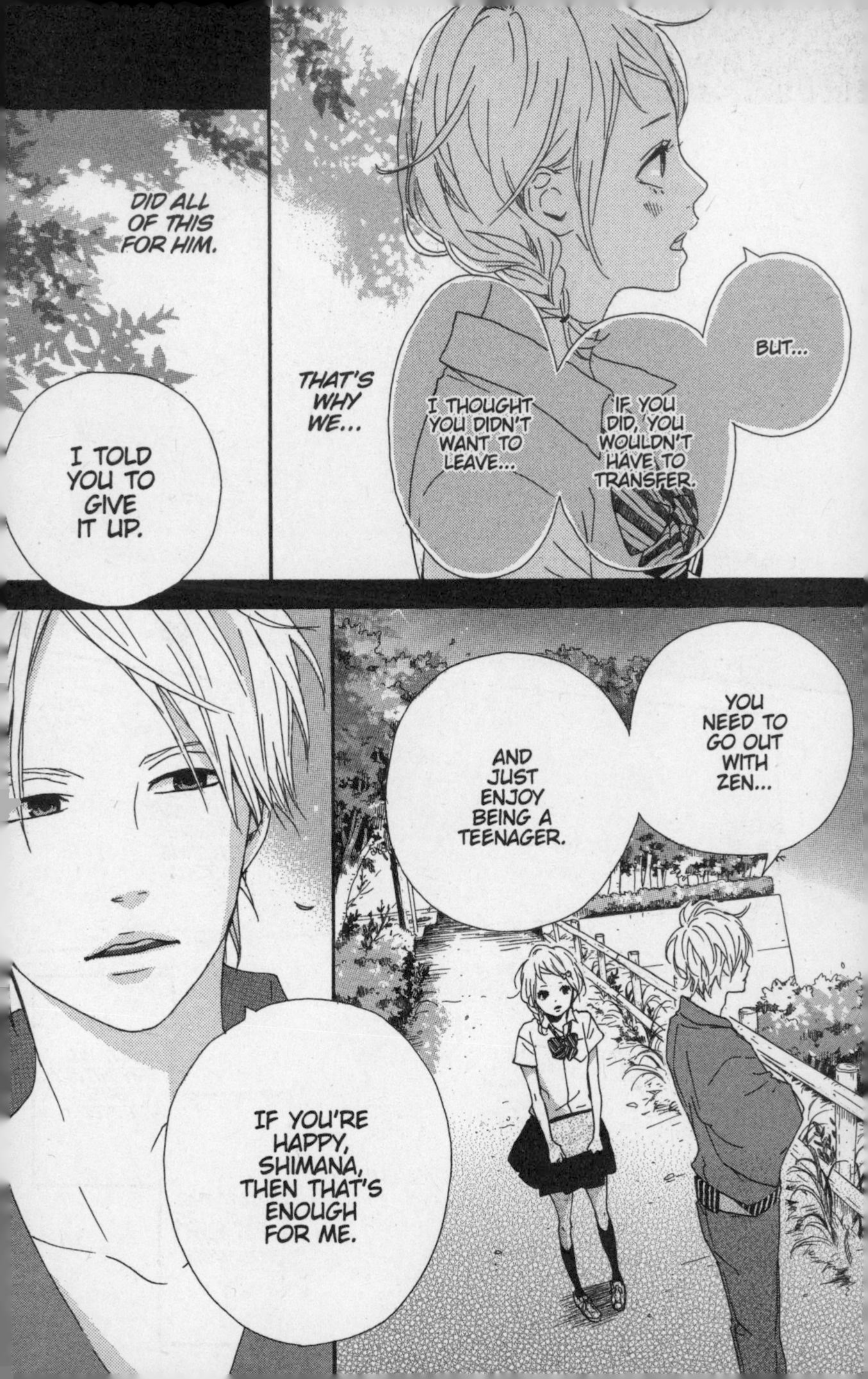
BUT...
IF YOU DID, YOU WOULDN'T HAVE TO TRANSFER.
I THOUGHT YOU DIDN'T WANT TO LEAVE...
THAT'S WHY WE...
DID ALL OF THIS FOR HIM.
I TOLD YOU TO GIVE IT UP.
YOU NEED TO GO OUT WITH ZEN...
AND JUST ENJOY BEING A TEENAGER.
IF YOU'RE HAPPY, SHIMANA, THEN THAT'S ENOUGH FOR ME.

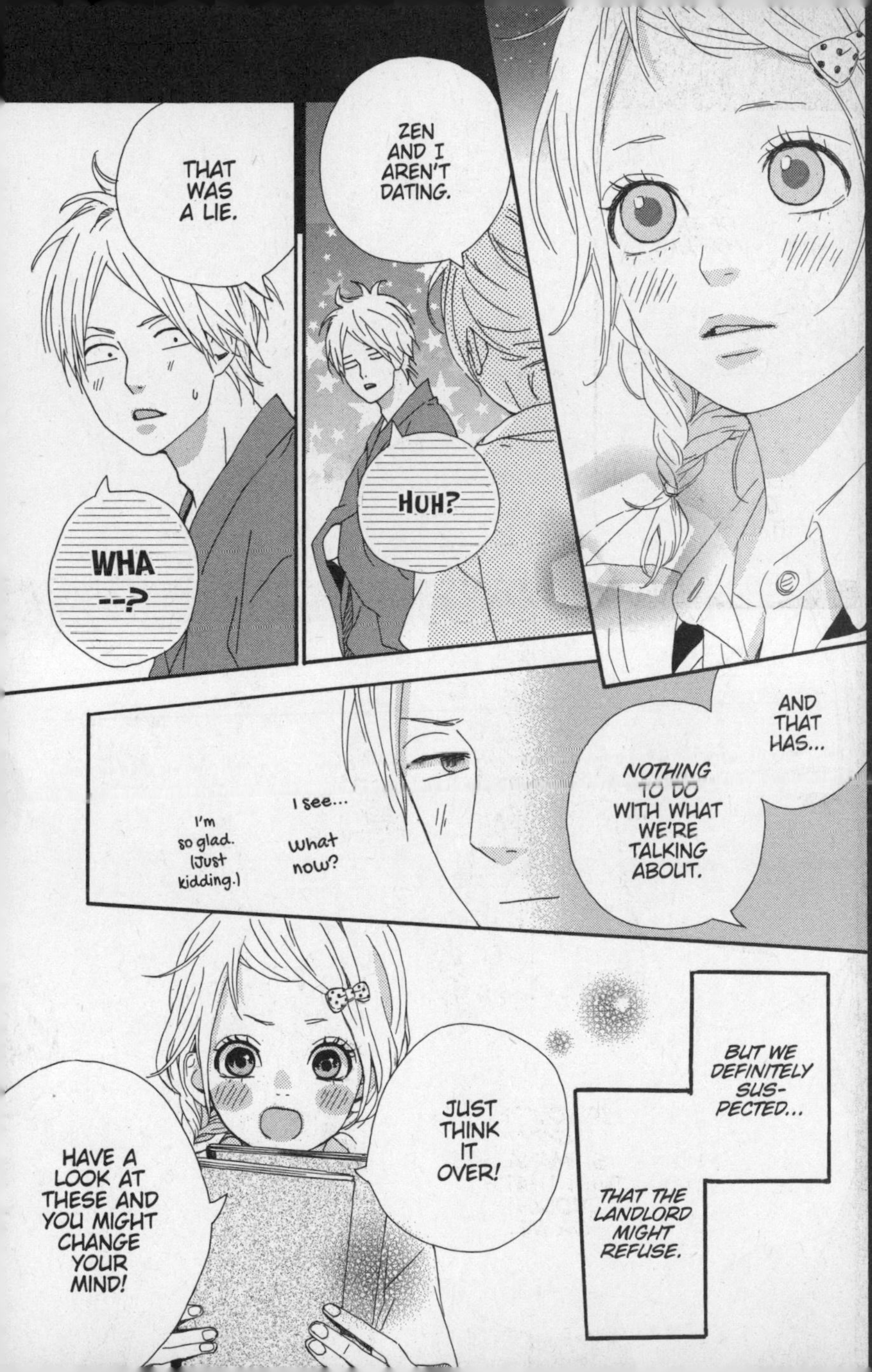
ZEN AND I AREN'T DATING.
HUH?
THAT WAS A LIE.
WHA--?
AND THAT HAS...
NOTHING TO DO WITH WHAT WE'RE TALKING ABOUT.
I see...
What now?
I'm so glad. (Just kidding.)
BUT WE DEFINITELY SUS-PECTED...
THAT THE LANDLORD MIGHT REFUSE.
JUST THINK IT OVER!
HAVE A LOOK AT THESE AND YOU MIGHT CHANGE YOUR MIND!

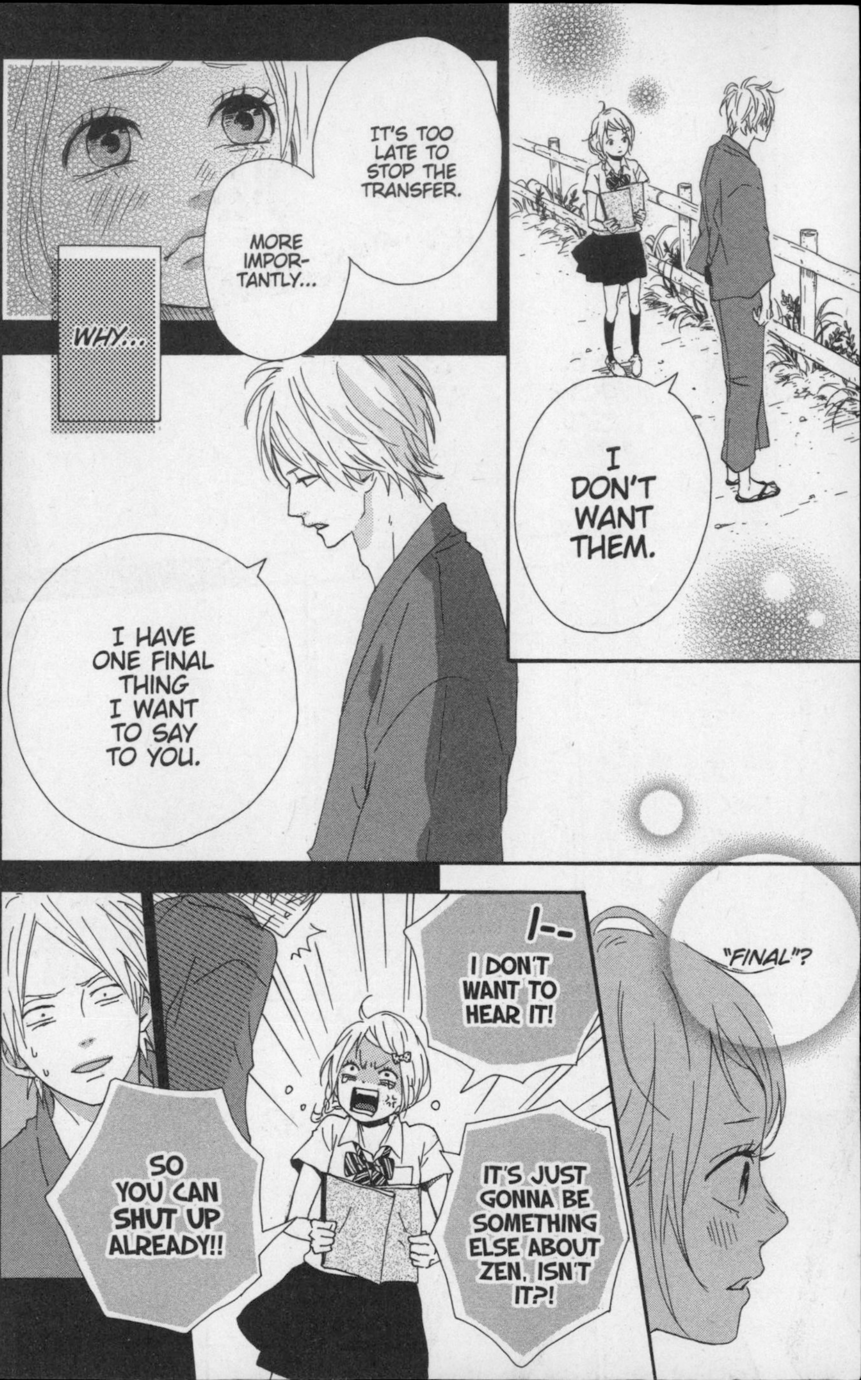
I DON'T WANT THEM.
IT'S TOO LATE TO STOP THE TRANSFER.
MORE IMPORTANTLY...
WHY...
I HAVE ONE FINAL THING I WANT TO SAY TO YOU.
"FINAL"?
I-- I DON'T WANT TO HEAR IT!
IT'S JUST GONNA BE SOMETHING ELSE ABOUT ZEN, ISN'T IT?!
SO YOU CAN SHUT UP ALREADY!!

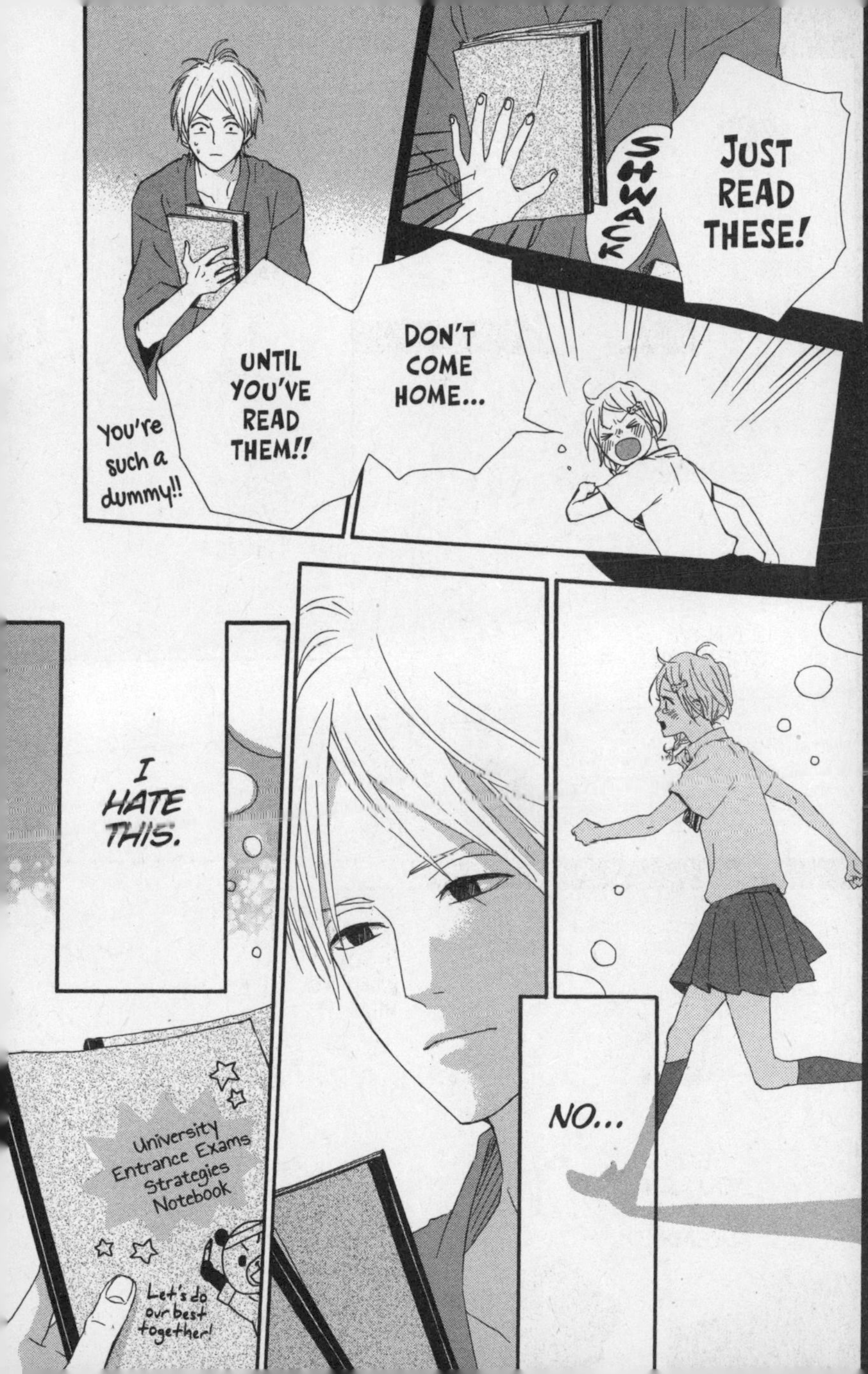
SHWACK
JUST READ THESE!
DON'T COME HOME...
UNTIL YOU'VE READ THEM!!
You're such a dummy!!
NO...
I HATE THIS.
University Entrance Exams Strategies Notebook
Let's do our best together!

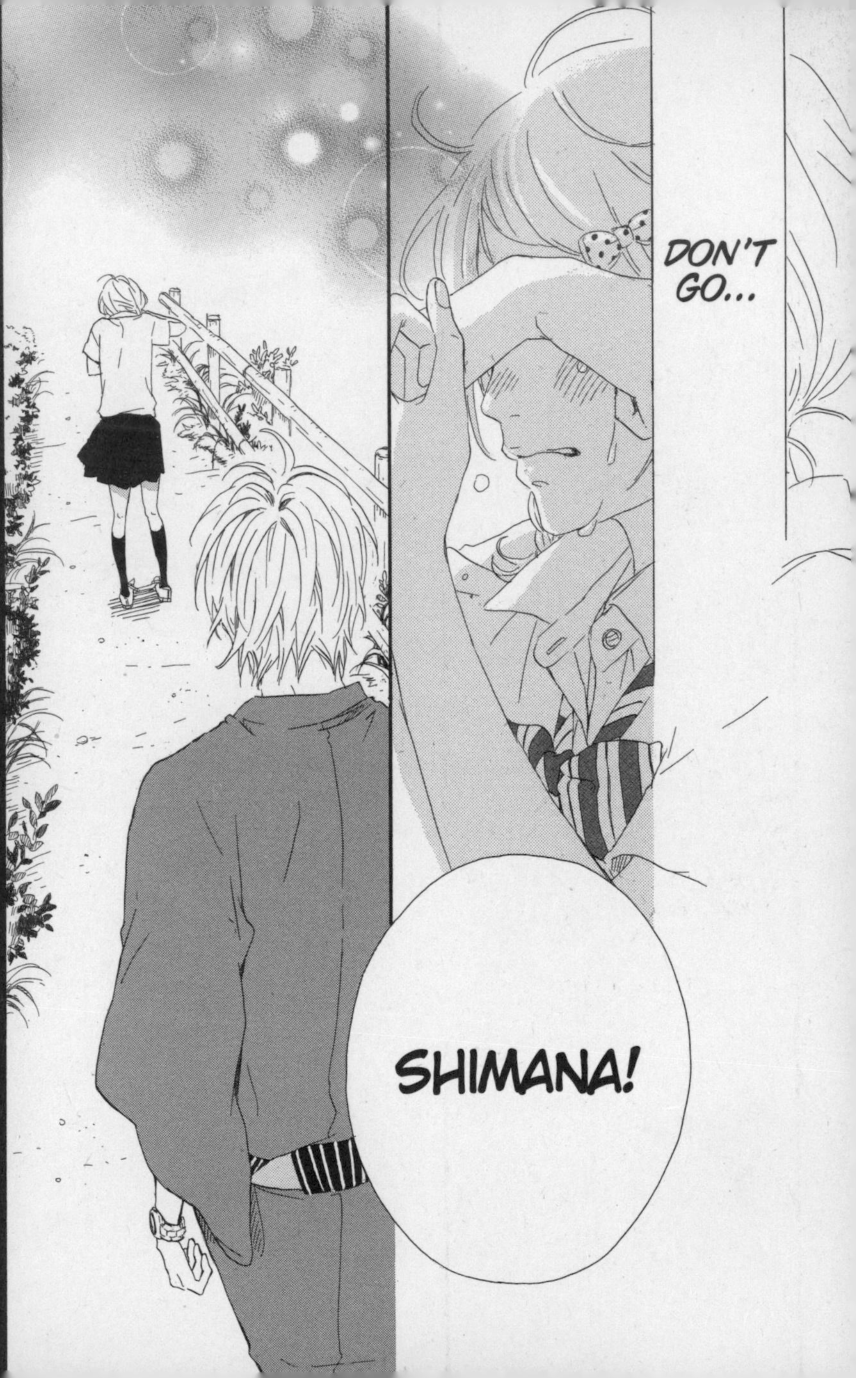
DON'T GO...
SHIMANA!

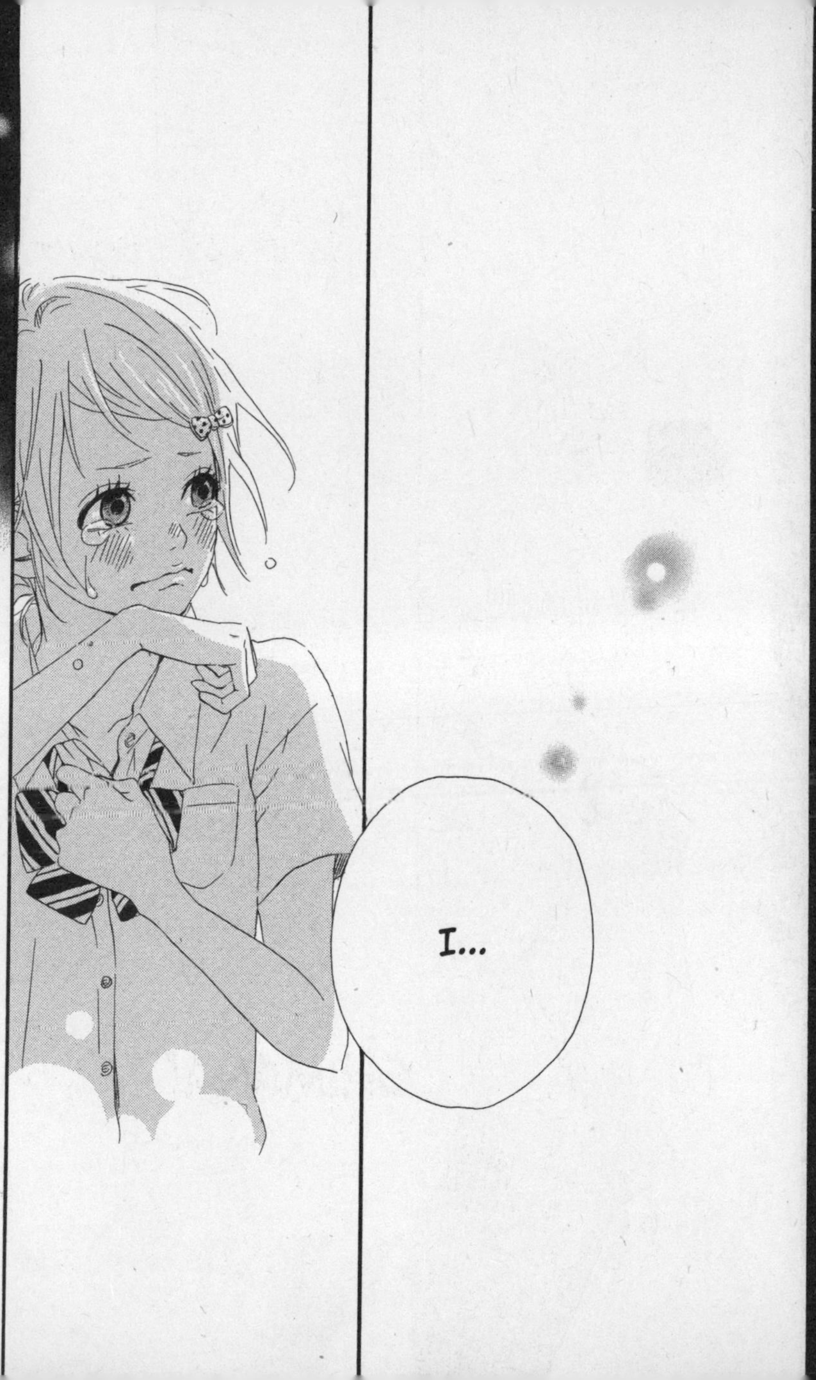
I...

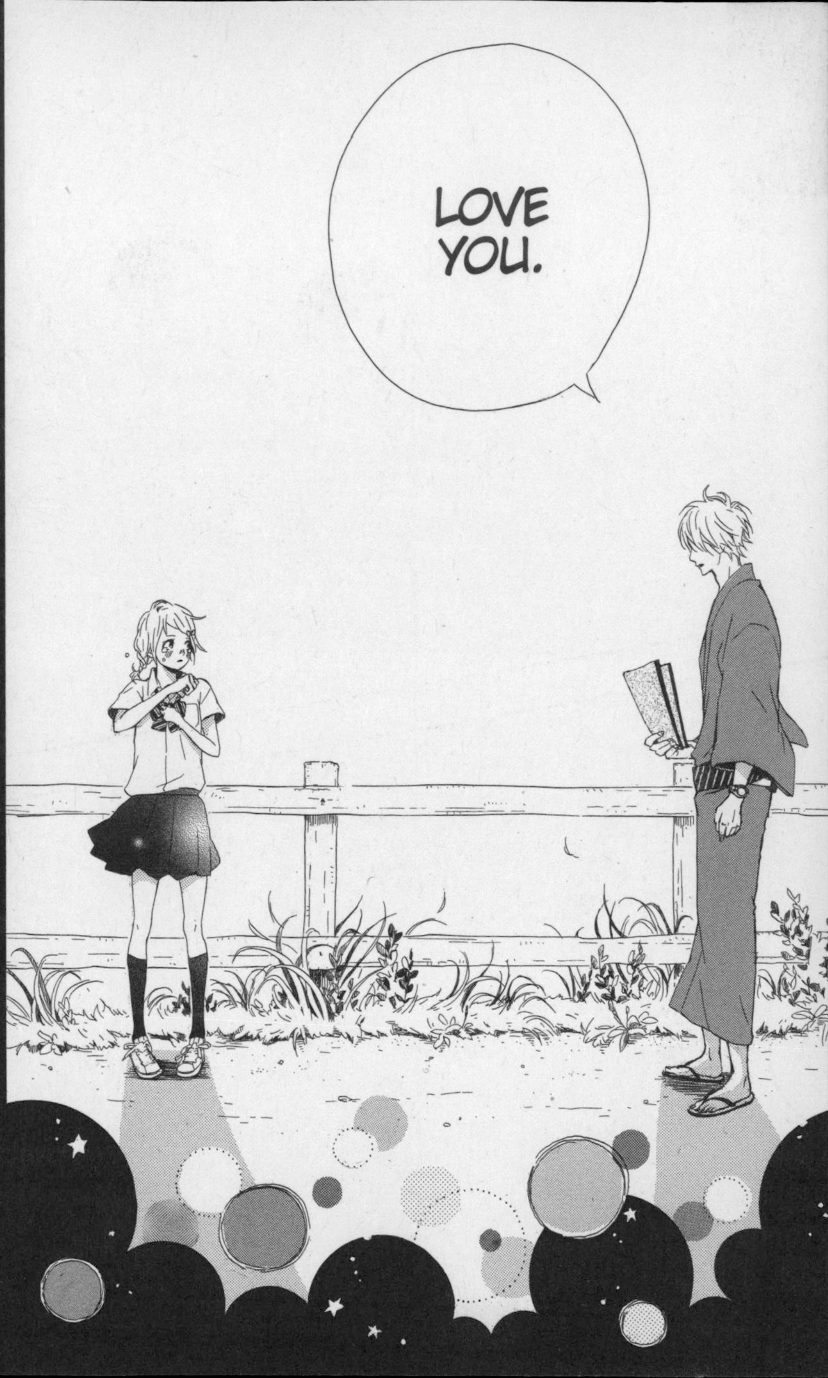
LOVE YOU.

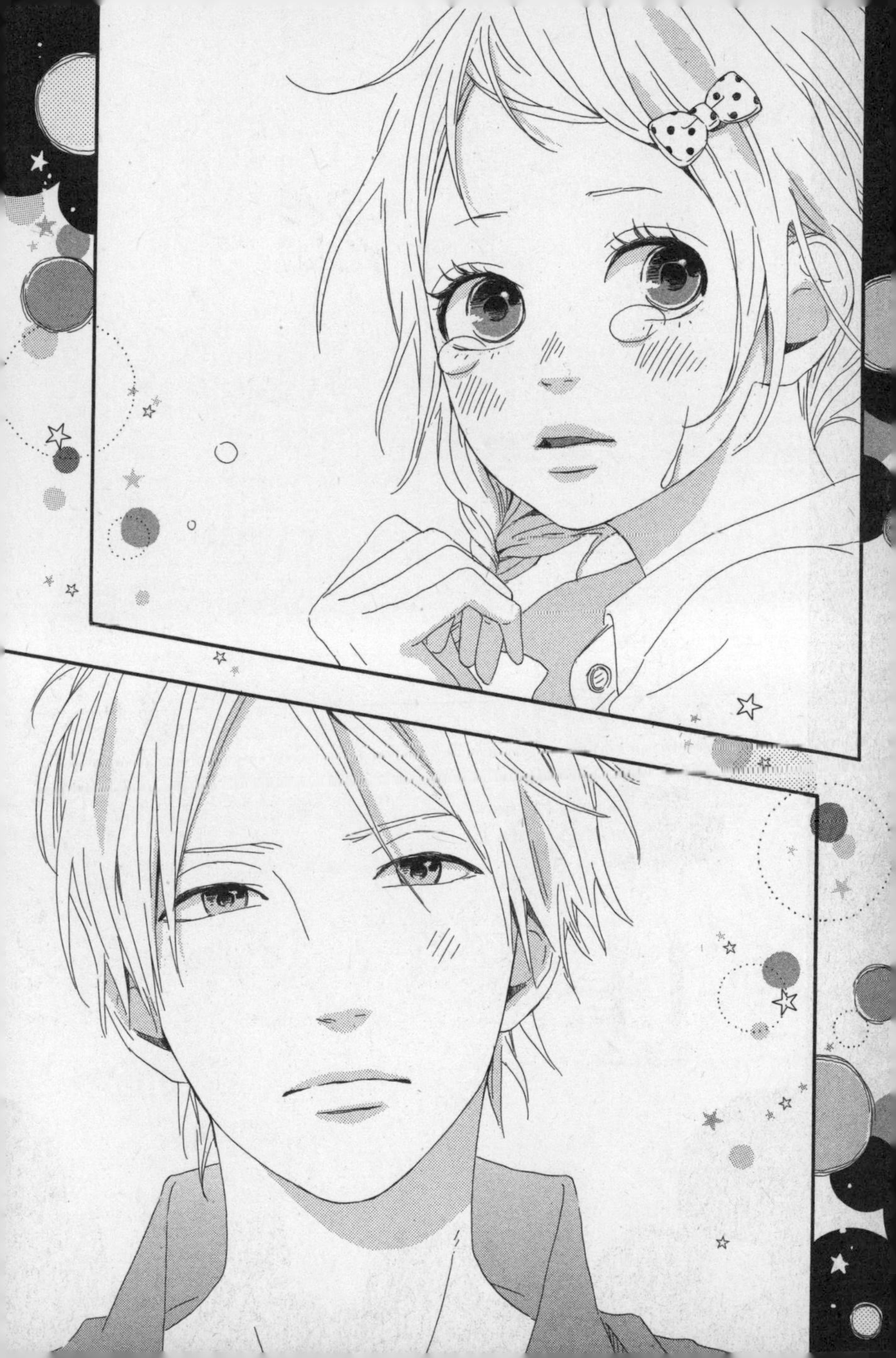

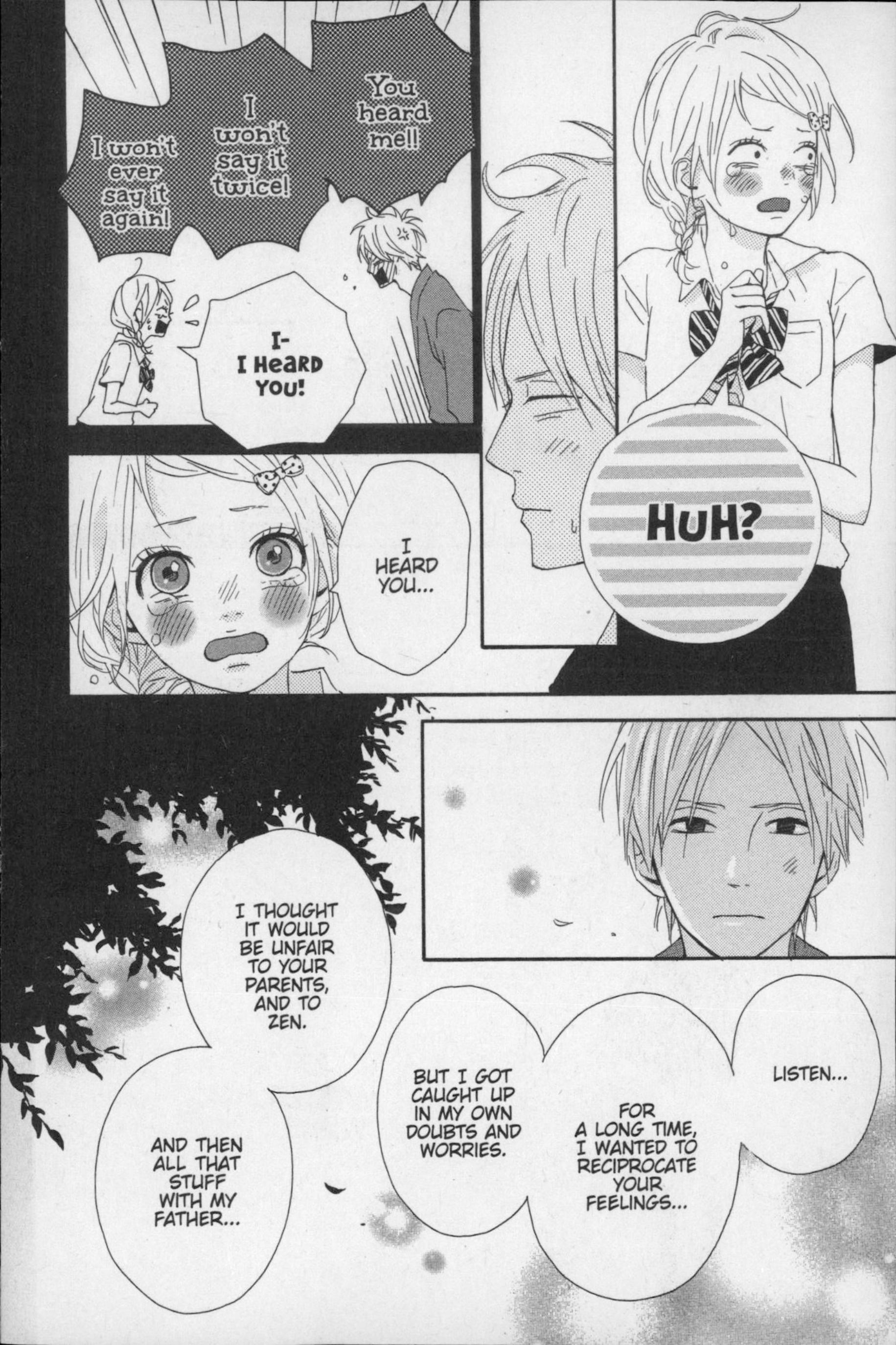
HUH?
You heard me!!
I won't say it twice!
I won't ever say it again!
I- I heard you!
I heard you...
Listen...
For a long time, I wanted to reciprocate your feelings...
But I got caught up in my own doubts and worries.
I thought it would be unfair to your parents, and to Zen.
And then all that stuff with my father...

I WAS AFRAID THAT IF YOU WENT OUT WITH ME, YOU'D EXPERIENCE EVEN *MORE* SADNESS AND HEART-ACHE...
LIKE SENSEI DID.
......
BUT THAT...
DOESN'T MATTER ANYMORE.
I'LL MAKE YOU HAPPY, SHIMANA.
NO MATTER WHAT.

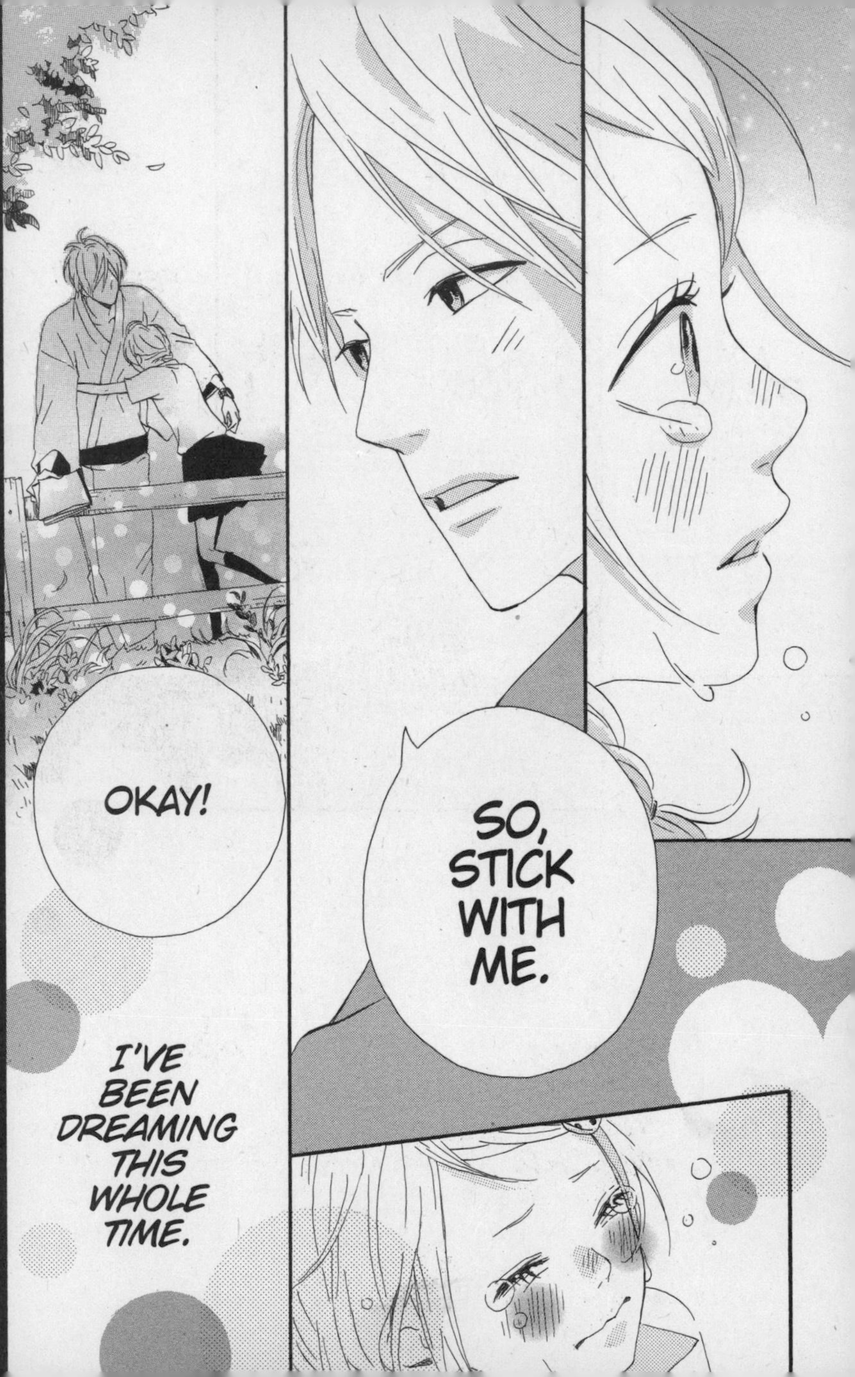
SO, STICK WITH ME.
OKAY!
I'VE BEEN DREAMING THIS WHOLE TIME.

TODAY...
FEELS LIKE A DREAM.
I LOVE YOU!
......
MY DREAM CAME TRUE.
I KNOW.
DREAMS DO COME TRUE, LANDLORD.

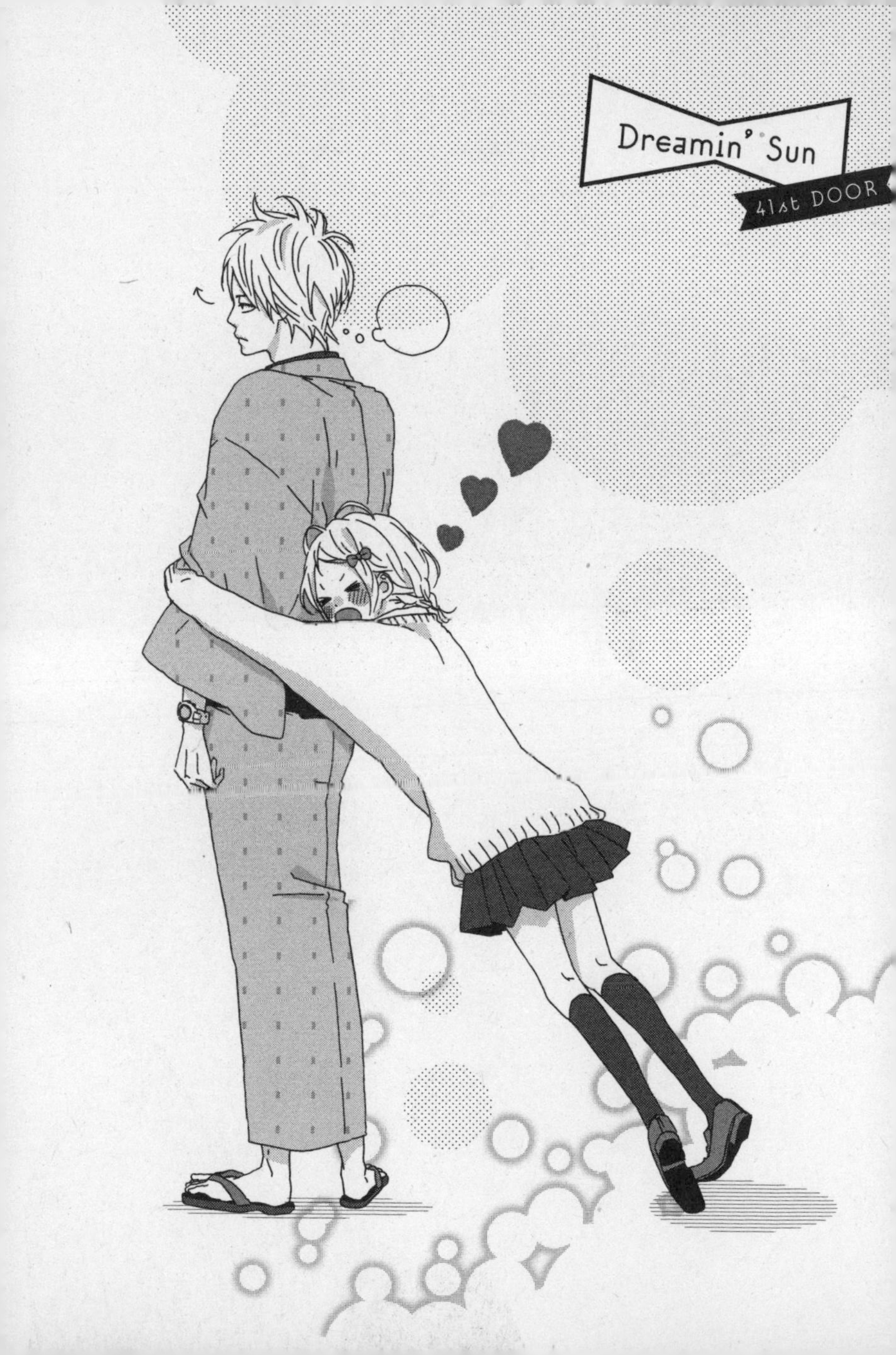
Dreamin' Sun
41st DOOR

Sniffle...

UWAH... UWAH...

ZEN...

Waaagh!

I'M SORRY...

FIGURES.

CONGRATS!

MAN, I'M GLAD WE DIDN'T KISS.

We saw the whole thing.

My heart was pounding! I was so happy when Taiga-san said he loved you!

I was right there with you, Shimana!

I'm so happy for you *Shima-naaa~!!*

I'm so *glaaaad~!!!*

UH, WHY?

SHIMA-NAAAA~!

ZENN-NNN~!

H-HEY!! DON'T GRAB HER LIKE THAT!

AND NOW, IT'S FINALLY HAPPENED.

YOU'VE LOVED HIM FOR SO LONG...

AH, THAT'S RIGHT! THE LANDLORD WAS SO FUNNY HERE.

KNOCK IT OFF!

GYAH HA HA HA!

The landlord's birthday. After Shimana rejected him

WOW! THANKS SO MUCH! ♡

I'VE COLLECTED ALL THE PICTURES OF THE TWO OF YOU.

Camp

The landlord, gazing at Shimana

WHAT THE HELL?! IT'S EMBARRASS-ING!!

when'd you take these?!

At school.

SHIMANA.

I'VE PREPARED THIS JUST FOR THIS OCCASION.

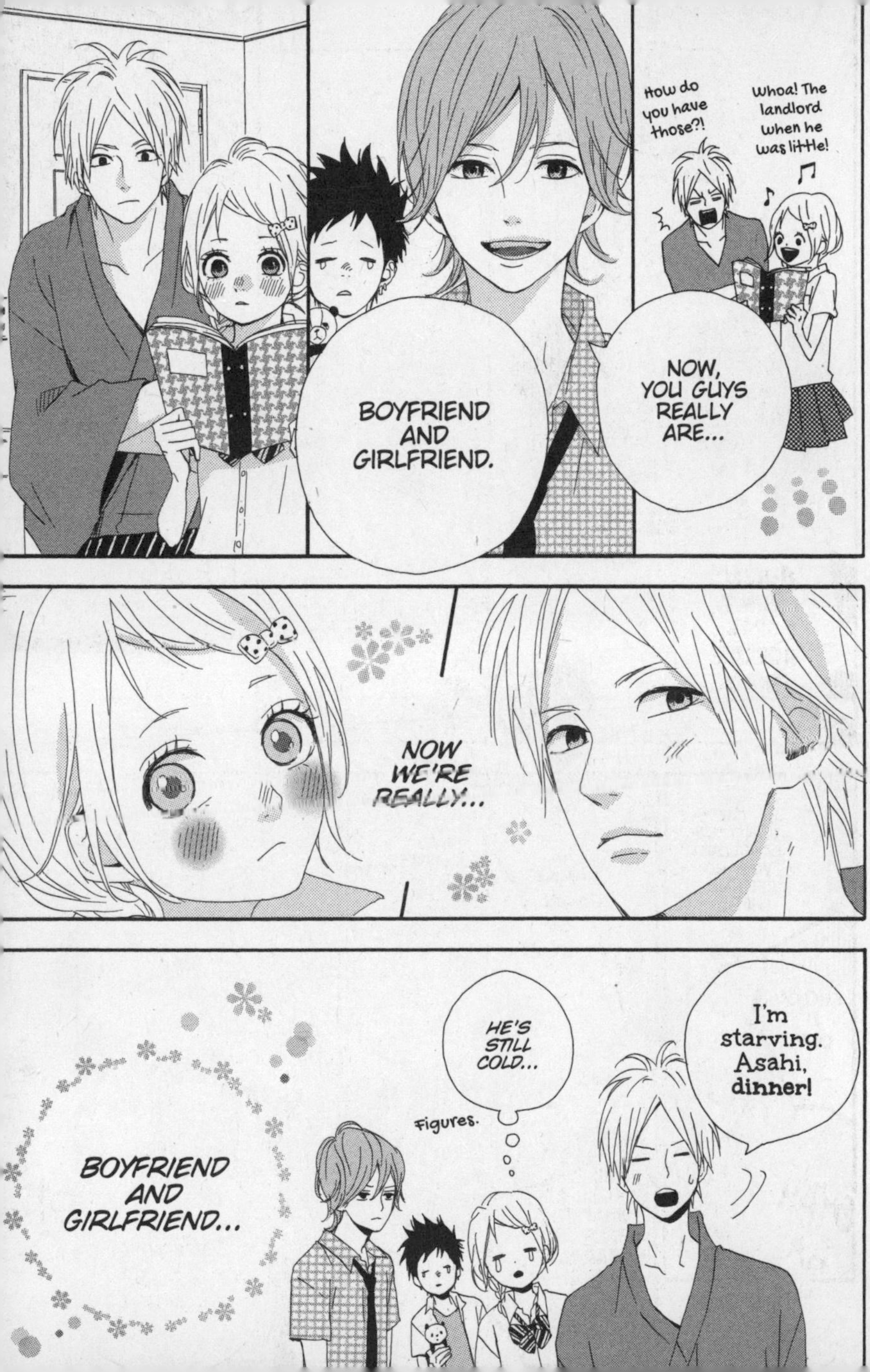
Whoa! The landlord when he was little!
How do you have those?!
NOW, YOU GUYS REALLY ARE...
BOYFRIEND AND GIRLFRIEND.
NOW WE'RE REALLY...
I'm starving. Asahi, dinner!
HE'S STILL COLD...
Figures.
BOYFRIEND AND GIRLFRIEND...

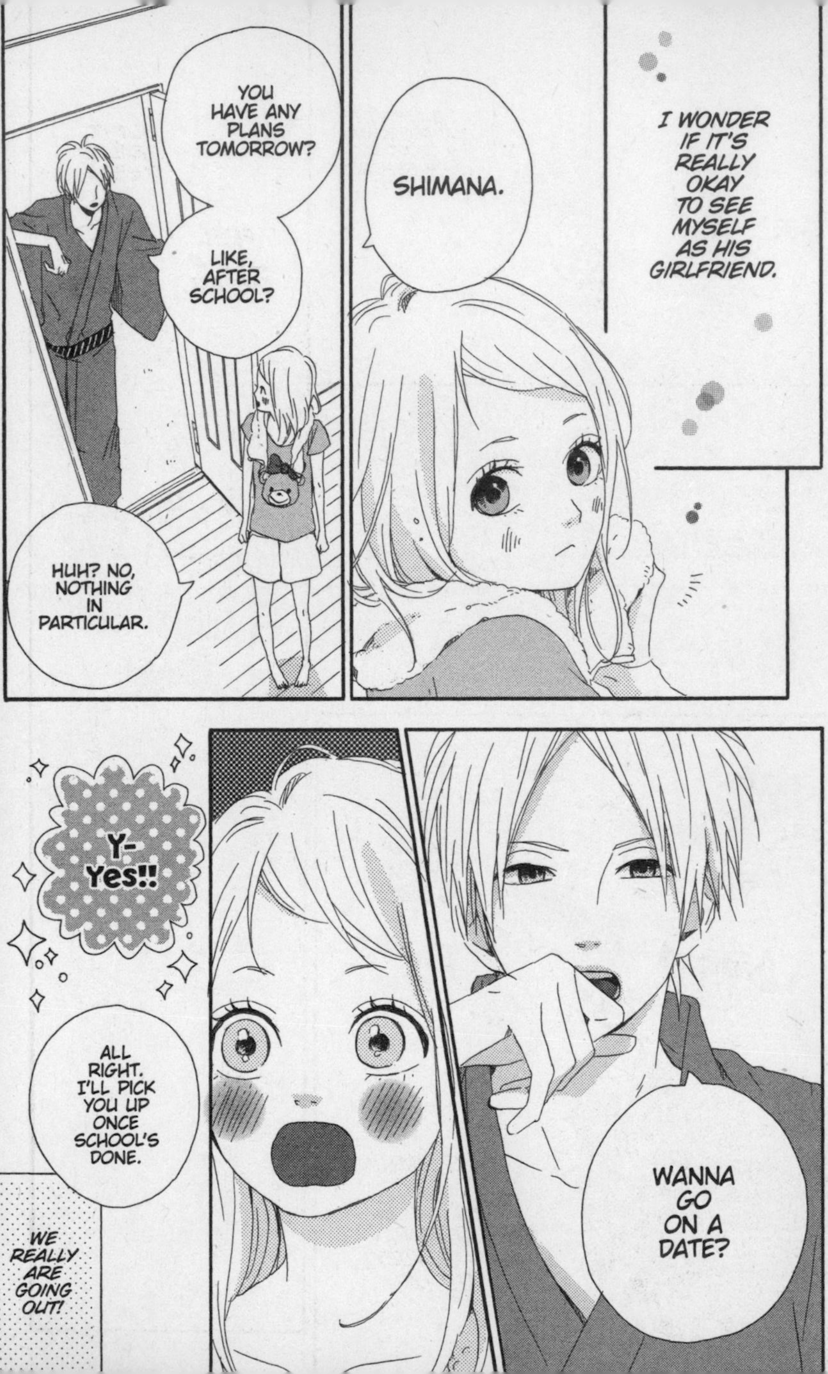
I WONDER IF IT'S REALLY OKAY TO SEE MYSELF AS HIS GIRLFRIEND.
SHIMANA.
YOU HAVE ANY PLANS TOMORROW?
LIKE, AFTER SCHOOL?
HUH? NO, NOTHING IN PARTICULAR.
WANNA GO ON A DATE?
Y-Yes!!
ALL RIGHT. I'LL PICK YOU UP ONCE SCHOOL'S DONE.
WE REALLY ARE GOING OUT!

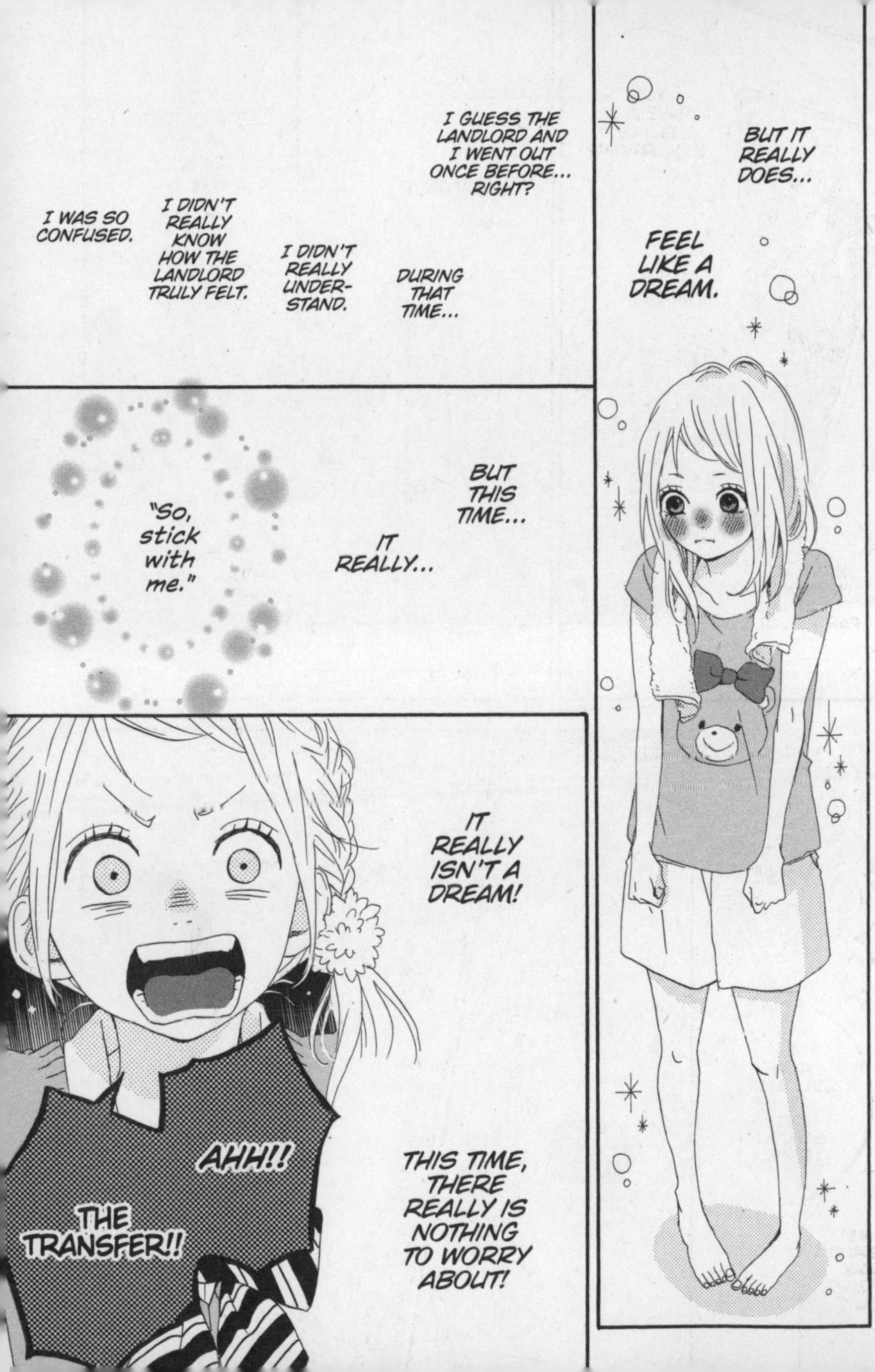
BUT IT REALLY DOES...
FEEL LIKE A DREAM.
I GUESS THE LANDLORD AND I WENT OUT ONCE BEFORE... RIGHT?
DURING THAT TIME...
I DIDN'T REALLY UNDER-STAND.
I DIDN'T REALLY KNOW HOW THE LANDLORD TRULY FELT.
I WAS SO CONFUSED.
BUT THIS TIME...
IT REALLY...
"So, stick with me."
IT REALLY ISN'T A DREAM!
THIS TIME, THERE REALLY IS NOTHING TO WORRY ABOUT!
AHH!!
THE TRANSFER!!

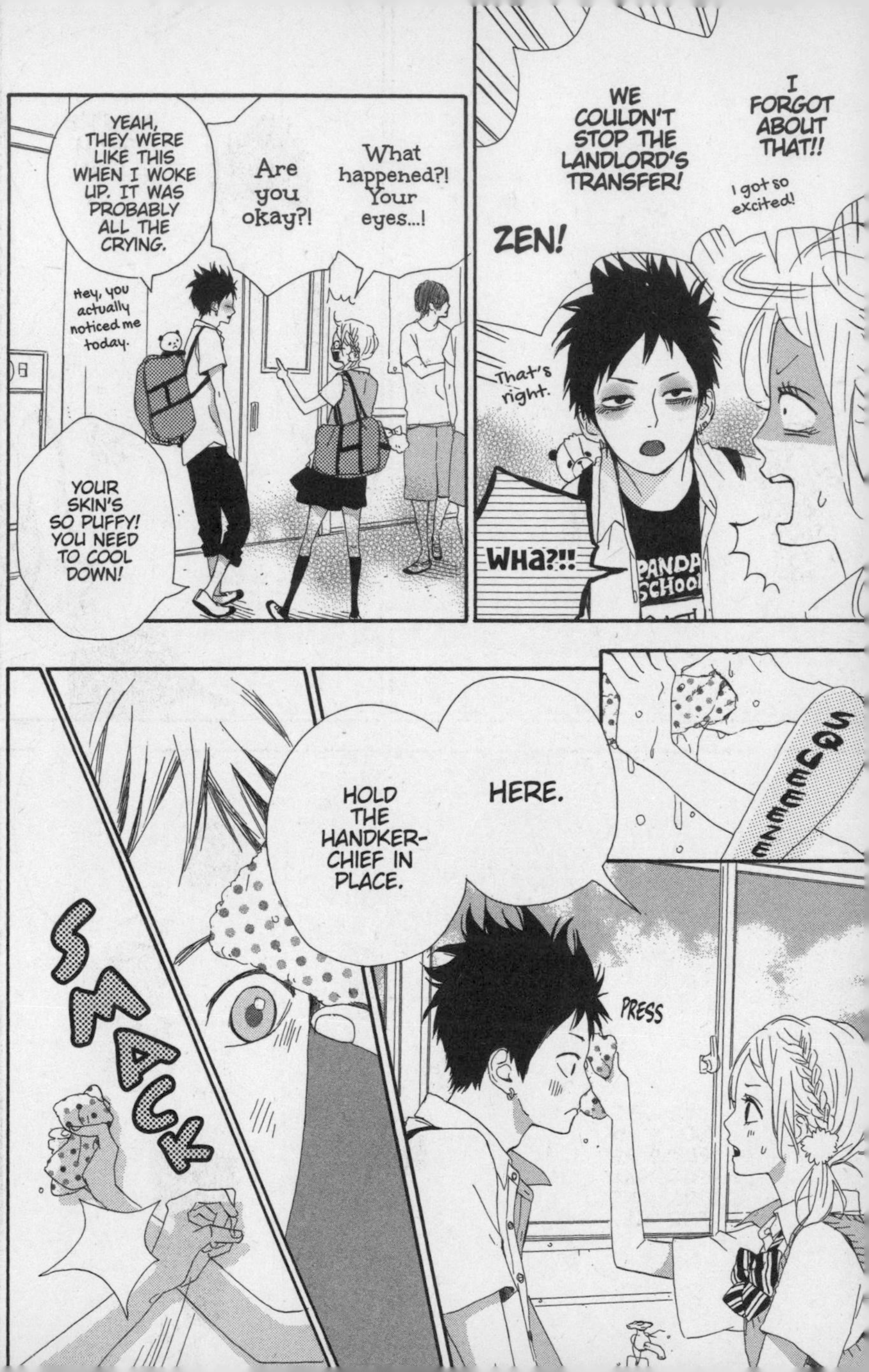
I FORGOT ABOUT THAT!!
I got so excited!
WE COULDN'T STOP THE LANDLORD'S TRANSFER!
ZEN!
That's right.
WHA?!!
What happened?! Your eyes...!
Are you okay?!
YEAH, THEY WERE LIKE THIS WHEN I WOKE UP. IT WAS PROBABLY ALL THE CRYING.
Hey, you actually noticed me today.
YOUR SKIN'S SO PUFFY! YOU NEED TO COOL DOWN!
SQUEEEEZE
HERE.
HOLD THE HANDKER-CHIEF IN PLACE.
PRESS
SMACK

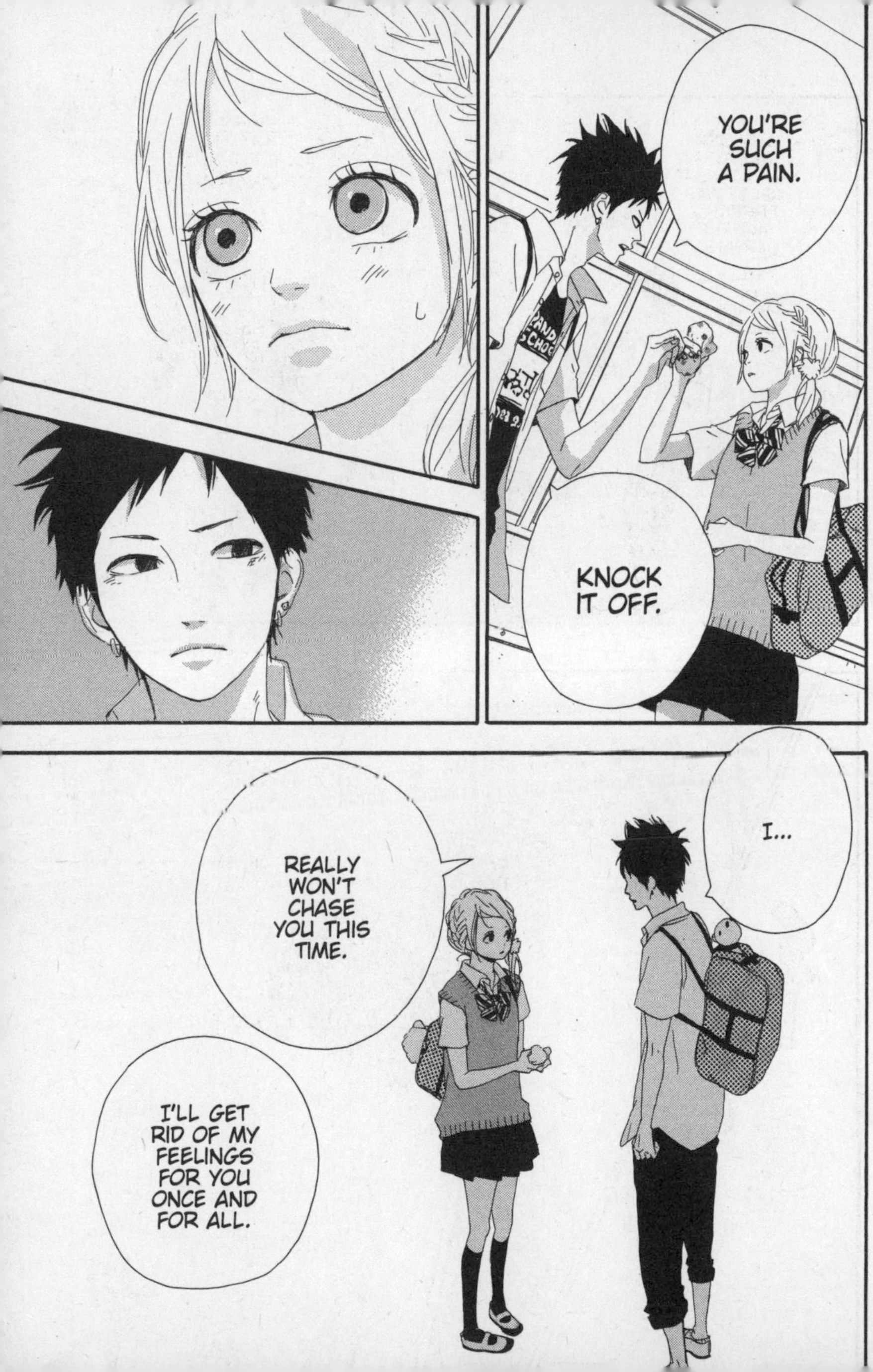
YOU'RE SUCH A PAIN.
KNOCK IT OFF.
I...
REALLY WON'T CHASE YOU THIS TIME.
I'LL GET RID OF MY FEELINGS FOR YOU ONCE AND FOR ALL.

BORROW YOUR HAND-KERCHIEF.

BUT I WILL...

Huh?

YEAH.

You're still annoying!!

I'M *HAPPY* ABOUT IT OR ANY-THING!

B-BUT IT'S NOT LIKE...

SORRY...

GOOD MORNING.

Ah!

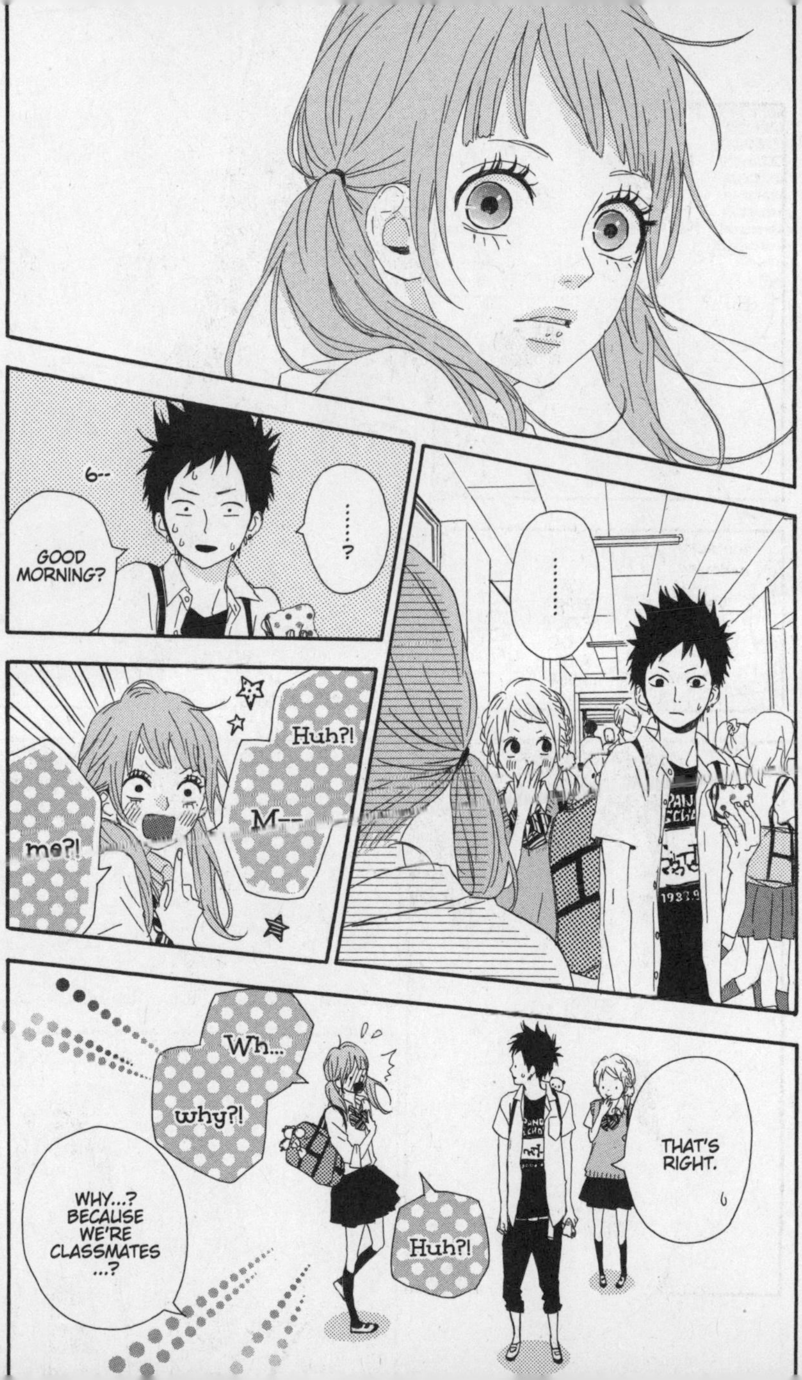
......
......?
G--
GOOD MORNING?
Huh?!
M--
me?!
THAT'S RIGHT.
Huh?!
Wh...
why?!
WHY...? BECAUSE WE'RE CLASSMATES ...?

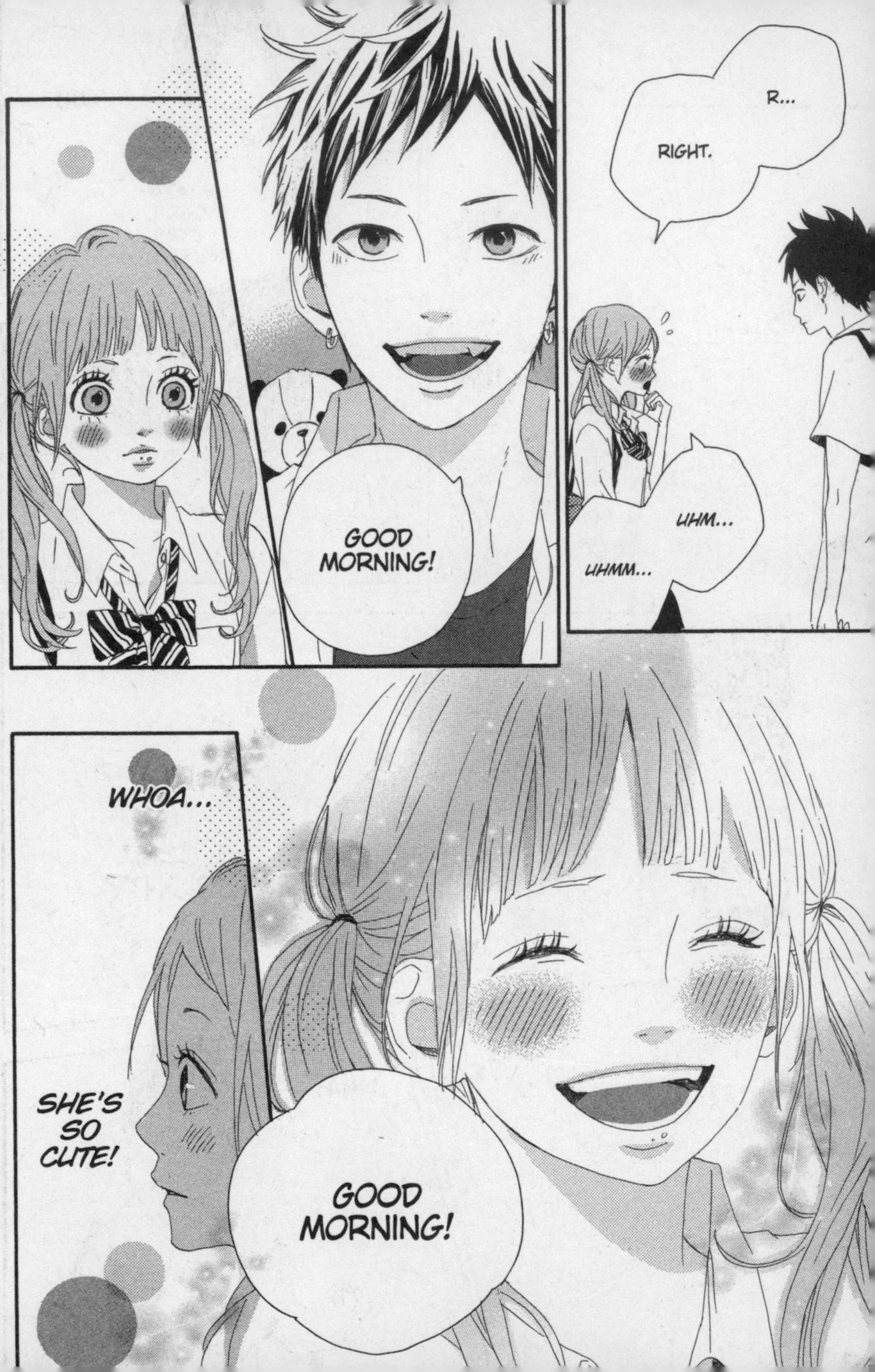
R... RIGHT.
UHM... UHMM...
GOOD MORNING!
WHOA...
SHE'S SO CUTE!
GOOD MORNING!

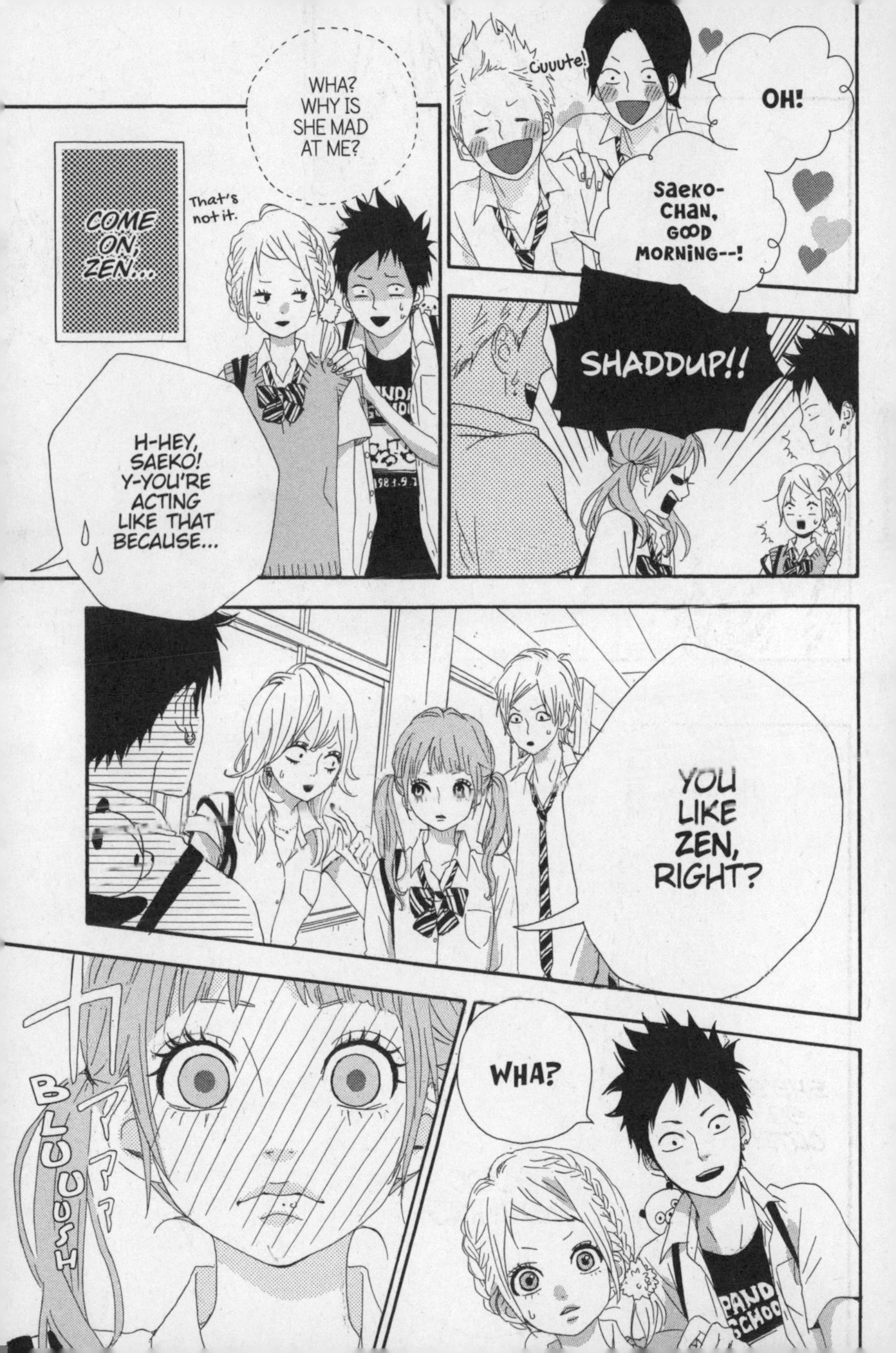
OH!
Saeko-chan, good morning--!
Cuuute!
SHADDUP!!
WHA? WHY IS SHE MAD AT ME?
That's not it.
COME ON, ZEN...
H-HEY, SAEKO! Y-YOU'RE ACTING LIKE THAT BECAUSE...
YOU LIKE ZEN, RIGHT?
WHA?
BLUUSH

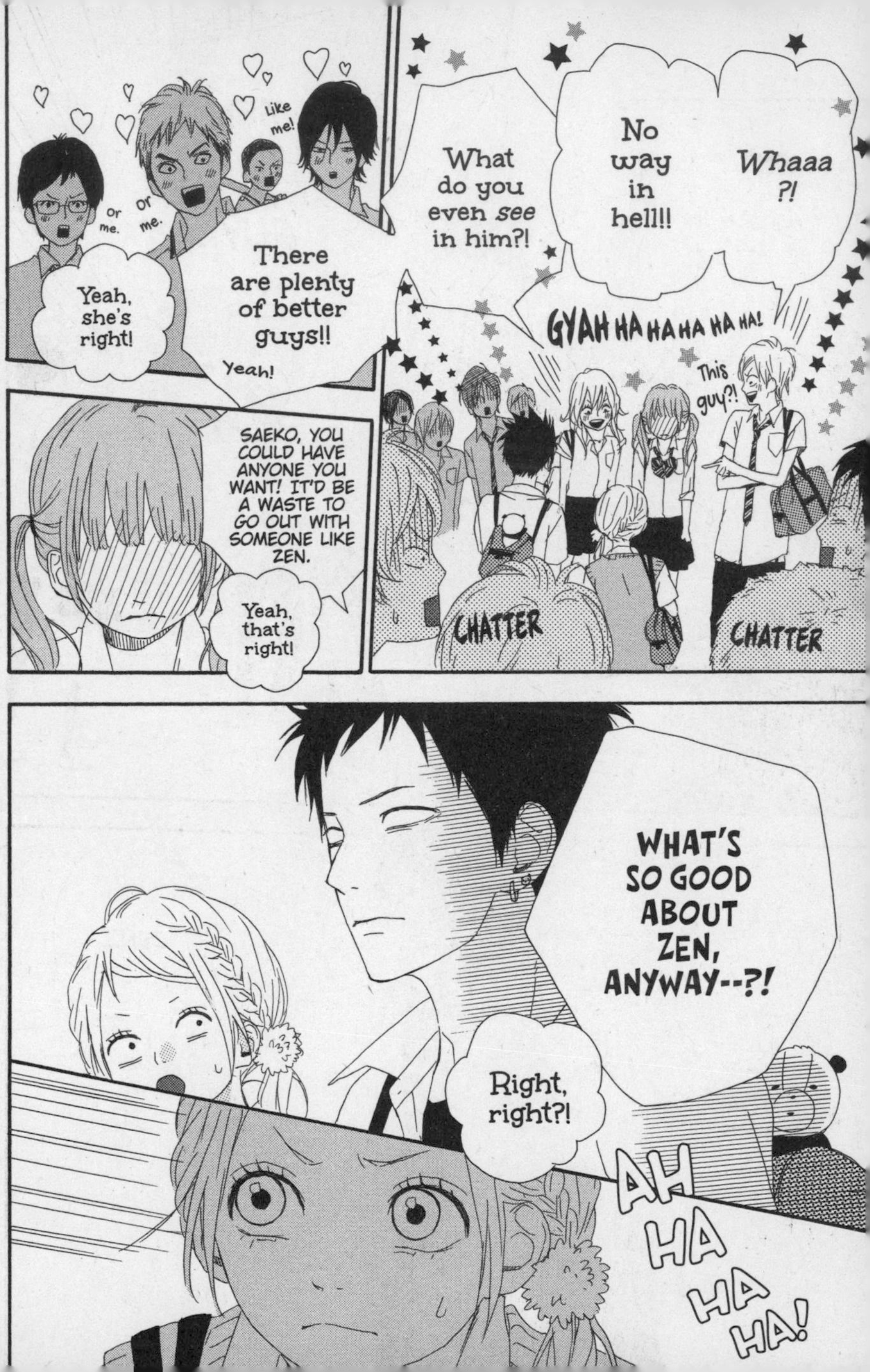
Whaaa?!
No way in hell!!
What do you even see in him?!
GYAH HA HA HA HA HA!
This guy?!
CHATTER
CHATTER
Like me!
Or me.
Or me.
There are plenty of better guys!!
Yeah, she's right!
Yeah!
SAEKO, YOU COULD HAVE ANYONE YOU WANT! IT'D BE A WASTE TO GO OUT WITH SOMEONE LIKE ZEN.
Yeah, that's right!
WHAT'S SO GOOD ABOUT ZEN, ANYWAY--?!
Right, right?!
AH HA HA HA!

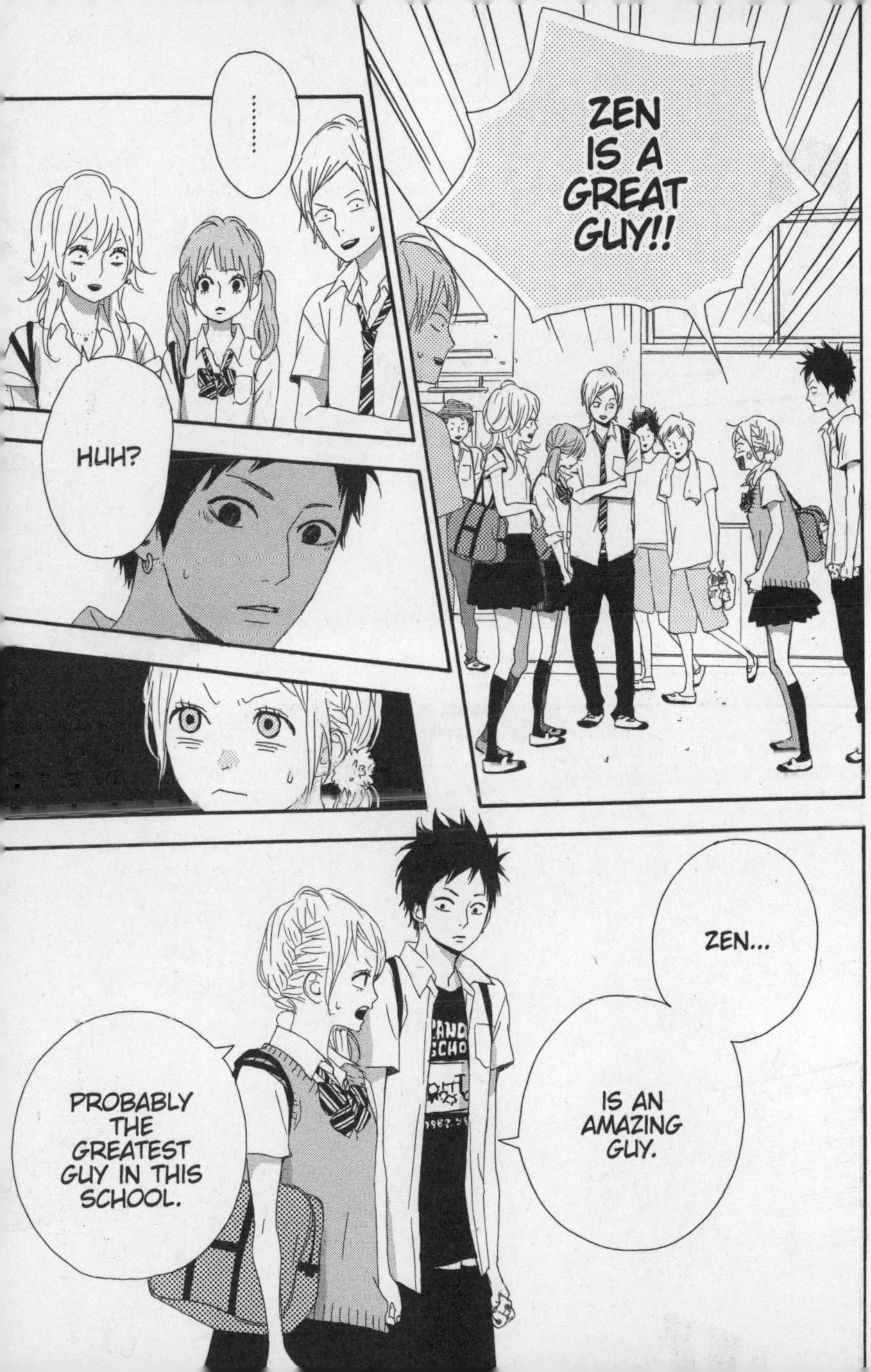
ZEN IS A GREAT GUY!!
......
HUH?
ZEN...
IS AN AMAZING GUY.
PROBABLY THE GREATEST GUY IN THIS SCHOOL.

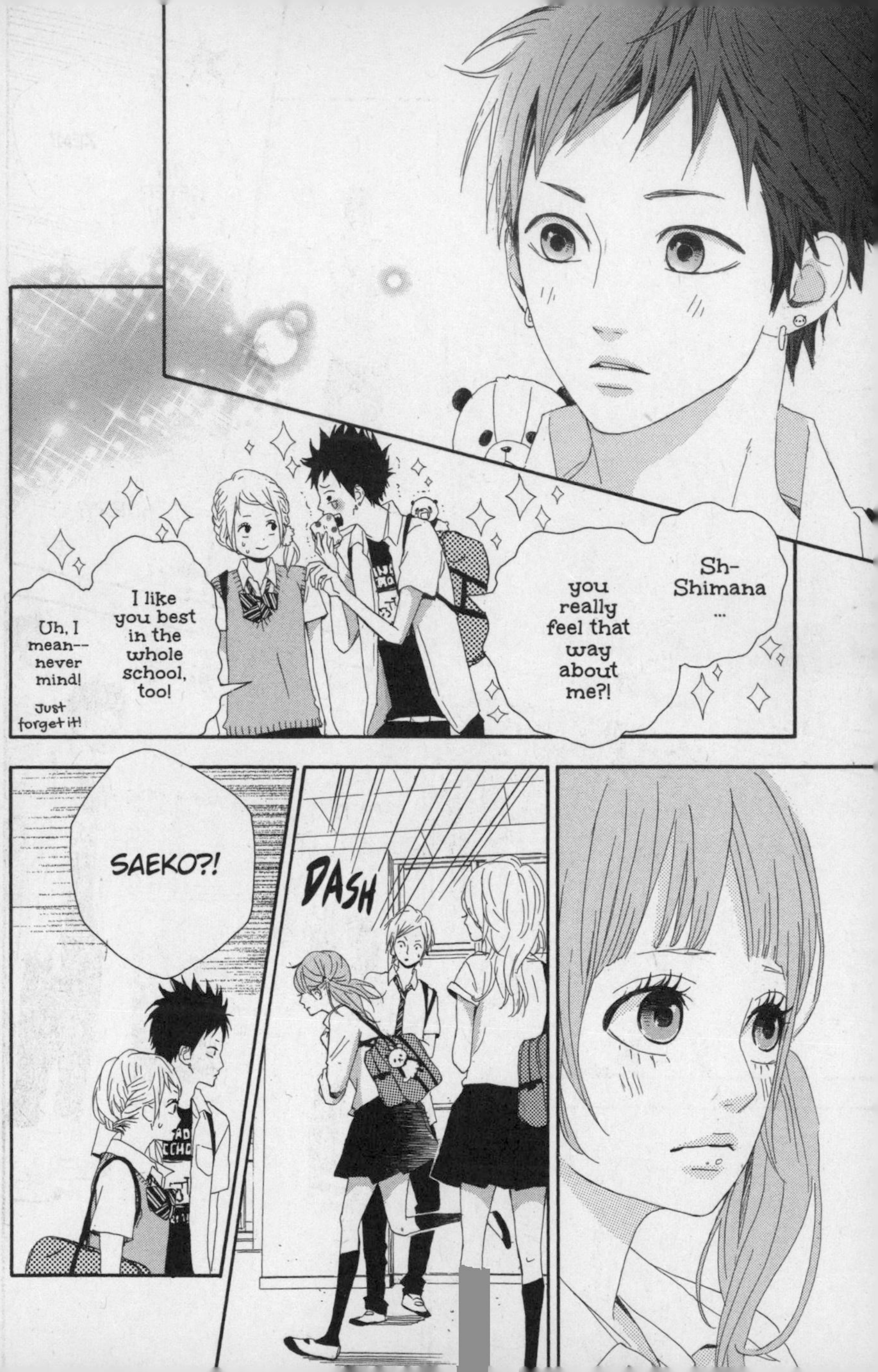
Sh- Shimana ...
you really feel that way about me?!
I like you best in the whole school, too!
Uh, I mean-- never mind!
Just forget it!
DASH
SAEKO?!

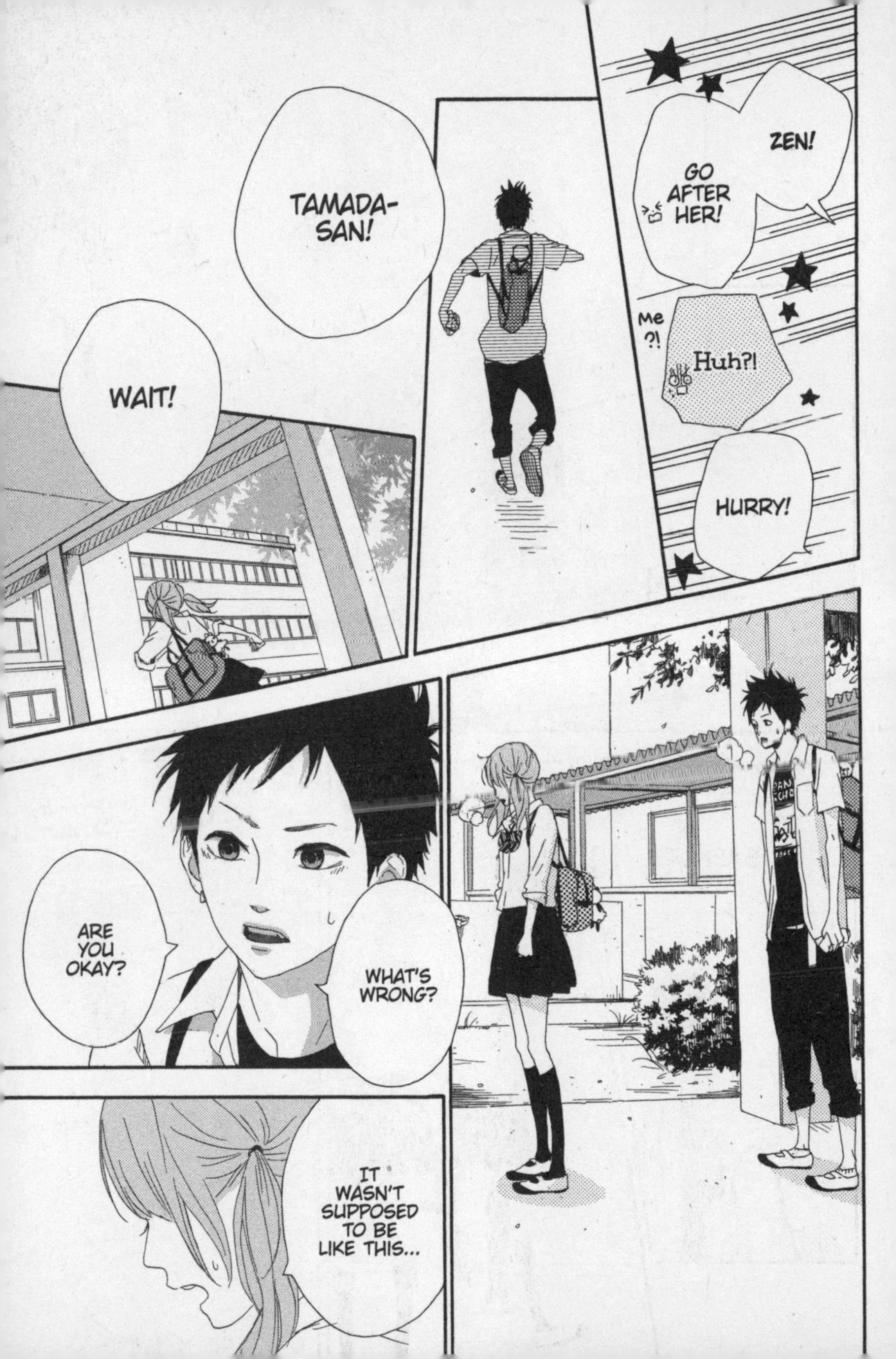
ZEN!
GO AFTER HER!
Me ?!
Huh?!
HURRY!
TAMADA-SAN!
WAIT!
WHAT'S WRONG?
ARE YOU OKAY?
IT WASN'T SUPPOSED TO BE LIKE THIS...

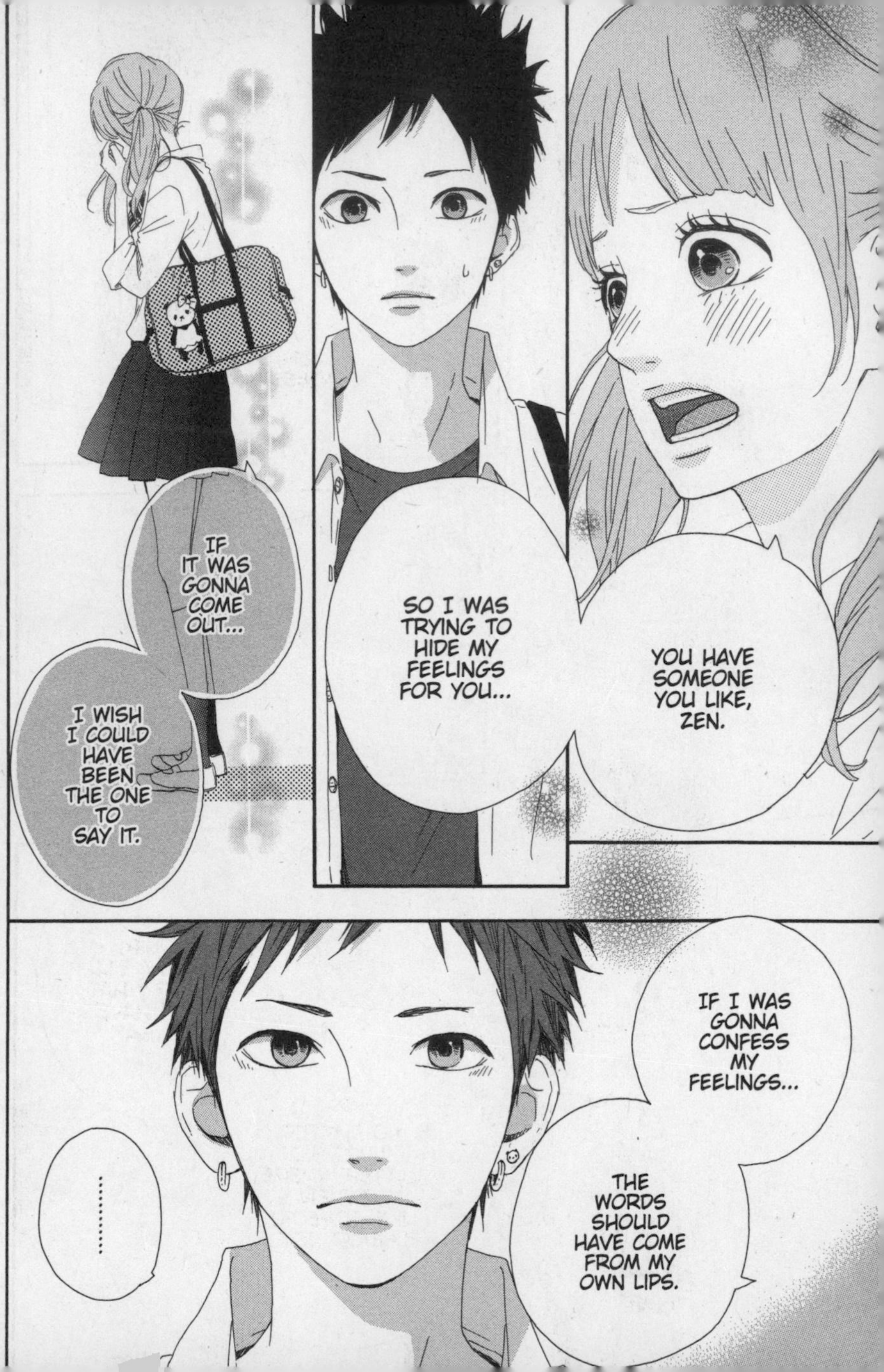
YOU HAVE SOMEONE YOU LIKE, ZEN.
SO I WAS TRYING TO HIDE MY FEELINGS FOR YOU...
IF IT WAS GONNA COME OUT...
I WISH I COULD HAVE BEEN THE ONE TO SAY IT.
IF I WAS GONNA CONFESS MY FEELINGS...
THE WORDS SHOULD HAVE COME FROM MY OWN LIPS.
......

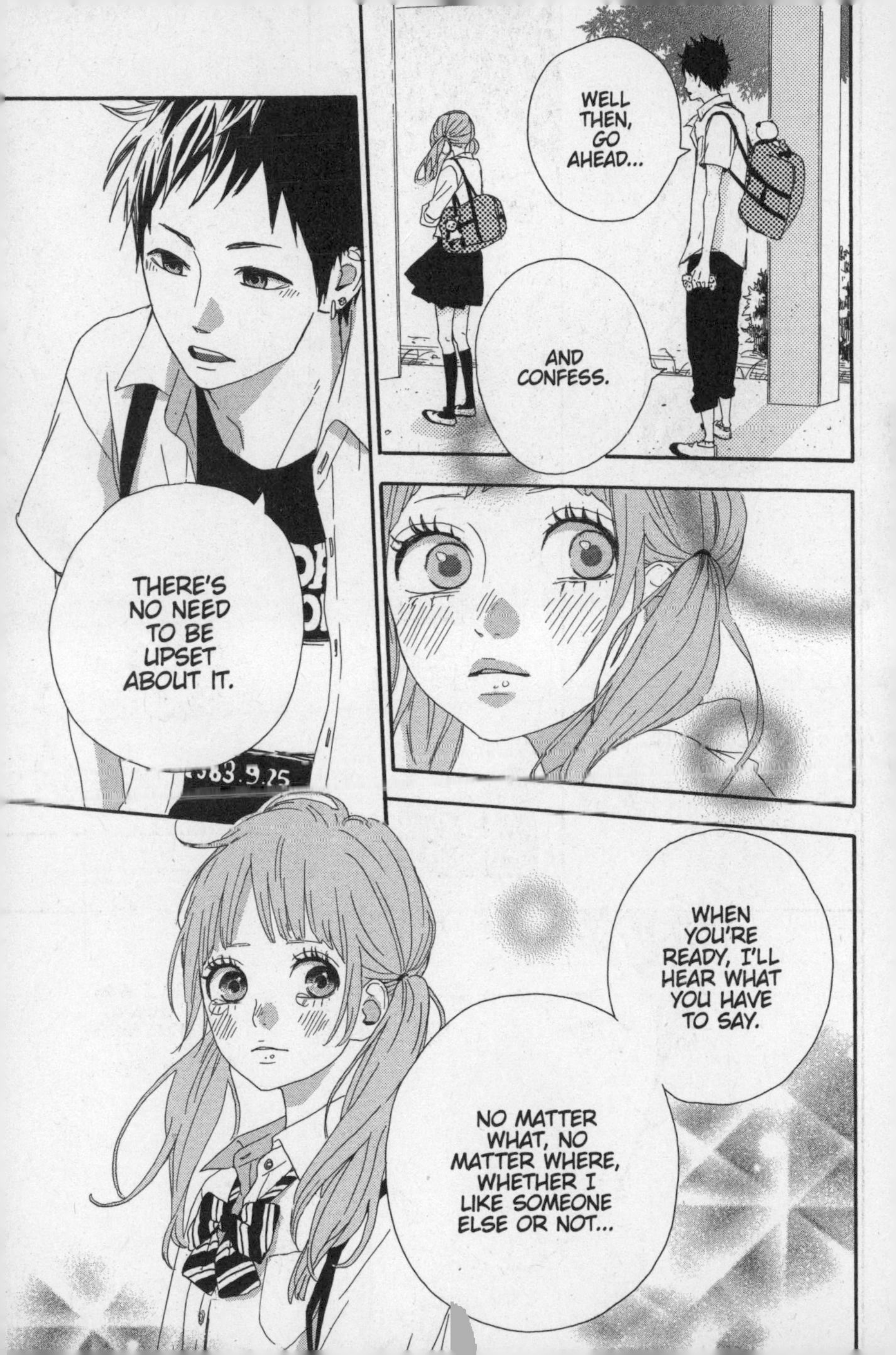
WELL THEN, GO AHEAD...
AND CONFESS.
THERE'S NO NEED TO BE UPSET ABOUT IT.
WHEN YOU'RE READY, I'LL HEAR WHAT YOU HAVE TO SAY.
NO MATTER WHAT, NO MATTER WHERE, WHETHER I LIKE SOMEONE ELSE OR NOT...

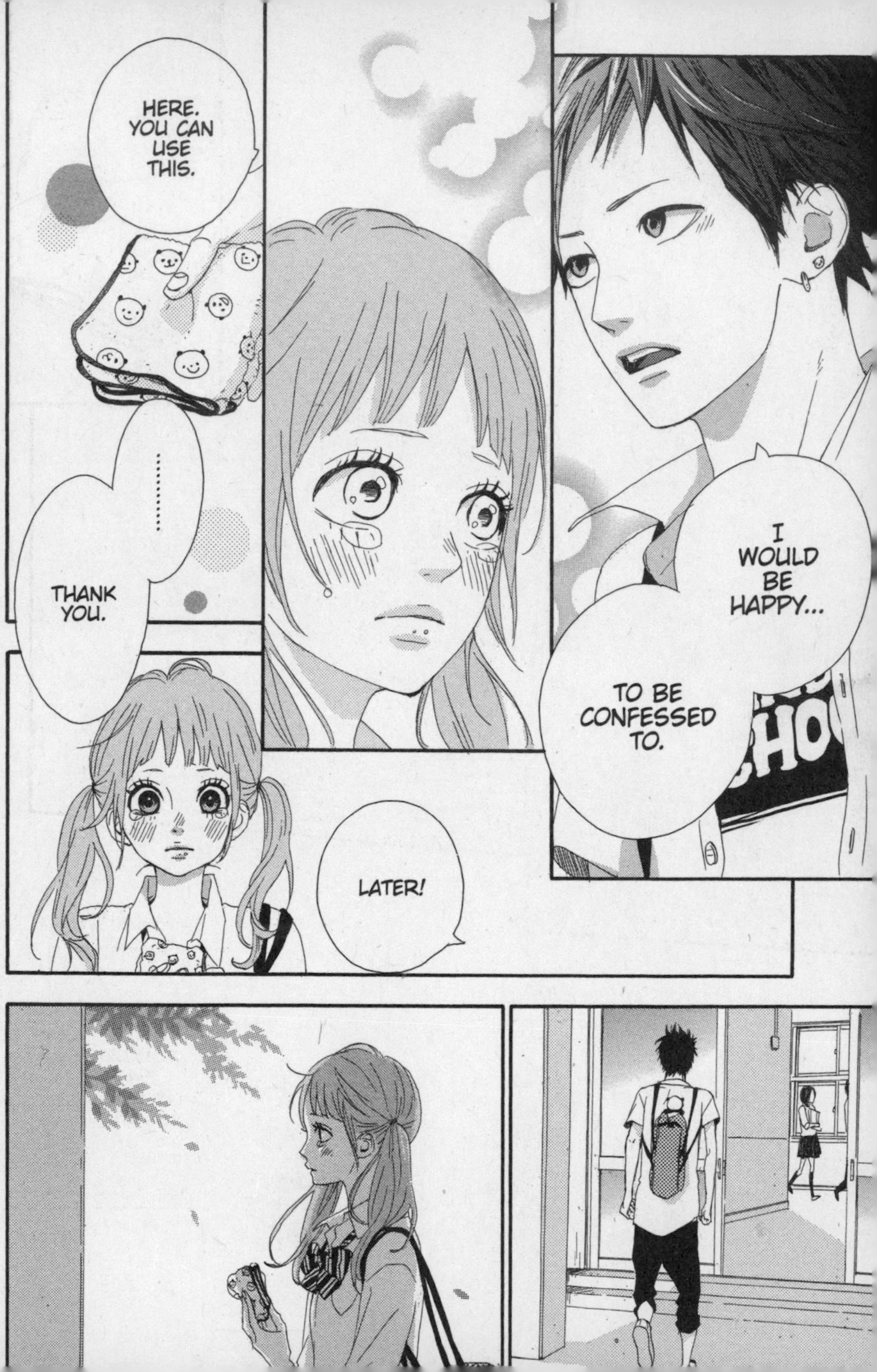
I WOULD BE HAPPY...
TO BE CONFESSED TO.
HERE. YOU CAN USE THIS.
......
THANK YOU.
LATER!

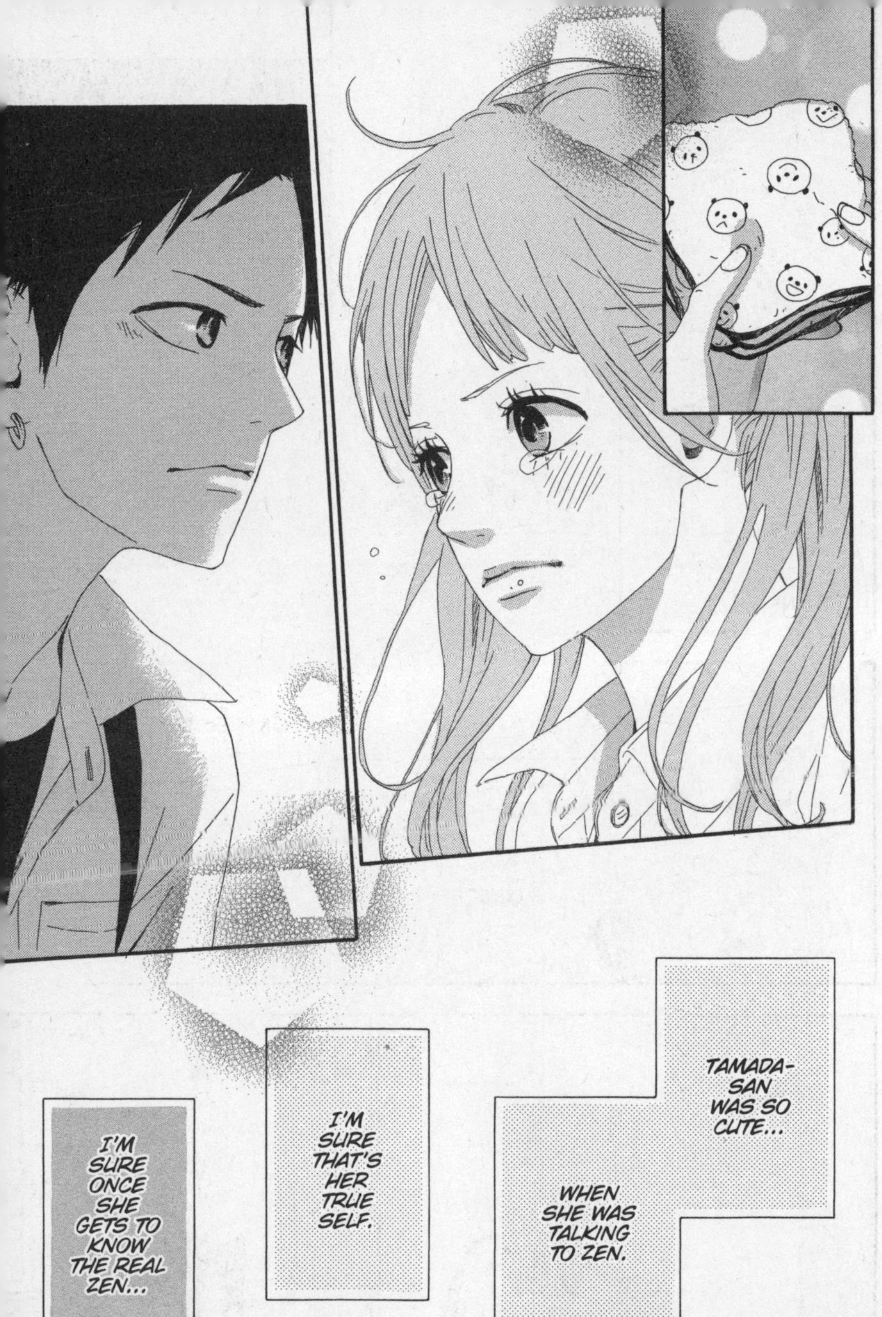
TAMADA-SAN WAS SO CUTE...
WHEN SHE WAS TALKING TO ZEN.
I'M SURE THAT'S HER TRUE SELF.
I'M SURE ONCE SHE GETS TO KNOW THE REAL ZEN...

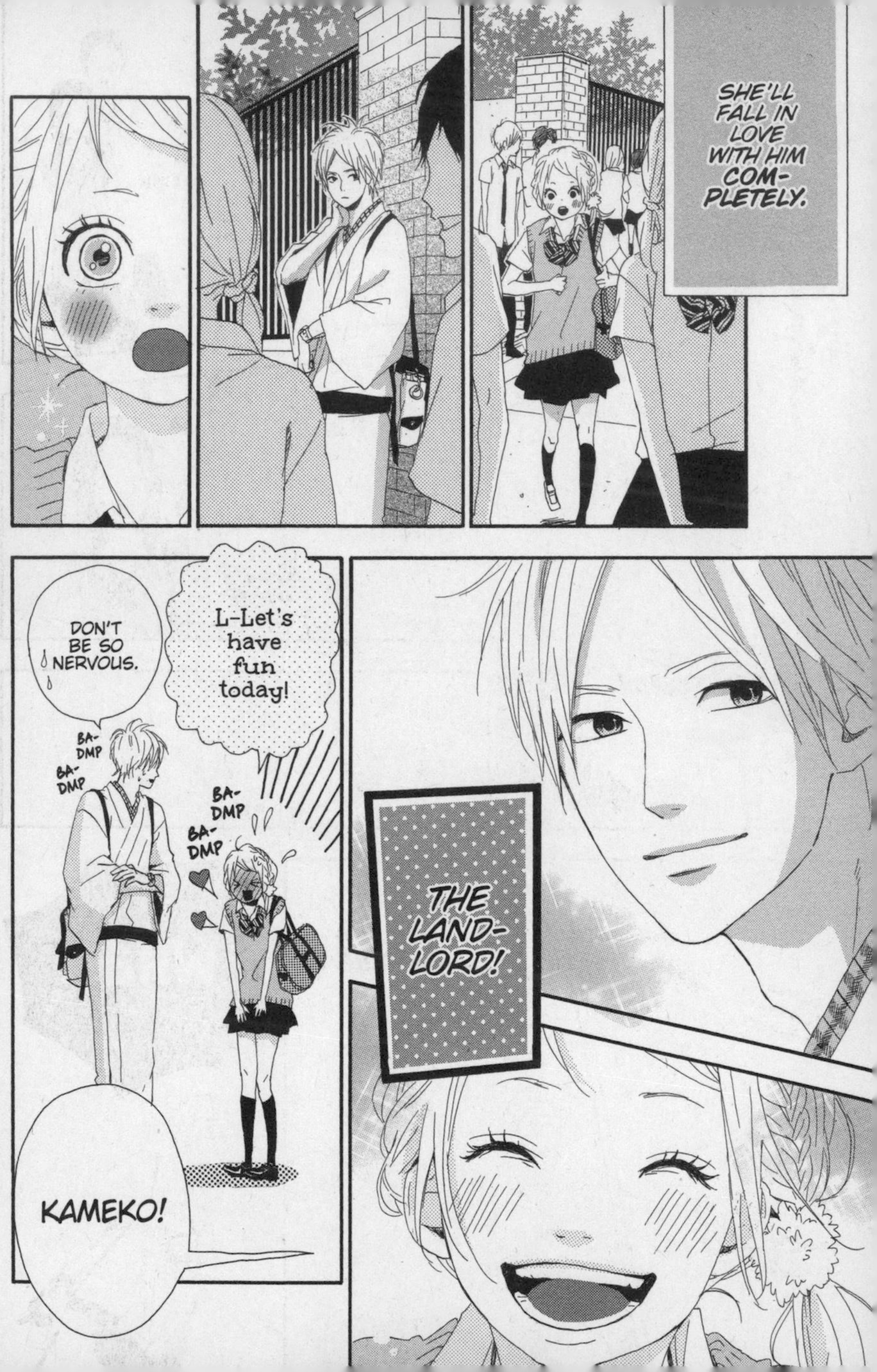

SHE'LL FALL IN LOVE WITH HIM COM-PLETELY.
THE LAND-LORD!
L-Let's have fun today!
DON'T BE SO NERVOUS.
BA-DMP BA-DMP
BA-DMP BA-DMP
KAMEKO!

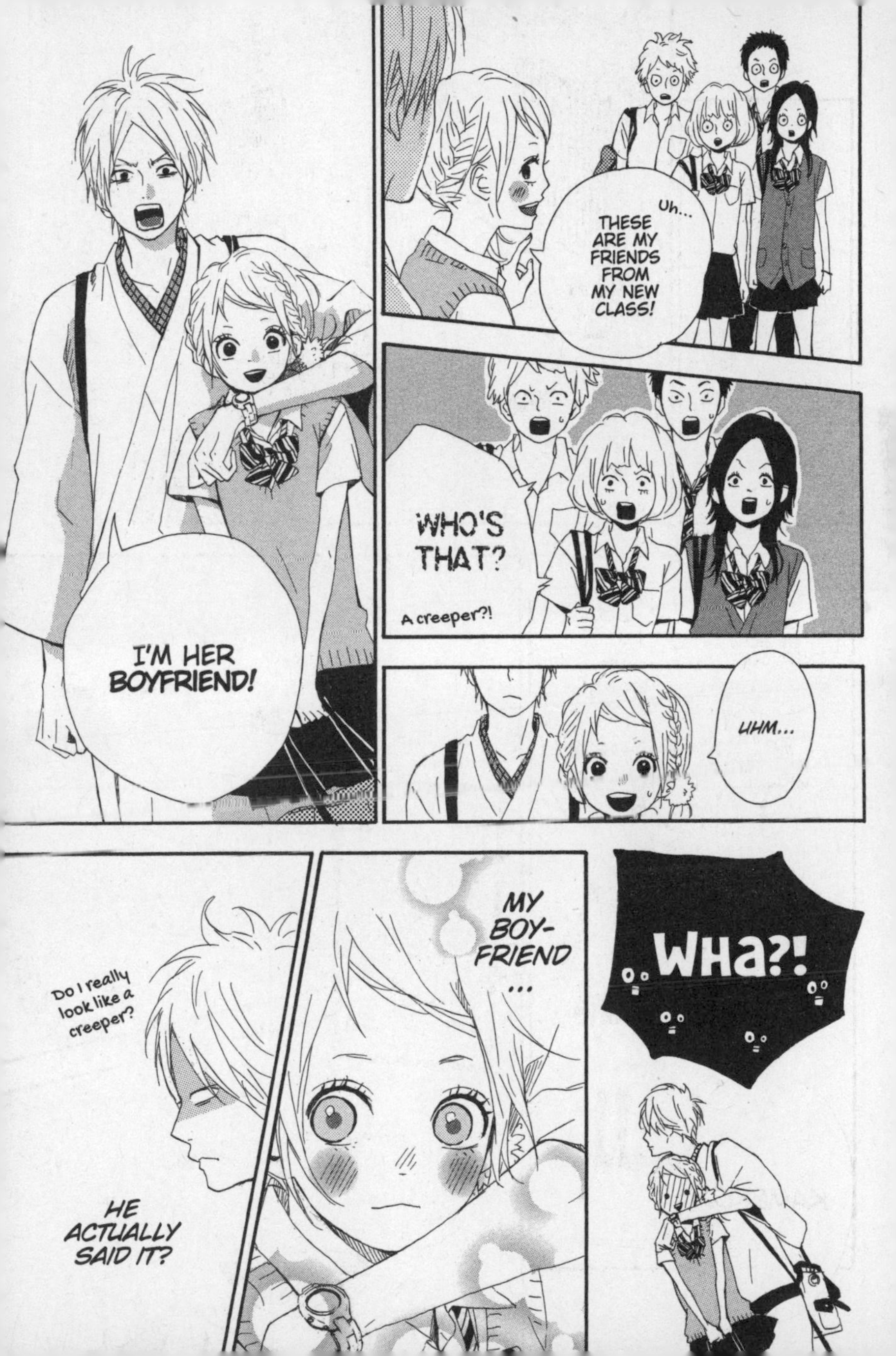
Uh... THESE ARE MY FRIENDS FROM MY NEW CLASS!
WHO'S THAT?
A creeper?!
UHM...
I'M HER BOYFRIEND!
WHA?!
MY BOY-FRIEND ...
Do I really look like a creeper?
HE ACTUALLY SAID IT?

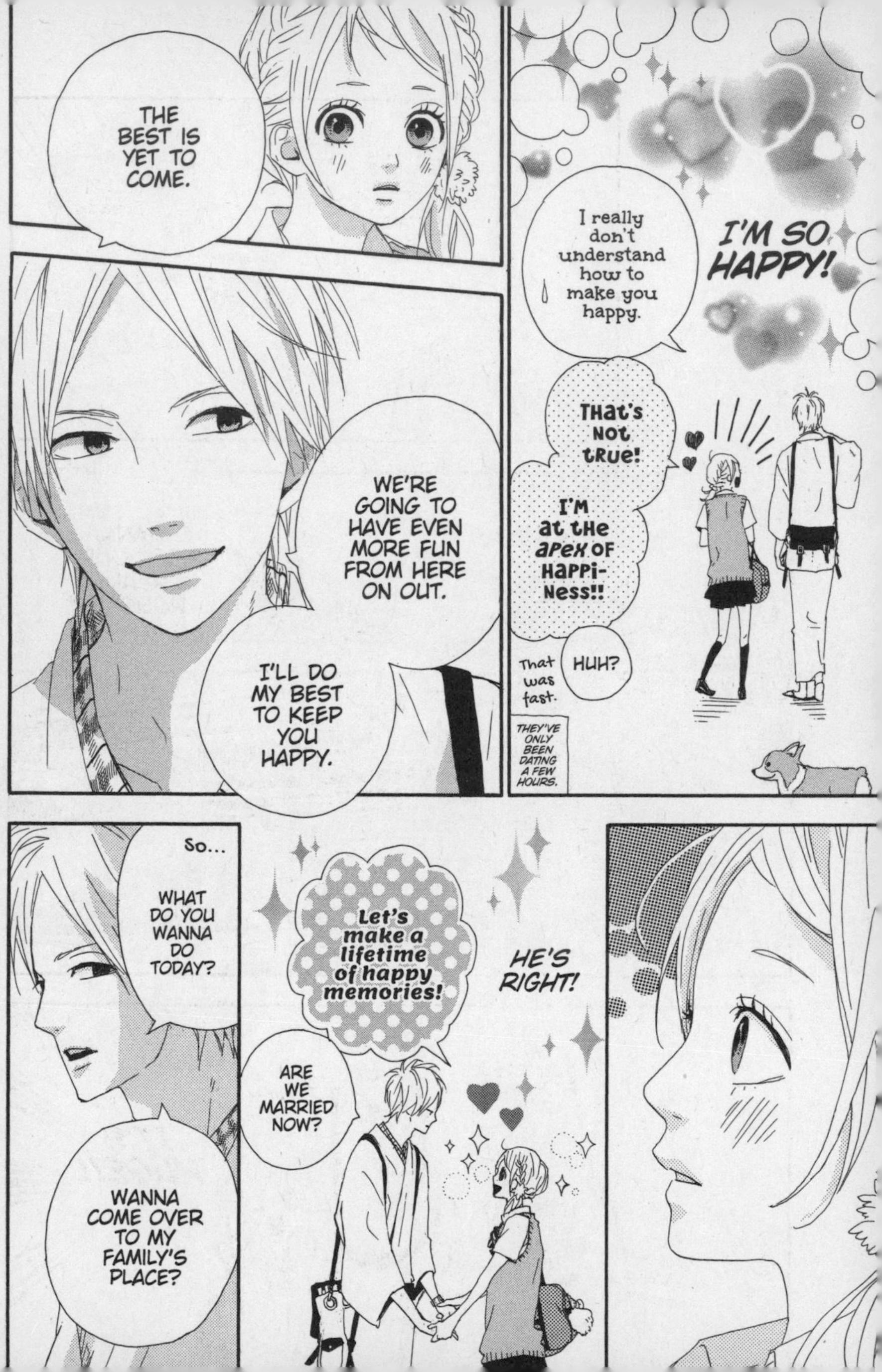
I'M SO HAPPY!
I really don't understand how to make you happy.
That's not true!
I'M at the apex of happi-ness!!
HUH?
That was fast.
THEY'VE ONLY BEEN DATING A FEW HOURS.
THE BEST IS YET TO COME.
WE'RE GOING TO HAVE EVEN MORE FUN FROM HERE ON OUT.
I'LL DO MY BEST TO KEEP YOU HAPPY.
HE'S RIGHT!
Let's make a lifetime of happy memories!
ARE WE MARRIED NOW?
So...
WHAT DO YOU WANNA DO TODAY?
WANNA COME OVER TO MY FAMILY'S PLACE?

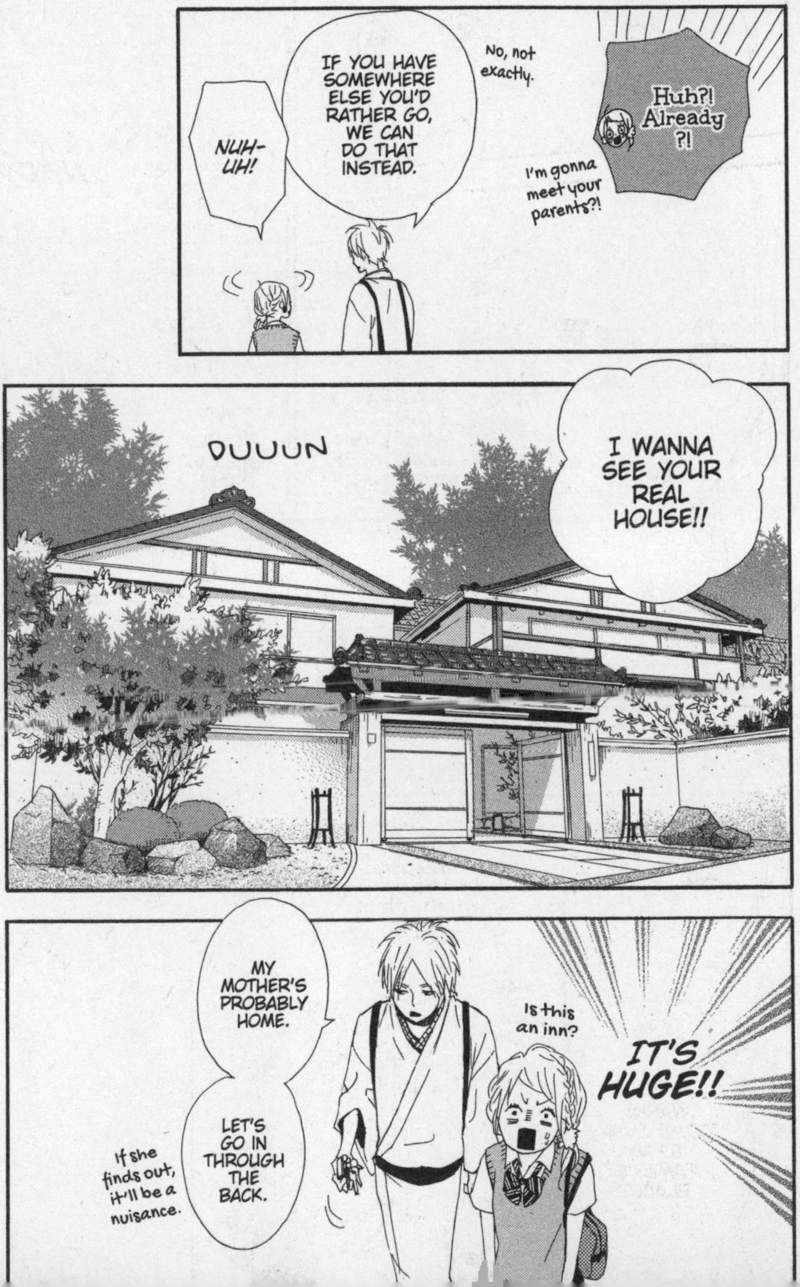
Huh?! Already ?!
I'm gonna meet your parents?!
No, not exactly.
IF YOU HAVE SOMEWHERE ELSE YOU'D RATHER GO, WE CAN DO THAT INSTEAD.
NUH-UH!
I WANNA SEE YOUR REAL HOUSE!!
DUUUN
IT'S HUGE!!
Is this an inn?
MY MOTHER'S PROBABLY HOME.
LET'S GO IN THROUGH THE BACK.
If she finds out, it'll be a nuisance.

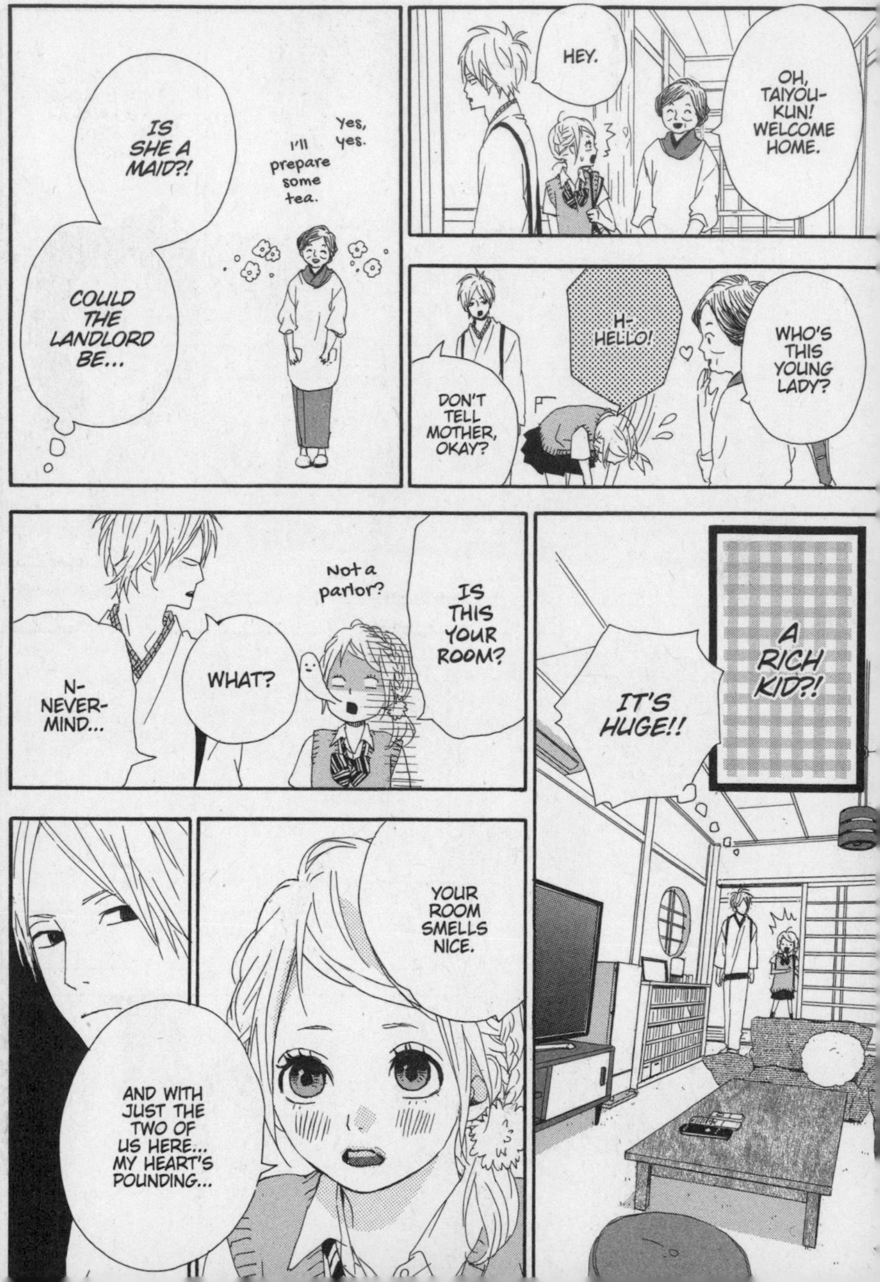
OH, TAIYOU-KUN! WELCOME HOME.
HEY.
WHO'S THIS YOUNG LADY?
H-HELLO!
DON'T TELL MOTHER, OKAY?
Yes, yes.
I'll prepare some tea.
IS SHE A MAID?!
COULD THE LANDLORD BE...
A RICH KID?!
IT'S HUGE!!
IS THIS YOUR ROOM?
Not a parlor?
WHAT?
N-NEVERMIND...
YOUR ROOM SMELLS NICE.
AND WITH JUST THE TWO OF US HERE... MY HEART'S POUNDING...

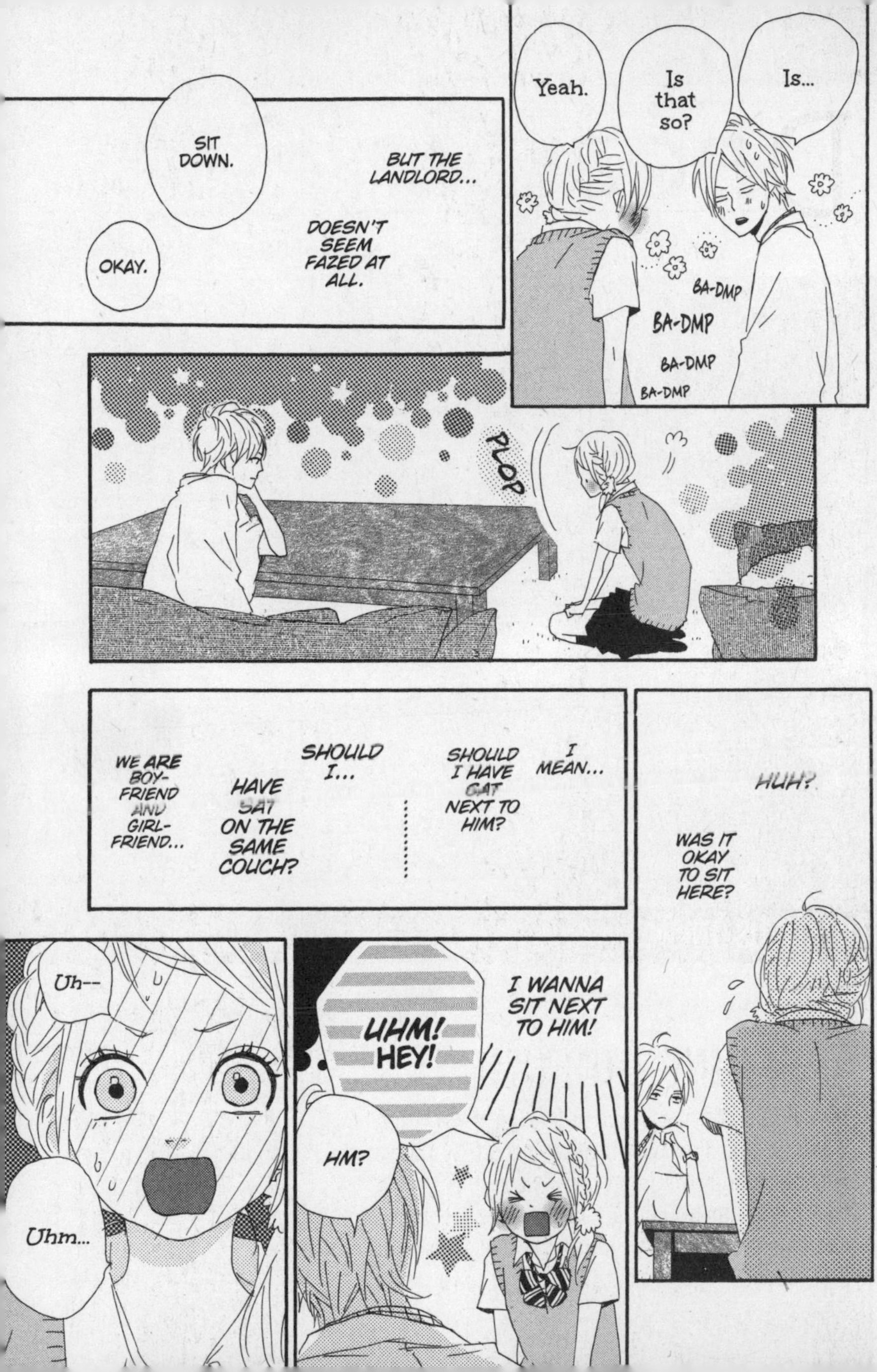
Is...
Is that so?
Yeah.
BA-DMP
BA-DMP
BA-DMP
BA-DMP
SIT DOWN.
OKAY.
BUT THE LANDLORD...
DOESN'T SEEM FAZED AT ALL.
PLOP
HUH?
WAS IT OKAY TO SIT HERE?
I MEAN...
SHOULD I HAVE SAT NEXT TO HIM?
......
SHOULD I...
HAVE SAT ON THE SAME COUCH?
WE ARE BOY-FRIEND AND GIRL-FRIEND...
I WANNA SIT NEXT TO HIM!
UHM! HEY!
HM?
Uh--
Uhm...

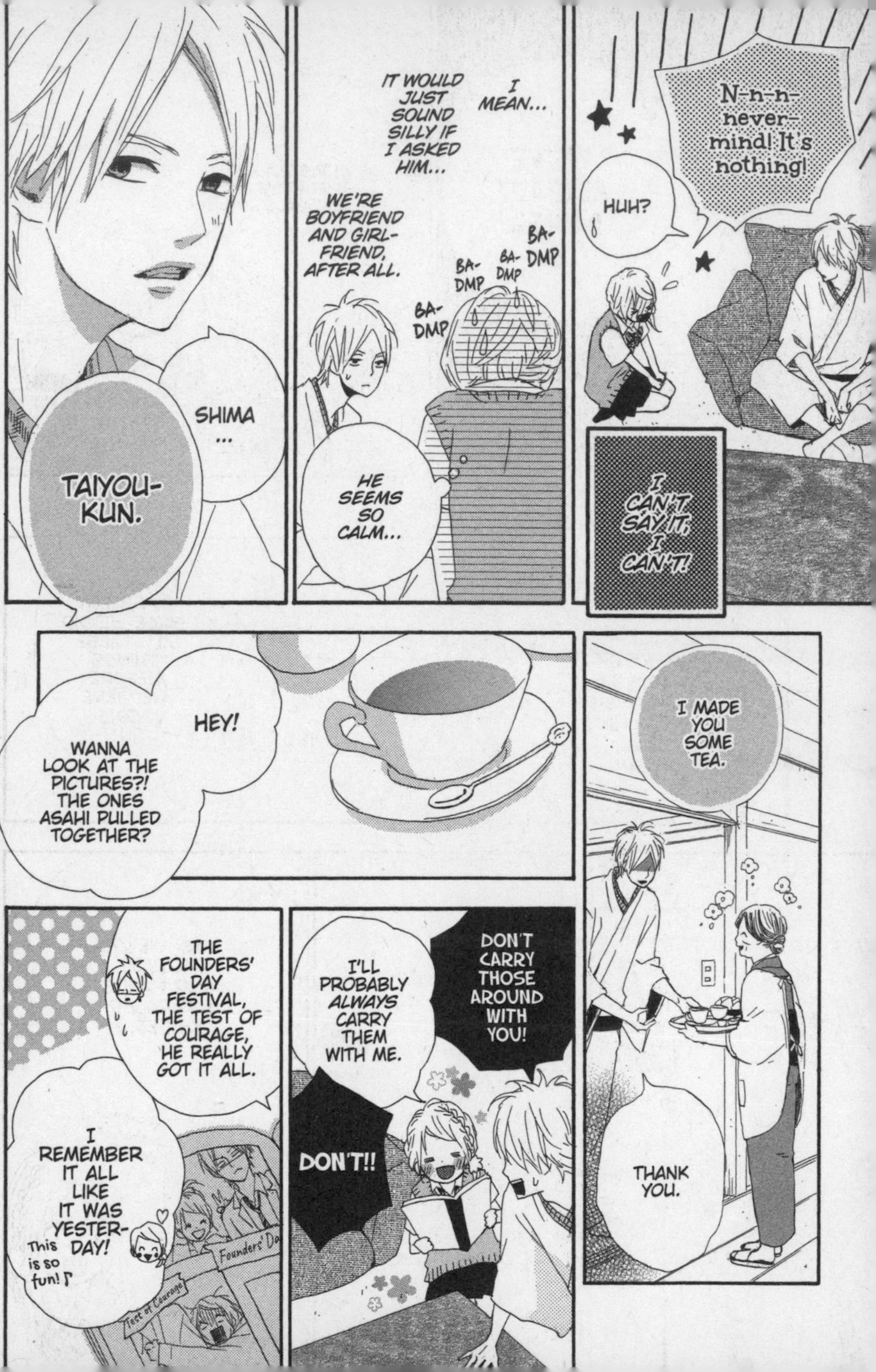
N-n-n-never-mind! It's nothing!
HUH?
I CAN'T SAY IT, I CAN'T!
I MEAN...
IT WOULD JUST SOUND SILLY IF I ASKED HIM...
WE'RE BOYFRIEND AND GIRLFRIEND, AFTER ALL.
BA-DMP
BA-DMP
BA-DMP
BA-DMP
HE SEEMS SO CALM...
SHIMA...
TAIYOU-KUN.
I MADE YOU SOME TEA.
THANK YOU.
HEY!
WANNA LOOK AT THE PICTURES?! THE ONES ASAHI PULLED TOGETHER?
DON'T CARRY THOSE AROUND WITH YOU!
I'LL PROBABLY ALWAYS CARRY THEM WITH ME.
DON'T!!
THE FOUNDERS' DAY FESTIVAL, THE TEST OF COURAGE, HE REALLY GOT IT ALL.
I REMEMBER IT ALL LIKE IT WAS YESTERDAY!
This is so fun! ♪
Founders' Day
Test of Courage

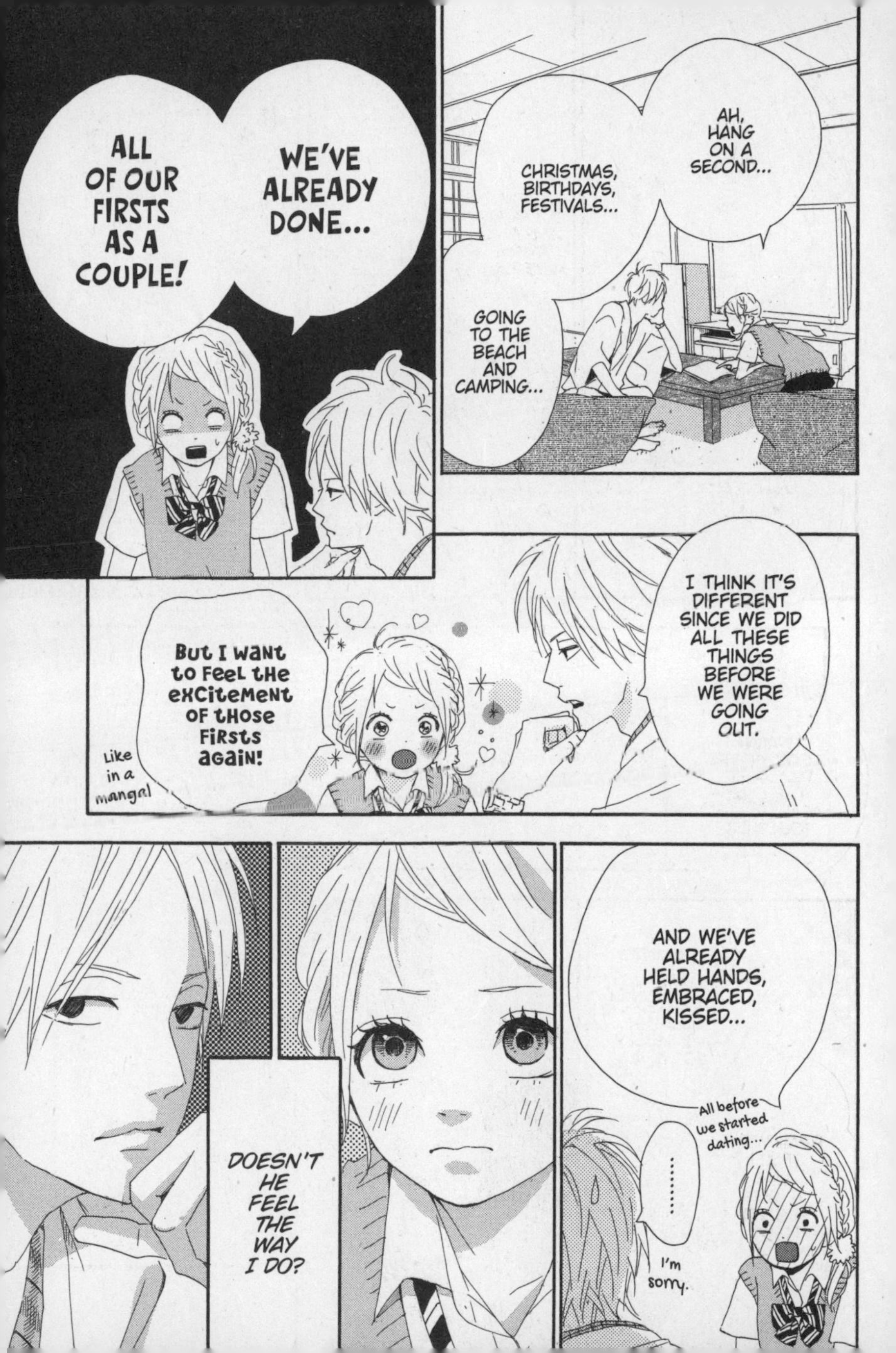
AH, HANG ON A SECOND...
CHRISTMAS, BIRTHDAYS, FESTIVALS...
GOING TO THE BEACH AND CAMPING...
WE'VE ALREADY DONE...
ALL OF OUR FIRSTS AS A COUPLE!
I THINK IT'S DIFFERENT SINCE WE DID ALL THESE THINGS BEFORE WE WERE GOING OUT.
But I want to feel the excitement of those firsts again!
Like in a manga!
AND WE'VE ALREADY HELD HANDS, EMBRACED, KISSED...
All before we started dating...
....
I'm sorry.
DOESN'T HE FEEL THE WAY I DO?

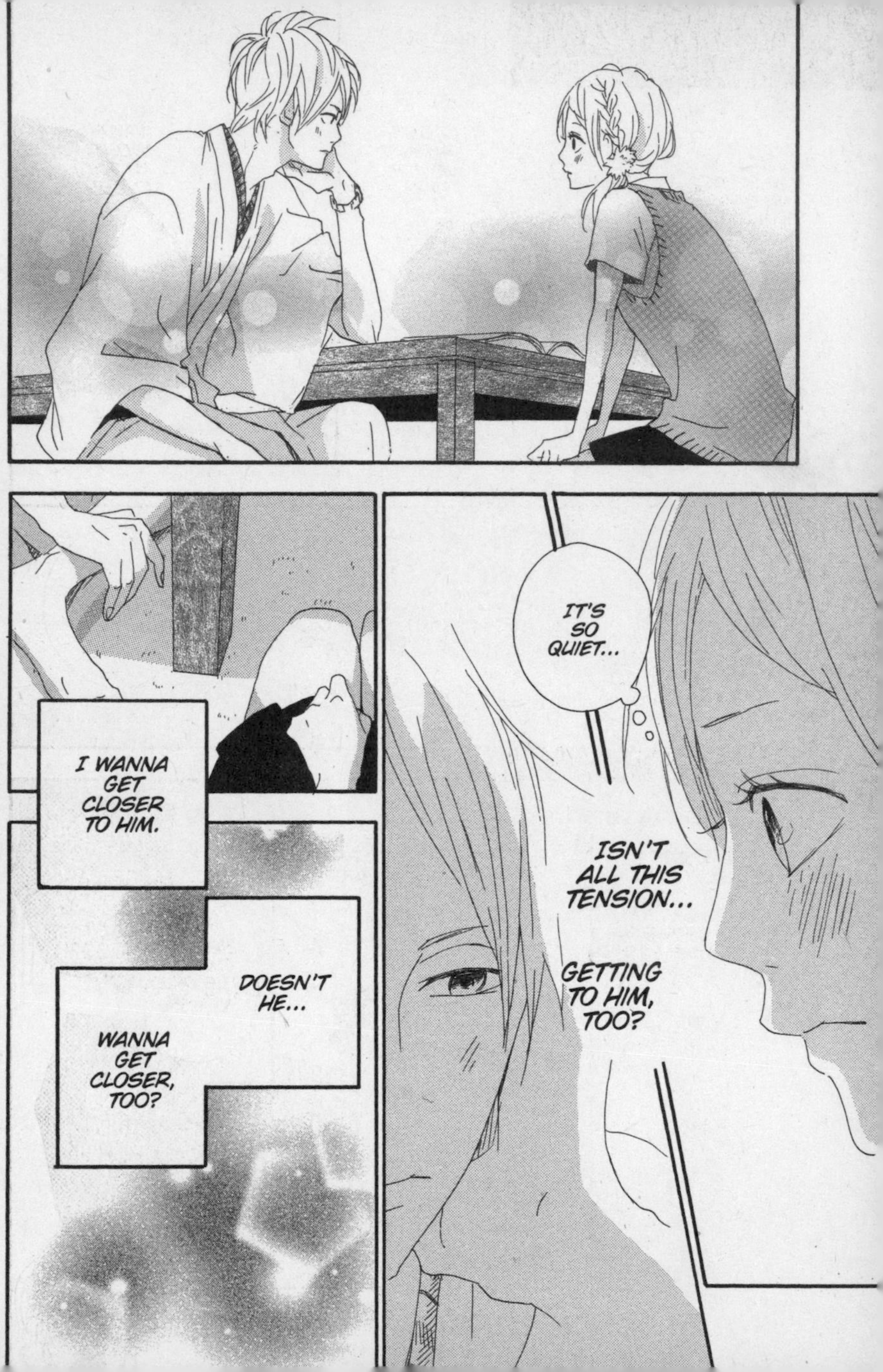
IT'S SO QUIET...
ISN'T ALL THIS TENSION...
GETTING TO HIM, TOO?
I WANNA GET CLOSER TO HIM.
DOESN'T HE...
WANNA GET CLOSER, TOO?

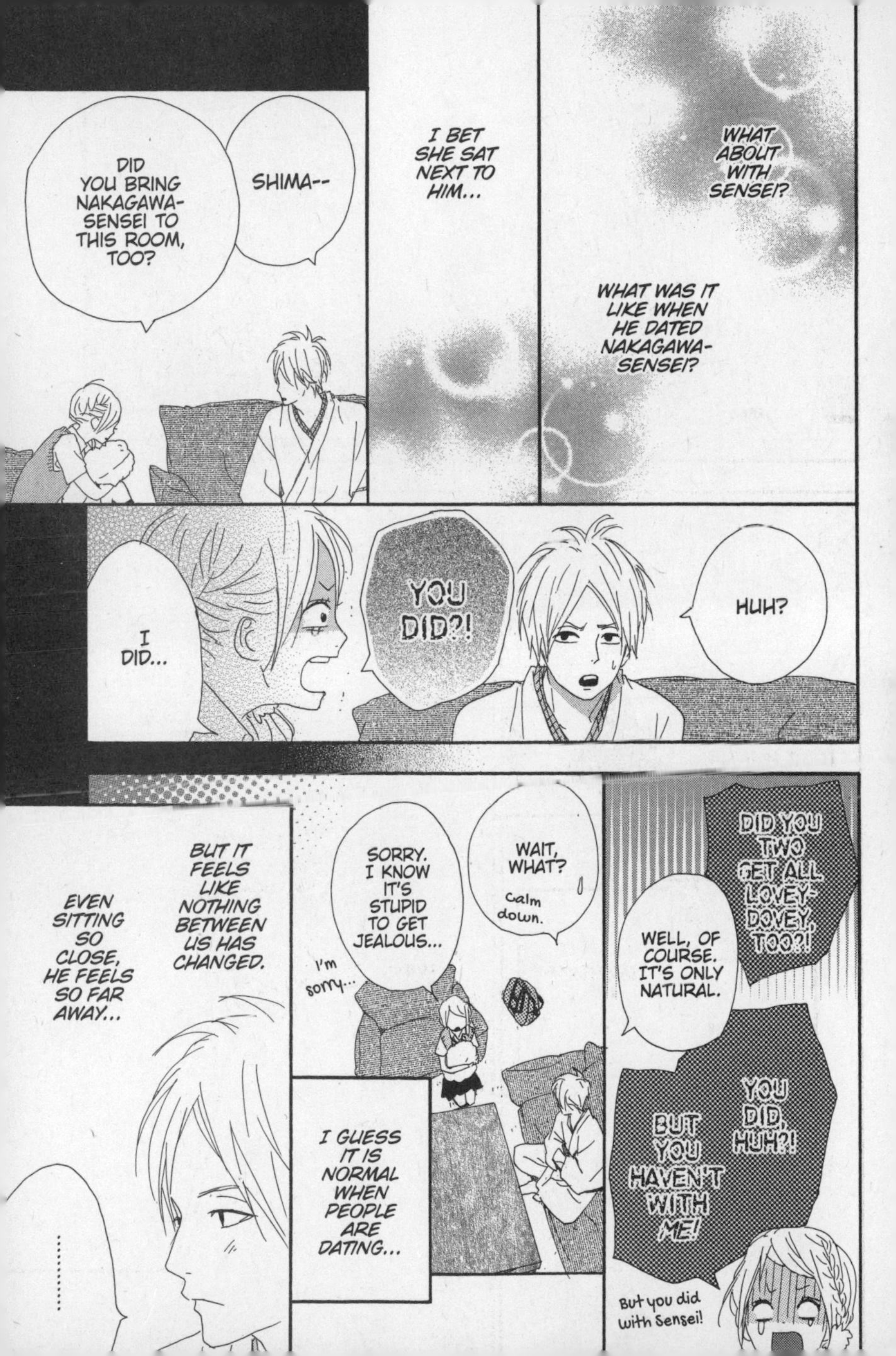
WHAT ABOUT WITH SENSEI?
WHAT WAS IT LIKE WHEN HE DATED NAKAGAWA-SENSEI?
I BET SHE SAT NEXT TO HIM...
SHIMA--
DID YOU BRING NAKAGAWA-SENSEI TO THIS ROOM, TOO?
HUH?
YOU DID?!
I DID...
DID YOU TWO GET ALL LOVEY-DOVEY, TOO?!
WELL, OF COURSE. IT'S ONLY NATURAL.
YOU DID, HUH?!
BUT YOU HAVEN'T WITH ME!
But you did with Sensei!
WAIT, WHAT?
Calm down.
SORRY. I KNOW IT'S STUPID TO GET JEALOUS...
I'm sorry...
I GUESS IT IS NORMAL WHEN PEOPLE ARE DATING...
BUT IT FEELS LIKE NOTHING BETWEEN US HAS CHANGED.
EVEN SITTING SO CLOSE, HE FEELS SO FAR AWAY...
......

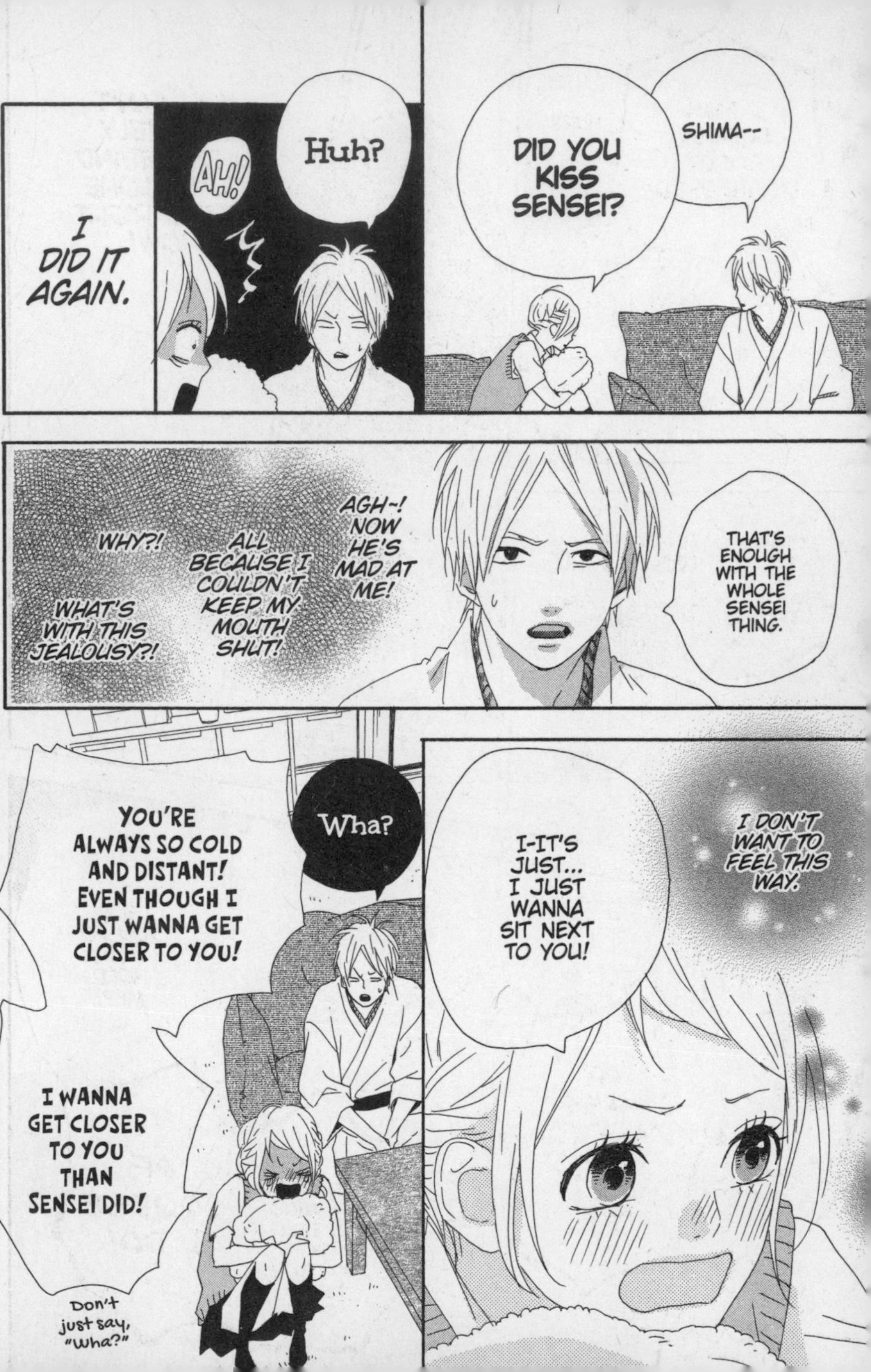
SHIMA--
DID YOU KISS SENSEI?
Huh?
AH!
I DID IT AGAIN.
THAT'S ENOUGH WITH THE WHOLE SENSEI THING.
AGH~! NOW HE'S MAD AT ME!
ALL BECAUSE I COULDN'T KEEP MY MOUTH SHUT!
WHY?!
WHAT'S WITH THIS JEALOUSY?!
I DON'T WANT TO FEEL THIS WAY.
I-IT'S JUST... I JUST WANNA SIT NEXT TO YOU!
Wha?
YOU'RE ALWAYS SO COLD AND DISTANT! EVEN THOUGH I JUST WANNA GET CLOSER TO YOU!
I WANNA GET CLOSER TO YOU THAN SENSEI DID!
Don't just say, "Wha?"

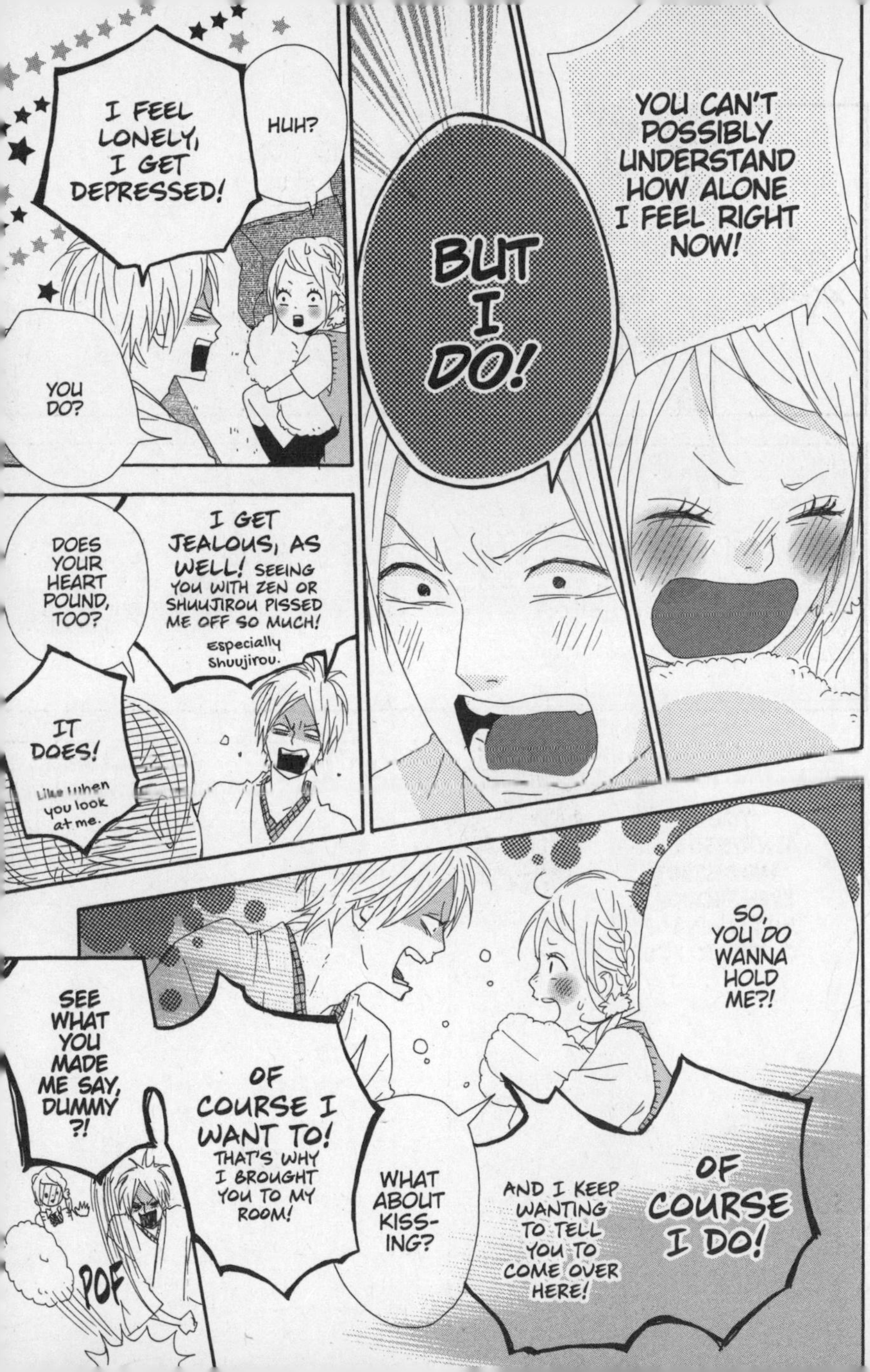
YOU CAN'T POSSIBLY UNDERSTAND HOW ALONE I FEEL RIGHT NOW!
BUT I DO!
HUH?
I FEEL LONELY, I GET DEPRESSED!
YOU DO?
I GET JEALOUS, AS WELL! SEEING YOU WITH ZEN OR SHUUJIROU PISSED ME OFF SO MUCH!
Especially Shuujirou.
DOES YOUR HEART POUND, TOO?
IT DOES!
Like when you look at me.
SO, YOU DO WANNA HOLD ME?!
OF COURSE I DO!
AND I KEEP WANTING TO TELL YOU TO COME OVER HERE!
WHAT ABOUT KISS-ING?
OF COURSE I WANT TO! THAT'S WHY I BROUGHT YOU TO MY ROOM!
SEE WHAT YOU MADE ME SAY, DUMMY?!
POF

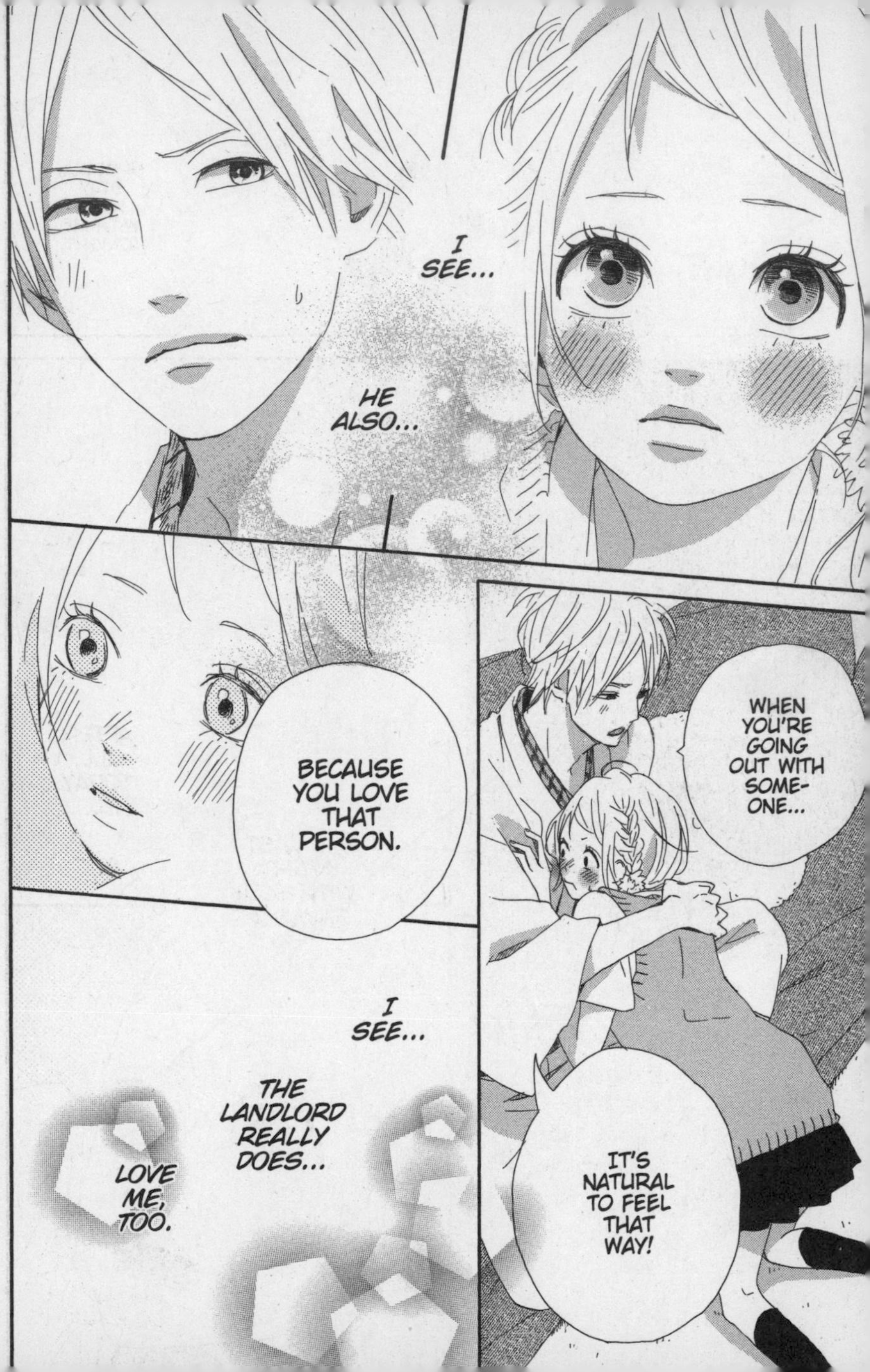
I SEE...
HE ALSO...
WHEN YOU'RE GOING OUT WITH SOME-ONE...
IT'S NATURAL TO FEEL THAT WAY!
BECAUSE YOU LOVE THAT PERSON.
I SEE...
THE LANDLORD REALLY DOES...
LOVE ME, TOO.

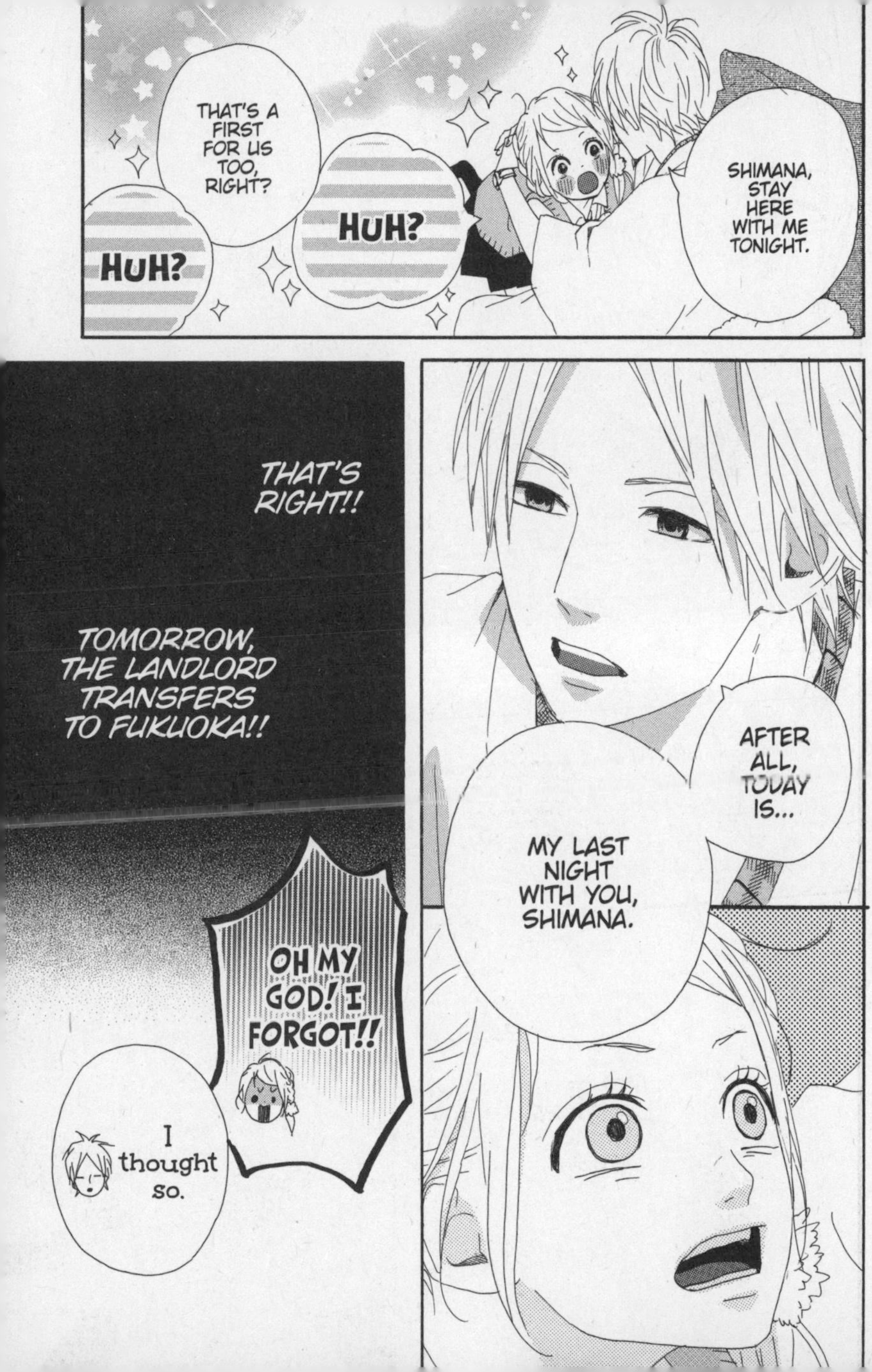
SHIMANA, STAY HERE WITH ME TONIGHT.
HUH?
THAT'S A FIRST FOR US TOO, RIGHT?
HUH?
AFTER ALL, TODAY IS...
MY LAST NIGHT WITH YOU, SHIMANA.
THAT'S RIGHT!!
TOMORROW, THE LANDLORD TRANSFERS TO FUKUOKA!!
OH MY GOD! I FORGOT!!
I thought so.

THE FIND POKO GAME

Poko is hidden
throughout the manga!
Find him!

This time,
there are 5 Pokos.

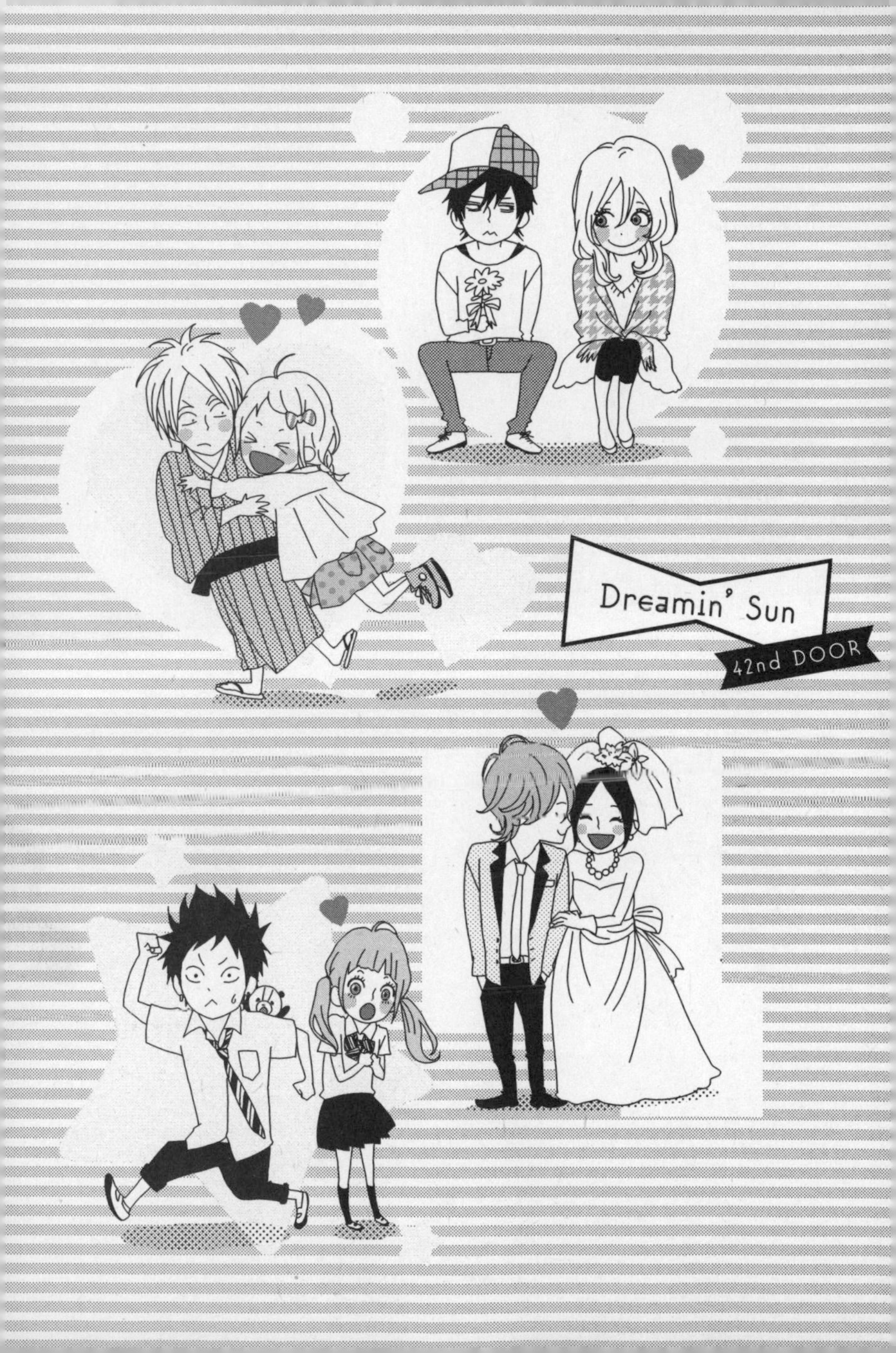
Dreamin' Sun
42nd DOOR

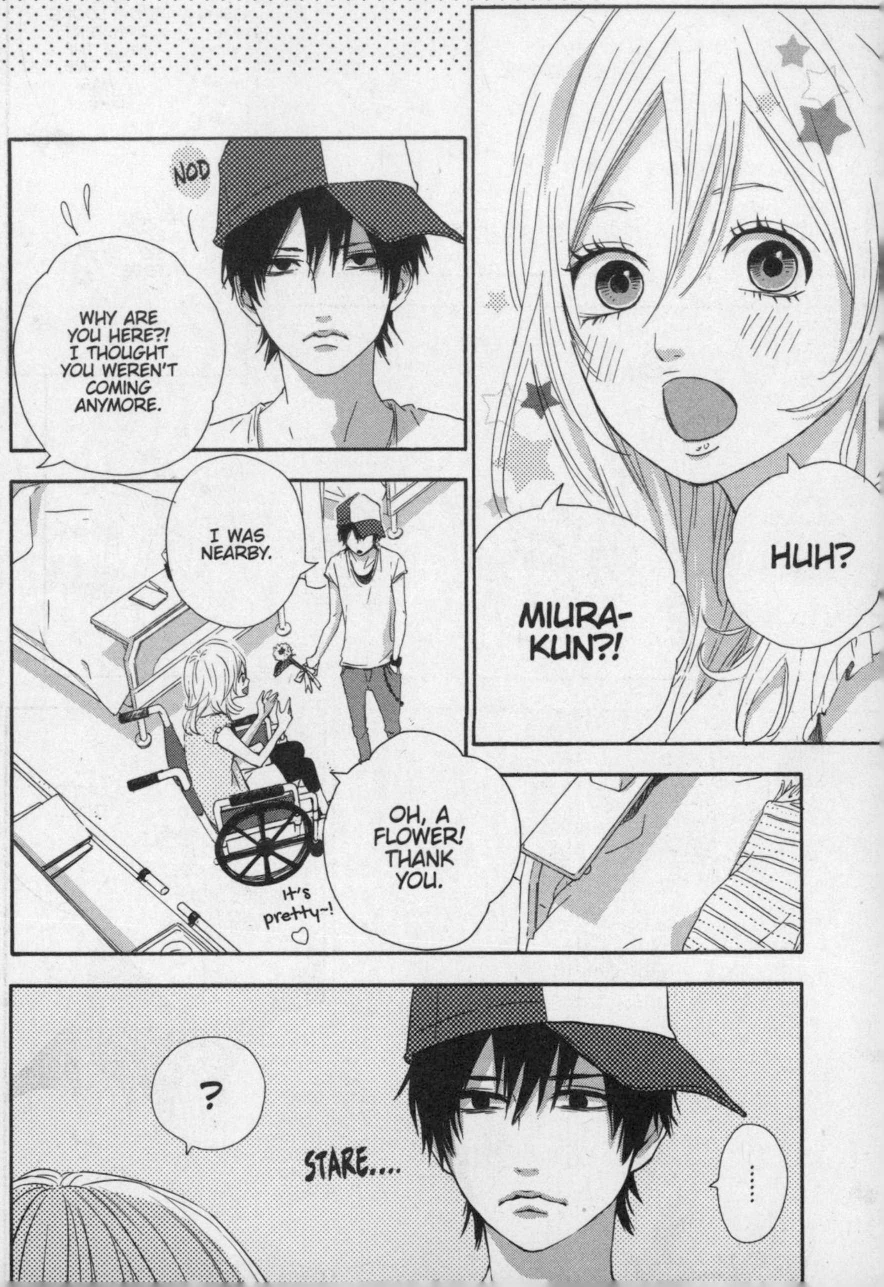
HUH?
MIURA-KUN?!
NOD
WHY ARE YOU HERE?! I THOUGHT YOU WEREN'T COMING ANYMORE.
I WAS NEARBY.
OH, A FLOWER! THANK YOU.
It's pretty~!
?
STARE...
......

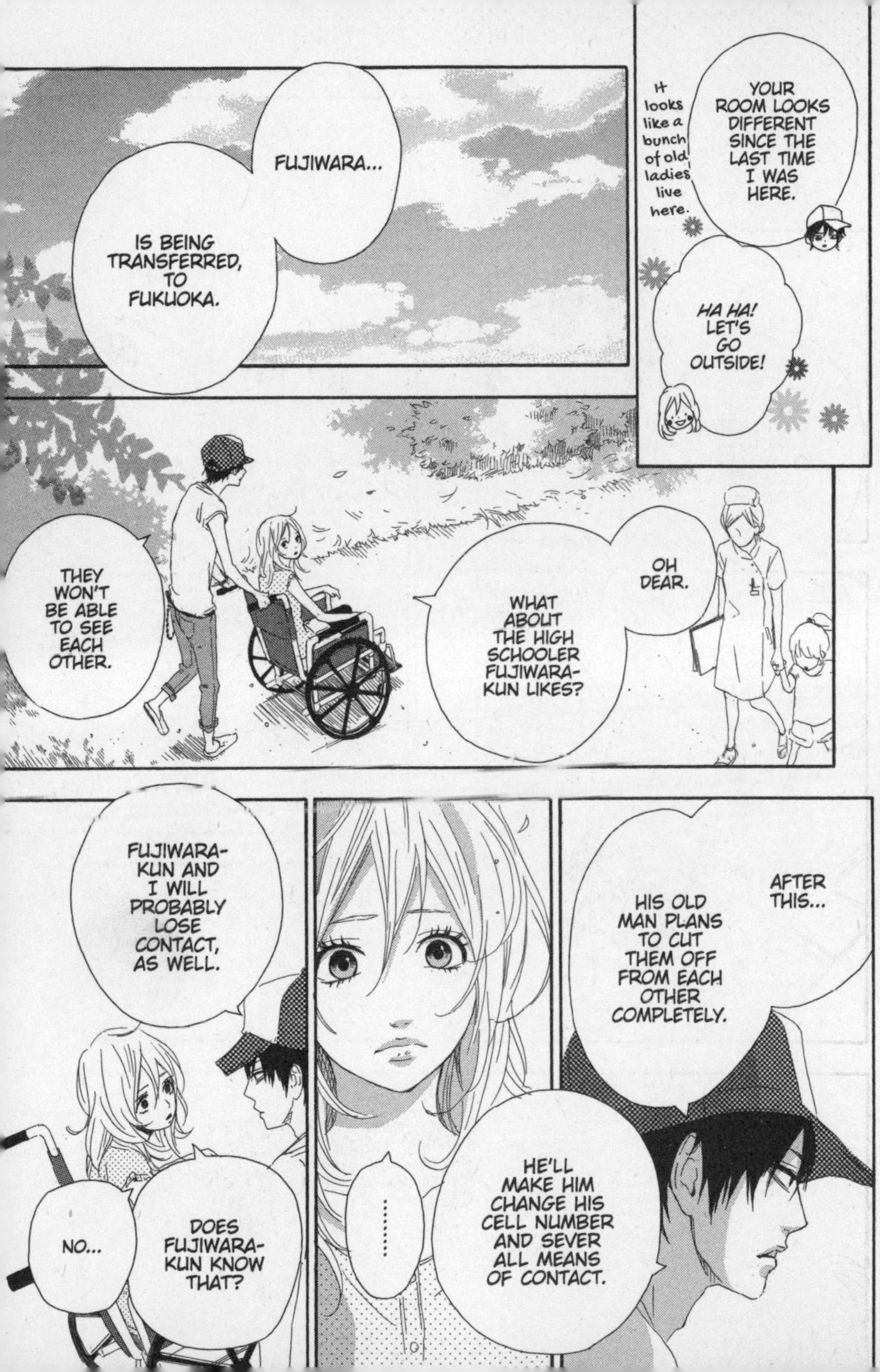
YOUR ROOM LOOKS DIFFERENT SINCE THE LAST TIME I WAS HERE.
It looks like a bunch of old ladies live here.
HA HA! LET'S GO OUTSIDE!
FUJIWARA...
IS BEING TRANSFERRED, TO FUKUOKA.
OH DEAR.
WHAT ABOUT THE HIGH SCHOOLER FUJIWARA-KUN LIKES?
THEY WON'T BE ABLE TO SEE EACH OTHER.
AFTER THIS...
HIS OLD MAN PLANS TO CUT THEM OFF FROM EACH OTHER COMPLETELY.
HE'LL MAKE HIM CHANGE HIS CELL NUMBER AND SEVER ALL MEANS OF CONTACT.
......
FUJIWARA-KUN AND I WILL PROBABLY LOSE CONTACT, AS WELL.
DOES FUJIWARA-KUN KNOW THAT?
NO...

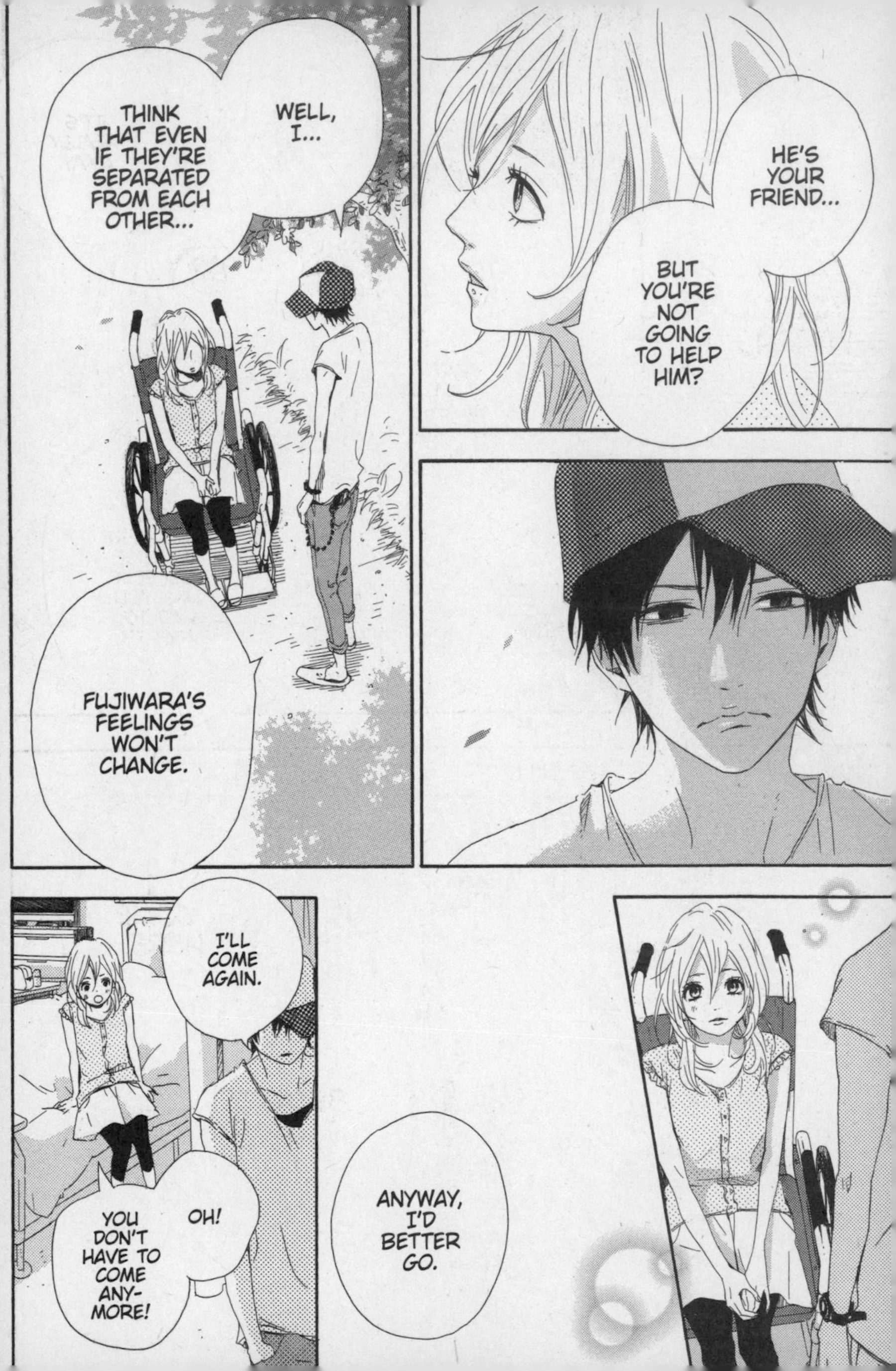
HE'S YOUR FRIEND...
BUT YOU'RE NOT GOING TO HELP HIM?
WELL, I...
THINK THAT EVEN IF THEY'RE SEPARATED FROM EACH OTHER...
FUJIWARA'S FEELINGS WON'T CHANGE.
ANYWAY, I'D BETTER GO.
I'LL COME AGAIN.
OH!
YOU DON'T HAVE TO COME ANY-MORE!

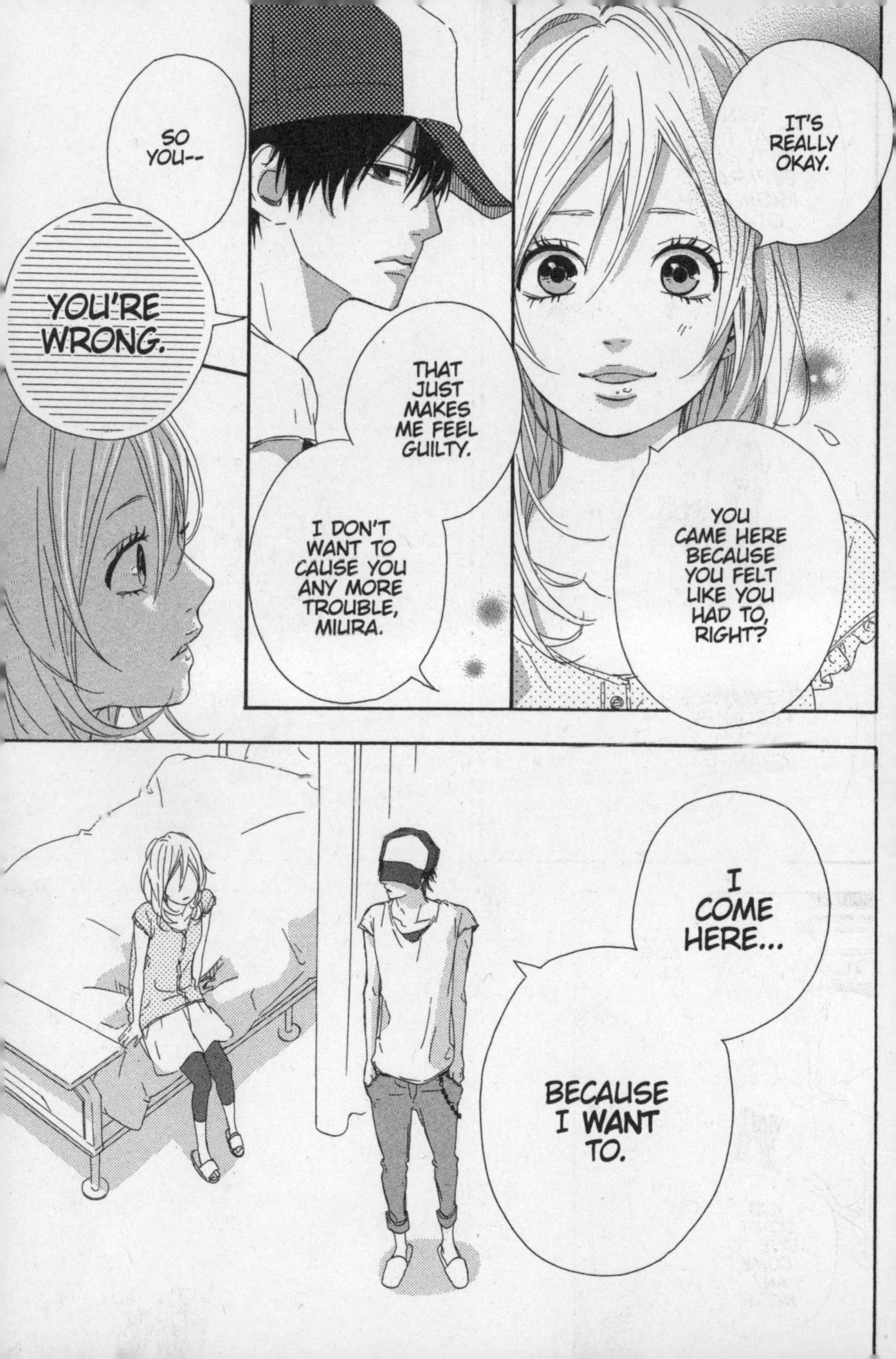
IT'S REALLY OKAY.
YOU CAME HERE BECAUSE YOU FELT LIKE YOU HAD TO, RIGHT?
THAT JUST MAKES ME FEEL GUILTY.
I DON'T WANT TO CAUSE YOU ANY MORE TROUBLE, MIURA.
SO YOU--
YOU'RE WRONG.
I COME HERE...
BECAUSE I WANT TO.

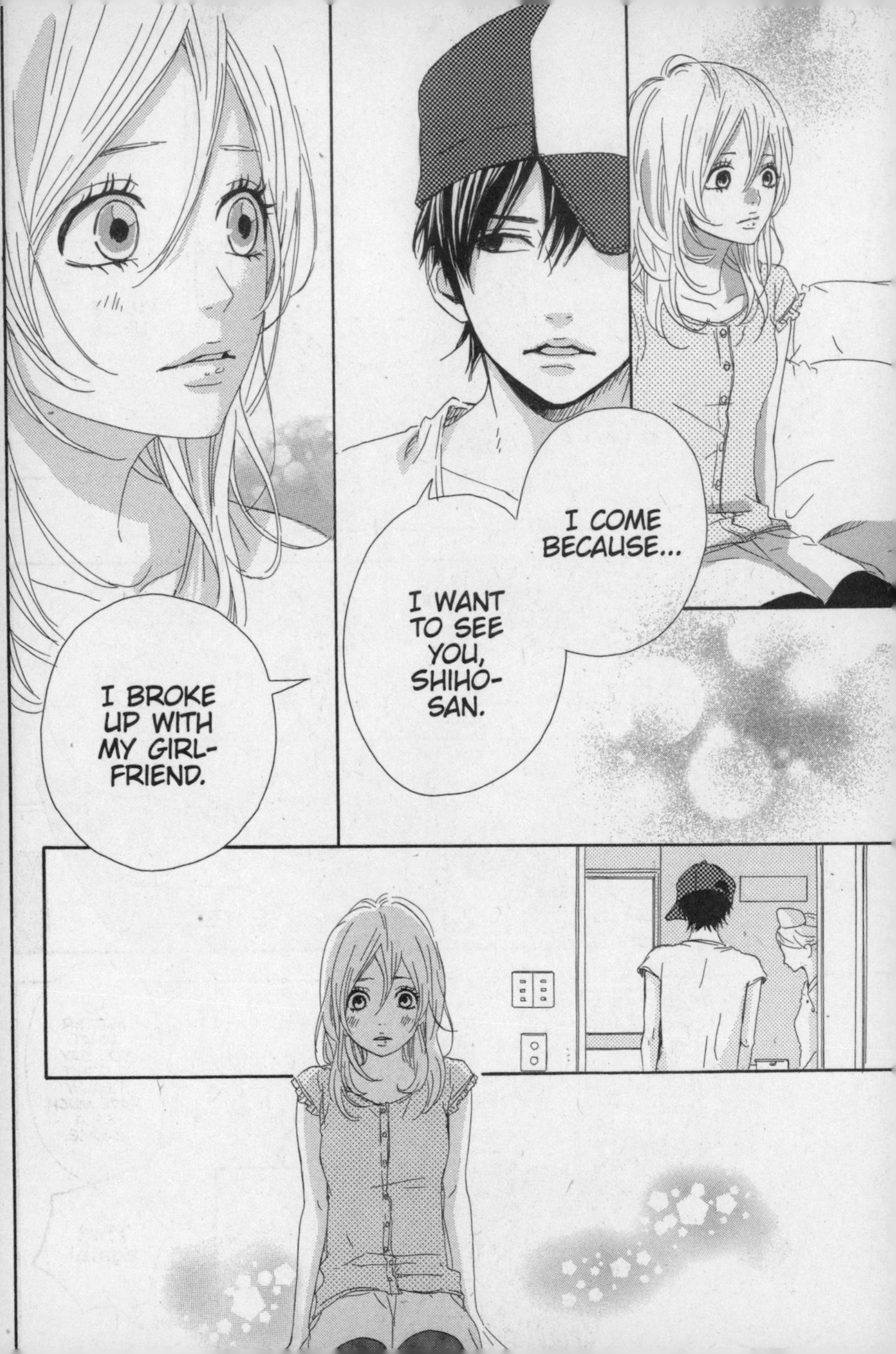
I COME BECAUSE...
I WANT TO SEE YOU, SHIHO-SAN.
I BROKE UP WITH MY GIRL-FRIEND.

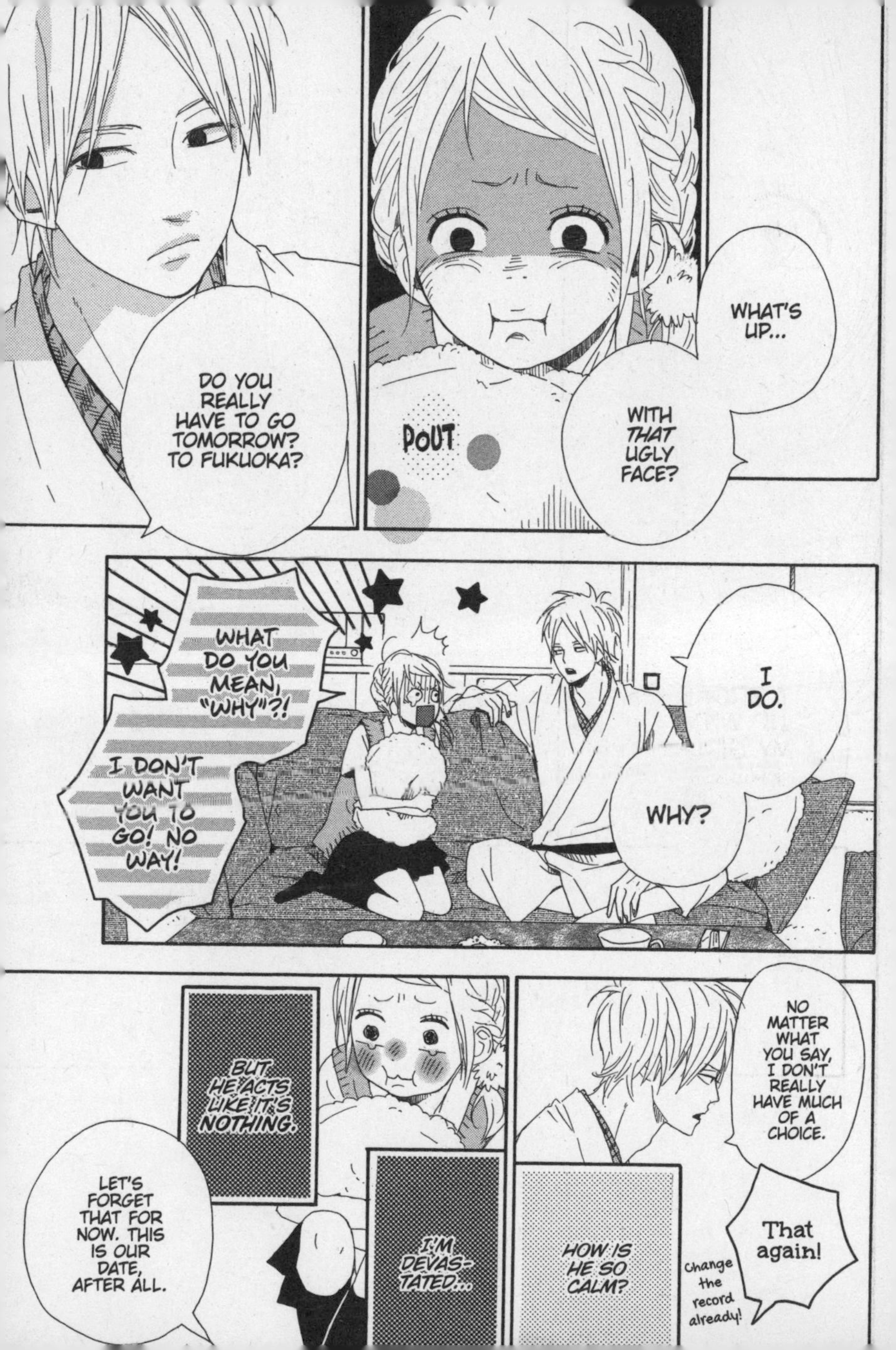
WHAT'S UP...
WITH THAT UGLY FACE?
POUT
DO YOU REALLY HAVE TO GO TOMORROW? TO FUKUOKA?
I DO.
WHY?
WHAT DO YOU MEAN, "WHY"?!
I DON'T WANT YOU TO GO! NO WAY!
NO MATTER WHAT YOU SAY, I DON'T REALLY HAVE MUCH OF A CHOICE.
That again!
Change the record already!
HOW IS HE SO CALM?
BUT HE ACTS LIKE IT'S NOTHING.
I'M DEVAS-TATED...
LET'S FORGET THAT FOR NOW. THIS IS OUR DATE, AFTER ALL.

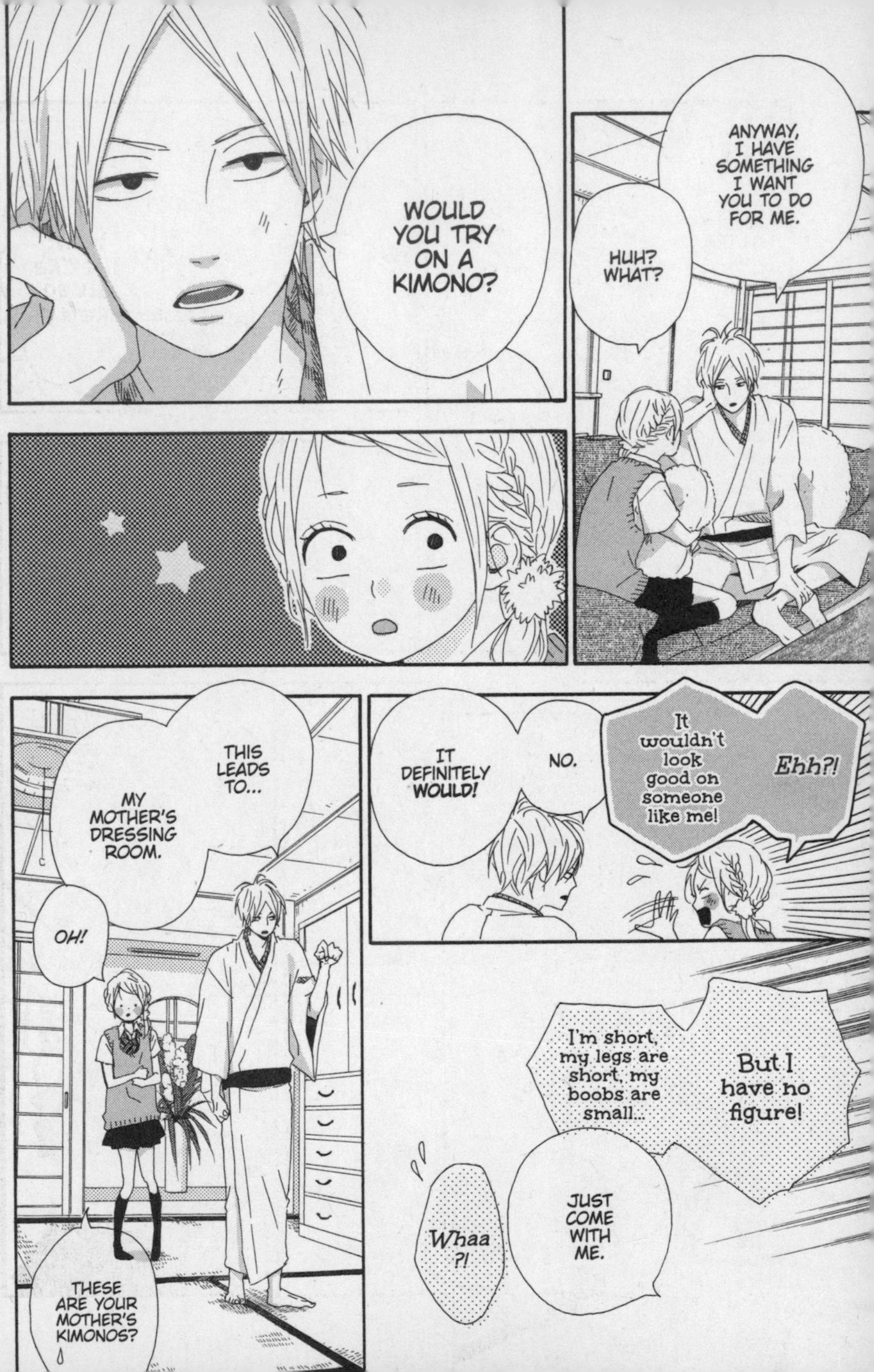
ANYWAY, I HAVE SOMETHING I WANT YOU TO DO FOR ME.
HUH? WHAT?
WOULD YOU TRY ON A KIMONO?
Ehh?!
It wouldn't look good on someone like me!
NO.
IT DEFINITELY WOULD!
But I have no figure!
I'm short, my legs are short, my boobs are small...
JUST COME WITH ME.
Whaa ?!
THIS LEADS TO...
MY MOTHER'S DRESSING ROOM.
OH!
THESE ARE YOUR MOTHER'S KIMONOS?

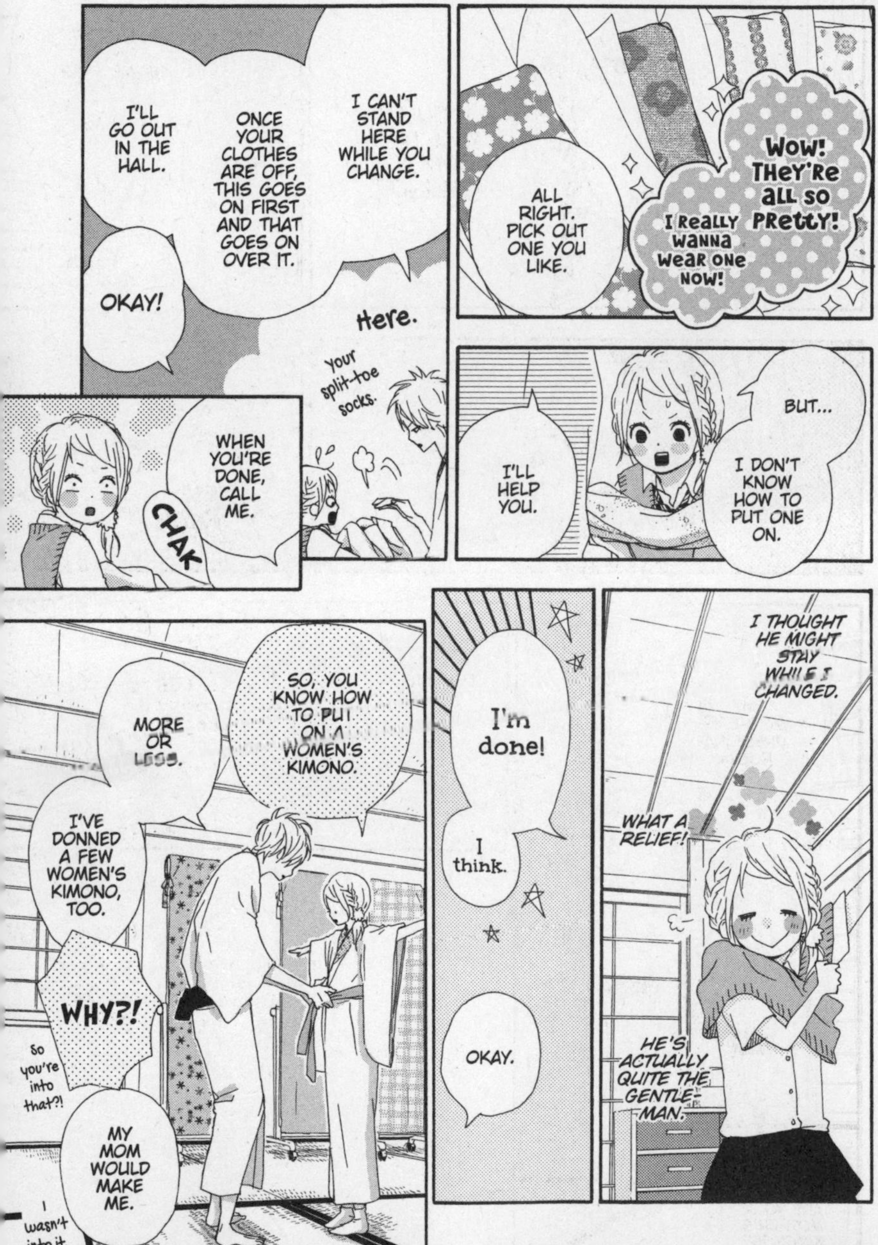
Wow! They're all so pretty!
I really wanna wear one now!
ALL RIGHT. PICK OUT ONE YOU LIKE.
I CAN'T STAND HERE WHILE YOU CHANGE.
ONCE YOUR CLOTHES ARE OFF, THIS GOES ON FIRST AND THAT GOES ON OVER IT.
I'LL GO OUT IN THE HALL.
OKAY!
BUT...
I DON'T KNOW HOW TO PUT ONE ON.
I'LL HELP YOU.
Here.
your split-toe socks.
WHEN YOU'RE DONE, CALL ME.
CHAK
I THOUGHT HE MIGHT STAY WHILE I CHANGED.
WHAT A RELIEF!
HE'S ACTUALLY QUITE THE GENTLEMAN.
I'm done!
I think.
OKAY.
SO, YOU KNOW HOW TO PUT ON A WOMEN'S KIMONO.
MORE OR LESS.
I'VE DONNED A FEW WOMEN'S KIMONO, TOO.
WHY?!
So you're into that?!
MY MOM WOULD MAKE ME.
I wasn't into it.

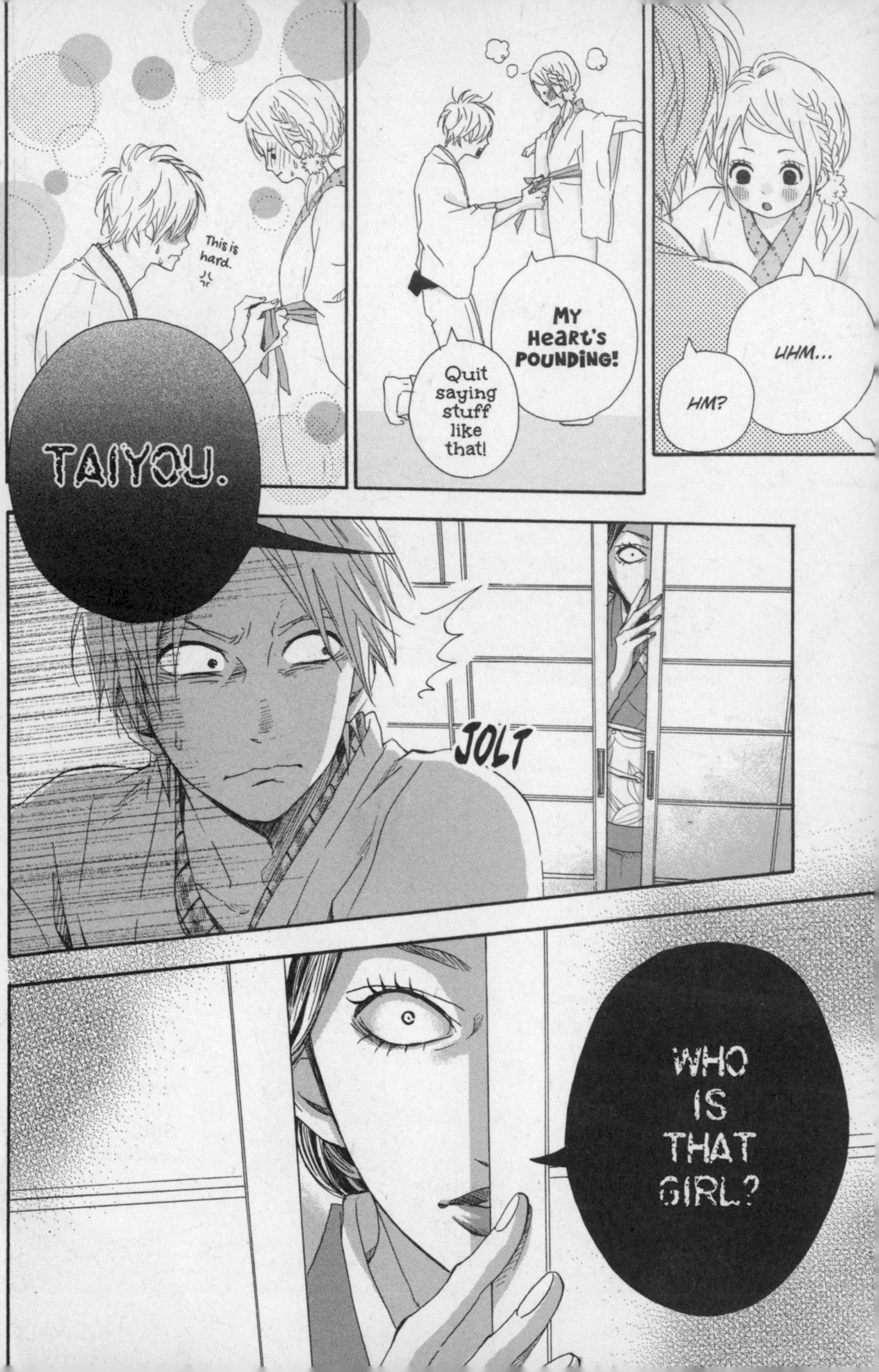
UHM...
HM?
MY Heart's POUNDING!
Quit saying stuff like that!
This is hard.
TAIYOU.
JOLT
WHO IS THAT GIRL?

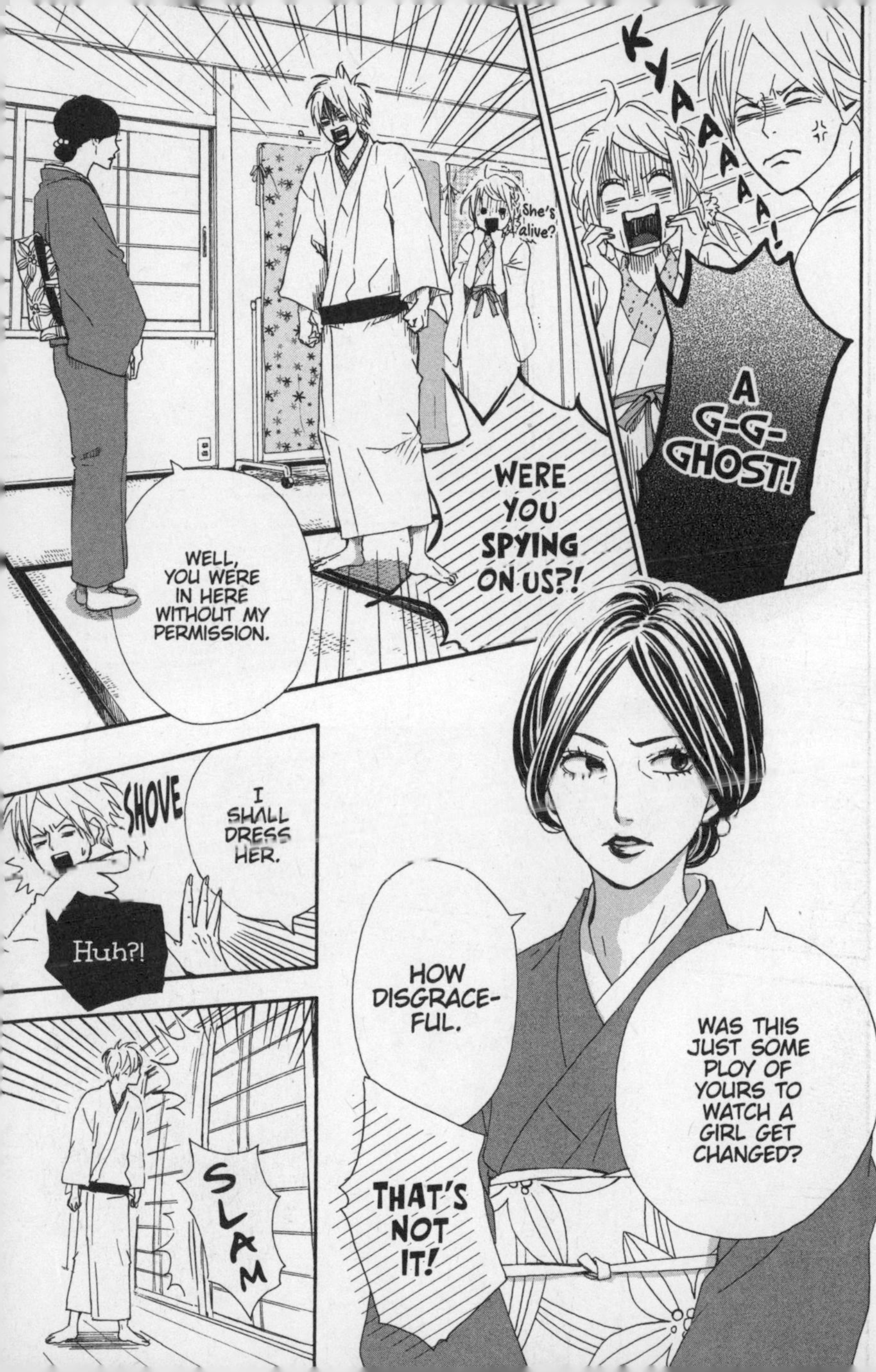
KYAAAAAA!
A G-G-GHOST!
She's alive?
WERE YOU SPYING ON US?!
WELL, YOU WERE IN HERE WITHOUT MY PERMISSION.
WAS THIS JUST SOME PLOY OF YOURS TO WATCH A GIRL GET CHANGED?
HOW DISGRACE-FUL.
THAT'S NOT IT!
I SHALL DRESS HER.
SHOVE
Huh?!
SLAM

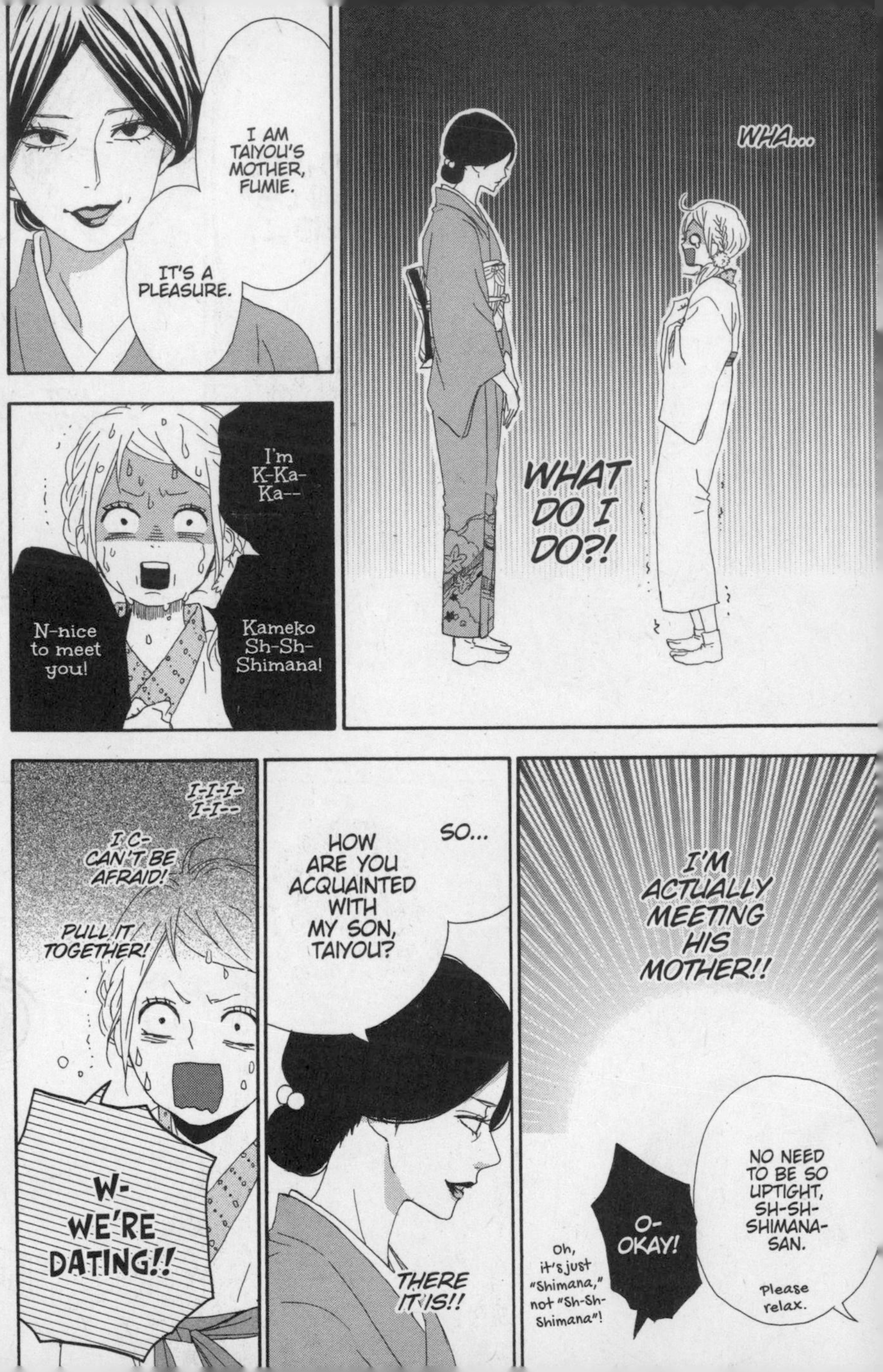
WHA...
WHAT DO I DO?!
I AM TAIYOU'S MOTHER, FUMIE.
IT'S A PLEASURE.
I'm K-Ka-Ka--
Kameko Sh-Sh-Shimana!
N-nice to meet you!
I'M ACTUALLY MEETING HIS MOTHER!!
NO NEED TO BE SO UPTIGHT, SH-SH-SHIMANA-SAN.
Please relax.
O-OKAY!
Oh, it's just "Shimana," not "Sh-Sh-Shimana"!
SO...
HOW ARE YOU ACQUAINTED WITH MY SON, TAIYOU?
THERE IT IS!!
I-I-I-I-I--
I C-CAN'T BE AFRAID!
PULL IT TOGETHER!
W-WE'RE DATING!!

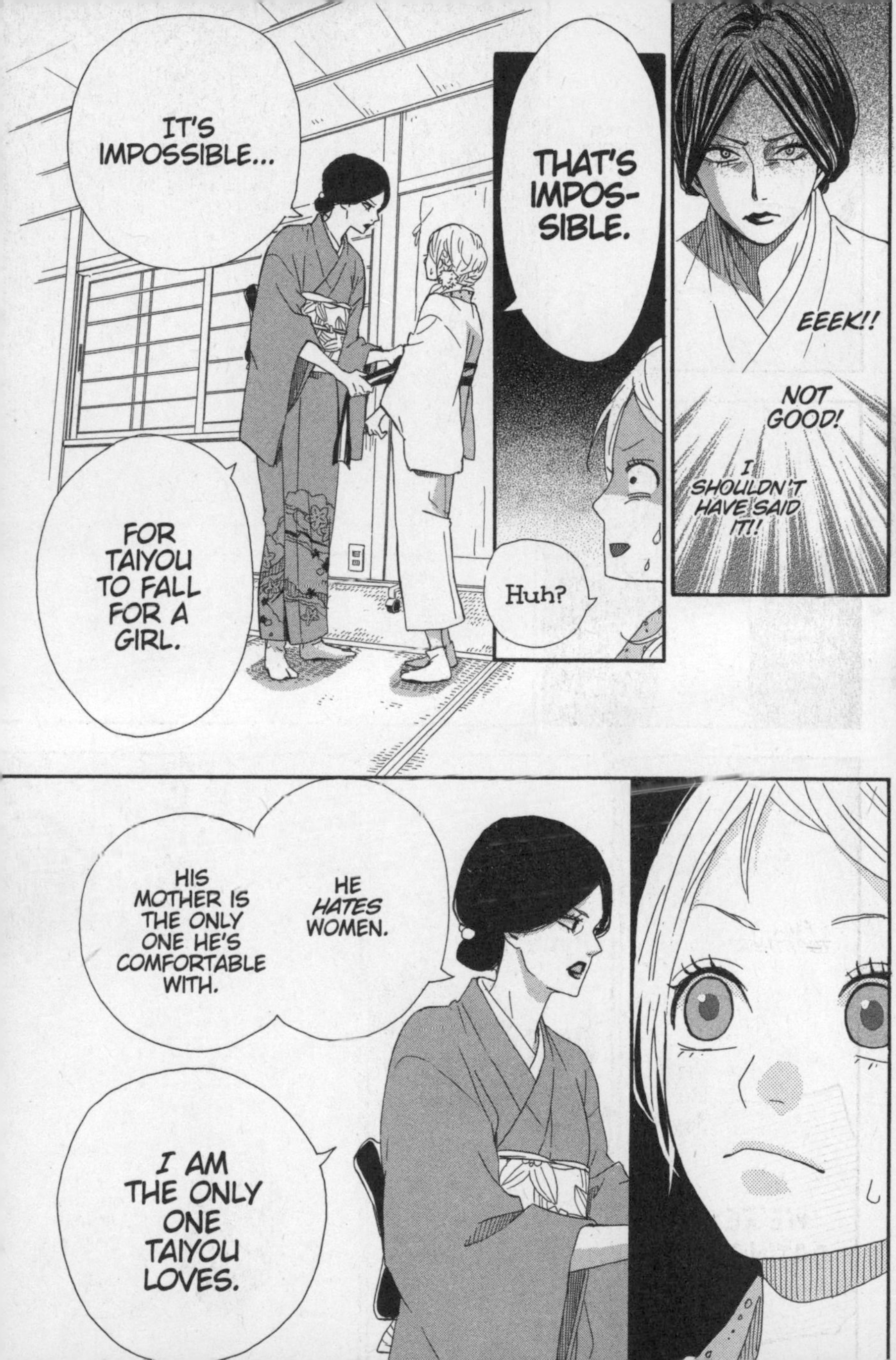
EEEK!!
NOT GOOD!
I SHOULDN'T HAVE SAID IT!!
THAT'S IMPOSSIBLE.
Huh?
IT'S IMPOSSIBLE...
FOR TAIYOU TO FALL FOR A GIRL.
HE HATES WOMEN.
HIS MOTHER IS THE ONLY ONE HE'S COMFORTABLE WITH.
I AM THE ONLY ONE TAIYOU LOVES.

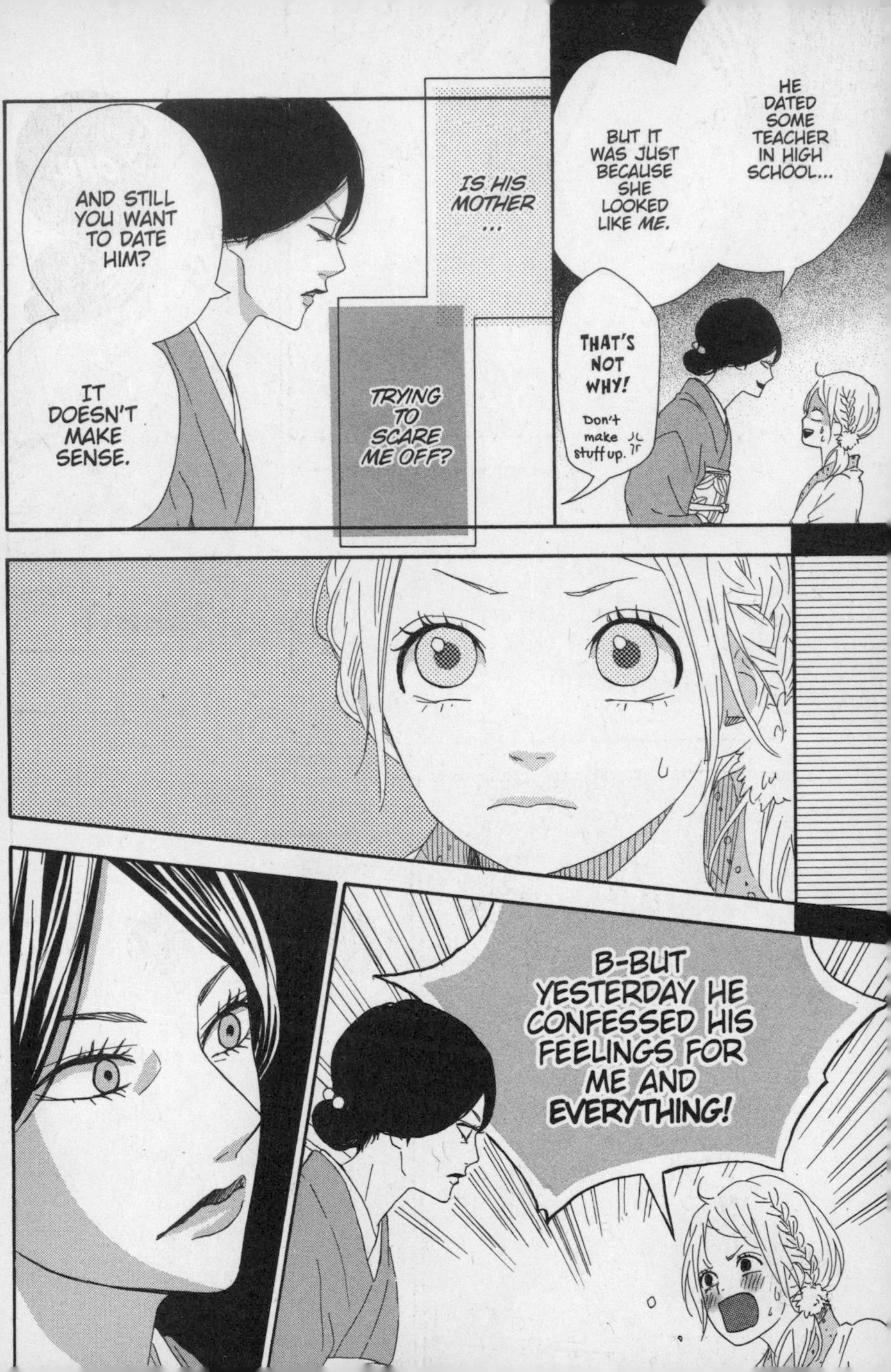
HE DATED SOME TEACHER IN HIGH SCHOOL...
BUT IT WAS JUST BECAUSE SHE LOOKED LIKE ME.
THAT'S NOT WHY!
Don't make stuff up.
IS HIS MOTHER ...
TRYING TO SCARE ME OFF?
AND STILL YOU WANT TO DATE HIM?
IT DOESN'T MAKE SENSE.
B-BUT YESTERDAY HE CONFESSED HIS FEELINGS FOR ME AND EVERYTHING!

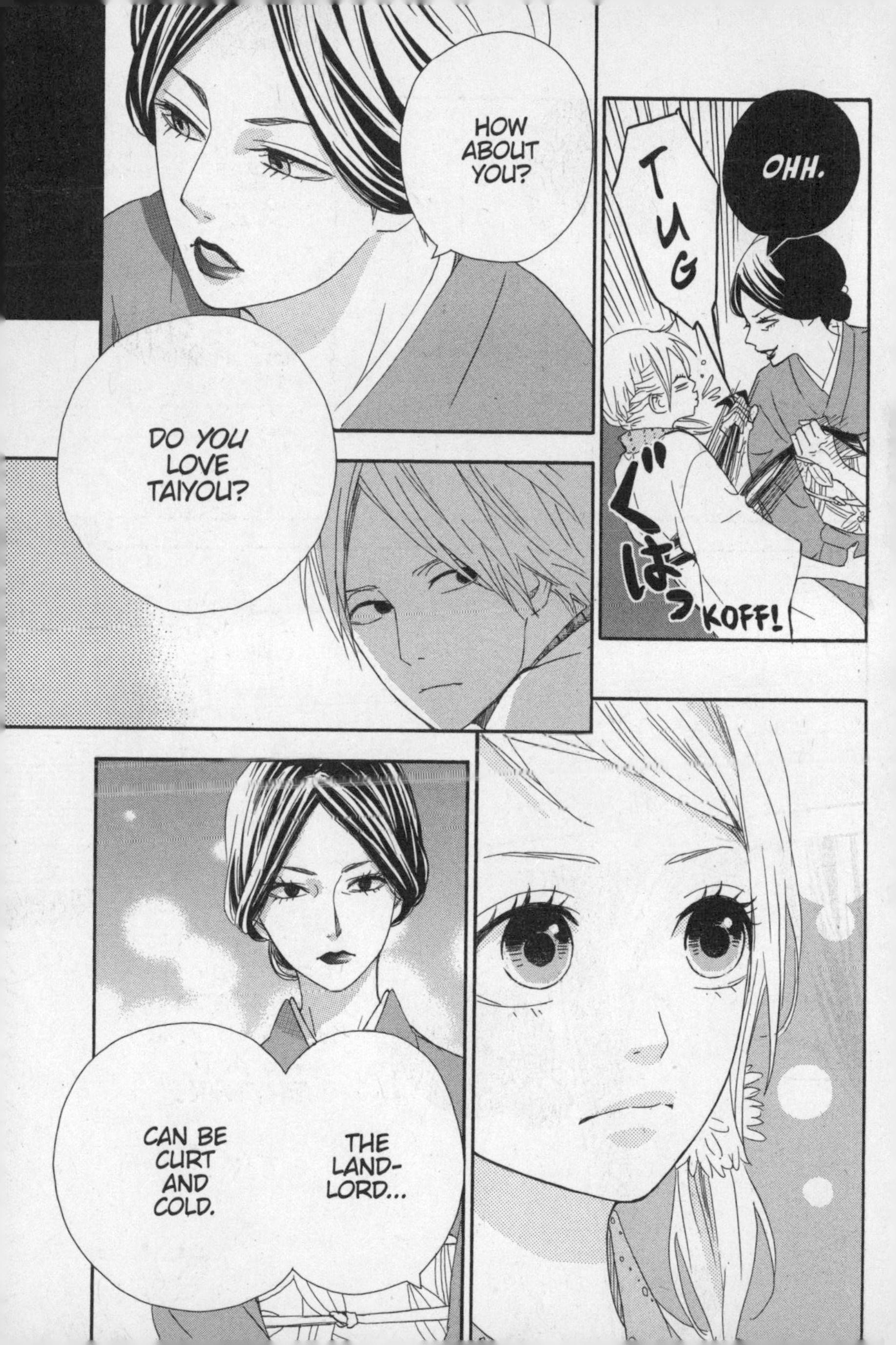
OHH.
TUG
ぐぱっ
KOFF!
HOW ABOUT YOU?
DO YOU LOVE TAIYOU?
THE LAND-LORD...
CAN BE CURT AND COLD.

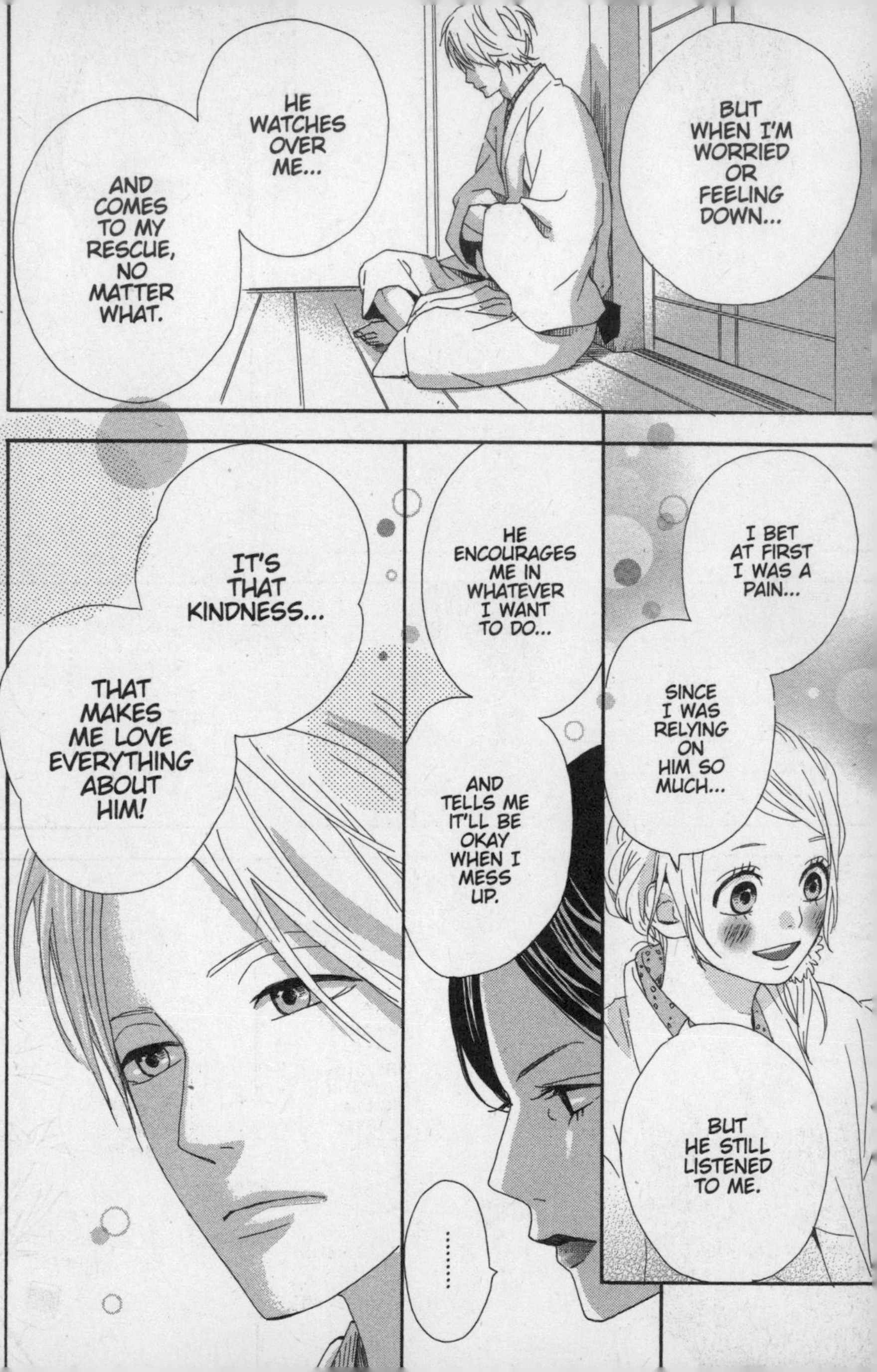
BUT WHEN I'M WORRIED OR FEELING DOWN...
HE WATCHES OVER ME...
AND COMES TO MY RESCUE, NO MATTER WHAT.
I BET AT FIRST I WAS A PAIN...
SINCE I WAS RELYING ON HIM SO MUCH...
BUT HE STILL LISTENED TO ME.
HE ENCOURAGES ME IN WHATEVER I WANT TO DO...
AND TELLS ME IT'LL BE OKAY WHEN I MESS UP.
......
IT'S THAT KINDNESS...
THAT MAKES ME LOVE EVERYTHING ABOUT HIM!

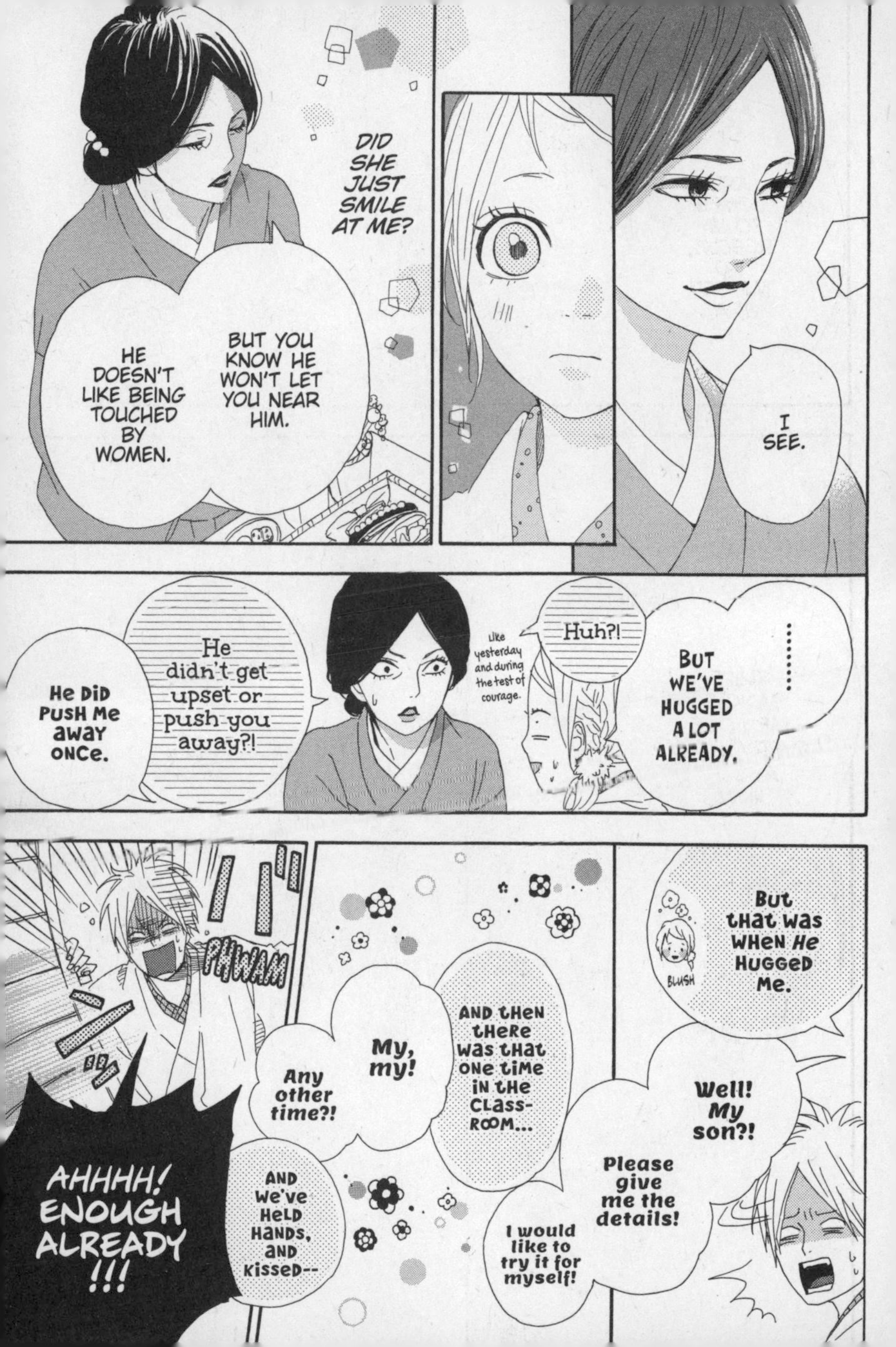
I SEE.
DID SHE JUST SMILE AT ME?
BUT YOU KNOW HE WON'T LET YOU NEAR HIM.
HE DOESN'T LIKE BEING TOUCHED BY WOMEN.
......
BUT WE'VE HUGGED A LOT ALREADY.
Huh?!
Like yesterday and during the test of courage.
He didn't get upset or push you away?!
He DID push me away once.
BLUSH
But that was when He hugged me.
Well! My son?!
Please give me the details!
I would like to try it for myself!
AND then there was that one time in the CLASS-ROOM...
My, my!
Any other time?!
AND we've HELD HANDS, AND KISSED--
PHWAM
AHHHH! ENOUGH ALREADY!!!

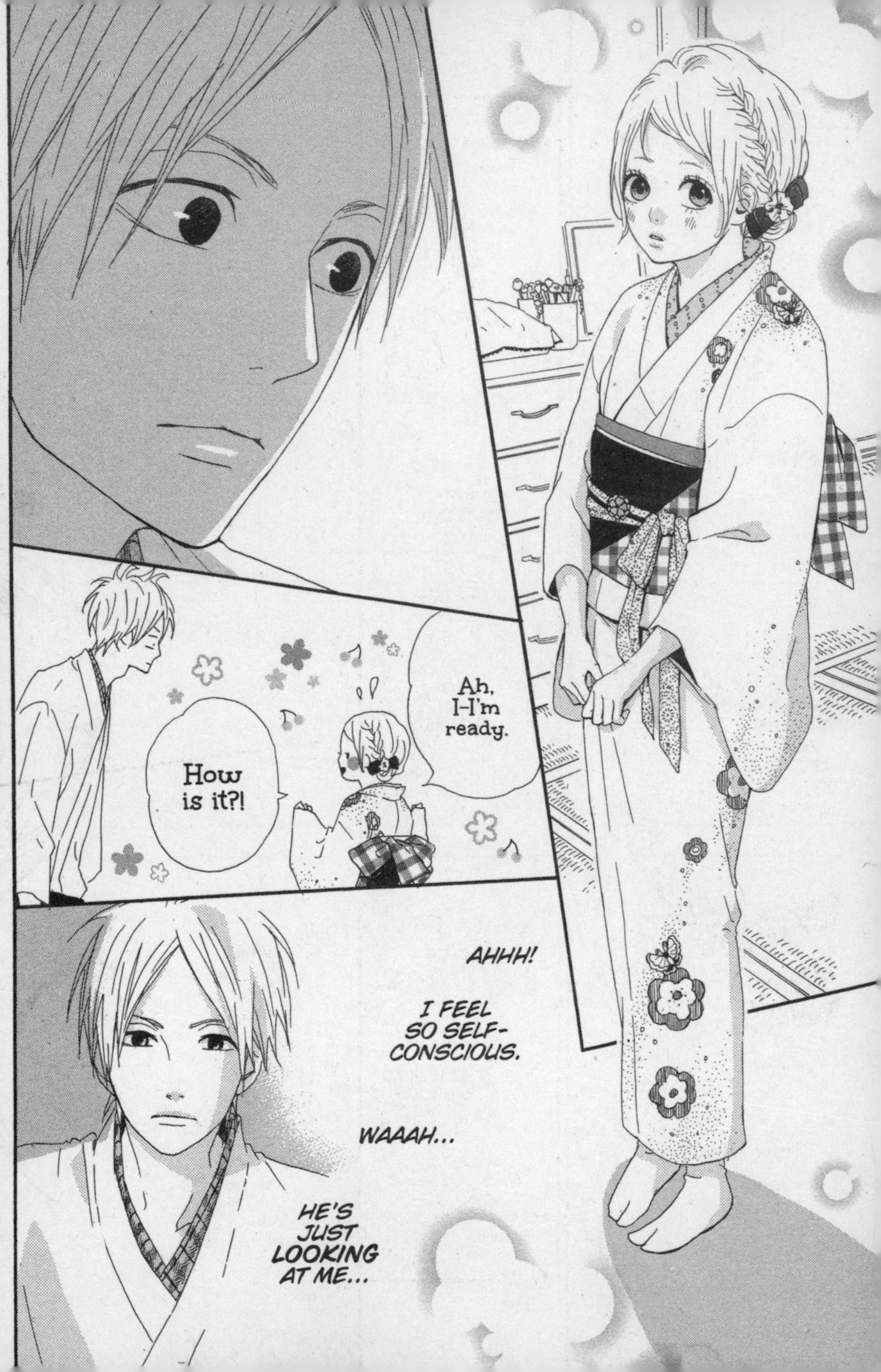
Ah, I-I'm ready.
How is it?!
AHHH!
I FEEL SO SELF-CONSCIOUS.
WAAAH...
HE'S JUST LOOKING AT ME...

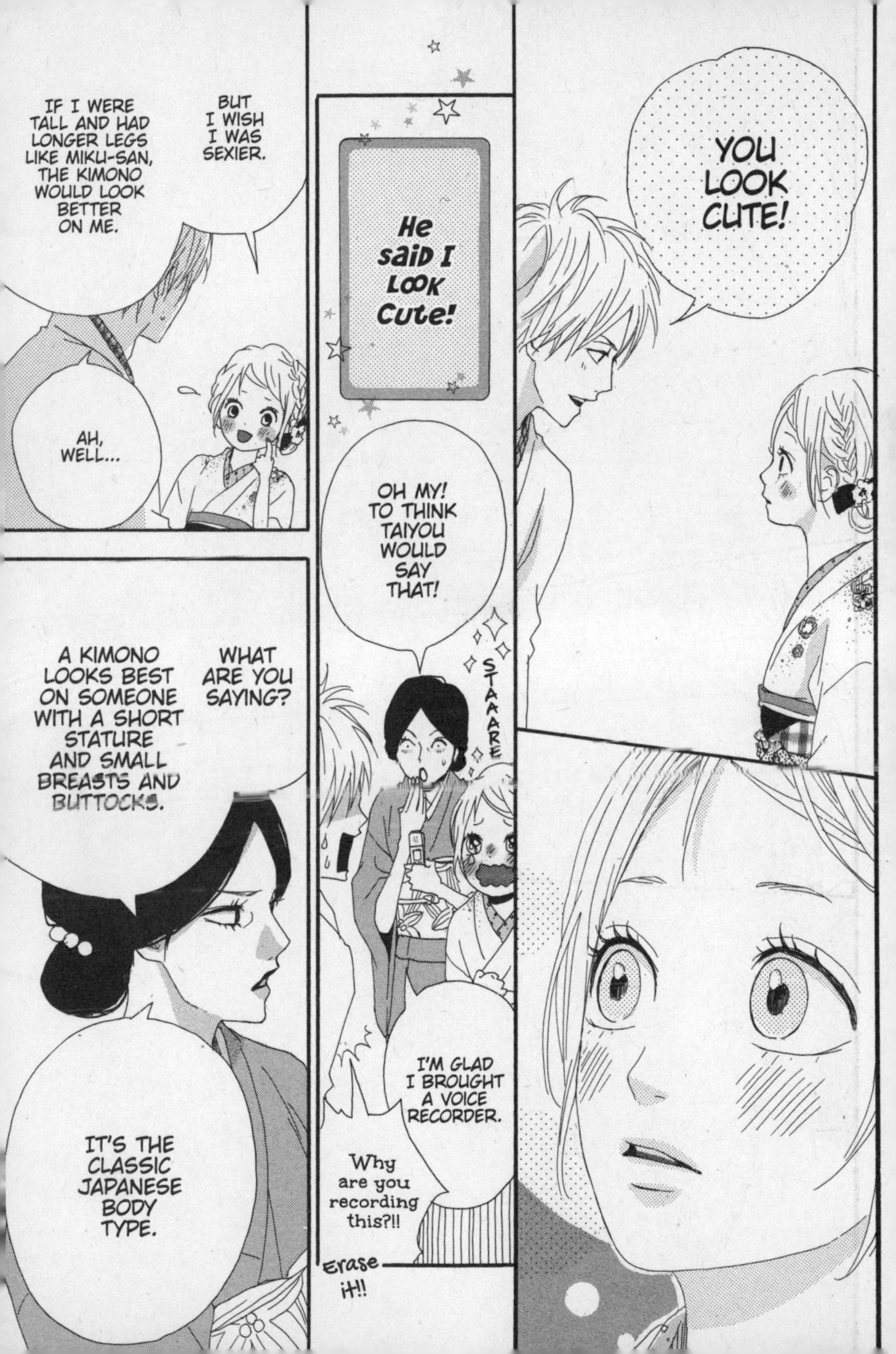
YOU LOOK CUTE!
He said I look cute!
OH MY! TO THINK TAIYOU WOULD SAY THAT!
STAAARE
I'M GLAD I BROUGHT A VOICE RECORDER.
Why are you recording this?!!
Erase it!!
BUT I WISH I WAS SEXIER.
IF I WERE TALL AND HAD LONGER LEGS LIKE MIKU-SAN, THE KIMONO WOULD LOOK BETTER ON ME.
AH, WELL...
WHAT ARE YOU SAYING?
A KIMONO LOOKS BEST ON SOMEONE WITH A SHORT STATURE AND SMALL BREASTS AND BUTTOCKS.
IT'S THE CLASSIC JAPANESE BODY TYPE.

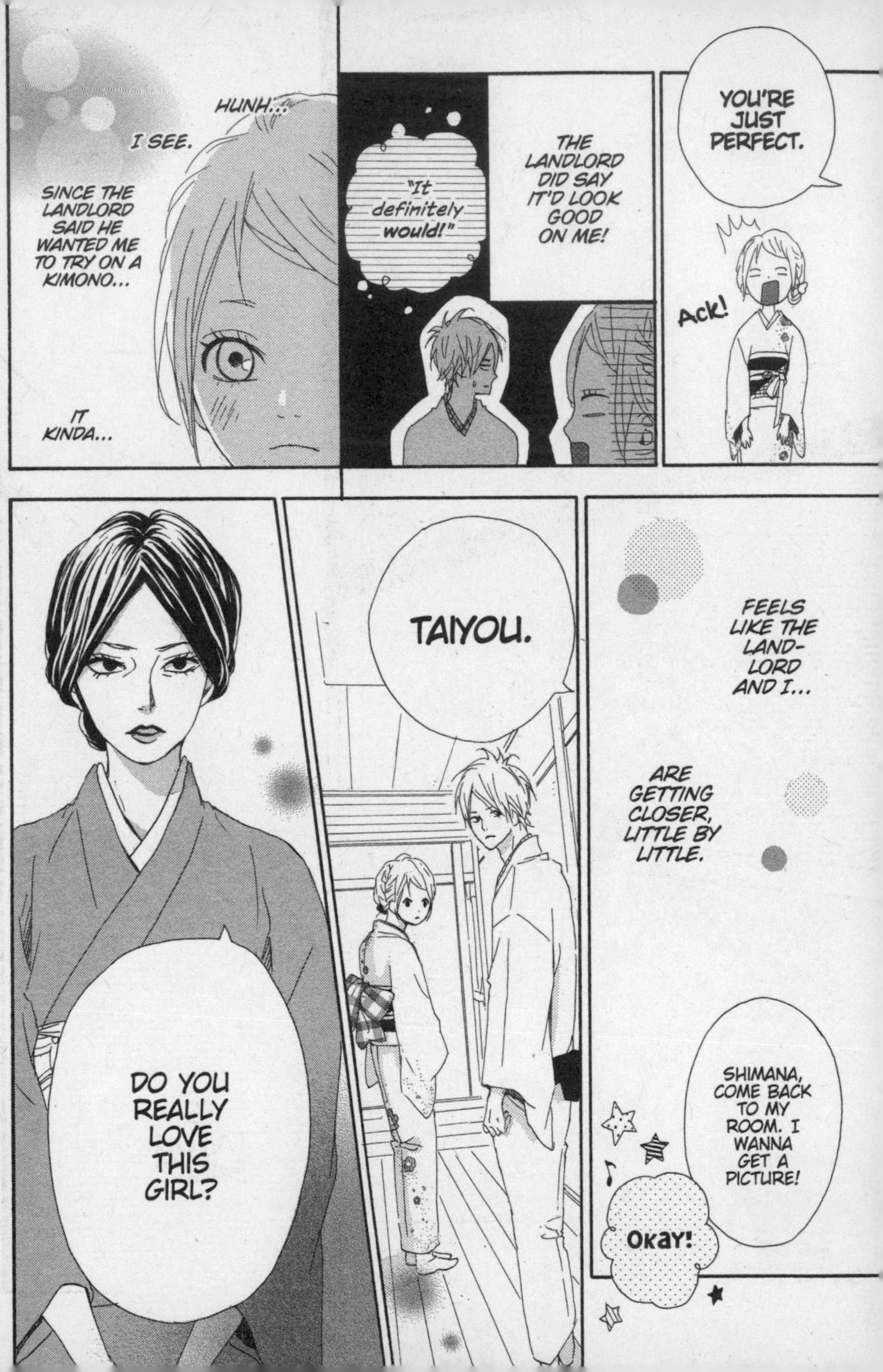
YOU'RE JUST PERFECT.
Ack!
THE LANDLORD DID SAY IT'D LOOK GOOD ON ME!
"It definitely would!"
HUNH... I SEE.
SINCE THE LANDLORD SAID HE WANTED ME TO TRY ON A KIMONO...
IT KINDA...
FEELS LIKE THE LAND-LORD AND I...
ARE GETTING CLOSER, LITTLE BY LITTLE.
SHIMANA, COME BACK TO MY ROOM. I WANNA GET A PICTURE!
Okay!
TAIYOU.
DO YOU REALLY LOVE THIS GIRL?

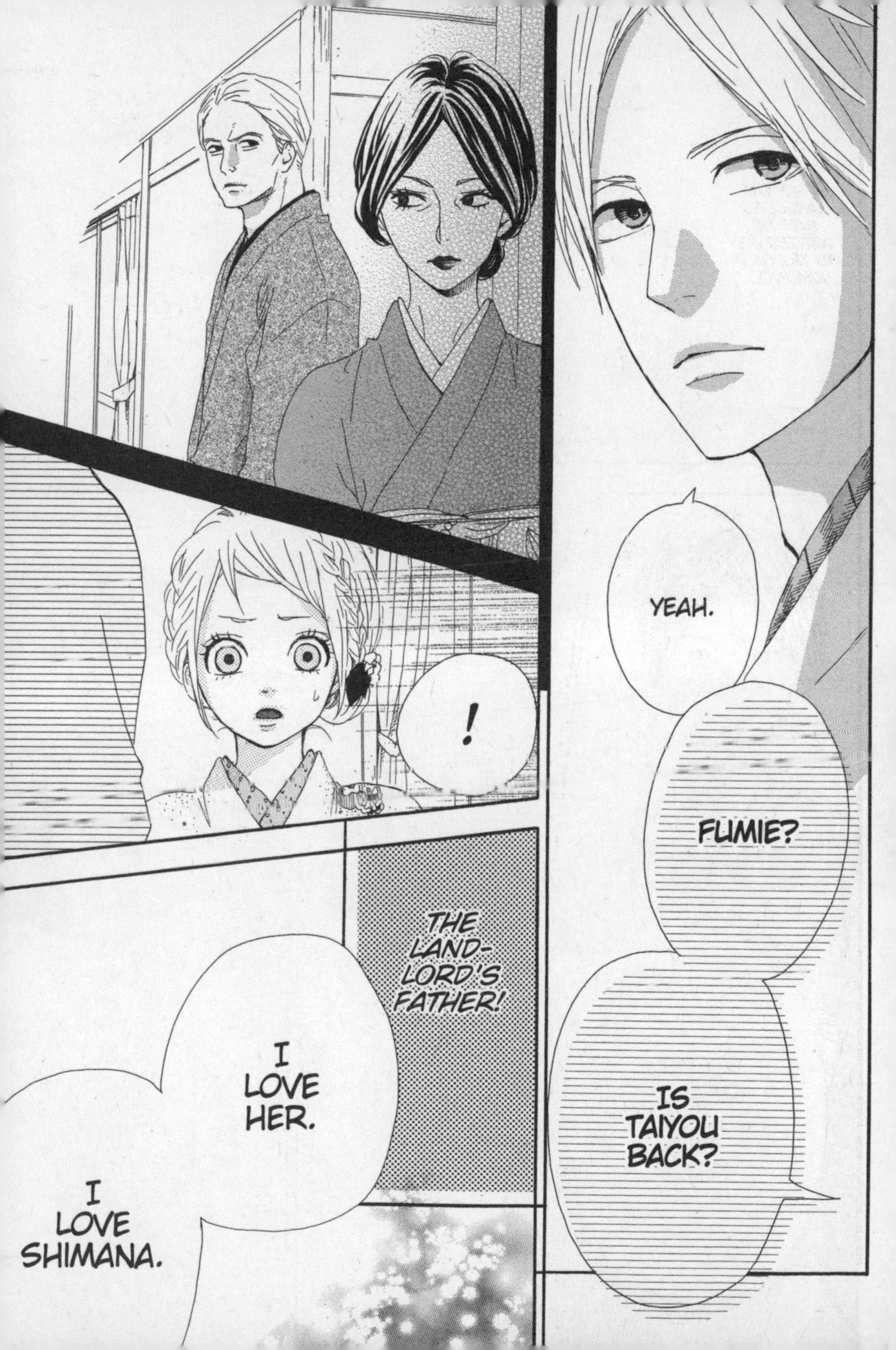
YEAH.
FUMIE?
IS TAIYOU BACK?
!
THE LAND-LORD'S FATHER!
I LOVE HER.
I LOVE SHIMANA.

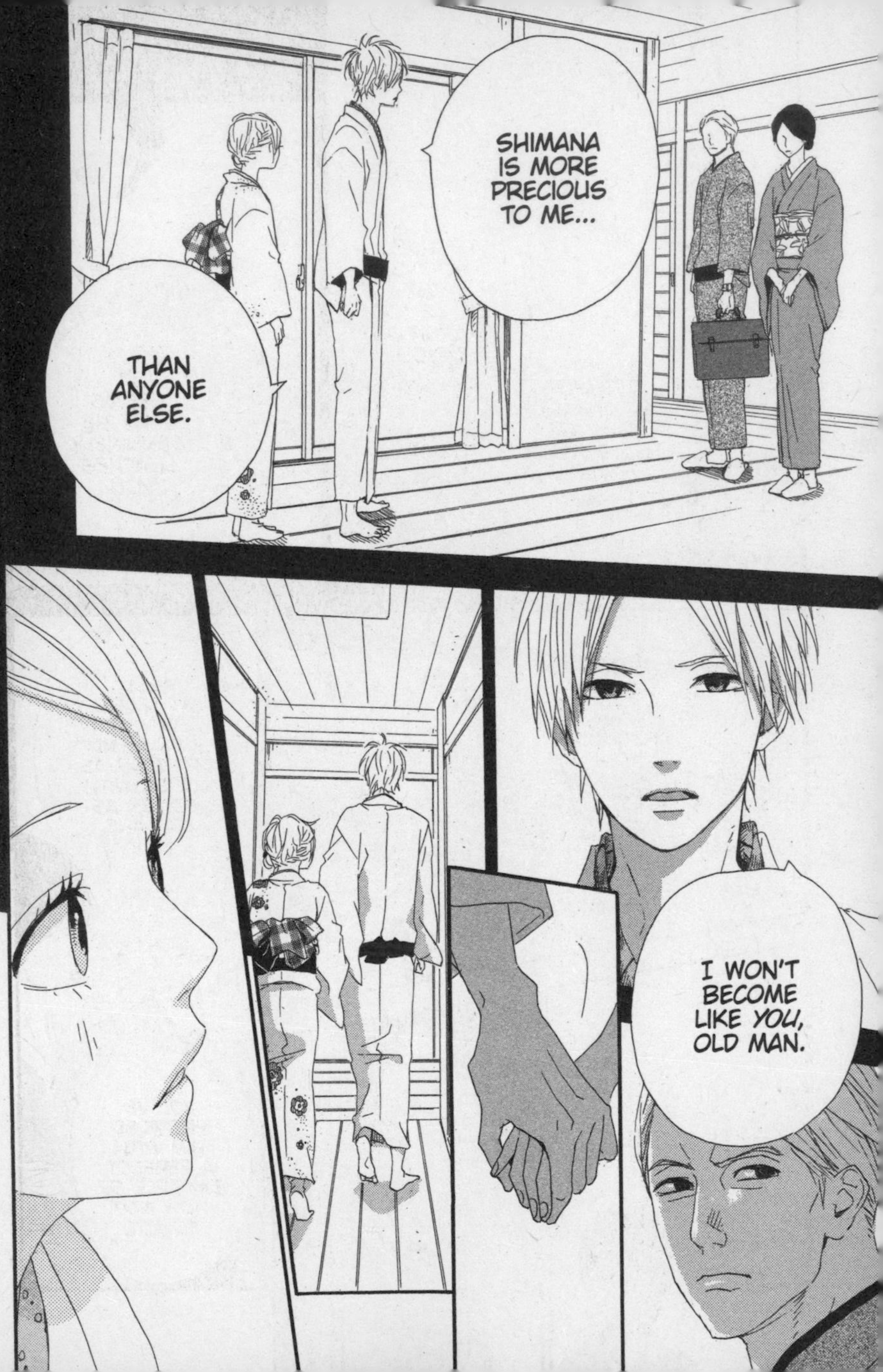
SHIMANA IS MORE PRECIOUS TO ME...
THAN ANYONE ELSE.
I WON'T BECOME LIKE *YOU*, OLD MAN.

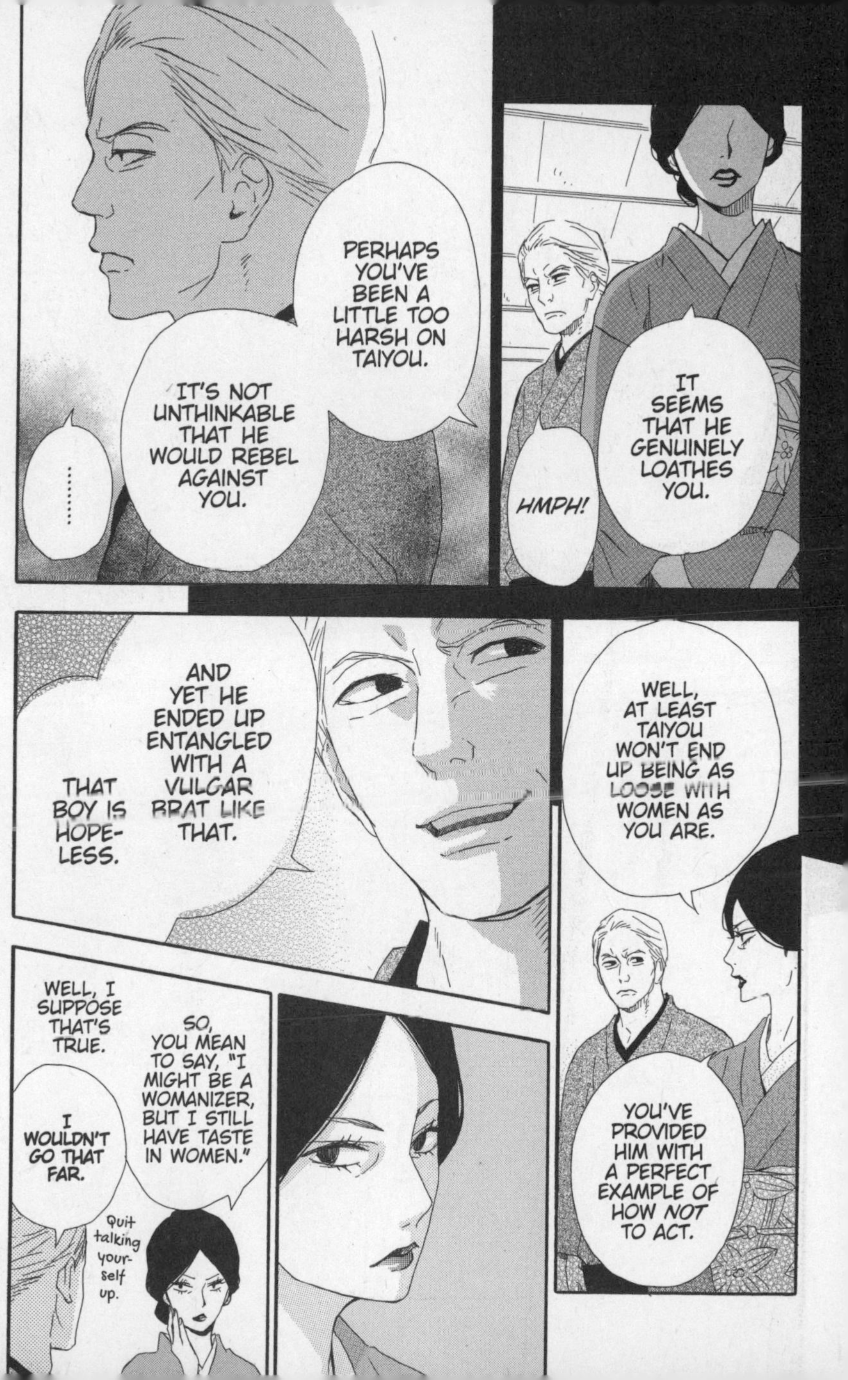
IT SEEMS THAT HE GENUINELY LOATHES YOU.
HMPH!
PERHAPS YOU'VE BEEN A LITTLE TOO HARSH ON TAIYOU.
IT'S NOT UNTHINKABLE THAT HE WOULD REBEL AGAINST YOU.
......
WELL, AT LEAST TAIYOU WON'T END UP BEING AS LOOSE WITH WOMEN AS YOU ARE.
YOU'VE PROVIDED HIM WITH A PERFECT EXAMPLE OF HOW *NOT* TO ACT.
AND YET HE ENDED UP ENTANGLED WITH A VULGAR BRAT LIKE THAT.
THAT BOY IS HOPELESS.
SO, YOU MEAN TO SAY, "I MIGHT BE A WOMANIZER, BUT I STILL HAVE TASTE IN WOMEN."
WELL, I SUPPOSE THAT'S TRUE.
I WOULDN'T GO THAT FAR.
Quit talking yourself up.

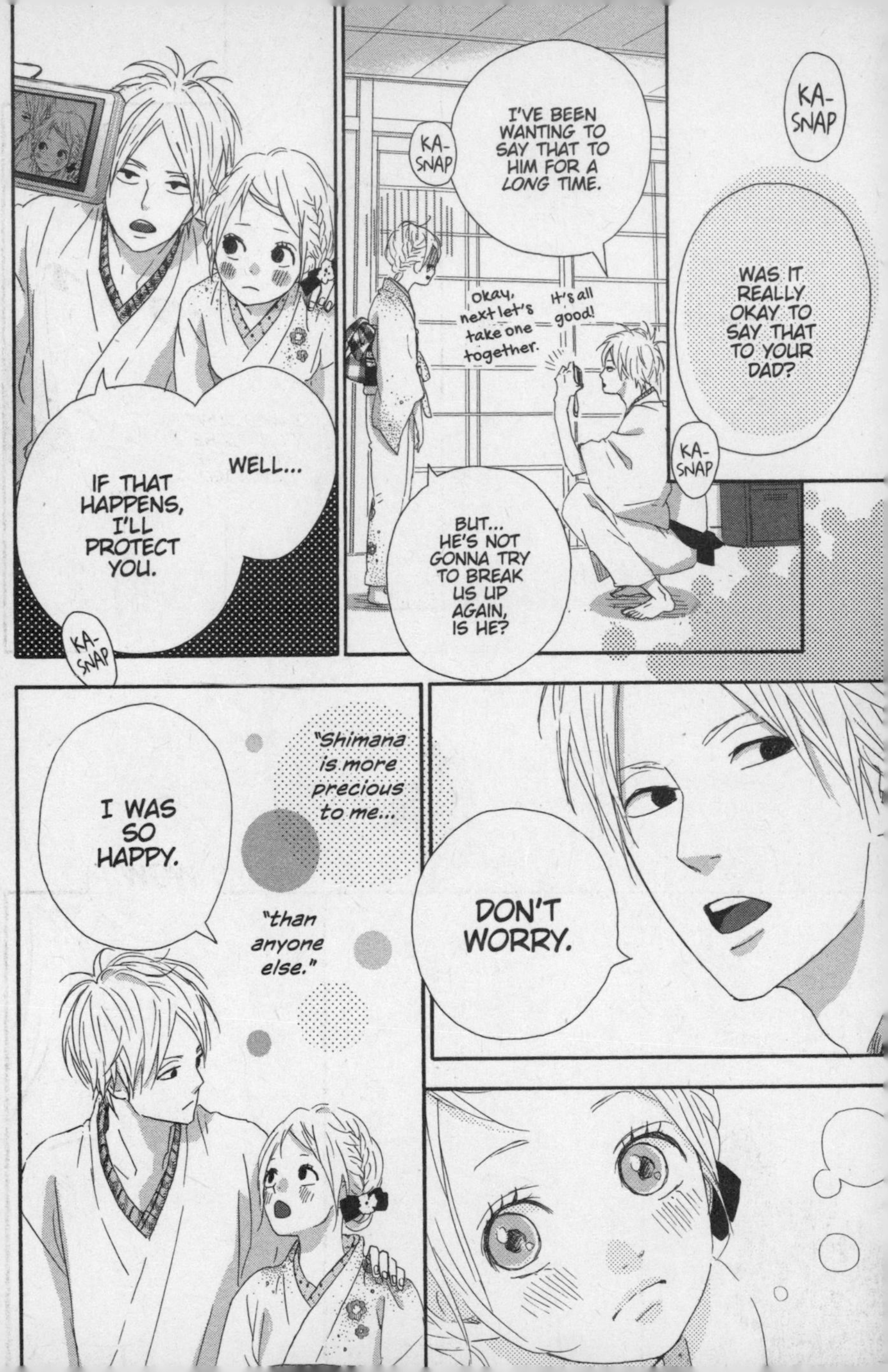
KA-SNAP
WAS IT REALLY OKAY TO SAY THAT TO YOUR DAD?
KA-SNAP
I'VE BEEN WANTING TO SAY THAT TO HIM FOR A LONG TIME.
KA-SNAP
It's all good!
Okay, next let's take one together.
BUT... HE'S NOT GONNA TRY TO BREAK US UP AGAIN, IS HE?
WELL...
IF THAT HAPPENS, I'LL PROTECT YOU.
KA-SNAP
DON'T WORRY.
"Shimana is more precious to me...
"than anyone else."
I WAS SO HAPPY.

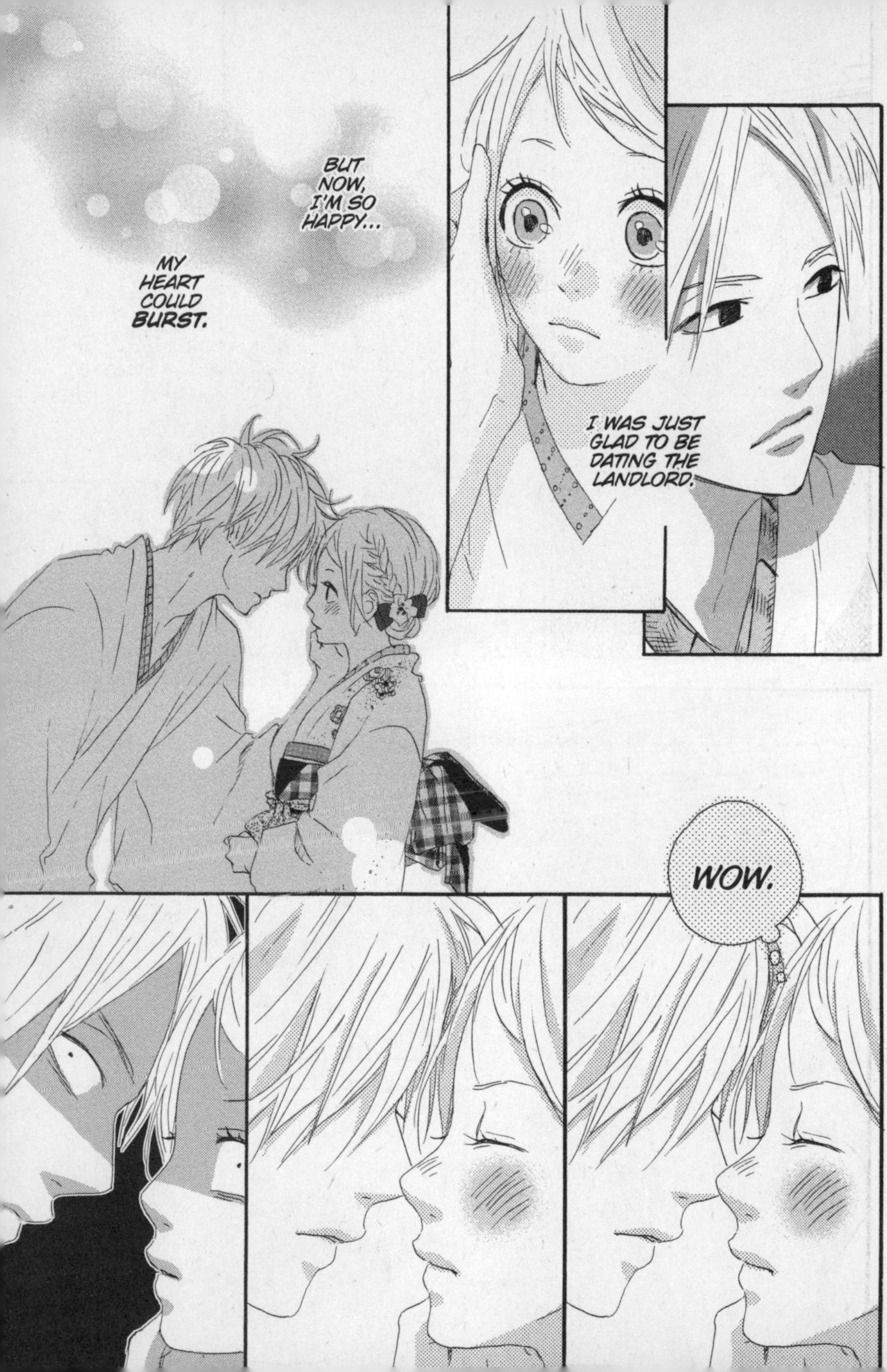
I WAS JUST GLAD TO BE DATING THE LANDLORD.
BUT NOW, I'M SO HAPPY...
MY HEART COULD BURST.
WOW.

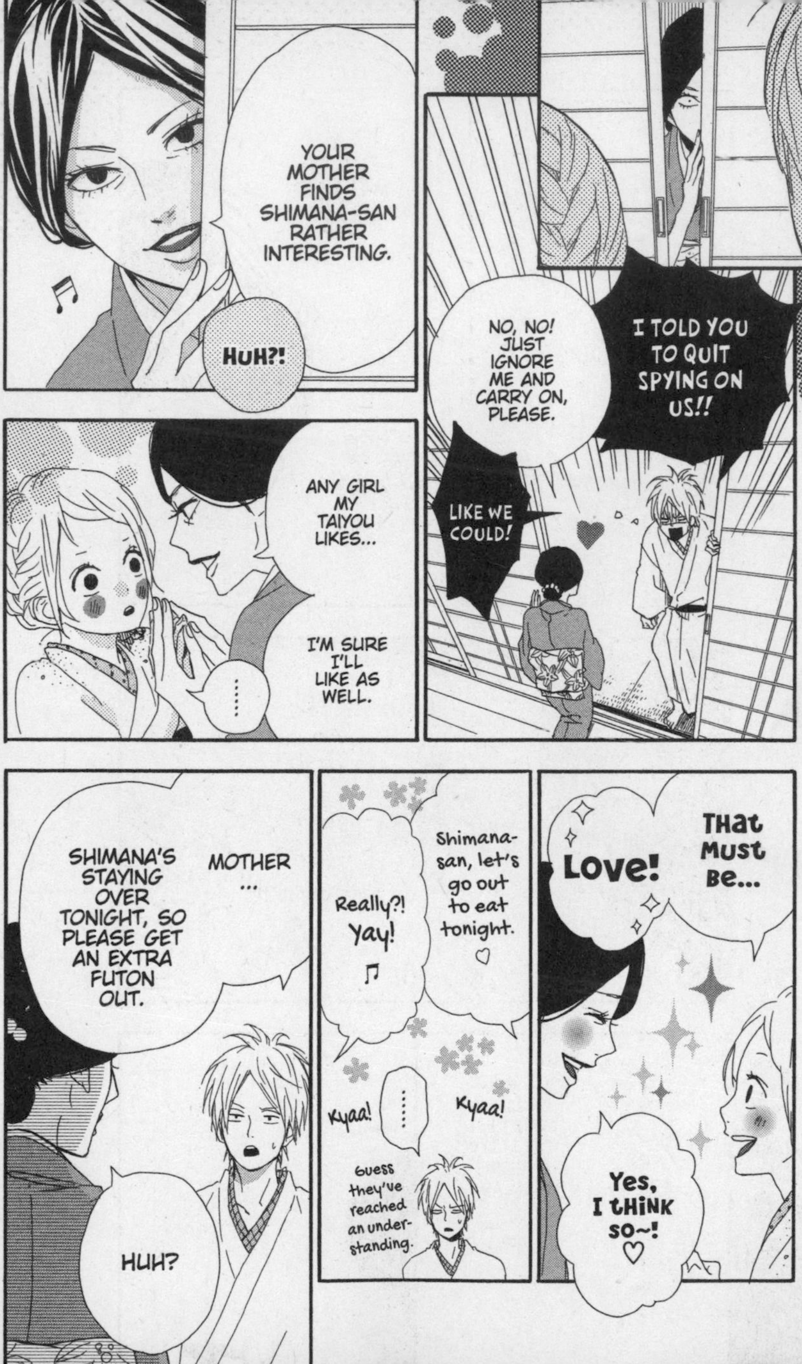
I TOLD YOU TO QUIT SPYING ON US!!
NO, NO! JUST IGNORE ME AND CARRY ON, PLEASE.
LIKE WE COULD!
YOUR MOTHER FINDS SHIMANA-SAN RATHER INTERESTING.
HUH?!
ANY GIRL MY TAIYOU LIKES...
I'M SURE I'LL LIKE AS WELL.
......
That Must Be...
Love!
Yes, I tHink so~! ♡
Shimana-san, let's go out to eat tonight. ♡
Really?! Yay! ♫
Kyaa!
......
Kyaa!
Guess they've reached an under-standing.
MOTHER ...
SHIMANA'S STAYING OVER TONIGHT, SO PLEASE GET AN EXTRA FUTON OUT.
HUH?

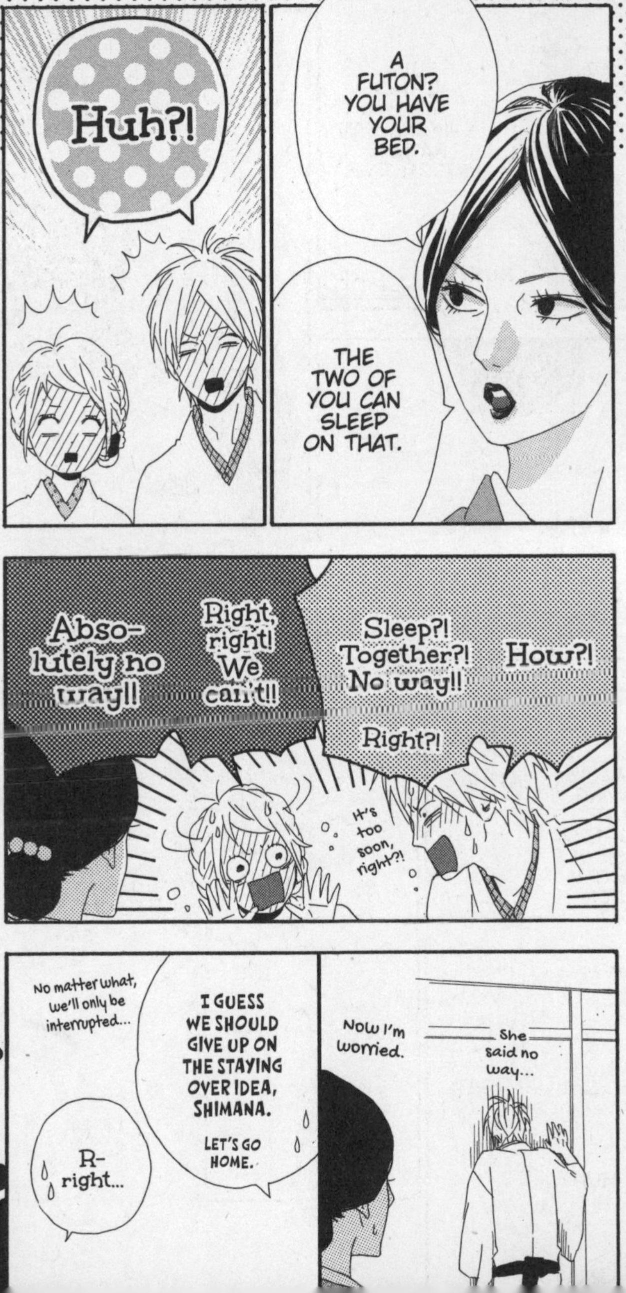
A FUTON? YOU HAVE YOUR BED.
THE TWO OF YOU CAN SLEEP ON THAT.
Huh?!
Sleep?! Together?! No way!! How?! Right?!
It's too soon, right?!
Right, right! We can't!!
Abso-lutely no way!!
She said no way...
Now I'm worried.
I GUESS WE SHOULD GIVE UP ON THE STAYING OVER IDEA, SHIMANA.
LET'S GO HOME.
No matter what, we'll only be interrupted...
R-right...

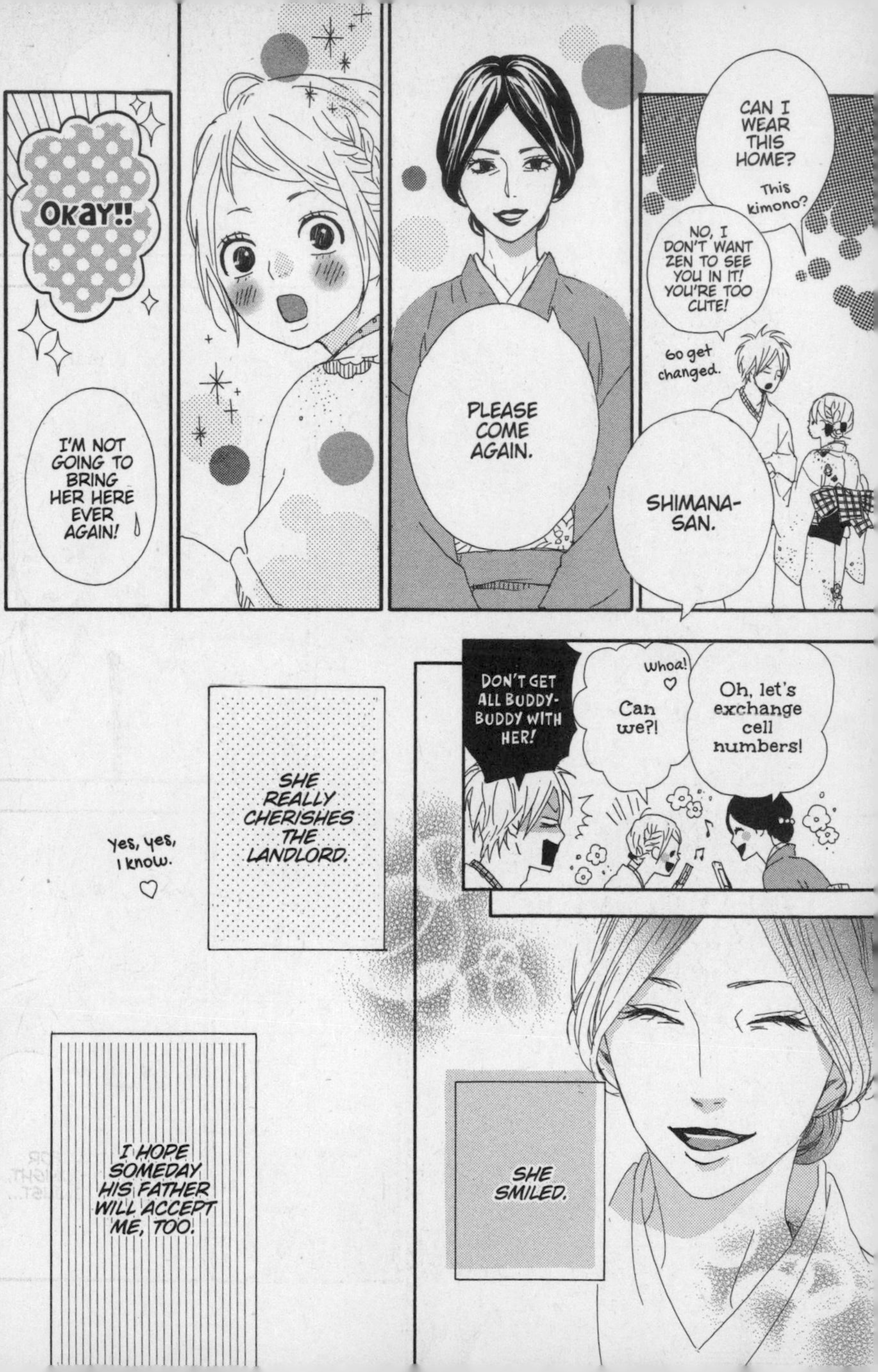
CAN I WEAR THIS HOME?
This kimono?
NO, I DON'T WANT ZEN TO SEE YOU IN IT! YOU'RE TOO CUTE!
Go get changed.
SHIMANA-SAN.
PLEASE COME AGAIN.
OKAY!!
I'M NOT GOING TO BRING HER HERE EVER AGAIN!
Oh, let's exchange cell numbers!
Whoa! ♡
Can we?!
DON'T GET ALL BUDDY-BUDDY WITH HER!
SHE SMILED.
SHE REALLY CHERISHES THE LANDLORD.
Yes, yes, I know. ♡
I HOPE SOMEDAY HIS FATHER WILL ACCEPT ME, TOO.

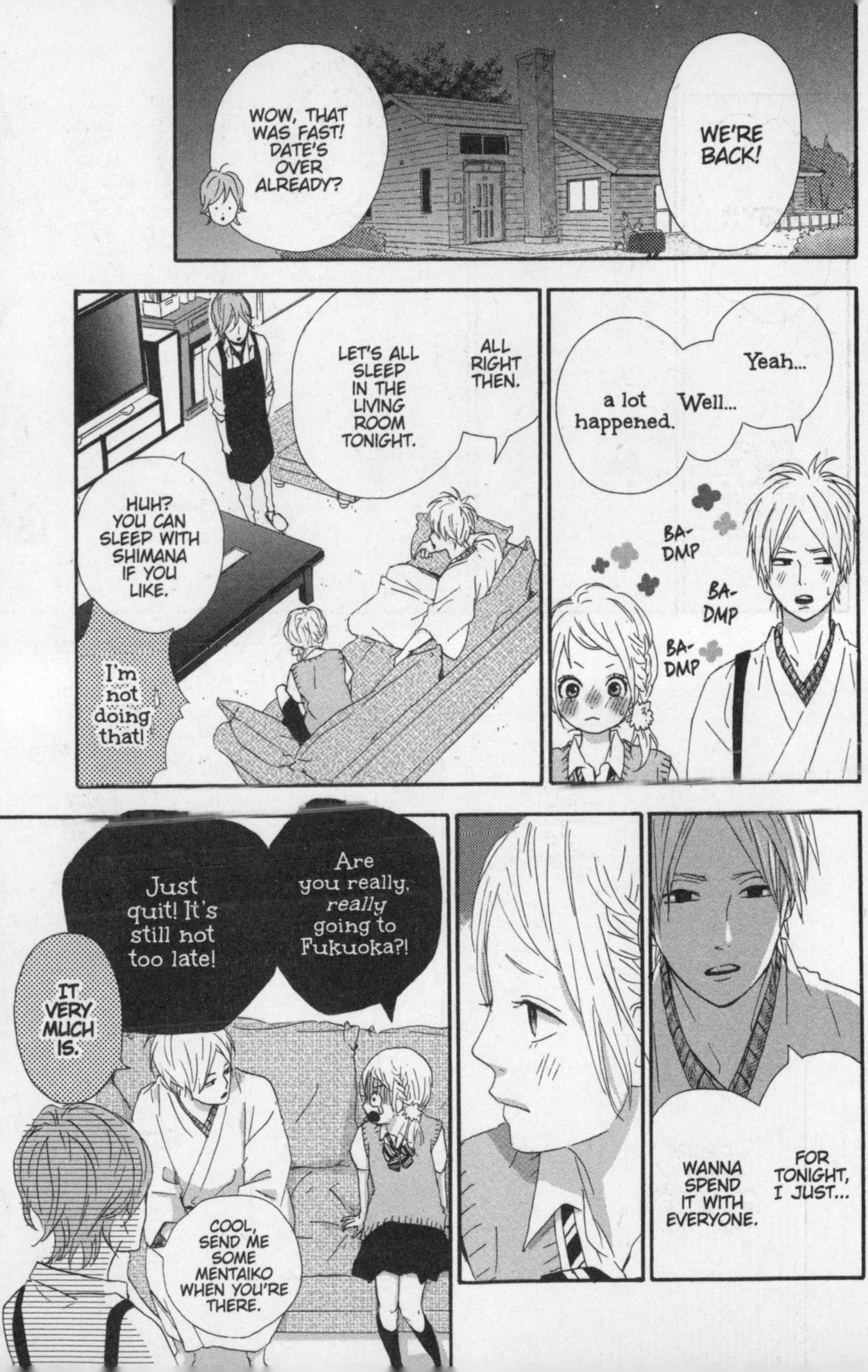
WE'RE BACK!
WOW, THAT WAS FAST! DATE'S OVER ALREADY?
Yeah...
Well... a lot happened.
BA-DMP
BA-DMP
BA-DMP
ALL RIGHT THEN.
LET'S ALL SLEEP IN THE LIVING ROOM TONIGHT.
HUH? YOU CAN SLEEP WITH SHIMANA IF YOU LIKE.
I'm not doing that!
FOR TONIGHT, I JUST...
WANNA SPEND IT WITH EVERYONE.
Are you really, *really* going to Fukuoka?!
Just quit! It's still not too late!
IT VERY MUCH IS.
COOL, SEND ME SOME MENTAIKO WHEN YOU'RE THERE.

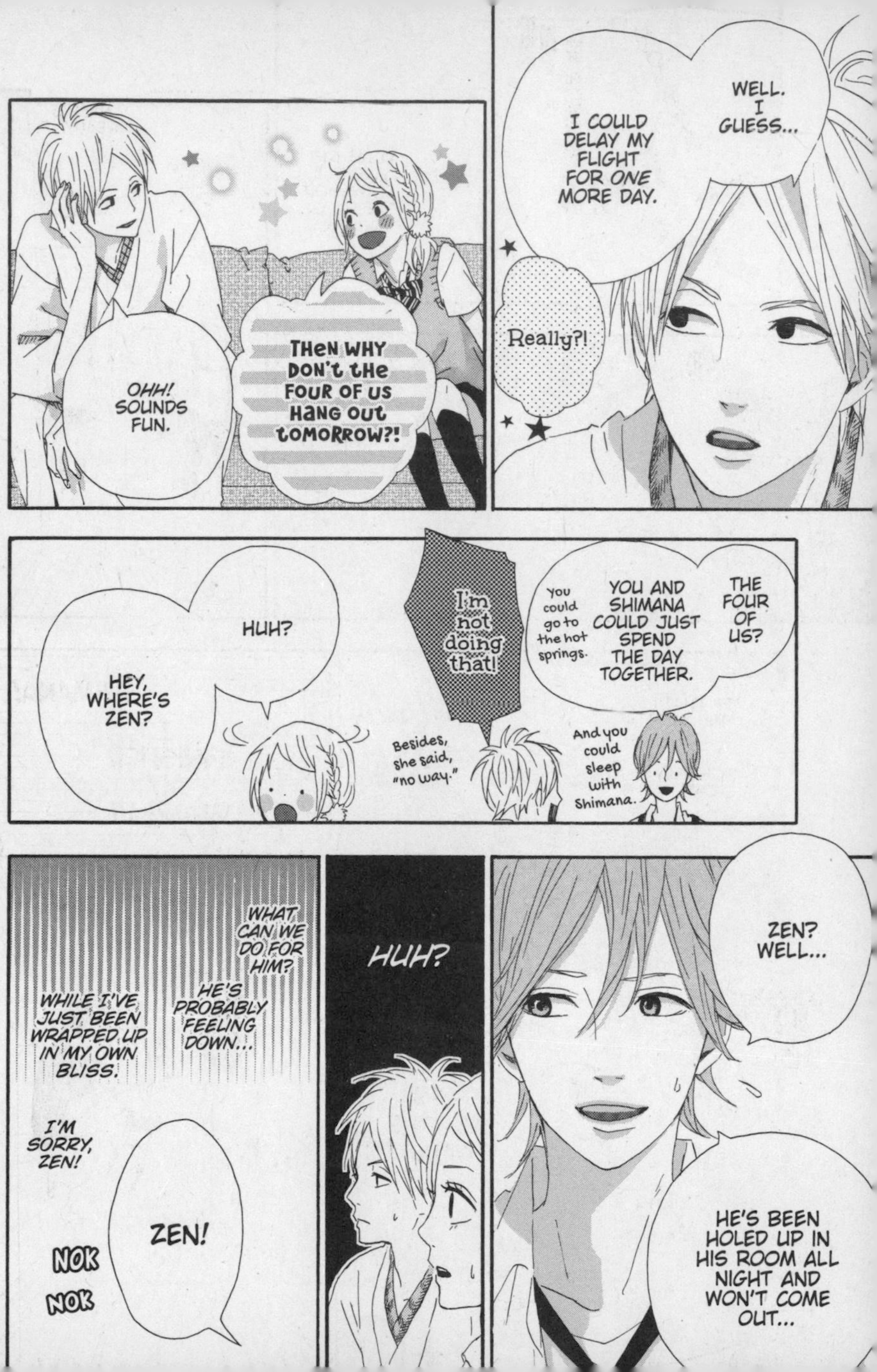
WELL. I GUESS...
I COULD DELAY MY FLIGHT FOR ONE MORE DAY.
Really?!
THEN WHY DON'T THE FOUR OF US HANG OUT TOMORROW?!
OHH! SOUNDS FUN.
THE FOUR OF US?
YOU AND SHIMANA COULD JUST SPEND THE DAY TOGETHER.
You could go to the hot springs.
And you could sleep with Shimana.
I'm not doing that!
Besides, she said, "no way."
HUH?
HEY, WHERE'S ZEN?
ZEN? WELL...
HE'S BEEN HOLED UP IN HIS ROOM ALL NIGHT AND WON'T COME OUT...
HUH?
WHAT CAN WE DO FOR HIM?
HE'S PROBABLY FEELING DOWN...
WHILE I'VE JUST BEEN WRAPPED UP IN MY OWN BLISS.
I'M SORRY, ZEN!
ZEN!
NOK
NOK

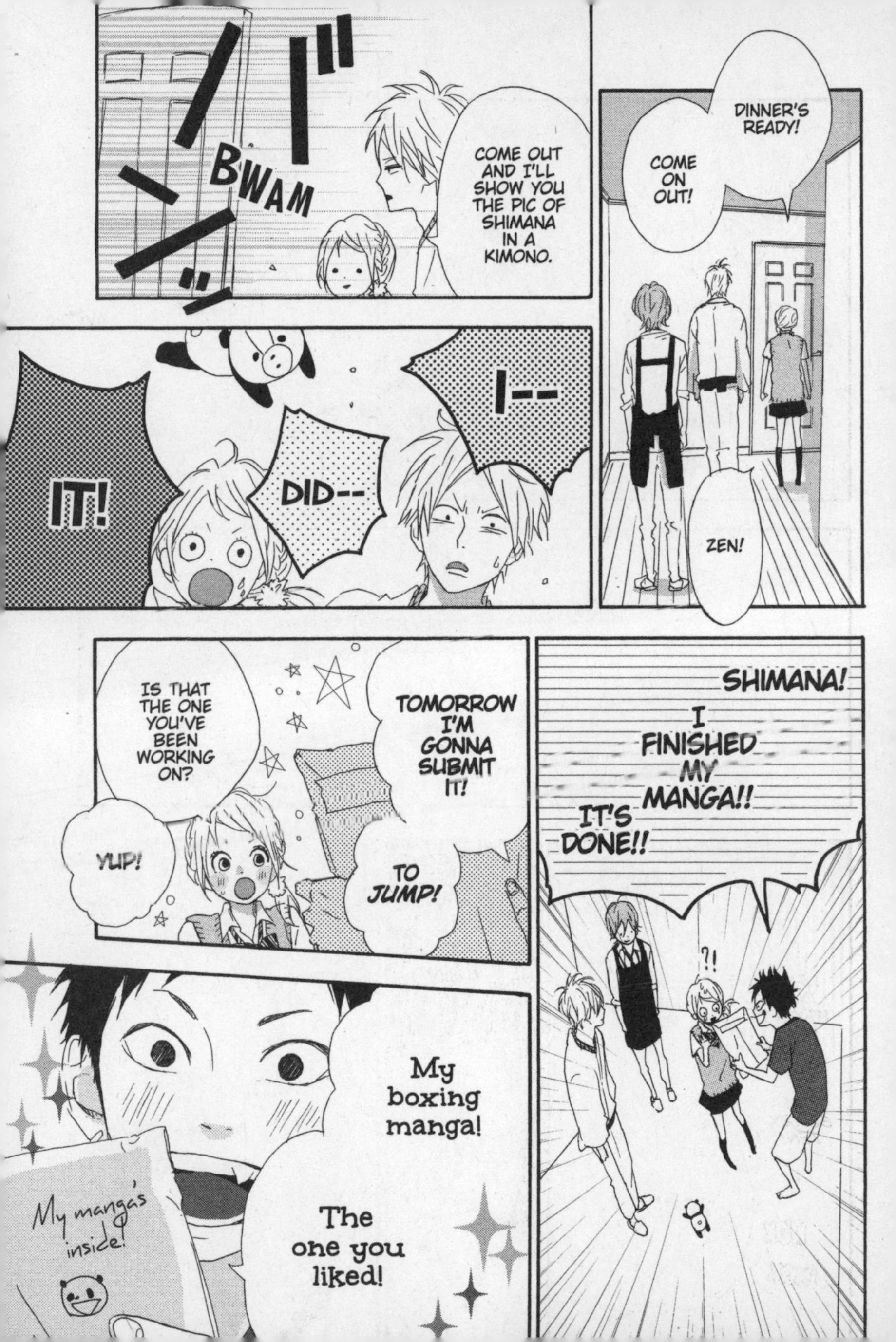
DINNER'S READY!
COME ON OUT!
ZEN!
COME OUT AND I'LL SHOW YOU THE PIC OF SHIMANA IN A KIMONO.
BWAM
I--
DID--
IT!
SHIMANA!
I FINISHED MY MANGA!!
IT'S DONE!!
?!
TOMORROW I'M GONNA SUBMIT IT!
TO JUMP!
IS THAT THE ONE YOU'VE BEEN WORKING ON?
YUP!
My boxing manga!
The one you liked!
My manga's inside!

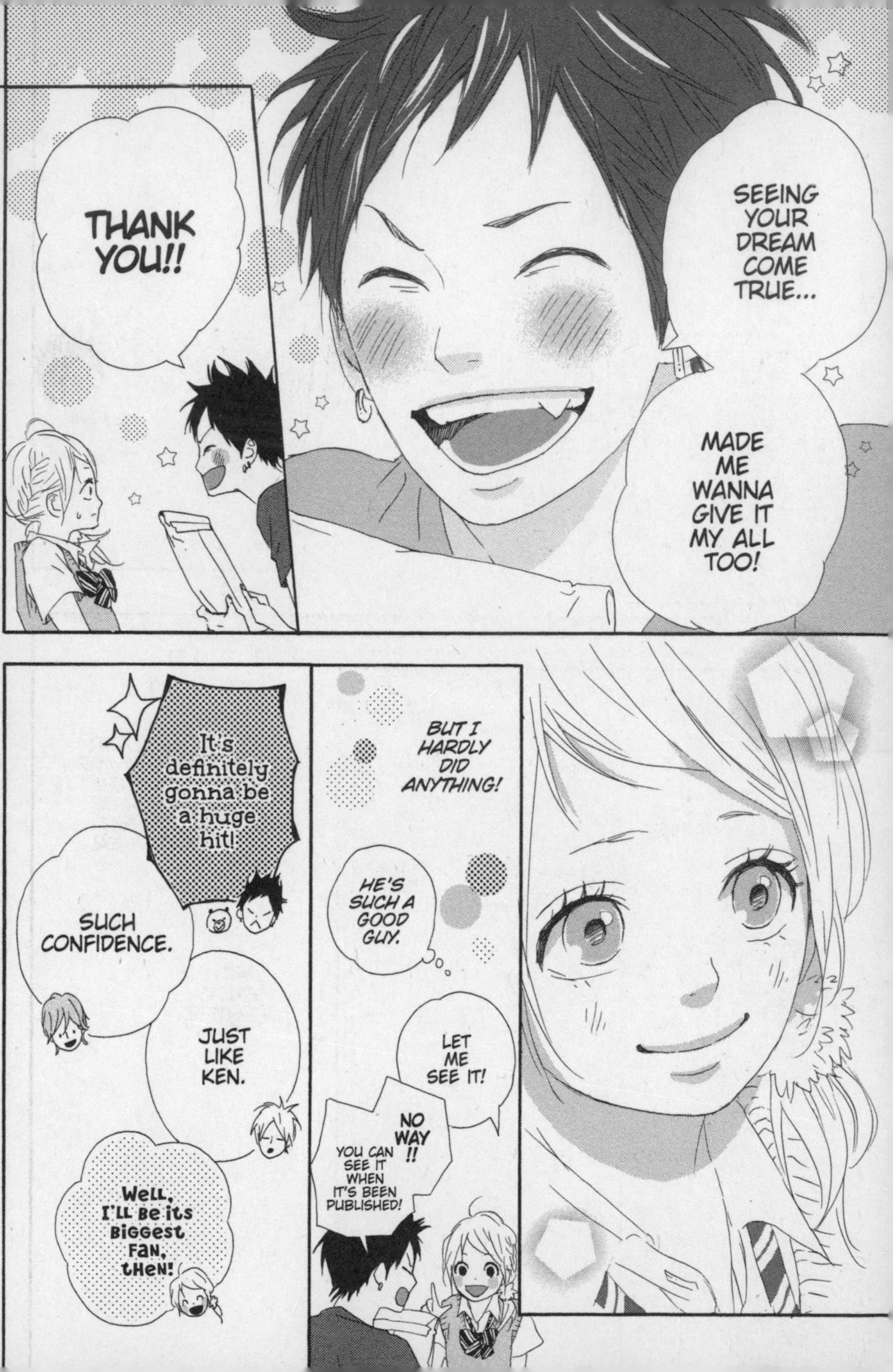
SEEING YOUR DREAM COME TRUE...
MADE ME WANNA GIVE IT MY ALL TOO!
THANK YOU!!
BUT I HARDLY DID ANYTHING!
HE'S SUCH A GOOD GUY.
LET ME SEE IT!
NO WAY!!
YOU CAN SEE IT WHEN IT'S BEEN PUBLISHED!
It's definitely gonna be a huge hit!
SUCH CONFIDENCE.
JUST LIKE KEN.
Well, I'll be its biggest fan, then!

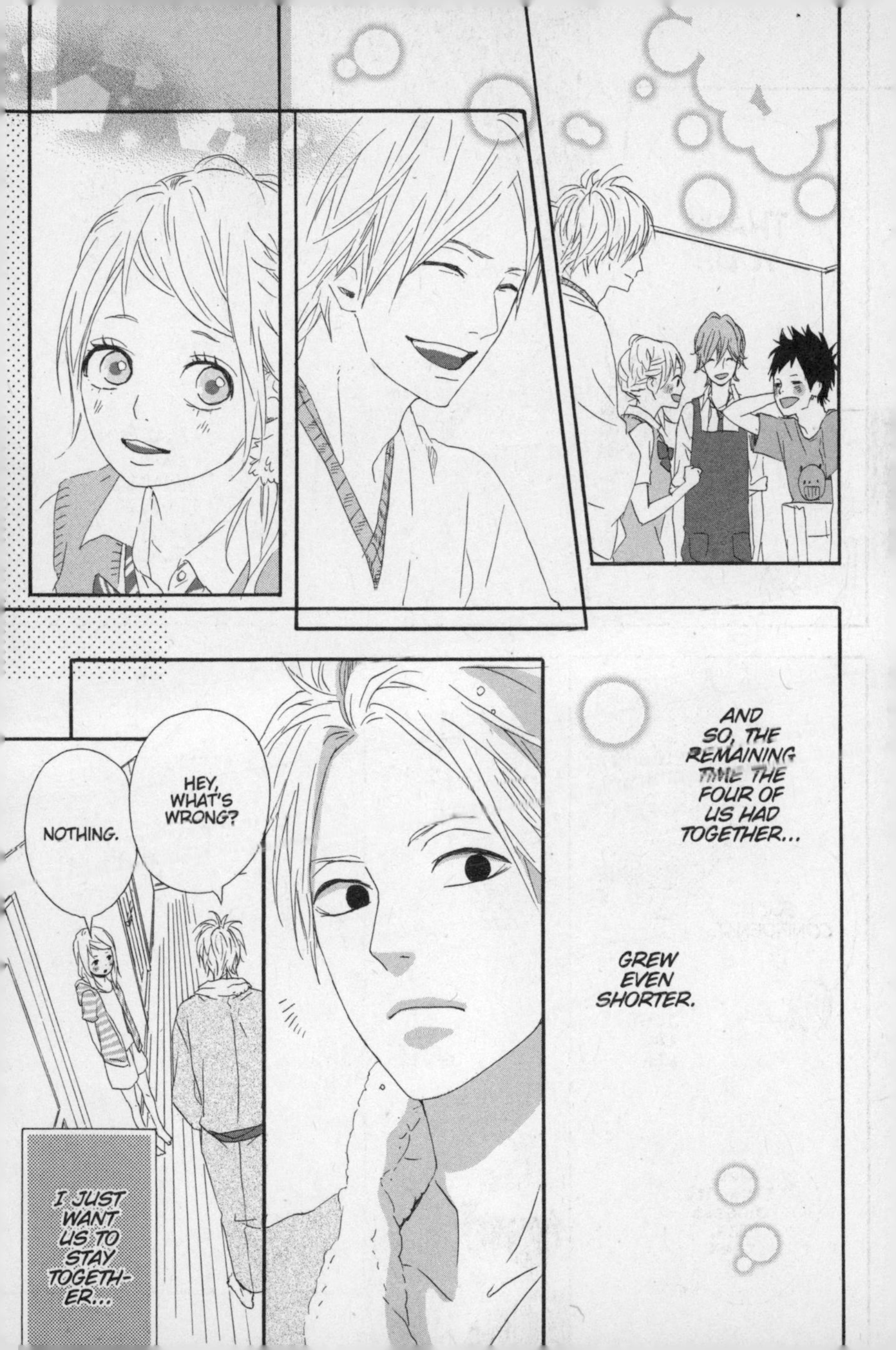
AND SO, THE REMAINING TIME THE FOUR OF US HAD TOGETHER...
GREW EVEN SHORTER.
HEY, WHAT'S WRONG?
NOTHING.
I JUST WANT US TO STAY TOGETHER...

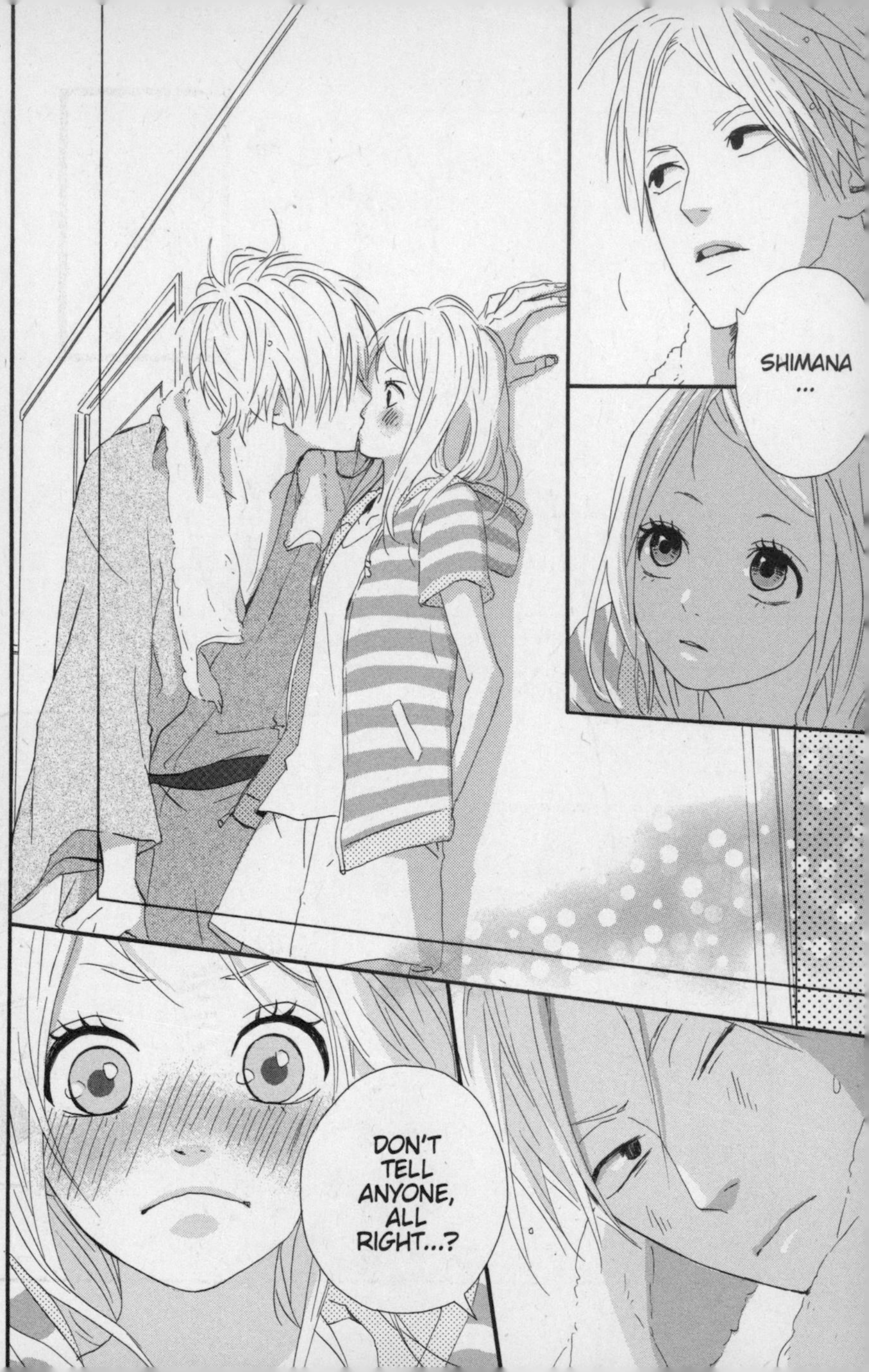
SHIMANA ...
DON'T TELL ANYONE, ALL RIGHT...?

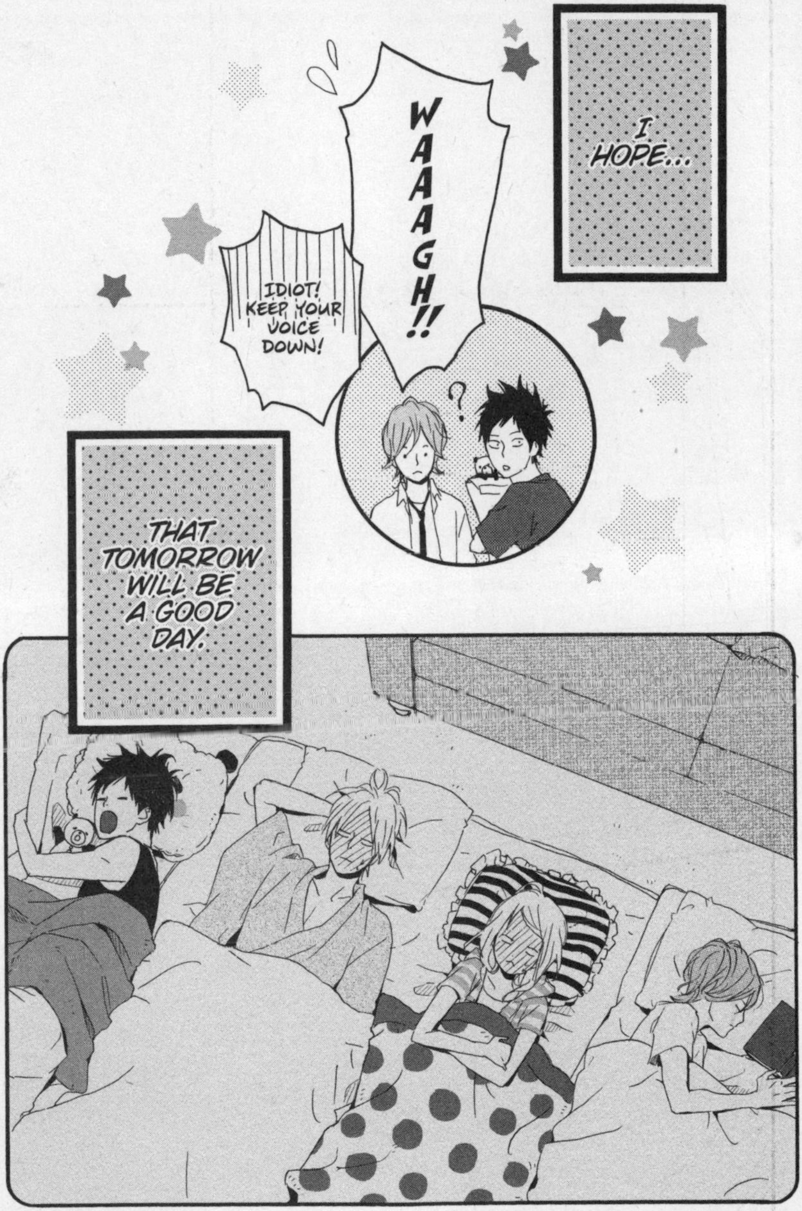
I HOPE...
WAAAGH!!
IDIOT! KEEP YOUR VOICE DOWN!
THAT TOMORROW WILL BE A GOOD DAY.

‹‹to be continued››

Bonus MANGA (After They Went to the Beach)

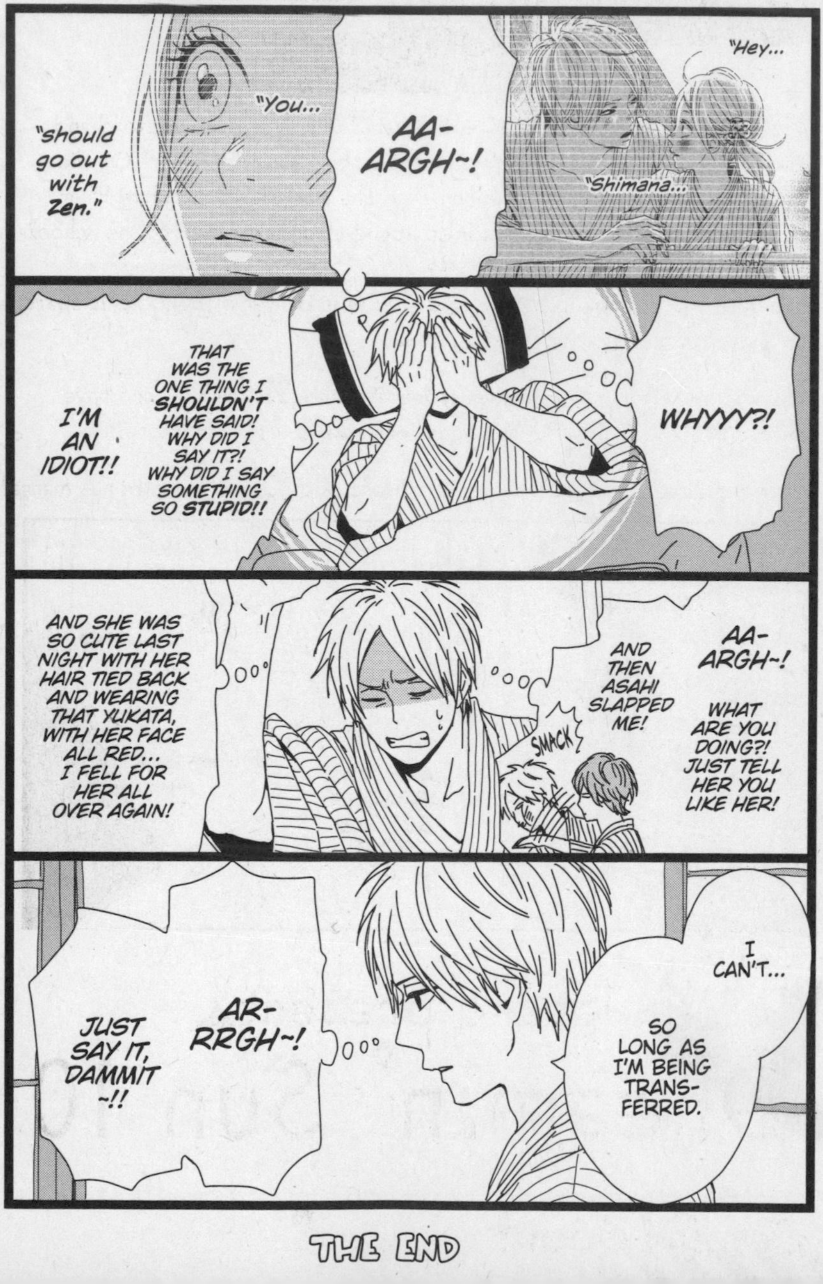
"Hey...
"Shimana...
"You...
"should go out with Zen."
AA-ARGH~!
WHYYY?!
THAT WAS THE ONE THING I SHOULDN'T HAVE SAID! WHY DID I SAY IT?! WHY DID I SAY SOMETHING SO STUPID!!
I'M AN IDIOT!!
AA-ARGH~!
WHAT ARE YOU DOING?! JUST TELL HER YOU LIKE HER!
AND THEN ASAHI SLAPPED ME!
SMACK
AND SHE WAS SO CUTE LAST NIGHT WITH HER HAIR TIED BACK AND WEARING THAT YUKATA, WITH HER FACE ALL RED... I FELL FOR HER ALL OVER AGAIN!
I CAN'T...
SO LONG AS I'M BEING TRANS-FERRED.
AR-RRGH~!
JUST SAY IT, DAMMIT ~!!

THE END

Next Volume Preview

"Today, I just want to be with the landlord."

After spinning their wheels for what seems like ages, the landlord and Shimana are both finally feeling the same thing for each other! On the day before the landlord's transfer--and the final day the four of them can spend together--they decide to spend their last hours at the school Shimana and the others attend...?!
But even though time is passing and they're in danger of being split apart, they're each ready to face themselves...

It's an emotional final volume that leads these four friends, who have shared dreams and heartaches under one roof, into their future!!

Includes *Dreamin' Sun* chapters 43 ~ finale, side story, and a bonus manga!

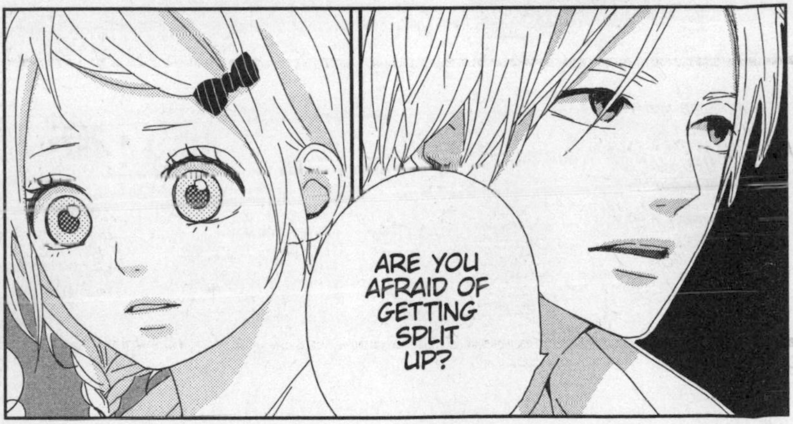
ARE YOU AFRAID OF GETTING SPLIT UP?

Ichigo Takano presents

Dreamin' Sun 10

Coming Soon!

SEVEN SEAS ENTERTAINMENT PRESENTS

Dreamin' Sun

story and art by **ICHIGO TAKANO**   VOLUME 9

TRANSLATION
Amber Tamosaitis

ADAPTATION
Claudie Summers

LETTERING AND RETOUCH
Lys Blakeslee

COVER DESIGN
KC F

Shannon Fay

PRODUCTION MANAGER
Lissa Pattillo

MANAGING EDITOR
Julie Davis

EDITOR-IN-CHIEF
Adam Arnold

PUBLISHER
Jason DeAngelis

DREAMIN' SUN VOLUME 9
© Ichigo Takano 2007
All rights reserved.
First published in Japan in 2015 by Futabasha Publishers Ltd., Tokyo.
English version published by Seven Seas Entertainment
under license from Futabasha Publishers Ltd.

No portion of this book ... any form without ... f fiction. Names, ... r's imagination ... es, or persons,

NO LONGER PROPERTY OF
SEATTLE PUBLIC LIBRARY

... enquiries can be sent to Marketing Manager
Lianne Sentar at press@gomanga.com. Information regarding the distribution
and purchase of digital editions is available from Digital Manager CK Russell
at digital@gomanga.com.

Seven Seas and the Seven Seas logo are trademarks of
Seven Seas Entertainment. All rights reserved.

ISBN: 978-1-626929-74-6

Printed in Canada

First Printing: July 2019

10 9 8 7 6 5 4 3 2 1

JUL 14 2021

FOLLOW US ONLINE: *www.sevenseasentertainment.com*

READING DIRECTIONS

This book reads from *right to left*, Japanese style.
If this is your first time reading manga, you start
reading from the top right panel on each page and
take it from there. If you get lost, just follow the
numbered diagram here. It may seem backwards at
first, but you'll get the hang of it! Have fun!!

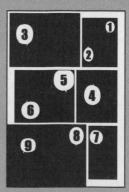